John Martin Littlejohn

The political Theory of the Schoolmen and Grotius

Parts I, II and III

John Martin Littlejohn

The political Theory of the Schoolmen and Grotius
Parts I, II and III

ISBN/EAN: 9783337134341

Printed in Europe, USA, Canada, Australia, Japan

Cover: Foto ©Suzi / pixelio.de

More available books at **www.hansebooks.com**

THE POLITICAL THEORY

OF

THE SCHOOLMEN

AND

GROTIUS.

PARTS I, II, and III.

BY

J. MARTIN LITTLEJOHN,
University Fellow in Political Philosophy.

Submitted in partial fulfilment of the requirements for the Degree of Doctor of Philosophy, in the Faculty of Political Science, Columbia University, N.Y.

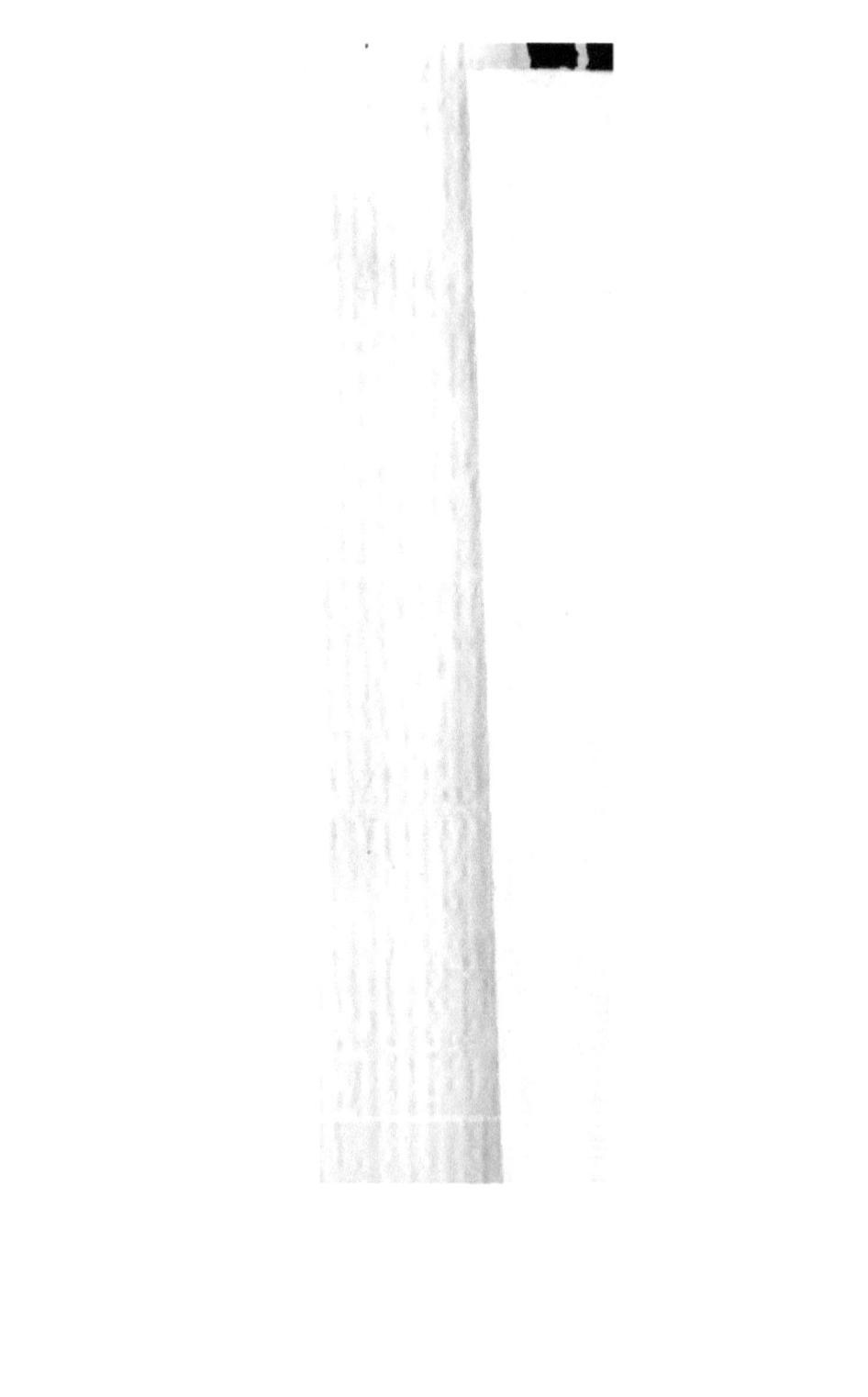

PREFACE.

The following pages are the result of investigations in the field of Medieval Politics. The topic was first selected and the original plan, which has been adhered to throughout, was first formulated under the inspiration of the ideas of the late Professor Lorimer of Edinburgh University. Valuable suggestions were received from Advocate W. G. Miller, lecturer on Political Philosophy and International Law in my *Alma Mater*, Glasgow University. Professor Reginald L. Poole, of Jesus College, Oxford, gave me hints which aided me in consulting the original authorities. My obligations to others are acknowledged in the course of the work.

As Fellow of Political Philosophy in Columbia College I selected this as the subject of my Dissertation. The materials were collected in this country and also in Europe where I had access to the great Libraries of Medieval Literature. Dr. W. A. Dunning, of Columbia College, to whom I owe grateful thanks for his constant suggestions in the course of the preparation of the Thesis, has carefully gone over all the materials, and on behalf of the Faculty of Political Science has accorded the work his approval as my Doctoral Thesis. To him and the other members of the Faculty of Political Science in conjunction with my *Alma Mater* I dedicate this contribution, in the hope that it may be serviceable as a means of calling attention to the lives and doctrines of men whose memories are almost forgotten.

I trust that its defects will be graciously pardoned on account of the fact that it is published under the pressure of many duties devolving upon me in my position as College President. Part IV., with the Bibliography of the whole subject will be published (D. V.) in the Fall.

May 1895.   J. Martin Littlejohn.
Amity College, Ia.

Errata.

A good many typographical errors have crept in but these will be easily corrected by the reader. Omissions are here corrected.

Page 1 line 19 read possessed.
" 2 " 10 " survive.
" 4 " 29 " Scholasticism.
" 8 " 11 " explicatio for plicatio.
" 22 " 13 " conditio for conditis.
" 25 " 14 " as for so.
" 26 " 14 " Dionysius de Moribus.
" 26 " 29 " Scotus for Scotua.
" 30 " 10 " Sismondi.
" 42 " 41 " Papae.
" 47 " 2 " et for et and ae juum.
" 47 " 15 " as for is.
" 60 " 16 " retrahitur.
" 66 " 4 " such after only.
" 67 " 41 " Arist. for Hist.
" 80 " 9 " lead for ead.
" 88 " 10 " master for matter.
" 91 " 22 " foreseeing.
" 94 " 4 " lack after but.
" 112 " 4 " ultimus and 37 divine.
" 117 " 7 " mundo.
" 118 " 27 " peccarent.
" 128 " 12 " be reached.
" 147 " 28 " vel for ve.
" 162 " 15 " Societies for cieties.
" 163 " 36 " utriusque.
" 181 " 18 " look.
" 201 " 10 " of before the Church.
" 202 " 7 " of before Schoolmen.
" 202 " 9 " Colonna.
" 202 " 26 " quatenus.
" 204 " 8 " higher, 20 food for good.
" 206 " 16 " Campsoria, 17 obolostatica.
" 207 " 5 and 6 read regnum for regum.
" 210 " 29 read tradito for traditis.
" 211 " 35 " mediis for medio.
" 213 " 17 " absolvi for abolvi.
" 216 " 13 " was after crisis.
" 224 " 38 " 851 for 8.51.
" 231 " 3 " there for ther.
" 232 " 14 " for t, †, 17 concessam.
" 232 " 21 " for †, ‡, 36 for †, §.
" 237 " 31 " solitary for itary.
" 248 " 11 " Church, 34 Anathemas.
" 257 " 42 " Die Moral und.
" 261 " 9 " ornat and munere.
" 262 " 42 " McIntosh.
" 263 " 14 " Granada.
" 274 " 2 " discursu, 17 naturale, 37 signum.
" 275 " 17 " foedus.
" 282 " 4 " prince for price.
" 292 " 38 " dispensing.
" 293 " 1 " (VII) for (VI).

TABLE OF CONTENTS.

INTRODUCTION.—1. Aristotle.—2. Science of politics.—3. Why unite Schoolmen and Grotius?—Estimate of the Schoolmen.—4. Grotius.—Estimate of Grotius.—5. Transition to Scholasticism. Origin and Character.—Work of Grotius and predecessors..pp. 1-9.

PART I.
SCHOLASTIC POLITICAL THEORY BEFORE AQUINAS.

CHAPTER I.—PREPARATION FOR SCHOLASTICISM.—METHOD OF SCHOLASTICS.

1. Age of Church Fathers and early Middle Ages.—2. The Conflict of Secular and Spiritual power.—3. Rise of Scholastic philosophy.—Study of dialectics..pp. 11-16.

CHAPTER II.—POLITICAL THEORY BEFORE AQUINAS.

1. Where Scholasticism takes up political theory.—2. General character of Scholastic philosophy.—3. Scholastic political Theory begins with Augustine.—Political principles of Augustine:—(1) property; (2) slavery; (3) the origin and character of government; (4) the state and the Church; (5) the Unity of humanity.—4. The influence of Stoicism.—Stoic principles.—Boethius.—Alcuin.—Joannes Scotus Erigena.—Anselm.—Abelard.—5. Hincmar, Archbp. of Rheims.—His theory.—6. The Ecclesiastical system of politics.—Gregory the Great, and his works.—Growth of the Church power.—Nicolas I.—Hildebrande and his position.—Manegold.—Waltram.—Innocent III. and Summit of papacy.—7. Divisions of Scholasticism.—8. First period of Scholasticism.—Bernard.—Hugh St. Victor.—9. Peter Lombard.—Alexander Hales.—Bonaventure.—Albert the Great.—Works of Albert.—10. John of Salisbury.—(I) Theocratic idea of the state.—(II) The State as an organism.—(III) Doctrine of Tyrannicide.—11. Hugh of Fleury..pp. 17-48.

PART II.
THE POLITICAL THEORY OF THOMAS AQUINAS.

CHAPTER I.—PRELIMINARY.

1. Political Science of Middle Ages untouched.—Revival of interest in Science.—2. Who was Thomas?—His works.—Estimate of Thomas.—Works on politics.—3. Aquinas great representative Schoolman.—Authority in Scholasticism.—Method..pp. 49-57.

CHAPTER II.—ETHICAL PRINCIPLES AT THE FOUNDATION OF POLITICS.

1. Political Science in Thomas.—Division of Sciences.—Natural and supernatural.—2. Law.—(1) eternal, (2) natural, (3) human, (4) Divine law.—Law of nature in the history of political Science.—3. Justice.—Definition and nature of justice and right..pp. 58-68.

CHAPTER III.—CIVIL SOCIETY AND ITS SOCIAL ELEMENTS.

1. Association and concept of civil society.—(1) association; (2) the idea of power; (3) community of interest.—2. Right of property.—Private property distinguished from community.—Community in use.—3. Political disabilities.—Slavery.—(1) psychological, and (2) theological basis for slavery, not opposed to natural law.—Mitigation of slavery...pp. 69-83.

CHAPTER IV.—THE ORIGIN AND NATURE OF THE STATE.

1. Origin of the state.—Natural and actual origin.—Idea of contract.—It is establishment of government.—2. Nature of the state.—(1) The state is an order of social life.—(2) The state is a natural order of social life.—(3) The state as an organism.—3. Psycho-physical character of the state.—Moral and physical elements.—Physical basis of the state.—Territory.—Climate.—An agricultural state.—Beauty of landscape.—4. People.—One people.—Cultured people.—Elements of state-population.—Farmers, intermediate classes, governors.—Land in relation to the people.—Citizenship.—5. Nature of the ideal state..pp. 84-103.

CHAPTER V.—THE END OF THE STATE.

1. The end in general—Same for individual and state-happiness.—2. Twofold end in the state.—(1) Union of social beings; (2) making them good citizens.—3. Temporal aim of the state, unity and peace.—Aim of rulers of the state.—Aim of state in as far as subjects are concerned.—4. Summary...pp. 104-114.

CHAPTER VI.—ACTIVITY OF THE STATE. SOVEREIGNTY. THE FUNCTIONS OF THE STATE.

1. Activity.—Power and government.—2. Sovereignty in the state.—Power in itself, in its origin, and in its use.—Sovereignty of political virtue and sovereignty of the people.—3. Functions of the government.—The relation of government to the unity and peace and welfare of society.—A complete ruler.—Political virtue, prudentia.—Executive, legislative, and judicial....pp. 115-127.

CHAPTER VII.—FORMS OF GOVERNMENT.

1. Form of government, not of state.—Governments are just or unjust.—Governments classified according to the ends of the society and the numbers in the governing body.—Constitutions of the State, Kingdom, Aristocracy and Polity.—2. Actual forms.—Monarchy.—Tyranny. Aristocracy and Oligarchy.—Republic and Democracy.—3. The best form of government.—Difference between the best in theory and practice.—Two kinds of kingdoms.—In the De Reg. Prin. practical theory.—The ideal form in the Summa.—4. The worst form of government.—Tyranny the worst.—Tyranny under the three

forms..pp. 128-143.
CHAPTER VIII. RULE AND OBEDIENCE. LIMITATIONS UPON THE ACTIVITY OF THE GOVERNMENT AND STATE.

1. Idea of the power. Mode of acquisition and manner of use. Despotic, royal, and political power.—2. Limitations arising from the position of the rulers.—Motives that lead to rule well. Love of right and fear of punishment. Limitation in qualification for office. Constitutional government. 3. Limitations arising from the position of the subjects. Is obedience absolute. 4. Positive limits.—The right of revolution. Sedition.—Tyrannicide. 5. To prevent corruption.—Resistance to the judgment of the ruler. Confiscation, restitution..pp. 144-161.

CHAPTER IX. THE RELATION OF THE TEMPORAL AND SPIRITUAL. CHURCH AND STATE.

1. Temporal and spiritual power. Differs from Aristotle. 2. The believing and unbelieving. 3. Intolerance.—Inquisition. Persecution. pp. 162-176.

CHAPTER X. ECONOMIC AND SOCIAL VIEWS OF AQUINAS. GERMS OF NATIONAL-POLITICAL ECONOMY.

1. Introduction.—Trade and commerce.—2. State regulation. Marriage. Education. Progress. 3. Wealth.—Taxation.—Money.—4. Usury.—Reasonable price...pp. 177-194.

CHAPTER XI. CONCLUSION OF AQUINAS.

1. View of the anonymous continuator of Thomas.—Theocratic idea of politics. 2. Estimate of Thomas..pp. 195-199.

PART III.
POLITICAL THEORY OF THE LATER SCHOOLMEN.

CHAPTER I. AEGIDIUS ROMANUS AND TRIUMPHUS.

1. Transition to later Schoolmen. Change. (1) the assertion of national consciousness, (2) Imperialism becomes a dream; (3) In the decline of the Empire the Church is gradually becoming stronger. 2. Aegidius Romanus. (I) Ethical basis of political theory. (II) Economic basis of political theory. —3. (III) Political theory proper: (1) The philosophy of civil rule; (2) the best polities in time of peace; (3) policy of war. (IV) Ecclesiastical polities. —4. Augustinus Triumfo.—Temporal and spiritual powers........pp. 200-215.

CHAPTER II. DANTE. MARSILIUS. OCKHAM. WYCLIF.

1. Contest of the 14th Century. Nationality. Papal bulls.—Philip of France and Louis of Bavaria.—Peter du Bois.—De utraque potestate. Raoul de Presles.—2. Dante.—(I) Is universal temporal monarchy as represented in the empire necessary to the good of the human race? (II) Did the Roman people rightly possess Imperial power?—(III) Is the Imperial authority derived from God or from the Vicar of God? 3. Marsilius of Padua. I. General Theory of the state.—Legislative, executive, official and military power. —(II) Theory of the civil and religious orders.—Doctrine of toleration. III Conclusion.—Distinguishing theology from politics. The State as an organ-

ization of free men.—The people is sovereign.—4. William of Ockham.—Position in the Imperial contest.—Position in the Franciscan struggle.—(I) Nominalist ideas at the basis of politics.—(II) Theological politics. (1) Liberty. (2) Authority.—Pope or Emperor. 5. John Wyclif.—Position. (I) General theory of lordship.—(II) Application of the theory of lordship.

No one guilty of mortal sin has any right to property.—Righteousness is the fundamental principle of lordship.—The gospel law alone is necessary in the exercise of lordship.—Lordship implies service.—Summary....pp. 216-252.

CHAPTER III. SPANISH JURISTS. VICTORIA. SOTO. SUAREZ.

1. Introduction.—Humanism.—Spanish Jurists.—The Jesuit schools.—2. Vasquez.—Francis de Victoria.—Relectiones Theologicae.—Antonio Augustino, author of Emendationes Juris Civilis.—Dominic Soto.—De Justitia et de Jure.—Topics treated.—3. Francis Suarez.—Position and Life.—(I) First principles in politics.—(II) Law.—Divisions of law and definition.—Justice.—(III) Civil society.—Man as a social being and a being of law.—(IV) Sovereignty and temporal power.—Tyranny and tyrannicide.—(V) Government, its elements and forms.—Potestas which is delegated and alienated.—Legislative power.—(VI) The Civil and Ecclesiastical.—Position of papal and civil powers.—Liberty of conscience.—(VII) International law............pp. 253-296.

INTRODUCTION.

1. Not inappropriately may we invoke the name of the great father of Political Science upon the effort to set forth a philosophy that was in a great measure inspired by his genius. The memory of Aristotle formed the grand inspiration of the men who cover this wide field of Scholasticism and Reniscence. From Greece, or better through Greece, came to modern civilization almost every contribution that has been made to the advance of learning. Chiefly through the tempering and humanizing influence of the logical system of the Stagyrite, although it came at first through the adulterated medium of Saracenic philosophising, learning arose out of the corruption of the age of darkness, to take its place as the guiding star of the world towards happiness and greatness. In no Science does the Greek influence occupy a position of such commanding importance as in that of politics. The spirit that founded the Science brought it forth from the womb of time to a second birth, more than a thousand years after its first conception. Aristotle, as the first great writer on the Science of Politics, gathered into complete system the scattered fragments of an earlier antiquity, basing it upon an analytical study of over one hundred and fifty constitutions, and gave an impetus to Political studies that has only been intensified with the lapse of ages. It is not wonderful that the introduction of a system possessed of such scientific completeness, even in imperfect translations, should tend to dispel the darkness which had enveloped every science within its mazes and produce the first awakening of a promised scientific reformation.*

2. In order to define our field the question may be asked, is there such a Science as Politics? This question has been answered by other writers. It is a question of importance, where does Politics stand in the great edifice of human knowledge. There is a political science just as there is a natural and mental science. The attempt to discover the principles that guide moral conduct and the rules that are followed in such actions as we call moral,

---

* Coleridge, Table Talk 101; Townsend, Great Schoolmen of the Mid. Ages, p. 318, 9.

justifies the existence of moral philosophy. Men cannot help being moral creatures, nor can they help meditating on moral questions. In the same way men cannot help thinking of the state, the office of the public government and the province of civic life. The influence of the contract theory upon the historical development of states and of political philosophy, and its reaction upon the concept of the state in France and in the United States is a proof of this.*

Political Science is the generic term and in the main deals with states that exist and as they exist, their laws and history and the conditions under which they continue to survive and develop. It investigates the life-history of states, to work up the varying elements economic, financial and legal into the present status. But philosophers are not content to deal with the facts of state life; they take account of the ideal condition of the state and the best means of attaining to it. Political Philosophy therefore does and must exist for the purpose of playing the part which Kant claimed for speculative philosophy, namely, that of scientific and rational criticism, to establish the truth of theories that receive practical illustration in states and the falsity of others that ought to be rejected. Political Philosophy looks mainly to the ideal state and tries to discover under what conditions and by what principles it can find realization. It looks down from the standpoint of the ideal state by means of scientific principles and applies these principles to states in their living evolution, in solving unsolved problems of human social life and of the world. This ideal theory of the state is not necessarily abstract, nor should it be so. It is a theory to meet the aspirations and to satisfy the conditions under which man exists as a Political being, aiming at the most perfect political organization of human society. Politics as a science is the science of the state.†

Such a statement is necessary in order to define and limit the field of our investigation among the writings of the Schoolmen to whom Theology was the SUMMA SCIENTIA. Without adopting any classification of the sciences as final,‡ it is sufficient in endeavoring to indicate the province of politics, firstly, to mark off the natural sciences, which treat of man in his animal and material organism; secondly, to exclude the mental science which treats of man as an intelligent being, logical, psychological and metaphysical; thirdly, to distinguish the moral science in which man is treated as a rational as well as an intelligent and physical being, not only possessing an animal nature in some sense conditioning his higher life and a capacity for knowledge, but being endowed with a free moral power of acting in accordance with which he regulates his conduct as an individual and his relations as a member of society with the politically organized social community known as the state.

---

* H. L. Osgood, Pol. Sc. Quar. VI. 1; D. G. Ritchie, Pol. S. Q. VI. 668; What is Political Science, W. J. Ashley.

† Monroe Smith Pol. S. Q. I. p. 1. Domain of Political Science.

‡ Compare Spencer on Classification of the Sciences.

It is in this last aspect of man's being that we find the basis for politics. Man is a member of society, but in particular he is a member of a politically organized body of which he is a citizen, and in which account is taken of his physical, intelligent and moral being as well as the social community of his nature with others. Politics, roughly speaking, deals with the origin and constitution of civil society, the forms and organization of government, the rights and duties of members, the organs and functions of legislation, the definite personality of the state as a unit distinct from all others of the same nature and the limiting conditions under which the state and government continue to exist and act.

3. It may be asked, why do we combine the schoolmen and Grotius? It is because we desire to do justice to a class of men who have received, from men of letters, more ridicule and less consideration than any other writers in the whole field of political literature. It may seem a thankless task to subscribe our faith in the Schoolmen. Yet we are confident a closer study of their writings will give to us a deeper regard for men who, writing under circumstances never paralleled in human evolution, produced ideas that are not yet exhausted. Taking in the Theology and Philosophy from Augustine to Hugo Grotius, we may say that there is nothing which has been produced in modern times that has not found its archetype in these writings. For several centuries it was a literary habit to condemn the schoolmen as literary gymnasts, no account being taken of the services they rendered to the world or to literature by their untiring labors. In the days of the Reformation when Humanism began its positive work of upbuilding, it was almost a necessity that the Reformers should declare war against the method and the principles of the Scholastics, in order to break the galling chains of dogmatism and pave the way for the intellectual renascence. But the spirit of these iconoclasts, bitterly opposed as it was to the method of scholasticism, became even more bitter towards the schoolmen, and the age that ushered in the new learning condemned without consideration the Doctors of the School in no measured terms. Hobbes declares, "those who wrote volumes of such stuff were mad." (1) Brucker characterizes their works as "philosophical skirmishes with the help of verbal disputes, worthless mental abstractions." (2) The editors of Hume, Green and Grose, put in a single epithet the sentiments of the learned since Hobbes' time, when they speak of "the mire of scholasticism." (3) Of the same nature are the words of Mosheim, (4) Hallam, (5) Spanheim, (6) Enfield, (7) Tait, (8) Lewes, (9) and Schlegel. (10)

1. Leviathan I. C. 8.
2. Hist. of Phil. II. lib. II.
3. Hume's Human Nature. Introd. p. 7.
4. Eccl. Hist. I. 329.
5. Europe in Mid. Ages. 684.
6. Eccl. Annals, trans. by Wright. 408.
7. Hist. of Phil. p. 453, 485.
8. Lectures on recent Science, 54.
9. Hist. of Phil. Trans. Per. I. 3.
10. Phil. of Hist. p. 376.

Now, however, in the light of researches made in the vast field of Scholastic literature a truer estimate has been formed of the learning and worth of these men of a former age. Aside from the works of Mohl, Janet, Bluntschli, Stockl and Blakey in which we have a true, though brief account of the labors of these men, there is amassing a comprehensive literature in praise of the schoolmen, in which there is a recognition of the indebtedness of the modern world to these writings so long unread. Sir William Hamilton, than whom no brighter figure shines in the philosophical history of Europe, speaks of them with much appreciation: (1) among others are Maurice, (2) Sir J. McIntosh, (3) Pope, (4) Hampden, (5) Lord, (6) Guizot, (7) Neander, (8) Cousin, (9) Townsend, (10) Draper, (11) Coleridge, (12) Stoughton, (13) Thomas Harper, S. J., (14) D'Aubigne. (15)

We trust that the result of a fuller acquaintance with these men and their writings will justify the most laudatory sentiments of recent writers. "In treating of the subject of jurisprudence," writes Townsend of Thomas Aquinas, "he was led by the principles he adopted into conclusions which, if followed out to their last result, would produce the most complete overthrow of all tyranny both civil and ecclesiastical. He insists that in the reason of man law is dominant. It is a standard of human action and must be considered as the rule and measure of all acts of the reason. A law thus existing is powerfully operative and the acts of the reason are within its operations. But this touches also the action of the will in the attainment of the ends for which reason co-operates actively and effectually. These ideas he applies to social and political life; he affirms that the will of the majority of the people is the only really governing and legislative authority; that the Prince is only the interpreter of the will of the great body of the Nation. Thus he anticipated some of the most earnest pleaders of Constitutional liberty in laying down this principle as a corner stone of his system, and especially as Prof. Maurice has well pointed out, he anticipated Locke in advocating a view of so democratic a tendency, which could not fail to produce final fruit in the course of succeeding ages." (16) "The Schoolmen were the first great reformers in Europe.... leaders on the side of a wronged humanity .... there was never wanting a Schoolman to fight on the side of liberty of conscience and freedom of thought until the grand result was obtained, "the right of thinking as we will, and of speaking as we think." (17) "They did not

1. Discussions, 118.
2. Mor. and Met. Phil. I. 616.
3. Works vol. I. 48, 49.
4. Compend. of Theol. I. 21.
5. Bampton Lect. VIII.
6. Beacon Lights of History.
7. Cours d' Hist. Mod. I. 220.
8. Ch. Hist. Vol. VI. 439; VIII.
9. Mod. Phil. II. 12.
10. Gr. Schoolmen in Mid. Ages.
11. Intel. Devel. of Eur. II. 3.
12. Table Talk. 240
13. Ages of Christ. 361.
14. Metaph. of the School. Introd.
15. Voice of the church.
16. pp. 234, 5.
17. Heeren, Hist. Res. 340; Townsend, p. 327.

succeed in obtaining for the world the full blessing of liberty....they were a powerful force in preparing for the battle in the future; they sowed the seeds of political, moral, metaphysical and religious truth....they succeeded in evoking a love of wisdom and a spirit of enquiry which could not, and would not be restrained....they were left behind by new generations who, without due acknowledgement of the services or tender gratitude for the sacrifices of their predecessors...were borne on to triumph. Meantime those who had done so much....were left to neglect and contumely until in the far distant future the morning should dawn when their services should have recognition and their reputation a bright resurrection."*

4. By a remarkable coincidence Hugo Grotius has been subjected to the same measure of reproach as these scholastic precursors whose system he frees from the fetters of Ecclesiasticism. His works were composed amid circumstances of personal adversity; his life, one of exceptional honour, was largely spent in exile, while his sympathies towards the free rights of man were called forth by the struggles of blood through which the nations of Europe were then called to pass. In his great work, the Summa of all his other works, his design was "to settle the grounds of the rights of men in civil society,"† being one of the first great political philosophers who attempted to establish a basis for society and human government apart from the dictation of the Church and independent of Theological Dogmatism. But this attempt to revolutionize the ideas at the basis of the political system brought upon him the contempt of others. Voltaire scoffs at Grotius. "On est partagé, dans les ecoles entre Grotius et Puffendorf. Croyez-moi, lisez les Offices de Ciceron."‡ De Quincey has said, the book is equally divided between empty truisms and time-serving Dutch falsehoods.§ Dugald Stewart, speaking of Grotius and Puffendorf, says, "notwithstanding all their industry and learning, it would be very difficult to name any class of writers, whose labors have been of less utility to the world."‖ This is well answered in the Edinburgh Review.¶

The work of Grotius is in reality the climax of the better part of Scholasticism, the resurrection of what was eternal from the sepulchre of these decaying systems, the transition from the freer spirit of the Spanish Schoolmen, who by the principles of the Roman jurisprudence, accommodated to the casuistical character of Jesuitism, departed from the iron-bound yoke of scholastic philosophy and pointed the way, to the emancipation of reason

---

* Townsend pp. 3/5, 6. NEED FOR EXPLORING THE FIELD OF THE SCHOOLMEN. Tenneman. Geschicte der Philosophie VIII. Band, 1817; Cousin, Cours de l'hist. de la Phil, p. 29. Paris 1828.
† Enfield Hist. of Phil. p. 624.
‡ Hamilton's Ed. of Stewart, works I. p. 178. Note.
§ Encyc. Brit. Grotius; Hely. Etude sur le droit de la guerre de Grotius Paris 1875. Stewart's Diss. III.
¶ Vol. XXVII. pp. 230-244.

characteristic of modern times. It set before Kings and Governors the sentiments of all whom learned men held in reverence, and contributed "to diffuse a reverence for principles of justice" which commended itself to the the approbation of all thinking men. The key-note of a new order is sounded in the sentiment expressed with pathos by Grotius at the very close of his Masterpiece, "*non potest diu perdurare doctrina quæ hominem hominibus inamicabilem facit.*"* "That doctrine can have no permanent validity which renders man the enemy of his fellow-men." Doctrines cannot work well which make men unfit for society. It is the prophecy with which a regenerated political theory is presented to mankind. Bluntschli, speaking of Grotius, justly declares, "The eloquence of his diction, the pearls of classical antiquity with which he adorned his pages, the temper of humanity which pervaded his argument, his effort to mitigate the horrors of the thirty years war, in the midst of which he wrote, and the warmth of his sympathy for a moral opposed to a material order, enlisted men's hearts on the side of his reasoning, while the deficiencies of his doctrine were not as yet detected."† The reputation of Grotius and the enduring influence of his writings need no recommendation in the light of to-day. The most effective answer to the unmeasured censure of pseudo-apologists is the fact that political science gathered around the centre which Grotius set up in defense of the rights of men and the liberties of nations as well as the political sovereignty of the people for more than a century.

5. There is a natural sequence in the order of thought from the Schoolmen to Grotius. Aquinas, "The Saint, Scholar and Monk of the Medieval ages,"‡ is the most conspicuous figure in the five centuries preceeding the general reformation and his SECUNDA SECUNDAE remained during that period the Ethical Code of Christendom. The later Schoolmen all speak of the superior character of Aquinas' works. Fontenelle says of him, "in another age Aquinas might have been a Descartes." But it was reserved for Leibnitz, the illustrious philosopher, to strike the key-note of the relation of Grotius to the Schoolmen in that saying of his so often repeated, "There was a gold in the impure mass of Scholastic Philosophy and Grotius discovered it."§ This judgment avoids the two extremes and presents the truth that there is very much gold in these writings.

Scholasticism properly speaking was a system of the Theologians who made use of their philosophical weapons in defence of Christianity. The originator of the system was Augustine, the Bishop of Hippo, a man of great

---

* De Jure Pel. ac Pac, Lil. 25.

† Encyc. Brit. Grotius; Schmidti Vit. Grot. Frankf. Ad Moen. 1722; Thom's. Hist. Jur. Nat. p. 48; Goering. Lit. Jur. Gent. p. 234; Bib. Jur. Imperant. p. 16; Hallam. Lit. Mid. Ages II. 543; Carmichael, Lects. on Puffendorf.

‡ Beacon Lights. Lond. II. 255

§ Hampden's Life of Aquinas. Encyc. Metropol.; Blakey's Hist. of the Phil. of Mind. II. 59, Edin. Review XXVII. 1788.

genius and commanding power in the work of systematising. There is found among his works a system of Logic, mainly Stoic, which is that followed during the Middle Ages.* Under the guise of Augustine's name the subtleties of dialectics were taught in the schools of the Monks.† The writings of Aristotle were known only in the manual of Augustine till the beginning of the 12th Century.‡ In the 12th Century the system of dialectics which had been taught for centuries in a manufactured translation, was studied in the original language.§ The position of the Schoolmen may be described. Aquinas was the most distinguished champion of Aristotelian Augustinianism. He represented the more moderate views, declaring that the civil powers possessed the supremacy in purely temporal affairs, while the Church was limited in her authority to spiritual matters.‖ Moral duty is based upon man's nature and the social welfare. Ockham the celebrated English Schoolman modifies this doctrine by making the absolute will of God the ground of morality, so that "if God had commanded his creatures to hate him" it should have been man's duty to obey.¶

The Schoolmen derived their name from those who taught in the Cathedral Schools. These Schools or Colleges were erected adjacent to the Cathedral Churches, or in the Monasteries, and were given into the charge of the learned doctors whose duty it was to attend to the education of those entrusted to them. After the regime of these schools passed out of the hands of the Church teachers into the professional class they still retained the old name. Out of the Monastic Schools sprang the public institutions of learning in which philosophy was taught by those professors, named Scholastics, who vied with one another in the use of dialectics. The Institutes of Augustine, and latterly the works of Aristotle, until the scholastics prepared commentaries, Summas, etc., were the text-books in these schools of learning, applied chiefly to the study of Theology. Scholasticism thus gradually rose up from the beginning of the 5th to the 12th Centuries, after which it flourished for three centuries.**

During the sixteenth century, in Spain, then the leading nation of Europe, we notice the appearance of an independent spirit in the study of political subjects. Taking as their basis the Scholastic writings the Spanish Jourists with a keen insight into the essential principles of justice, apart altogether from positive law, began to publish treatises on Justice and Right, in which, though not freed from the authority of the Doctors and though still fettered by the influences of the confessional, they presented the duties of men and of

---

* Biblioth. Lat. Fabr. III. p. 519.
† Launoius de Scholis. (ed. C. 5) art. 1. p. 178. Hanck 1717.
‡ Enfield, Hist. Phil. 481.
§ Gassend. Exerc. Parad. adv. Arist. Ex. III; Launoius de Fort. Arist. C. 1. Aquinas. Vol. VIII. fil. Opera. Paris 1556; McIntosh, Philosophy, p. 411. 2. note II.
‖ Cudworth's Immutable Morality, p. 16.
¶ Tratt'ss. Gen. de Doy s. 9. d. C. 1-3. Cum Praef. Hannoni; Buddi. Isag. Hist. Theol. II. 1; Aristot Freye. 1 4. 167, Malthew. Circl. ad. Arist. II; Lnko G. Hist. Ph. Po s. or Smith, Fel. Hist. Vol. II. Pt. II. s. 28. p. 60 sq.

nations on the foundation of human nature apart from any Code of morals or legal institutions of states. Francis de Victoria was the first, to whom Grotius acknowledges his obligations, who broke the spell of scholasticism. His illustrious pupil Dominic Soto, the oracle of the Council of Trent, dedicated his work *De Justitia et de Jure* to Don Carlos. We notice in this work the movement towards freedom. The necessity of manuals for the guidance of priests in the advice given in the Confessional produced in this great stronghold of Catholicism many works on Natural Right. Francis Suarez, "the acutest of philosophers and divines" according to Grotius, the last of the Schoolmen, presents even more clearly than Grotius himself the practical application of justice to men and nations.* Spain having now under Charles and Philip become the foremost nation in Europe felt the need of the help which Natural Law could give in the conduct of military operations. The war of Independence between the Netherlands and Spain produced the treatise of Balthazar Ayala and the Spanish English Naval contest directed the attention of Albericus Gentilis to the right of a state of war. Gentilis was the Counsel in Spanish claims in the English Prize Courts and as such is the first exponent of Maritime Jurisprudence. The ground prepared by the skill and erudition of Gentilis was cultivated by Grotius whose attention was called to the subject by the Thirty Years' War.† The Spanish revolution directed his mind to the limitations placed upon human power; the war in Flanders full of terrific stories of atrocity called his attention to the subject of a reasonable war-policy; the insolent and autocratic policy of the Medicis created in him an intense desire to assert the sacred character of right against the Egotism of human will; his habits of classical study, his keen insight into the Science of law, and his reverence for the universal voice of mankind set forth in the utterances of the wise men of all ages made a deep impression upon his nature and moulded the character of his work. He was scholastic in his reverence of antiquity, in the vast collection he made of human authorities from poets, historians and others; but his mind was of the renascence type in this, that he viewed these authorities not by numbers, nor by the weight of official standing, but he regarded them as "the repositories of those moral sentiments with which civilized men had sympathized from age to age."‡ Grotius looked upon men, not as poets or philosophers or church-fathers, but as men in whom during all the ages, and in all lands, the spirit of reason, of liberty, and of justice was exhibiting itself, bringing all his doctrines, as Zouch declares, to the touchstone of reason. He was a reviewer of the history of blood, a peace-maker in the age of atrocities, the embodiment in embryo of the spirit of tol-

* Epist. Apol. Anton, Bibl. Hist. Nova. Madrid 1783.
† Thomas. Hist. Nat. Juris Feenalis sive juris inter gentes pileatio 1850. R. Zouch. Praet. oho. Europ society and its Philosophy. Dean.
‡ Edin. Rev. Vol. XXVII 1831 p. 39.

eration that could embrace within its catholic charity heretics as well as the orthodox; himself a sufferer, at one time a bigoted controversialist, he gathers from all that men hold dear the solace of his exilic career, in order to present to the world that fraternity which should characterise mankind. It is now political philosophy, not for a nation, but for the world; it is peace, not for the sake of a people or their prince, but for mankind; it is the victory of learning raised above the jealousy and rivalry of schools and sects.*

If such is a true picture of the influence of those principles dug from the mine of scholasticism by the deft hands of Grotius, filled with the lustre of his own personality, and handed on through others to us, we may be pardoned if we make the attempt to trace the evolution of the political theory from the Schoolmen to Grotius so as to set it forth in the clearest light. The closing words of Grotius may be regarded as the watchword of the movement from the dark ages to the present moment, "*Monita ad fidem et ad pacem.*"

* "That the book of Grotius became the companion of Gustavus Adolphus during the war undertaken by that virtuous hero for civil and religious liberty is a very striking proof of its extraordinary fitness for its purpose.... The name of Grotius gave lustre to this part of knowledge for more than a century. His successors rather derived credit from his name than improved the science which he left them. From the peace of Munster to the French Revolution writers on this subject incessantly succeeded each other. It became a principal part of the education of all politicians; the treatises concerning it were appealed to by all sovereigns and states in their controversies. It was thought an advantage by the most powerful and ambitious prince to have them on his side; and whatever was positive and practical in these systems, whatever regulated the conduct and rights of individuals under the general usage of European War was adopted by the tribunals of one country from the writers and courts of foreign and even hostile communities. No other age of the world had witnessed such an appearance. The opinion of men without power or office or even superior genius was appealed to by conquering Monarchs, discussed by statesmen and never publicly disregarded but by those who had renounced all pretensions to the exterior of morality. Every such appeal was a lesson taught by the sovereign to his subjects of the homage due from both alike to the Supreme authority of reason." Edin. Rev. XXVII. p. 204-5.

PART I.

SCHOLASTIC POLITICAL THEORY BEFORE AQUINAS.

CHAPTER I.

PREPARATION FOR SCHOLASTICISM. METHOD OF SCHOLASTICS.

1. From the time of the Church Fathers during what is termed the dark ages there is little that can be described as philosophy. The doctrines established in the elaborate treatises of the Fathers of the Church, as the Christians increased in numbers so as to embrace the greater part of the Roman Empire, so far as they were political, concerned chiefly the relations of the Church and the State. The Church of the Apostles, living so near its founder, was governed by the principles enunciated in the gospel system of Political Ethics. In opposition to the Stoics who based their Ethics upon reason, the Christians took their stand upon the platform of brotherhood and developed their system on the basis of Christian love. Under the persecutions to which the Christians were subjected, the estimate they formed of civil government was in harmony with the teachings of their Master who declared that his Kingdom was not of this world. Civil government they regarded as an ordinance of God. Wherever man is found, this ordinance finds a place. The duty of the subject is that of obedience within the limits of "the law of God." While civil government itself is a divine institution, civil governors are not necessarily divinely appointed, and when they antagonize the will of God, it is the duty of Christians to dissent from their policy by separation from the governing body which opposes the will of God. After the Church rose into importance, especially after Christianity became the established religion in the Roman Empire in the time of Constantine, the great question around which all philosophic thinking clustered was the relation of the Secular and Ecclesiastical powers. The superiority of the spiritual was set forth in the promulgation of the codes of Justinian's Law "in the name of the Lord Jesus Christ."

The History of the Middle Ages is largely the history of the long struggle between these two powers as embodied in the Latin Church and the Roman Empire.* In the old Roman Empire, when Christianity became the state religion, the Emperor became the recognized head in civil and ecclesiastical affairs. The first evidence of a change is to be found in the decline of the Empire, when the Church Bishops are entrusted with important functions bearing upon the position of those unsound in the faith, and the relations they sustain to the civil government. The large issue before the Church, aside from the purely Ecclesiastical one of the superiority of one central authority in the Church herself, is that of the right of the spiritual power to priority and superiority over the civil power. First the Bishop of the Imperial city becomes the embodiment of Church dignity and the receptacle of Ecclesiastical authority. This was first set forth in an official manner in 445 A. D. in the decree of Valentinian III., in which it is declared that the Bishop of Rome shall form the ultimate court of appeal from the other Bishops of the Church. Then followed the decadence of the Papal supremacy in the period succeeding the Justinian administration, and during the supremacy of the Byzantine Empire. During the Lombard incursions into Italy, there arose a succession of politic and wise popes, who upon the basis of the rupture of the Eastern Empire built up the supremacy of the Papal power and attached to the Papal See a large amount of territory, still administered in name under the Eastern Emperors in opposition to the Lombards. In the struggle that ensued the Popes were able to establish their own independence. In the separation from the Eastern Empire, consummated principally by a religious dispute, the popes fearing the growing importance and the combined force of the Lombards had recourse to the Franks. The Franks came to the aid of the Popes and were successful in defeating the Lombards. The Bishops of Rome secured the papal territories in return for their favor towards the Carolingian family. The last of the Merovingians was deposed by papal decree and Pepin Le Bref was crowned king by Pope Zacharias, while Charles, Pepin's son, was placed at the head of the Empire. In this way in Charlemagne, who had conquered nearly the whole of Europe, was established the Imperial Empire, when Charles the Great was crowned at the hands of Leo III in Rome, 800 A. D., nominally, at least in the Papal view, under the Pope's suzerainty. With the decay of the imperial authority in the successors of Charlemagne, and the consequent disorder in the secular affairs of the Empire, the popes were able to establish their own authority, under a centralized and well-organized system of unity. The principles of this spiritual supremacy are to be found, not in the political theories, but in the concrete facts of history.† During the eleventh and twelfth centuries the

---

* Milman's Hist. of Latin Christianity Vol. I; Smith's Eccl. Hist. Vol. II. Pt. I; Bryce's Holy Roman Empire, p. 39; Encyc. Britan. Popedom, 9th Ed.

† Riezler, Die Literarischen Widersacher der Päpste zur Zeit Ludwig des Baiers, 1874; Niehues, Kaiserthum und Papsthum im Mittelalter, 1883; Laurent, L'Eglise et l'Etat, 1866; Baxmann, Politik der Päpste Von Gregor I. bis Gregor VII. 1868.

theory of spiritual ascendancy gained its greatest triumphs and in the person of Innocent III the secular power is completely under the control of the Ecclesiastical. He exercised his power in the deposition of kings and in the settlement of secular affairs to establish a purely theocratic rule under the Roman See.*

2. But what part had been played by the Secular power itself? Did it present no claim to independence? During the confusion of the Carolingian disintegration the chief feature of all the political struggles was the use of brute force. Disorder everywhere prevailed, even among the sentiments of the people there was no settled thought. The feudal chiefs took advantage of every opportunity afforded of exercising their tyrannical lordship, in robbing one another and plundering their own wealthy vassals. While the Church protested against anarchy, she had no force to support her protests. The Barons had little need for the clergy, because the principle of their religion and morality was "might is right." All authority fell into disrepute, and the warriors had the benefit of any victory they gained: but these warring classes were so much disunited that there was little, if any, centralized power. Hence, when through the growing influence of the papal power the Church started the crusade for unity, the secular powers were placed at an enormous disadvantage, because of their disorganization, while the Church presented a solid organization with a definite aim. The demand of the Popes was for the submission of the feudal lords, and in this they succeeded to a large extent, because secular authority had been weakened by the fierce struggles of the warrior class, and by the selfish policy of the feudal lords. Out of this struggle in reference to the relations of the secular and Ecclesiastical powers there sprung up two counter theories, the theory of SECULAR INDEPENDENCE and the theory of SPIRITUAL SUPREMACY.

The great support of the spiritual supremacy was found in the Church authorities. Its earliest introduction took place, when by a side issue, the bishops were successful in securing control over secular questions that involved issues of morals. In the Isidorian decrees, falsely attributed to the first century, there is an assertion and vindication in the ninth century, that all clerical disputes are to be settled by Episcopal judgment, not by civil jurisdiction, and that the penalties of excommunication are to be used by the Church to bring the secular princes into subjection. In the celebrated work of Hincmar, Archbp. of Rheims, we have the separation of Church and State in the Christian dispensation, the former founded by Christ, the latter continuing to exist from ancient times. The Church possesses the superior authority, exercising the limiting power over the secular princes, to prevent tyranny, to outroot heresy and to keep the Secular powers in allegiance to the Divine being through the Church which is God's representative on earth.

* Baronius Annal. Eccles. A. D. 1076; Fleury, Hist. Eccl. XIII.

Gregory VII, maintained and extended the doctrines of Hincmar, he being the first pope to establish the supremacy of the papal court over the secular rulers. In the deposition of Henry IV, Gregory vindicates his authority on the ground of scripture precedent, historical precedent and abstract principle as set forth in the Church fathers and papal decrees. This theory received sanction in the codification of the decrees, writings and declarations of the popes, prepared in the twelfth century under the name of *Discordantium Canonum Concordia* by Gratian, the foundation of the Church law (*Jus Canonicum*). This collection was prepared to support papal authority. In it we find the oath taken by the Emperor Otho, in placing himself under the papal surveillance as a feudal vassal of the pope; and also the alleged donation of Constantine in which is set forth the gift of Constantine the Emperor to Silvester, Bishop of Rome in 324 A. D., of the Western Empire of which Rome is the chief city, as a free gift of love in gratitude for the miracle which had cured his leprosy. The political doctrine formulated by the Church at this time ascribed to political sovereigns a two-fold dignity—(1) that of upholding the imperial office; (2) of championing the Church and truth, because the soul is of greater concern than the body.*

The Theory of secular independence which was developed in opposition to the doctrine of spiritual supremacy was based, first of all, on the revived conception of universal monarchy. The idea of the old Roman Empire, embracing within it the whole civilized world, led to the conception of the imperial dominion as universal. But it was chiefly by the renascence and revival of the Justinian Law in the holy Roman Empire that the theory of civil independence became enforced. By the renewed study of the Justinian system in the universities, the Doctors of law became enthused with the imperial ideas and worked out the principle of a continuous *imperium* as the basis of their defence against the spiritual power. It was pleasing to Emperors like Barbarossa to be told that they were the lineal descendants and successors of Augustus Cæsar in authority, and that the *imperium* they exercised was *quidquid placuit*.†

3. In the very midst of this strife, disorder and conflict of theory arose the Scholastic Philosophy. It was not the product of a single mind, nor was it the growth of a single generation. "The Scholastic philosophy appears to have risen up by almost imperceptible degrees from the twelfth century,

---

* Love, De jurisdictionis Ecclesiasticæ progressu, 1855; Raffel, Geschichtliche Darstellung der Verhältnisse Zwischen Kirch und Staat, 1845; Gibbon's Hdy Rom. Empire Bk xv, Vol. I. C. 6 p. 184; Ziegler, de orig. et increm. Jur. Can.; Decrees of Gratian. Janet, Sc. Polit. Vol. I pp. 341-350.

† Gibbon, Holy Rom. Emp. Ch. 65; Bryce, Holy Rom. Emp. C. 10; Fitting, Die Rechtsschule zu Bologna, 1888; Muther, Romisches und Kanon. Recht im Mittelalter, 1871; School of Bologna—M. Laferriere, Hist. du droit franc. IV; Imperial supremacy, M. Hindy, De Juribus Sancti Imper. Romani.

when it attained its maturity."* The seeds of it were sown in Stoicism, as Lorimer says, the Summas of the Scholastics being imitations of the systems of the Stoics. The church fathers were the first to nourish this seed especially those who ranked as authorities on church dogma. For the system exists in germ the moment we notice the method, and the content of that theological current of thought which supersedes as well as swallows up philosophy. It arose during the dark ages when the church became the incarnation of learning, authority and organization. This meant that the church had become the sole channel through which knowledge, power, civil as well as ecclesiastical, and organic unity were received. The old philosophic schools of antiquity have disappeared from the world, only remnants of the bright intelligence of ancient ages gleam through the thick crust that covers it. Christianity had destroyed much of the refinement and had thrust from her the works of the philosophers because they were pagan and opposed to the christian spirit. The Saracens in their zeal to gain supremacy for themselves had done what they could to destroy what christianity had left of ancient learning, because it was opposed to their spell-bound revelations. Platonism had kept its hold upon the thought of these ages, blended as it was with rigid Stoicism. When Aristotle came to be studied in the Schools and Universities, at first through Arabic and Latin translations, the new learning was utilised in the defence of Theology. This fragmentary knowledge of Aristotelian principles led to the distorted method of the earlier Schoolmen, by which they sought to explain and philosophise upon the dogmas of the christian faith. This led to the use of dialectics in the explanation, interpretation and defence of Theology, resulting in hair-splitting analyses and vague conceptions of truth. The characteristic of the Schoolmen all through the centuries of their history is the attempt to reconcile the old philosophy and the theology of the Church fathers. The rationalism of pagan philosophy is wedded to the simple faith of the christian fathers: in that relation of wedlock there is born a hybrid offspring the characteristics of which we are to study.†

The study of dialectics, loaded with metaphysical subtleties, was the scholastic preparation of the schoolmen. Abelard tells us how he began his studies at Paris, "preferring the study of logic to all others and the disputation of the schools to the trophies of war, I entirely devoted myself to this pursuit, and like a peripatetic philosopher, travelled through different countries, exercising myself wherever an opportunity offered in these contests."‡ A philosopher says that it was "the employment of the philosophical world to disputed *loca Copulos*."§ While it is true the method they

---

* Enfield, H'st. of Phil. p. ———— Vol. II. Pt. II p. 475.
† Lorimer, Inst. of Law. p. ———— Vol. II. Pt. II. p. 456; Enfield, Hist. Phil. I. p. 287-91.
‡ Hist. Calamitatum Suarum. CHI. Paris 1616.
§ Enfield, p. 480.

employed was "an ostentatious display of ingenuity," in which they assumed unproved axioms, unfounded distinctions and delicate differences, yet we must not lose sight of the fact that the art of reasoning was used in their writings with much acuteness, if with little advantage. John of Salisbury complains of their spending not a few years but a lifetime in such disputes.* Lord Bacon's judgment is expressed in the simile, "if, like the spider, the human mind draws its materials from within itself, it produces cobwebs of learning, wonderful indeed from the fineness of the threads, and delicacy of the workmanship, but of no real value or use."† Like all other writers they "found their environment prepared for them. They were nursed and trained under the over-shadowing influence of the great politico-Ecclesiastical system, which called itself the Christian Church. Under its shadow and by its influence they were moulded and educated. They never had the opportunity of experiencing a different discipline or coming within the range of other forces."

The great question is, did they do the utmost they could under the circumstances in which they were placed? As systematizers of thought they deserve the grateful thanks of posterity. If they were bound to a method that was pernicious, they had no other they could use. The Aristotelian philosophy had established its supremacy among the Saracens in the East and the Moors in the West, and through them had placed the Key of Knowledge in the hands of Christian Europe. Do we wonder that as loyal sons of "the parent of Science, the Master of Criticism and the founder of logic," as Coleridge calls him,‡ they used the mould that he cast, for the purpose of presenting to humanity the truth they held dear in a well-fashioned form. To rebuke their use of the logical method is "to blame providence for not having given to them a different mental constitution and a more penetrating insight into abstract principles and things."§

* Metal. II, 10.
† De Aug. Scient. I, Op. I, C, 9.
‡ Table Talk, 101.
§ Townsend, p. 340, 349; Confess. Lud. Vives de Corrupt. Art. III. p. 112; V, p. 155; Conf. Thomas de Caust. Inept. Schol. Praefat. 82 p. 511; Melanchthon Apolog. p. 62.

CHAPTER II.

POLITICAL THEORY BEFORE AQUINAS.

1. At what point does Scholasticism take up political theory, or what is the theory at the point when the Schoolmen appear on the scene? In order to understand Scholastic political theory we must know its connection with the historical evolution of philosophy. The doctrines associated with the political power of the state and the authority of the Church in Secular and Ecclesiastical matters slowly became a general theory. As Christianity developed the Church grew in importance and strength, accommodating itself to the political life and becoming in the end a part of civil polity. As Christian principles were opposed to Paganism, the early Christians found themselves in a position of antagonism to the existing governments. Starting in opposition to civil authorities under whom they suffered persecution, the ultimate conversion of these powers to Christianity meant the dominance of theology in the sphere of politics, because Christianity itself had become corrupted. Christ and his apostles recognized the principle of government as an ordinance of God for man's well being; but as the existing authorities were hostile to Christianity, they maintained an attitude of indifference towards them, at the same time yielding obedience to the powers that be for conscience sake, in so far as this did not lead them into disregard of the will of God. The Apostolic fathers assumed the same attitude, their indifference becoming opposition under the cruel persecutions of the Emperors, inspiring the watchword they bequeathed to the ages to come, *"human freedom and justice."* The Church took up this war-cry of religious liberty and brought to bear all the influence her Christian doctrines could command, and all the enthusiasm of her religious life in defence of this liberty. The Church secured peace in the establishment of Christianity as the state religion by Constantine in 324 A. D., and by the promulgation of the Justinian Code of Law in the name of Jesus Christ in the years 528-533 A. D.

The Christian system is not only a theological system, it contains a political theory, and hence Christianity accommodated itself to civil polity. Human freedom has its best defence in Christian toleration. Christian freedom embraces both religious and civil liberty, or equality and independence in the civil and religious life. These two kinds of freedom had a struggle to pass through in the political history of the coming ages. Through the writings of the Church fathers the despotic policy of heathen rulers was exposed, clearing the way for the Church in advising and ultimately in commanding obedience to the demands of Christianity. The learning of the clergy and the close relations they sustained to the people brought the religious influence into state-life. Hostility to the rulers led to the upraising of a rival system which found its climax in *papalism*. The old polity that had never been reformed by Christianity, but had simply attached Christianity to itself to save its life, became too weak to stand against the powerful organism that had been built up on the historic foundation of Christianity. As the civil power failed, the Church power was strengthened. It was not pure Christianity, but an outgrowth from early Christianity and pagan philosophy, the combination being accomplished by reason of the fact, that these were the two great forces arrayed against misrule, and that they united in a common struggle, when the civil power threatened to destroy them both. The Church was a new organization, and it had the new force of a spiritual victory already achieved. The ancient learning had been buried, but a resurrection was taking place and that new life was easily drawn into the Church organism. For nearly four centuries the Church had known no political party in the state. But as it enters upon its new career under state sanction, it receives from Constantine the organized form in which it is at a later date to subject the state to itself. On the model of the civil power it became the ideal of the Church to attain external unity. Forgetting the war-cry of some of the early Christians for human freedom, and Christian toleration, a toleration extending to private judgment in religion and a free inquiry after truth,* she used her organization and the power she had secured, to maintain unity in her government and in her doctrine. Encouraged by the Imperial presence the Council at Nice altered its first anathemas against the heretics, and thereafter invoked civil help against all refractory members. The one great principle which had pressed to the front during the first four centuries, was the right of private judgment in religion, free from civil pains and penalties. Many of the clergy protested against persecution to death for religious opinions. But the two great lights whose voices are raised against the world in which they stand alone, were Lactantius and Athanasius. From the fifth to the eleventh centuries another great principle is added to political philosophy, namely, the superiority of the Church over the civil power, in granting to the civil authority its privileges and investing it with the inspiration of heaven under the sanction of God's representative on earth.†

2. At this point Scholasticism comes in. Of the philosophy as a whole we may state that it is more theological than political. However, as it

---

* Tertullian Apolog. 24; Cyprian Epist. 51; Lactantius, Instit. Divin. II. c. 7; Eusebius Ec. Hist. Bk. V; Lardner's Credibility II. c. 65.

† Blakey l. c. 6; Smith Eccl. Histy. Vol. I; Vol. II. Pt. I. Review of Centuries up to 1000 A. D.; Erdmann, Hist. Phil. I. 290 f. Hough, London, 1890.

dealt largely with ethics and with theology in an ethical manner, we have the foundation principles of politics or political ethics. All the Scholastics take the ethics and the politics of Aristotle, and blending them with Christian principles, produce not in reality a science of politics, for no such science existed in those days, but a science of civil government. The greater Schoolmen present in the form of handbooks for the rulers and ruled their treatises on this important subject. The only social science with them is religion; yet this religious science has as its fundamental basis brotherhood, however exclusive, as the Christian foundation of social being in man as man. The wide field they cover in their intellectual contemplations, and the freedom they use in applying reason and rational principles to all matters of faith in the social life, elevates human freedom to the very highest place in their system, although in practice they often deny it, especially in their relations with heretics and refractory civil rulers. "Scholastic philosophy," says Blakey, "gave a unity of design and scientific arrangement to political speculations with which they had not been previously invested since Aristotle and Plato. The Schoolmen took up the science of government and formally installed it as a distinct branch of knowledge in the collegiate curriculum. This exercised a great and marked influence directly and indirectly on its future progress and prospects. Its principles were more gradually separated from the other elements of human nature; they were more minutely scrutinized and more fully tested by appeals to well-established facts. Students in the Universities carried with them many of the elements of civil polity and often bore good fruit. The maxims of political philosophy came to be regarded in different aspects, truth elicited by discussion."* The reason why they did not frame a science is to be found in the fact, that their political ideas were not based upon historical facts, but gathered from the "instinctive impulses" of human nature; they began the edifice in the Divine being, and brought it down to human realization in the abstract ideas of right and duty found in the mind of man, the intuitive principles, as they conceived it, at the foundation of human relations with God.

3. Scholastic political theory begins with the celebrated church father Augustine.† Augustine was a Schoolman in this sense, that his high reputation in the church and in the schools led to the adoption of his philosophic method of applying the subtleties of stoic reasoning to sacred doctrines, and also as Lorimer points out, his doctrines themselves form part of the Scholastic system, because the Schoolmen, even St. Thomas, could not contradict what Augustine had said, and only upon points not referred to by Augustine or upon which he left the matter an open question could Thomas exercise an independent judgment. Augustine's contribution to

* Hist. of Polit. Liter. Vol. I, C. 10, p. 218.
† MacIntosh, Philosophy, p. 93-95.

politics, like his theological doctrines, were accepted as the voice of churchmen and even of Christendom.*

Augustine was born at Tagaste in 354 A. D. He studied philosophy at Carthage and received his first inspiration from the writings of Cicero. Not satisfied with Cicero, he studied the Scriptures; but soon he abandoned them because of their unadorned simplicity of style. He next studied Aristotle under whose abstract philosophy he adopted the Manichaean conception of two independent principles, the good and the evil. He became disgusted with this system and fled to Rome, and later to Milan, where he studied and taught oratory. At Milan he met Ambrose, a christian teacher of great eloquence and profound knowledge. Under the influence of Ambrose's pure life and eloquent teaching, aided by the platonic conception of the Divine being, he embraced christianity, returning to Africa where he became a renowned churchman and a vigorous defender of the christian faith, especially applying the platonic doctrine to Natural Theology.† There are in Augustine two influences apparent, that of the church and that which springs from his study of pagan philosophy. In all human relations the church does not keep the upper hand, because man is a political being as well as a religious being. The fact that a man has accepted of christianity ought not to lessen but rather to intensify his desire to be a good citizen. Augustine repudiates the insinuation that political interests will lead man to oppose christianity, and refuses to believe that human passion can be led into antagonism to religion. It cannot be doubted that his conception of the two cities, the city of God and the city of the world, introduces an element of contradiction. But he did not believe that the dwellers in the city of the world could exercise a prejudicial effect upon the inhabitants of the city of God, because all human good was to find its permanent abiding in the city of heaven. If there is an opposition for the present, it springs from the fact of the corruption of man's nature by reason of sin, which sets defective man in antagonism to true man in God's likeness. Augustine‡ was well acquainted with Cicero's definition of the state, in which there is an association of people united on the basis of a mutual understanding in regard to law and common interest, in fact a society of men united under the bond of law, the law preceeding the organization of the society, the law of nature. Augustine places the human state on a different basis. Cicero's definition of the state he applies exclusively to the Divine state, in which there is a fixed law and definite forms of justice, whereas in the purely human society which results

* Lorimer, Instit. of Law, p. 181. Influence of Augustine on the centuries up to the 15th century. Nourrisson, La philosophie de St. Augustine Vol. II. pp. 153-175.

† August. confess. and De Civitat. Cred.

‡ "Est igitur, inquit Africanus, respublica res populi; populus autem non omnis hominum coetus quoque modo congregatus, sed coetus multitudinis juris consensu et utilitatis communione sociatus. Civitas est constitutio populi." De Repub. L. 2o. 25.°

from a voluntary association of individuals, there is the absence of law and justice in the proper sense, all human law being tentative and preparatory to a divine state. With him earthly society is imperfect, at best it is a temporary union to preserve social peace and prepare man for entering a higher state in which his aspirations after perfection can find complete realization. As distinct from the aim of the state which presents itself as the idea of the state, namely self-preservation, there springs up from the christian conception of the state, the idea which Augustine presents, that the state being the immediate work of God is destined to exalt and advance the glory of God. Hence he naturally speaks of the divine will as the law which is supreme in the state and in him we find the first tendency towards the acceptance of *lex aeterna*, as the highest law; and in subordination to this *lex aeterna* we have the human order in the conception of a law in harmony with and answering to the eternal law, the divine will being the fundamental foundation of all law in the universe. An unjust law does not merit the name of law, *mihi lex esse non videtur quae justa non fuerit*.* The law is written in the heart of men. Augustine looks upon the city or the state just as ancient philosophers had done, as of the highest importance, while the individual and the family are in subordination. The church is uppermost in his mind. The political principles of Augustine may be classified under five heads:—(1.) property; (2.) slavery; (3.) the origin and character of government; (4.) the state and the church; (5.) the unity of humanity.

(1.) *Property.* The basis of property according to him is to be found in Divine Right, consequently the only right which any one has to possession and dominium springs from the gift of God. But how is this gift bestowed and upon whom? Only those who render obedience to the true God can have any property by right. Barbeyrac, regarding this as a precarious right according to Augustine, characterizes it as an abominable idea.† Only the faithful have any right to possess anything. The unfaithful have and possess only by sufferance. He thus makes the right of property purely subjective. He qualifies this harsh idea as to property later, by ascribing a human right to property, which comes to be possessed by the dispensatory power of the sovereign. The prince, receiving by Divine delegation the right to all property, dispenses the human right to it, but this only on the condition of a good and proper use of what is received.‡ According to this theory the use legitimates the right of property, not as it is conceived with us property legitimating use. Property objectively is the result of a proper use of what comes from the prince, and the will of the prince is the conditioning determination upon which it rests. Use or abuse is determined by

  * De lib. art. II, C. I. Confess. lib. IV.
  † Puffendorf, Transl. p. 237.
  ‡ Apologie de la Morale des Peres de l'Eglise, contre les Injustes accusations du Barbeyrac, p. 119. Paris, 1748.

the prince. The prince has the right and it is his duty, to combat heretics: hence it is his will to demand conformity to the church, property is an enjoyment at the pleasure of the sovereign. There is a confusion of a natural right and a civil right of property, the latter being the same as the former only under guarantee; there is a confusion of the use of property and the right which gives the use. The prince is God's representative and what he has by divine right, he has a right to give or take *civilitu e* according as men are faithful or unfaithful. Nourrisson characterises his idea of property as *communisme theocratique*, a theocratic communism.*

(2.) *Slavery.* His idea of property led to the idea of slavery. According to the natural order established by God at first, man was not destined to command man, but this order has been reversed by sin, and servitude is a just chastisement for sin. *conditi quippe servitutis jura intelligitur imposita peccatori.* Slavery is an effect of God's judgment, who measures the penalty by the sin.† He was led astray in his conception of property by considering the use of it rather than the fact of its existence; so he was misled in slavery, by viewing man in his history rather than man in himself. He prefers the idea of the Stoics, giving up that of Aristotle. He looks upon slaves, not as chattels, but as individual beings, who have the dignity of human beings and who but for accidental circumstances should have enjoyed the privilege of human nature, namely, freedom. Slavery is a result of sin. It is an essential quality of innocent human nature that it be free. How did slavery originate? The ancients declared that it arose from war, when the conqueror gave life to his captives upon condition of degradation into slavery. But, says Augustine, war sprung from the evil passions of men, and passion has its origin in sin. Slavery therefore is one consequence of the fall of man. Just as property is legitimated by use, slavery is legitimated by the fall, or by the history of man in which the chief fact is sin. Slavery is incompatible with man's uncorrupted being; but since human nature has lost its original purity and become corrupted, slavery is possible, even necessary. So close is the relation between sin and slavery that in the present condition of society, slavery is ineradicable; nay, slavery is a blessing to those who are subjected to it. It is a part of the penalty attaching to the fall and as man under it is subjected to divine chastisement on account of sin, it is an expiation offered by man to the inexorable divine justice, leading in some measure to the restoration of man's natural primitive state of liberty. Man has fallen out of the city of God in his fall into the city of the world. His aspiration is to regain his liberty in this city of heaven. While he is compelled to make his habitation in this prison house upon earth, he cannot but expect that those who keep the prison-house will gall him with the chains of bondage. In order to

* Vol. II. p. 102.
† De Civit. Dei. c. 15.

reorganize our being we must be content to suffer humiliation. Liberty is reserved for man's restoration.

(3.) *The origin and character of government.* He unites various disparate elements in his conception of authority. The prevailing element is the ecclesiastical. All power flows from the Divine being and as such is possessed of a sacred character. It is a first principle that nothing can have a place in politics contrary to the will of God. Cicero ascribed the real origin of the State to the social nature of man, yet he introduced the secondary element of *utilitarianism* as leading man to find in the state the best means of preserving life and property. Augustine introduces a new idea, due to the persecution to which the Christians were subjected. He ascribes the origin of the state to the defective constitution of man under the regime of sin since man's fall. Cain and Romulus are the founders of this human civil government. Yet the human state is in accord with the divine will as a lower and more imperfect realization of what the will of God presents in the more exalted, divine and perfect city. This idea kept its hold upon Medieval political philosophy, for the fact that the secular government was in some way connected with human corruption presented the reason for the exaltation of the spiritual power above the inferior organization of the state. Forms of government are of no consequence. The patriarchal principle however gives the nearest approach to a perfect model of governmental authority. Paternalism is the keynote of government. The end of government is, as the platonic philosophy had pictured it, virtue; but with Augustine true virtue is to live according to orthodox Christianity. The ideal to which government tends is the complete infusion of Christian principles into the political organism, the head of which, the prince, is God's defender of the faith. In this character he speaks of the prince as "a prosecutor of crime" that he may become "a liberator of humanity."* It is not only his right but his duty to use this coercive and protective power. The circumstances of Augustine's life no doubt account for these ideas. Amid the conflicts of Donatists, Pelagians and Pagans, he felt the need of some guardian of the peace and champion of the truth. He preaches in his mildest tones and yet he invokes the secular power to defend religion because he feels it a necessity. The punishment of heresy is as necessary in the interests of public peace as the punishment of civil crimes. The prince is lord of the conscience as he is owner of the goods of the citizens. His law must be obeyed because in willing the right he acts in the name of God. Resignation and humility are the duties owed in the spirit of christianity to the civil power and to the prince as God's ruler.

4. *Conception of the state and the Church.* Having established the prince as the divinely appointed and commissioned governor, whose will is law, we must see how he is kept in check. The state is not a society of men working

1. Epist. 153.

for common ends and united by a common bond of peace. The state is a "Monastery," as Noarrisson puts it, the peace enjoyed is christian peace, and the subjects are true members of the orthodox faith. The great idea in his mind is that of the Church and Church-unity. The state is synonymous with the Church, except in officers. Only the faithful can be citizens in the commonwealth. It is from the Church that the state receives its power and through the Church it attains its highest end, the unity and government of Christians. Therefore the check upon the government would be found in the fact that the Church would be judge of the orthodoxy of the prince and therefore of his qualifications to rule. The sovereign power is vested in the Church, so that we have a theocratic state, in which an autocractic orthodox sovereign rules with a limitless power, save that in the matter of orthodoxy he is subject to the Church.

(5.) *The Unity of humanity.* His belief in and adoption of Christianity led him to that universal idea of union and unity among all the faithful. There is a unity of race which among Christians is the highest ideal of all social relations. He studied in detail all the elements in human society. He speaks in the highest terms of a state of virginity, yet he does not condemn marriage, but rather vindicates its sanctity. He sustains parental authority, but distinguishes it from the absolute power of the old *patria potestas*. In the marriage relationship he asserts a perfect and natural equality between husband and wife. Christianity has been the means of vindicating marriage and the family relationships. In the same way he speaks of the social character of city and state life. He deprecates the practice of devoting time and attention to speculation that ought to be given to the duties of the civil and political life. While preaching liberty of conscience, it is to obey the prince when he declares the law of God. He strenuously resists the barbarous practice of torture. The grand aim of war is not conquest or aggrandizement, but peace. It is impossible, he thinks, to separate politics from ethics, because justice is the foundation of peace, the basis of prosperity and the only motive of obedience to duty. Justice which finds its happiest expression in religion is the only means of rising superior to the corrupt world; specially in princes religious duty tempers the exercise of a seemingly autocratic authority. As with Plato a philosophic king is the ideal, so with Augustine, a Christian king is his ideal of goodness and good government. With Augustine man cannot be confined within the limits of individuality; he cannot find a proper sphere for his energies in the family or in the city. Christianity had broken down the barriers of nationality, at least exclusive nationality such as we find in the old world, and removed the curse of selfish racehood, to launch man into the larger area of humanity. There is a community among men based on human rationality, a community that naturally arises from the fact of man's common origin and common destiny. Christian and non-Christian unite together in the formation of this unique society of humanity in which God is the all pervading principle. Christianity becomes the universal regenerator. Man living in the old city of the world worshipped a multiplicity of Gods. Man under the new regime worships God. By the fall humanity became totally sin-infected. In the dispensation of Christianity that tends to restore man there is a twofold society, that of the world and that of heaven. In this life there is an absolute separation between these; in the future life only the elect enjoy the benefits of restoration in the city of God. The grand governing principle of history is the subordination of everything to the interest and destiny of the people of God. This idea of human unity springs from the fact of common origin from a single family, and it is in keeping with the entire progress of history that all men, the bad as well as the good, all facts and events, profane so well as sacred move towards

"the one far off divine event
To which the whole creation moves."

Upon the ashes of this general movement in the two camps in time and space Augustine builds the future life of the imperishable city in which he incarnates the universal society of the good.*

4. We must not forget the influence of Stoicism. As a system it belongs to Rome. The Stoics were the depositories and the teachers of the ethics of the Socratic Schools. They were the custodians of the principle of human freedom, namely, man as a law to himself, formulated in later times in relation to the individual, in the national and international relations of life. No other system has had such a great influence on the history of Europe.† It made its first impression upon Roman life in the late republic, and when during the Empire it came in conflict with Imperialism, it retained its influence over the individual citizen-life in the presentation of virtue as the *summum bonum*, and in the aim after freedom of individuality and universal benevolence. When society became corrupted in the decline of imperial vigor and gave place to a new order the sentiment that inspired the career of the dark ages, the principle that gave vitality to social institutions and that animated the feudal age by the spirit of lordly chivalry was the Stoic system. The "*D. Consolatione Philosophia*," written by the celebrated Boethius in the spirit of Stoicism, during his exile on account of the freedom with which he had censured the conduct of Theodoric and of his having desired the restoration of Roman freedom, is "one of the most important connecting links between the classical and the Christian world." The empire had begun to dissolve and in the midst of its dissolution barbarism overruns the domin-

---

* Nourrisson, Vol. II, pp. 398-418; Augustine, De Civitate Dei; De libero arbitrio and Confessions; Milman, Hist. of Lat. Christianity, Vol. I. 161; Barbeyrac, de la Morale des Peres; Janet, Sc. Pol. Vol. I, pp. 70-80; Fehr, Politische Theorien p. 95 seq; Ceillier, Hist. Generale des auteurs sacres ec Eccles. Vol. 15, p. 58 seq.

† Lorimer's Inst. of Law.

ions. Only a few scattered remnants of literature and science are preserved. Boethius is the one great light in these dark ages by whose presence in the world social philosophy is rescued from total destruction. Boethius seems to have been under the inspiration of ethical principles.* Alfred the Great and the poet Chaucer in his *King's Complete*, as translators of this work clearly identify the English civilization with these ideas in the Middle Ages. Boethius transmits the Stoic Electicism to the Scholastic age, blending together Plato, Zeno and Aristotle much as the schoolmen did Christianity and Aristotelianism.

The seeds of scholasticism were sown when philosophy and theology became intermingled, the one in illustration of the other, and especially when from the time of Alcuin, who died in 804 A. D., the spurious writings of Dionysius, of *Moribus*, received credit among christians and were used as text books in the schools. The learning of Boethius and of the venerable Bede gleamed through the darkness of the western world during several centuries. Alcuin, the celebrated professor of languages at Cambridge, used the influence of his massive genius in the confidence of Charlemagne, to establish schools in France, Italy and Germany, from 793 A. D., introducing morals in Gregory's *Moralia*, and philosophy and theology in Isidore of Seville and Augustine.‡ "It was in imitation of these expiring efforts of Stoicism that the Summa of the schoolmen and of the casuists began to be composed."‡ The efforts of Alcuin, the first of the schoolmen according to Dean, were directed to the establishment of a union between power and intellect, the former being embodied in Charlemagne whose throne he aimed to establish as the source of all intellectual development. These two social elements were displayed in the schools of France. Alcuin's contribution to the future of scholasticism §

Among the first of the schoolmen after Alcuin is to be ranked the name of Joannes Scotus Erigena, about 800 to 877, who translated for Charles the Bald the works of Dionysius the Areopagite, supposed to be the first Christian teacher in France, "*On the celestial monarchy*," "*the ecclesiastical hierarchy*," and on "*Mystic Theology*." Despite the prohibition of Pope Nicolas I, these works introduced the platonic elements of mystic theology into the western church and laid the foundation of the first opposition in Western Europe to the received faith of the Church of Rome. His system of philosophy was inseparably associated with religion and was a kind of science of everything which he derived from the fulness of nature and idealised in a nature-deity.‖

* Fabr. Bibl. Lat. I. and III.
† Mabillon, sec. IV; Conring Ant. Ac. Diss. III. p. 75; Launoius I. p. 15 and 31.
‡ Lorimer, Inst. p. 119
§ Dean, Hist. of Eur. Soc. 239-49; Schools of Charles the Great, J. B. Mullinger, 1877; Poole p. 84.
‖ Jourdan, IV. 19; Chron. scot. Ed. by Galueus; Conring. Ant. Ac. Supp. 31; Macbeth de Gest. Reg. Ang. I; F. Sac. West in Floc Lost. ad An. 887; Cedren. Hist. Gener. Aug. XII. c. 22. p. 509.

He wrote a work *on the nature of things,"* published by Gale at Oxford, 1681, under the title *Joanni Scoti Erigenœ de divisione naturæ libri quinque*, in which we have the scholastic idea of nature. Like the monk of later ages, he retires from the world of sense, into the material world of contemplation including God, the creator, and nature, the thing created. He divides nature into four parts:—(1.) that which creates and is not created; (2.) that which is created and creates; (3.) that which is created and does not create; (4.) that which neither creates nor is created. God is all things and all things are God.* He renounces this world for the next in which God will be all in all and nothing will remain but God alone.† The idea at the foundation of this system is the repudiation of external nature's teaching. It was this antagonism to nature in its phenomena that opened the way for the assertion on the part of the church of supreme authority over theology and philosophy. Men who retired into the unknown prepared the way for the voice of the unknown speaking through the ecclesiastics. Monkery and asceticism were the two pillars upon which scholasticism rested. It is this that has made the Catholic faith of the middle ages the irreconcileable foe of free thought and political autonomy. The enthusiasm of Erigena sprang from a deification of the divine which easily gave place to the mysteries of Ecclesiasticism. The one idea handed down from the church fathers through Augustine to this age was the Divine manifestation in humanity. This the church laid hold of, and giving forth the utterances of theology as the will of God, they descended into dogmatism. The grand problem of Scholastic writing therefore was the reconciliation of faith and human reason. It was in this sense that Anselm 1035-1109, the first reviver of Augustinianism wrote his *Fides quærens intellectum* in which he asserts that faith has nothing to fear.‡ That Abelard, 1079-1142, declares that his pupils demanded arguments to satisfy their minds and that he himself characterised christianity as *reformatio juris naturalis*.§

(5.) *Hincmar*, 806-882, Archbishop of Rheims, the most celebrated writer in the ninth century, distinguished himself by the earnestness and ingenuity with which he maintained the controversy of the times. In the conflict between Adrian II. and Charles the Bald he wrote a treatise on the "Character and office of a King," but his chief work is entitled *"De Potestate regia et pontificia."* ‖ In this work he treats of the relation of the civil and ecclesiastical powers. He draws a parallel between paganism and Christianity in reference to the two powers. He tries to separate the temporal from the spiritual power, by limiting the proper sphere of each. In the pagan system there is a perfect union of the secular and religious, there being no distinction between

---

* B. k. III. p. 185.
† p. 212.
‡ Trithemius de Script. Eccl. c. 351.
§ Blakey, Vol. I. C. 10, p. 218; Cousin's Intr. p. 142.
‖ Trithemius de S. E. c. 294.

the two; whereas in the Christian system there is a separation of the powers for the purpose of promoting human well-being and especially to carry out the instructions of the founder of Christianity Jesus Christ founded the Christian Church and gave to her laws, authority and organization. He had nothing whatever to do with the foundation of a state. He rather submitted to the power of the state, declaring that his Kingdom was not of this world. Jesus Christ alone held the twofold office of King and Priest. Knowing the weakness of men he has separated by definite acts and special characteristics the two powers, desirous of keeping the holders of the power from falling into undue pride, as did the Emperors under paganism prior to Christ. It was his will that Christian Kings should be in subjection, in all due humility, to the priests in matters concerning eternal life, while the priests as God's soldiers were not to take anything to do with temporal things, but to be subject to the Emperor in civil matters. Especially, men who are entrusted with temporal affairs should not preside over councils on spiritual matters.* Kings are subject to no law but that of God, the royal partisans say. Everything he has as King is by God's permission because God establishes the princes. "The heart of the King is in the hand of God," as it is written. The power of the King is absolute as against the clergy and Kings may not be excommunicated by Bishops or others. His armor opposes any limit to the power of the prince, save as it is in subordination to the spiritual power. Christ established his Kingdom and placed it where the priesthood of Moses stood. Jesus Christ accepted the foundation, laws and organization of the state as set forth in the Old Testament. In that revelation of the will of God, contained in the Old Testament, there is the vindication of the superiority of the Church, as possessing a higher because a spiritual authority. Nathan subjects King David to certain pennances, as his superior, the servant of the Lord. Saul is called to be King and anointed before the people by Samuel the priest; he is also commanded to be subject to the Divine authority. The apostolic injunction addressed to Kings is *ut reges obediant*, *non præsint ecclesiæ Domini*, that they be in subjection to those placed over them in the Lord, evidently quoting from the pseudo-Isidorian Decretals, as no such passage occurs in the New Testament writings.† In this way the secular power is limited by the authority of God, entrusted to the Church so as to prevent tyranny. He distinguishes between a King and a tyrant, the former is subject only to God, while the latter being a violator of God's law is subject to the judgment of God's representatives on earth the Church or the clergy. It is true, he says, the King is not subject to any law or judgment save that of God, if he is a true King. *Rex* is to exercise his office *regens*, on the principle of *recta regula*, that is rule according to right and oppose evil: but if a

* De Pot. Reg. c. I.

heretic, adulterer, slave of vice, then he is subject to be judged by the bishops who are the supporters of God's authority, in whom He resides and by whom He gives his judgments to men. In a letter written for Charles the Bald, he expresses a different idea, "Kings are not deputies of Bishops but masters of the country. They are not the serfs of Bishops."* Hincmar, while admitting the superiority of the spiritual over the the temporal power, does not admit that the Pope is above the other Bishops; he claims that the Bishops are responsible only to themselves as God's officers. He also denies the validity of the principle of heredity in the succession to royal power. It may be a means of determining who has the best claim to the succession, but it is subject to the judgment of the Church against any who may possess such a claim but who is a violator of God's law. He says, paternal nobility is not sufficient to secure the suffrage of the people to the children of Kings; because vice on the part of an individual tends to the forfeiture not only of rights of nobility, but even of liberty. There is no such thing as a divine right of Kings, and inviolability does not attach to the person merely as a person, but it depends upon the value of the person. There are here two liberal ideas, Kingship depends upon the suffrage of the people, and qualification for office is the determining principle of selection. The Ecclesiastical doctrine then comes in. As the Bishops say to Louis, "Jesus Christ created Bishops to govern and instruct thee," so says Hincmar. He joined in the conflict after Lothair's death in 855 which tended to strengthen the Ecclesiastical supremacy. After rescuing Charles from his own nobility, he said, "if Kings rule according to God's will they are subject to no one; if they be great sinners then is their judgment in the hands of the Bishops."†

6. Intimately associated with the Scholastic political theory, in fact forming a part of it, is the Ecclesiastical system of politics that sprung up during the conflict between the Church and state carried on between the Popes and Emperors and their respective followers. There were two great doctrines set up the one in opposition to the other—firstly, the sovereignty of the state and its independence in governing the nation, without Ecclesiastical interference; and, secondly, the divine right of the Church, as representing God's sovereignty, to control the secular government in the name of God. The controversy sprang up gradually and is to be found in the Ecclesiastical and political history of the early centuries of the Middle Ages.‡ *Gregory the Great*, whose blind zeal led him into the persecution of paganism and opposition to learning is the first in whom we discern the growing arrogance of

---

* M. Ampere, Hist. Litt. III. c. 10.

† Janet, Sc. Pol. I. 328-32; Encyc. Brit. Hincmar; Works of Hincmar, Ed. by Sirmond, 2 Vols., 1645; Migne's Cursus, Pat. Comp.; Prichard, Life and times of Hincmar, London, 1849; Noorden, Hincmar Erzbischof von Rheims, Bonn 1863; Gess, Merkwürdigkeiten aus dem Leben und schriften Hincmars, 1806; Cellier, Hist. Gen. des. auteurs Sacres, Vol. XII. c. 74.

‡ Account of the conflict Smith's Eccl. Hist. Vol. II. Pt. I.

Ecclesiastical power. His celebrated *Book of Morals* is itself the embodiment of the claims of religious supremacy above morality and even above grammar; and the claim of the Church to possess and guard all human knowledge. In a letter addressed to the Eastern Emperor he claims to oppose a law forbidding soldiers to be received in the Monasteries as a law contrary to the Sovereign Lord. As the servant of God and of the Emperor, for he does not refuse obedience as a subject, he says to the Emperor in the name of Christ, "I have made Caesar Emperor and the Father of Emperors." "I have entrusted my priests to thy care and thou art to give thy soldiers to my service," calling upon him to answer to these words at the judgment day. He distinguishes between the obedience he owes as still a subject of the Empire and that he owes to the truth of God.† The words of the Bishop of Rome are those of a subject speaking in terms of respect in the name of God to the Emperor. There is no idea of usurpation. When the King of Lombardy took possession of Ravenna the seat of the Eastern Exarchate, Pope Stephen, successor of Zachary, invoked the aid of Pepin King of France to repulse the Lombards. When the Lombards were defeated Pepin assigned the spoils of his victory to be held by the successors of St. Peter. The routed King signed the order, delivering up the Exarchate with all the cities "to be forever held and possessed by the most holy pope Stephen and his successors in the apostolic see of St. Peter." The Lombard King soon retook what he had given up. Stephen in order to gain the ear of Pepin presented the famous forged letter of St. Peter.‡ In the time of Charlemagne the relations of Church and state are still the same. The conqueror of Europe, however, aided in strengthening the temporal power and establishing the political pretensions of the Papacy. Charlemagne addresses Leo III on the occasion of his election, "We greatly rejoice at the unanimity of your election and the humility of your obedience and the promises of fidelity you have made." Leo III replies to the Emperor "if we have not followed the sense of the true law we are ready to reform after your judgment and that of your commissioners." About the same time was forged the second letter which appeared under papal sanction, known in history as the Donation of Constantine. We attribute to the Chair of St. Peter, all imperial dignity, glory and power. Moreover we give to Silvester and to his successors our palace of Lateran.... We give him our crown, our mitre, our diadem, and all our Imperial vestments; we resign to him the imperial dignity.... We give to the holy pontiff the city of Rome and all the western cities of Italy as well as the western cities of other countries. To make room for him we abdicate our sovereignty over all these provinces; and we withdraw from Rome, transferring the seat of our Empire to Byzantium since it is not just that a terrestrial Emperor shall retain any power where God has placed the head of religion."§ After Charlemagne the

Sarisberiensis, Policrat. L. 9; II. 35-9; VIII. 19.
Gregor. Magni Opera, Vol. II. p. 663, Ex. 66, Paris 1705.
‡ Codex Carolinus, Epistle 7.
§ Gibbon's Holy Roman Emp. VI. 16; Guizot, Hist. de Civilis. de France, Lec. 27; Janet, I. 335-6; Blakey, I. 177-81.

supremacy of the spiritual power becomes more pronounced. The church is the only real power in the state of confusion that prevails, and it is not slow to assert its controlling authority, and to centralize that authority in the Papacy above all other powers whether Civil or Ecclesiastical.

Accompanying the letter of St. Peter and the Donation of Constantine, there is a third series of forgeries, the false decretals, these three forged writings being the first, and by far the most important, of the documents used as foundations for Ecclesiastical supremacy. It is the first indication of the adoption by the Church of the Scholastic principle of authority in defence of Church politics. These letters and writings are attributed to the first papal successors of St. Peter after Clement, the immediate successor of Peter. They are generally attributed to Isidore, Archbp. of Seville who died in 636 A. D., a man of immense erudition and the influence of whose writings was great. His writings are of very great value on account of his general use of Latin authors. The design of these decretals was to establish the spiritual supremacy of the Church and the predominance of the Church of Rome over other churches. The jurisdiction of the Bishop of the Church is set up over the temporal, for if brethren have any matters to decide in their affairs, they ought to bring them, not before the judges of the age, but before the priests whose decisions they should obey.* Clement I, is represented as saying, *"Itanquam te omnibus praeesse moneris."†* All men, princes as well as subjects are commanded to render obedience to the church and in case of disobedience they are accounted infamous and expelled from the church.‡ The priests are exhorted to remember it is their office to instruct princes and it is the duty of rulers to obey the priests as they would obey God.§ The Roman Church has received her primacy direct from Christ; Peter and Paul both consecrated the Roman Church is above all others; and the spiritual judges must have the final decision in all matters because they are substitutes for God himself.‖ In a letter of Gregory the Great the climax is attained when it is asserted, if any king, prince, or secular ruler violate the authority of the apostolic see he ought to be divested of his secular authority.¶ Nicholas I, the earliest of the Popes to realize the idea of a universal dominion for the Church of Rome copying the example of Hincmar, lays down the principle upon which to make use of this power of deposition of rulers. Writing to Auxentius, Bishop of Metz, he says, "see if these kings and princes to whom you are subject are true kings and princes; see if they govern first themselves and after the people; see if they rule according to the right, for if they do not, they ought to be considered tyrants, not kings, and ought to be resisted. If we are subject to them, or favor them in any way, then we are reckoned to favor their vices."**

After a century of disorder and darkness the conflict between church and state revived with increased force during the eleventh century. Out of the

* Pseudo-Isidor Lett. I, p. 6. Geneva, 1628.   † I, p. 110; II, p. 121; III, p. 138.
‡ p. 9.   ‖ p. 533.
‡ p. 21.   ** Guizot, Hist. de Civil. Lec. 27; Janet, I, 378-8
§ Lett. III, p. 74.

conflicts of nations, amid intellectual and political renascence, the church raises herself as a united organism above the mass of confusion. It was now the mission of the church to regenerate society and to reform the state. It was the policy of the populace to bring the state into subjection to this church organism. It could not be done without a reformation in the church herself. It is because Hildebrand was animated by this ideal, the reformation of the church as a preliminary to the reformation and submission of the state, that we are able to see a better side to a policy that was carried out by dubious means, characterised by haughtiness and cruelty. This led to the strict separation of the clerical caste from the laity and ultimately to the elevation of the priest above the people and above social forms. This gave to the church organization which claimed to be divine, as against the civil power which was regarded as human, an influence it used in the warfare between church and state to the advantage of the former. Gregory VII. is the embodiment of this principle in the war he wages against the empire and in the use he makes for the first time of the power of deposition. The clergy of the empire make a loud protest against this fresh assumption of papal prerogative.* "He is raised above all as if he were God. He not only pardons sin, but he frees men from the force of the law of Christ, and from the obligation of oaths—all this he calls the law of God." Gregory is compelled to defend his position against the clerical protest. He does so in his two letters to the Bishop Hermann of Metz. Civil government he regards as an institution of man. It is so defiled by its origin among sinful men, for Cain and Nimrod are its founders, that it is itself sinful. Between the church which is divine and the state which is human and sinful there can be no permanent peace, until the latter is brought into harmony with the divine through the former. He argues from history, from the scriptures of the old and new Testaments, in favor of the superior power of the church. He ascribes the source of the power of the prince to God through his representative on earth. Wicked kings, he says, owe their power to the devil.† The *Dictatus Papal* which is ascribed to Gregory VII. 1075 A. D., embodies the papal conception of Ecclesiastical authority and supremacy. "The Roman church is founded by God alone. The Roman Pope alone is *jure* styled *universalis*. He alone can use imperial insignia. At the feet of the Pope only are all princes to bow. He can depose Emperors. By no one can he be judged. He can absolve subjects from allegiance to wicked rulers."‡ The long conflict between the papal and imperial powers drew forth many letters from both sides.§ Against the theory of Gregory it is argued that in the Scriptures God had said, "they have reigned but not by me; they have been

---

* Goldast, Monarchia Sanct. Imp. Rom. Apolog. pro Imper. Henr. IV. a ?c. Greg. VII. p. 46. Hanover, 1614.
† Mansi, Coll. of Councils XX. Ep. Greg. VII. bic. IV. Ep. 2. VIII Ep. 21
‡ Jancz, I. p. 344; Its authenticity is questioned. Pagius, Critica in Annales Baronii.
§ Goldast, Mon. p. 1-2; Hanover, 1611. Riezler, die Literar. Wider. der Papast. c.

tecmes per institutionem. Sovereignty therefore in making and unmaking the civil powers belongs to the Church.*

9. Peter Lombard, 1100-1164, who was educated in jurisprudence and philosophy at Bologna, the author of the first *Magister Sententiarum*, illustrates after the method of Augustine the church doctrines by sentences gathered from the fathers. Among the questions which he selected for disputation is the following, is it permissible to resist the power? Is resistance legitimate? He answers the question in the scholastic method, by the citation of numerous opinions on the the question pro and con. He answers himself, that obedience is absolute as laid down in the doctrines of the apostles and fathers, save only when that absolute obedience comes into conflict with that higher obedience which is due at all times and in all circumstances to God. Not only do the powers that are accounted good come from God; but evil power is of God, permissively allowed and used by God as the minister of God.†

Alexander Hales, who died in 1245, of the order of Minors was the first author of a *Summa*. He discusses the question of authority under the heading, *An justum sit homini in homini dominari?* Is it just for man to have rule over man? He quotes the authority of Gregory the Great against such domination. To this opinion he answers, as Paul had answered it, "let every soul be subject to the powers that be," and also in the language of St. Gregory, "nature hath made all men equal; yet the just dispensation of God hath subjected the one to the other according to the differing merits and capacities of each."‡ He also treats of the relations of the secular or civil and Ecclesiastical or spiritual powers more in detail. Does the Ecclesiastical power become a usurpation when it gives secular judgments? May it interfere in the civil domain? In favor of the separation of the two powers he instances the distinction of the earthly and the spiritual life, having different ends, and using different means to attain their ends. That the two powers are independent is according to the ideas of Scripture, for it ordains, "render unto Caesar the things that are Caesar's; and unto God, the things that are God's." As there are two swords, the temporal and spiritual, these ought to be used independently so as to avoid usurping the authority exercised by either of them. Against the separation of the two powers he cites the example of Christ, in driving out the money-changers from the Temple, in which case Christ exercised a temporal jurisdiction; Moses also was judge as well as pontiff; the priesthood is an institution of God, while royalty is of the priesthood by the command of God, the blessing being given by the hands of the priesthood to the people and rulers alike. His own opinion is presented by a scholastic distinction. The two powers, he says are distinct, *quoad exercitium*, in as far as their separate exercise is concerned; and they are so distinguished *quoad imperium*, but not *quoad unum*, that is in as far as they are both

---

* Hug. de S. Victor, De Sacramentis li. 2. c. 4; Jan. c. L. 315-9; Blakey, Pol. Lit. I. c. 19; Migne, Patr. Lat. Vol. 175-177.
† Trithemius, de Scrip. E., c. c. 377, p. 96; Launoius, de Fort. Arist. pp. 189-192; Migne, Patr. Lat. Vol. 191.
‡ Summa, Paris III. qu. 48, m. 1, a.

imperium, they are separate, but they have not a seperate *autum*. The spiritual power possesses its own *imperium* and *autum*; but the secular power while possessing its own *imperium* is subject to the *autum* (will) of the Ecclesiastical power. Hence Alexander puts it, "The relation of the secular to the Ecclesiastical power is not the same as the relation of the Ecclesiastical to the secular; for the Ecclesiastical is never subject to the secular, while in some things the secular is subject to the Ecclesiastical." It was in this way the pains and penalties of the state were meeted out to the heretics. The church professed to have no power to punish, but it had the will, that will handing over the refractory to the power of the state for its exercise in inflicting the penalty. This is also shown in the fact that the church possesses the power of determining who shall hold and exercise and how they shall exercise the civil power; that is, the sovereign power of instituting civil government and of judging who shall be civil rulers, as well as of impeaching and deposing them, rests with the church.*

Bonaventure, 1221-1274, was a member of the Franciscan order, a student and Doctor of philosophy at Paris and a Cardinal under Gregory X. He was a deputy at the celebrated Council at Lyons, dying during the session of the Council. His writings are chiefly of a mystical-theological character. According to him all human knowledge is divided into three branches, logical, physical and moral, all the branches being contained in the sacred Scriptures. Physical knowledge is concerned with the symbolical parts of Scripture; logical philosophy reasons from the external words or expressions, to the internal; while moral philosophy is the peculiar outcome of the monastic life of contemplation in communion with God.† In this we have the key to his political sentiments. All power, he says, in as far as it is power and by virtue of its relation to him who commands is just and comes from God. So far as the power itself is concerned it is just and good; but on account of the sin of man, man may get this power by unjust and unlawful means. If it is received in a lawful manner, it is from God and its exercise is just; if in an unlawful manner, it is not from God and its exercise is unjust. A good civil ruler is from God; a bad ruler comes from sin and is from the devil. Yet by reason of man's corruption, no power of man is wholly just; therefore we can only say of every power, it comes in part from God. The power ought to be in harmony with order and right; if it is against order and contrary to the right it is unjust. If all power comes from God, at least in part, we ought not to dispossess any of those who have the power. Power he answers to this, is not inviolable. If God gives power absolutely and without condition it would be inviolable; but if God gives it for a time or on a certain condition, then it would not be inviolable. Just as *justice* compels the

---

* Summ. Paris. II. qu. 119. m. 3. a. 1; III. qu. 40 m. 5; Janet, I. p. 353; Trithem. de Ser. Eccl. c. 451; Fabr. Bibl. Lat. Med. I. p. 60.

† De Reductione artium ad Theologiam, Bk. I. Opuscula. Lugd. 1647; Trithemius de Scrip. Eccl. c. 474 p. 112.

judge to take away the life of the brigand without injustice; so the abuse of the sovereign power demands that it be destroyed and its privileges taken away in order to vindicate right, and prevent wrong-doing. He next asks, if civil control is an institution of nature or simply a form of chastisement. In order to answer this question he distinguishes between the rule of a Master over a subject, which is according to nature, and the other two forms in which power presents itself, namely, that of a spouse or father over another spouse or child, and that of a person over a thing which are *extra natura*. The subjection of subjects to Masters arises from the corruption of the fall and is the penalty of sin. Christianity frees man from sin, but he is not wholly set free from the faculty of and inclination to servitude, which appears as the penalty of sin. It is a part of the Divine order that Christians should be subject to princes and rulers, but not in all things, nor in those which are against reason and custom. Christianity frees from the servitude of sin and the bondage of the Mosaic law; but not from human law which ought to lead us to the observance of the Divine law. On earth this distinction of ruling and ruled classes will continue as a discipline to lead man up to heaven, where there is a full enfranchisement from misery and domination such as man is subjected to in this life. Obedience then is not absolute in all things, and human power is not unlimited; yet obedience is a virtue like self-sacrifice with the monk. Self-sacrifice and charity become the foundations upon which he bases a kind of mystic socialism, such as has been developed more fully on somewhat different lines among the Christian socialists of later centuries.*

Albert the Great, 1193-1280, the predecessor and Master of Aquinas was possessed of much learning. He became a Dominican Friar in 1221, and a professor at Cologne and later at Paris, where he acquired a high reputation. Few men in that age possessed the same skill and knowledge of the natural sciences, and his skill in their use was attributed by the men of his times to magic or some other infernal art. No mere abstract truth, he thought can be accepted as a guide to legislative action. Political maxims cannot be laid down as universal postulates for permanent application in the course of the human history of society. Aside from the abstract, which cannot always be perceived, as divested of special circumstances of time and place, there are capacities of mind and sympathies of soul which exhibit themselves in political combinations of individuals, which cannot be influenced by naked maxims and which cannot be guided by general principles of politics. Human idiosyncrasies must be studied by him who would be an adept in politics in order to find out what is suitable to men's wishes and conditions of life; the subjective conditions of man, his feelings, desires, aspirations, and affections exercise an influence upon his social character and mould society itself. In every social

* Lib. Sentent. II. (I art. 2; Fabr. Bib. Lat. Med. IV. p. 121; Opera. Romax. Rome, 1598 Erdmann, I. 336.

change there are a variety of conditioning causes to be taken into account. We cannot assert positively that there is any principle or set of principles which can be applied with legislative sanction to regulate the movements of men in society. He is against the abstract in the sphere of politics, denying the rigidity of rule in social life. "The consciences of men, their affections, reason, sensitiveness to dishonor and coercion, desire of glory and happiness, benevolent affections and sympathies, their ideas of what is just, good, expedient, are all matters for the contemplation of the politician, and these are all matters which lie in vast abundance on the surface of society, and hence living and active agents of varied intensity in every symptom of change and innovation. Truth in politics, therefore, becomes hedged about with a peculiar sanctity, apart from its sacred character. It is truth in relation with many things and not truth barely contemplated in its own naked character."*

What is interesting in the political ethics of Albert is the fact that liberal ideas are not rejected by him simply because they are innovations. Although his knowledge of Aristotle and ancient philosophy cannot be regarded as very trustworthy, coming as it did through Arabian channels, on account of his ignorance of the Greek language; yet he gathered enough from these sources of independent thought to give him an insight keener than that of any of his predecessors, into the variable character of politics and political maxims. The rights, the conditions and the feelings of the people, as well as the external relations of things, these are ideas that break down, or at least modify in a large measure the unchangeable maxims of Hildebrandine politics. Derangement may naturally enough arise in political government and may influence the form of government. Sir Robert Filmer's contention that the doctrine, that men naturally born free from subjection by nature have a right to choose their own government and that the power of one over others was first bestowed at the discretion of the many, was hatched in the schools, does not fall far short of the mark, when we consider the democratic tendencies in politics in men like Albert.† Albert had no special preference for Monarchy and to him political theory was the product of so many internal and external causes, that with different surroundings and in a more enlightened age, he might have been the most radical of theorists. The man who through love of humility and dislike of the pride associated with the episcopal dignity, could abandon the chair of rule for the life of study is not the man to hanker after the Divine right of any person or to contend for a changeless system of authority. Elasticity is the law of life, it must be the law of institutions likewise.‡ The diligent study of Theology and his extensive acquaintance with natural science, led Albert to take a deep interest in the

* Blakey, Pol. Lit. I. c. 10.

† Filmer's Patriarcha, c. I, p. 2. 2nd. edition.

‡ Vinc. Justin. in Vita Alberti Mag.; Spanheim, Chronic. A. D. 1354; Trithemius, Ann. Hirs. I. p. 592.

world around him and in which he lived. One grand difference between him and his disciple Thomas is to be found in the fact that to Albert the world is the physical world of sense, while to Thomas it is the moral and political world. This marks off the politics of Albert from the politics of Thomas, giving to the latter just pre-eminence.

An examination of his political ideas might reveal many gems of thought for which others at present receive credit. Such a judgment is verified by the fact that his political speculations which are contained in eight books embrace the most extensive field of political ethics and of politics. One merit of his treatise on politics is that it is more philosophical than theological. He has digested the Politics of Aristotle as he got it from Latin translations, notes and Arabian commentaries. We notice two designs in all the works Albert, (1) an attempt to christianize Aristotle's philosophy; (2) a well defined effort to present the Christian faith in a philosophic system. He had the boldness in that early age of christian civilization to modify Aristotle's principals so as to unite the ancient philosophy and Christianity. Never before had Aristotle been the special subject matter of lectures in the Christian Schools and Albert deserves the praise as his first expositor, however imperfect his knowledge may have been. He exercised a strong influence on the mind of his pupil Aquinas.* The subjects of which he treats are as follows. (1) He considers the abstract nature of political power in itself and the various divisions into which it falls among different nations. He speaks of the *civitas* and its parts and rulers, of the power of governing in the household and state, of the difference between *dominatio* and *gubernatio*, the latter being the government of a state. (2) He enters upon a discussion of the principles and gives an analysis of governmental systems found in the history of Greece, Carthage, and Egypt. He refutes the opinion of Socrates that all union and community is found in the state, rejects community of goods, examining the different states of Solon's constitution, the Lacedæmonian and Carthaginian types. (3) He examines the abstract question of human society, the nature and origin of social combinations, and points out the differences in the different forms of the state-republic, Democracy, Aristocracy, Oligarchy and Monarchy. He defines the state and considers the end of the state, and the end of man as an individual. (4) He treats separately all these forms of government, giving a detailed account of the Politics of Aristotle. The different species of states, he points out, differ specially in the quality, not the quantity of each. He specifies various kinds of Democracies and Oligarchies, and treats of tyranny. He specifies the three parts of a governmental power, *consilium*, *magistratus* and *judicium*. (5) He mentions the causes which produce disorder in the exercise of political power, and examines the effect which these causes have upon the different forms of

* Life and labors of St. Thos. of Aquin. R. B. Vaughan. Vol. I, p. 115. 2 Vols. London. 1871.

government. He points out the causes of changes in states, by which one form gives place to another. (6) He treats of proprietorship and of the nature of polity, indicating the ends and purposes of popular government. 7. He shows what is the best life and the happy state, giving the activity to be employed and the means to be used in attaining these ends. He dwells upon the material situation, possessions, and enjoyments of the state, the fortifications necessary for its defence and the best division of the state. 8. He considers the subject of education and kindred subjects bearing upon the discipline of the citizens so as to prepare them for occupying their places with advantage to themselves and the state. How are good and free citizens to be made? He says that mental training and the acquisition of knowledge become proper instruments of extending the influence of good government. In order to promote good order among members of the community and to produce the best government on the part of the political body, it is the duty of legislators to attend to the interests of natural education among themselves and among the youth.*

10. John of Salisbury who died in 1182 was one of the most learned men of his age. He went to Paris in 1137 and attended the lectures of Abelard and other masters of Theology and Philosophy, acquiring an extensive knowledge of science, morals and languages, being a Greek and Hebrew scholar, a rare accomplishment in the 12th century. He was the friend, strenuous supporter of and after 1163 the companion in exile of Thomas a Beckett. Conscious of the frivolous nature of dialectics as taught and practised in his own time, he cultivated a high regard for true philosophy and exercised his fruitful genius with the correctest sense of literary taste he could foster in the elevation of true wisdom and enlightened principle above the ignorance of his time. There is no truer picture of the philosophical spirit of the age than that which he presents of his own visit to the former home of his student life in Mount St. Genevieve: "dialectic studies however useful they may be when connected with other branches of learning, are in themselves useless and barren."† His Polycraticus is the first production that can be characterized as a systematic treastise on politics. It is above all a philosophy of politics. We have no hint from beginning to end of the Polycraticus that there was a struggle going on between Frederick and Hadrian, just becoming ripe for open hostilities; there is nothing to indicate that John himself through his attachment to and advocacy of the policy of Beckett has been alienated from the royal favor and cause; there is not even a reference to the history of the time, or to the then existing forms of government, far less

---

* Albertus Magnus, Opera, 21 Vols. Lugduni 1651, 1654, Politics 4th. volume; 21 Vols. Lyons Ed. 1615; Blakey, Pol. Lit. I. c. 10 p. 228; Bach, Albertus Magnus, Wien, 1881, for general view of his relation to the Greeks, Latins, Jews and Arabians; Albertus Magnus, Sein Leben und seine Wissenschaft, Sighart, 1857; D'Assailly, Albert le Grand, 1870; Stöckl. Gesch. d. Schol. Phil.; Erdmann, Grund. d. Gech. Vol. I.

† Metal. I. 2, 3; II. 17, 19.

any account of the struggles through which the papal power has passed in its antagonism to the Greek Empire, and in its conflict with the barbarian forces and the Franco—feudal ideas. His forms are drawn from the ancient Scripture and Roman times; his theory of state is a reproduction of Plutarch's ideal; and his official designations are purely classical. Overlooking all conditions in human society that are changeful, such as the order of feudal lords and barons, he gets right into the principles of civil polity, as these are conceived by him to be enduring and unchangeable.*

(1.) *Theocratic idea of the state.* In the first books he lays down the general principles upon which he bases political speculation and thinking. When darkness and error prevail the truth disappears and the foundations of virtue are shaken. Who is so unworthy as the man who despises knowledge, for man borne away from truth and consequently from virtue becomes a brute, loses the image of the Divine and therewith loses his dignity as a rational creature.† In judging of what is right, we do not question, whether it brings pleasure or promotes utility, but we say that whatever opposes *natura* and *officium* ought to be characterized as *simpliciter alienum*.‡ We gather the idea of the distribution of duties, *officia*, from the political constitutions of the ancients; justice in its precepts and morals gives us the ground of prosperity in the great society of men.§ All things yield to the use of the wise, and they who are wise use all things in the exercise of virtue.‖ Public safety is the concern of man in general, individual safety of single lives, for nothing is more valuable than human life, nothing more durable than safety.* It is not only lawful but just and right to kill a tyrant, for he who takes a sword in his hand, deserves to die by the sword. He who receives power from God, serves the law and is a child of justice. But he who usurps it destroys right and subjects the laws to his own arbitrary will. No crime is so grave as treason, because it is against justice and the body of justice. Tyranny is worse than treason and more than a public crime, because it is a crime against the whole body of the earthly republic.** In book IV. he goes on with the treatment of tyranny, distinguishing the tyrant from the *princeps* who rules by law and according to the principle of *publica potestas* embodied in himself as the very image of Divine majesty upon earth; whereas the tyrant believes himself to be law, and rules for his own exclusive benefit. The *princeps* is the minister of God. The king is on a level with eternal law as its exponent and interpreter for the people, and is independent in the sense that he is the embodiment of the universal sense among the members who follow him as their Head. The prince's power comes from God and is not

* Baluck Hist. Ac. Par. II. p. 750; Fabr. Bib. Lat. Med. III. p. 580.
† Bk. I. c. 1.
‡ c. 2
§ c. 8.
‖ II. c. 1.
* III. c. 1
** III. c. 5.

the less divine in that it is exercised through his minister.* Equity as the jurists call it, *concenientia rerum*, the perfect adjustment of things, the natural law of the Stoics, the arrangement of the *ordo naturalis*, giving to each one what is his own under the guidance of reason, forms the basis of civil government, the foundation principle of the civil order. The prince and the law which is his ordinance, interpret justice for the people. The prince is the absolute legislator provided he be just. The *princeps* is to promote the good of others before his own private good, and he is to be guided by justice and equity. He may not deviate from the strict law of equity, his own opinion and judgment having legal force only if conformed to justice. He speaks of the prince as one freed from the bonds of law, not that he has freedom to do evil, but because the motive that leads him to promote the welfare of the state, should be, not the dread of punishment, but the love of justice. We cannot speak of the prince's will, for he has no will to do anything save what equity directs and what the public good commands. When his will is guided by equity and utility it forms a right judgment and his decree has the force of law to all the members of the commonwealth.† The *princeps* is thus raised above everything else, so as to elevate above him the Ecclesiastical power. The prince is the minister of God, but God is represented by the priesthood; therefore the prince is the minister of the priesthood, and thus inferior, for he receives the sword of power from the hand of the church, since the church cannot hold the sword of blood, but uses it in the hand of the prince to coerce the bodies of men. The temporal power exercises that part of the sacred office that seems to be unworthy of the hands of the clergy. The secular power derives its authority mediately from God, for the sacred laws are treasured in the church, which receives her power and dignity immediately from God.‡ The prince must be subject to the law of justice embodied in the Divine Law.§ All law is worthless if it does not bear the image of God's law and the prince's decree is void unless it conforms to the church's discipline.‖ The King ought to be a fearer of God and humble in the sight of God that his public authority be not lessened by reason of pride or presumption.¶ The state according to this reasoning is established upon the principles of eternal righteousness and as these are under the custody of the church, it is natural that the state, in its ideal of perfect conformity to righteousness, should be under the control of the church. The divine law is the rule of the prince's life, and the regulator of his public as well as his private actions. Justice and mercy and moderation are the virtues of his life and the attributes of his administration, executive and legislative. The reward of the good prince is prosperity and fixity of rule for himself and his sons. All political systems not founded upon these principles of truth and equity, fall into the category of tyranny, being based on these maxims of misrule, which arise from false ideas concerning the nature, position and purpose of the common

* IV. c. 1. † c. 2. ‡ c. 3. § c. 4. ‖ c. 6. ¶ c. 7.

wealth. When princes fall into such a position, involving injustice, injury to others, contumely and deceit, their kingdoms are and ought to be transferred to others. Injustice is a habit of mind which destroys equity and sweeps it out of the region of both morals and politics.*

(II.) *The State as an Organism.* Having established his theocratic and Ecclesiastical state, and constituted the ruler in it as the tool of the sacred Church, he proceeds to give an account of the state in itself and of the elements of the commonwealth. Finding no Biblical text-book which could guide his thoughts he had recourse to Plutarch's *Institutio Trajani.* The principate is the greatest of all human things, for it fills all things and by the force of virtue brings glory to the republic. The prince is conceived as the head of that living organism, the commonwealth, which is animated by the force of religion as the soul of the organism. As the head is governed and controlled by the soul, so the ruler is guided and controlled by religion in the republic, subject to God's will and authority. The different classes of society in the organism are represented by the separate and different members of the body. The heart is the Senate; the eyes, ears, and tongue represent the judges and presidents of provinces; the hands are the soldiers and other subordinate officials of state; the sides (latera) are those who assist the prince in his administration; the feet are husbandmen and common workers and laborers; the belly and intestines represent the administrators of finance, these being always inclined to extravagance and to luxury which threatens the body with destruction by means of dissipation and prodigality.† He gives an account of the division of duty, honor, and responsibilty among the different classes in the organic state. He does not repeat the doctrine of the subordination of the secular to the spiritual power; but the whole drift of his reasoning is that the secular is permeated by the religious element, religion as the soul of the republic caring for the interests of the spiritual nature. The qualifications of the Prince, the Judges and the rulers of all kinds are of a religious nature, justice and equity being demanded on the part of all. He censures severely the vices of the rulers, glorifying justice as the queen of all the virtues ‡ There is enjoined upon princes a fourfold duty, reverence of God, self-respect, discipline of officials, and affection towards and protection of his subjects.§ There is a special honor attaching to and reverence to be cultivated towards those who minister in sacred things.‖ He seems to favor the election of the king by the people, as when Samuel convened the people for the purpose of electing a King, but the appointment is made in reality by the ordination of God.¶ The Senate should be composed of just men who fear God. Nothing is more noble than a council of old men whose duty it is to counsel in matters of rule, who are endowed with strength of body and force of intellect, the wise men of the state.** Soldiers are not only to fight

*. c. S-12. † V. c. 2-13; VI. 1-20. ‡ VI. c. 24-26. § V. c. 3. ‖ C. 5. ¶ C. 6. ** C. 9.

for the temporal honor of the republic, but the special use of the military is to preserve the Church, to fight against perfidy and the perfidious, to reverence and cultivate a reverence for Sacerdocy, and to repel injuries offered to the poor.* The State must be ordered after the fashion of nature for the civil and political life imitates nature; if it does not, it becomes *incivilis*.† Every one rejoices in liberty, for slavery is the image of death, while liberty is the security of life ‡ Vices induce servitude, a servitude to vice which is far more miserable than the servitude of the person; for in the latter case the soul may be good and free, although the body is in chains, in the former the soul is in bondage even though the body is free.§

(III.) *Doctrine of Tyrannicide*. John jealously guards the principate by the exclusion of tyrants‖ from all the rights and privileges of Kingship. While he does not support the theory of contract, he adopts the principle of election as the mode of appointment under the divine will;¶ and he sets up the judgment of the people in the case of tyranny as the test, amounting to a negative proof of the contract idea, in its breach. Tyrants are not only to be deposed, they are to be slain. It is a sacred duty to resort to tyrannicide in the case of tyranny. He distinguishes between the moral value of different means used in tyrannicide. Poison is forbidden. It is lawful to use any other means besides that of poison, because poisoning is destitute of precedent as a means of getting rid of a tyrant. He who falls into tyranny has become a foe of the state, and it is the duty of the state-members to rid itself of such a pest of society.** Tyrannicide appears for the first time since Cicero in John of Salisbury. It is conceived as a necessity in order to carry out his distinction of tyrant and King. There are two instincts found in man, the love of justice and the love of the useful. From the first springs the love of liberty and of country, freedom and patriotism; from the second springs the passion for domination, which manifests itself in the spirit of inequality among men.†† The love of liberty gives rise to tyranny when it seeks liberty of self to the exclusion of and not for the liberty of others. To procure power he gathers forces and accumulates riches from all parts of the state by the oppression of those of equal nature and condition with himself.‡‡ The difference between a tyrant and prince consists in this, the true prince rules by the laws and fights for the laws and liberty of the people, while the tyrant is only satisfied by oppressing the people through violent domination and by reducing the people to servitude. The prince is the image of Divinity, the tyrant of Lucifer, the devil; the prince is and ought to be feared and reverenced, but the tyrant is to be and ought to be watched *plerumque occidendus*.§§ Law is the gift of God, the form of equity, the norm of justice, the image of the Divine will, the means of securing the safety, unity and consolidation of the people, as well as the exclusion and extermination of vices and the punish-

* VI. c. 8.   † C. 21.   ‡ VII. c. 17.   § C. 25.   ‖ IV. c. 1.   ¶ V. c. 6.
** IV. c. 15; VIII. c. 17²⁰.   †† VIII. c. 5.   ‡‡ VII. c. 17.   §§ VIII. c. 17.

ment of the violent, unjust and deceitful." It is lawful to lure a tyrant to his death, *ei namque licet adulari, quem licet occidere*. It is both *æquum* and *justum* to kill him.† The exception to this rule is to be found in the case of the priests, who are not allowed to use the material sword against the tyrant, out of respect to the sacraments and lest damage be done to religion, so that tyrannicide may be *sine religionis honestatisque dispendio*.‡ The end of all tyrants is misery and destruction and God's vengeance unless they are reclaimed by divine mercy.§ Such is the doctrine of John of Salisbury. The state is under the control of the church. It possesses a large amount of freedom in action, to develop itself on the lines of the social classes, provided these remain within the limits marked out for them by the ideas of justice. Injustice and oppression on the part of civil rulers are held in check by the obligation of removing and killing an oppressor.‖

11. Hugh of Fleury, Hugo Floriacencis, was a benedictine monk, who wrote in the beginning of the 12th century, a treatise *De regia potestate et sacerdotali dignitate*, in defence of the imperial independence and in opposition to the claims of supremacy made by the spiritual power. The foundation of the treatise is the text of scripture, "all power comes from God." It is part of the general plan of creation, he says, by which God set man over the other creatures and placed the head above the other members of the body, that God should distribute among men themselves different degrees of dignity and honor, just as he who is the sole monarch of the kingdom of heaven established the orders of archangel and angel in the heavenly world.* There are two great powers upon earth, the kingly and the priestly. These two powers are united in no one person, save in the Lord Jesus Christ. In the person of Christ, the kingly office is the image of the Fatherhood of God, and the priestly office of the sonship of the son of God, so that the priestly office is in subordination to the kingly. Just so in the earthly kingdom, the bishops are to be in subjection to the kings. It is the duty of the kingly power to promote the interests of the spiritual kingdom, and to bring the people into subjection to the right by means of the laws. The spiritual power is to use the word of God to bring the people to obedience and the temporal power is to exercise the disciplinary authority of law for the same end. The people are kept in check by the king, but the king is only checked by God. Bad Kings is well as good Kings are sent by God; in his anger he sends the bad as a chastisement to the people when they need correction; the people have no right to resist, save by spiritual means, such as prayer. It belongs to God alone to rebuke the pride of the haughty and to remove from their places the unworthy rulers.** Thus the doctrine of passive obedience is proclaimed in opposition to the doctrine of tyrannicide in John of Salisbury, in the twelfth

*. VIII. c. 17.   †. VIII. c. 18; III. c. 15.   ‡. VIII. 17, 18, 20.   §. VIII. 21.
‖. Polberaticus, Leyden, 1575; Migne, Patr. Lat. Vol. 199; Poole, Illust. of M. Th. pp. 232-9. Janet, Sc. Pol. I. 384-4; Blakey, Pol. Lit. I. c. 10.   * l. c. 1.   **. l. c. 2.

century, as the mainstay of the imperialism which is set up in opposition to the usurpation of temporal jurisdiction by the spiritual power.*

At this point we meet with the great light of the Scholastic Theory, the scholar and expounder of the Mediæval Theology, Politics and Philosophy: Thomas Aquinas.

* Melanges de Baluze, Bk. IV, A. D. 1426; Janet, Sc. Pol. I. pp. 378-90.

PART II.

THE POLITICAL THEORY OF THOMAS AQUINAS.

CHAPTER I.

PRELIMINARY.

1. The Political Science of the Middle Ages has until very recently been left untouched. Different writers have studied the institutions, laws, general literature and the natural science as found in the writings of that age; but few have thought it worth while to study the social and political theories, thinking the labor would not be repaid by its results. The more we investigate this so-called barren field, the more rich do we find it in the materials for science. One philosopher in bidding adieu to the thorny and intricate pathway of the middle ages on turning towards the renascence of literature and the revival of science, does so in the rather quaint language of Martial:—

"Turpe est difficile habere nugas,
Et stultus labor est ineptiarum,"

"'Tis a folly to sweat o'er a difficult trifle,
And for silly devices invention to rifle."*

The age of trifles, inventions and speculations was as essential in the progress of thought as that of the positive scientific thinking. It is not entirely a misfortune that Theology was the Science of Sciences in the Middle Ages, and that political science occupied only a secondary place in the scheme of knowledge. It was fitting that Christian thought which left in the background all purely philosophic systems and had brought the new civilization of humanity to bear upon ideal and semi-deistic conceptions of the world and man, should contribute its quota to the upbuilding of man's civil life. The Christian thinkers alone cared for knowledge in these dark ages, and if they threw their monastic spell over the thought of a freer political era, it was that it might be preserved in the shell of sacred tradition as the kernel of freedom to break forth in new forms and with fresher life in the resurrection of the ages. More than this, we owe a tribute of grateful praise to the

* Enfield, Phil. p. 517.

memory of the men who demonstrated to the world, that pagan philosophy was not an unmixed evil, that the better elements of its rationalistic system could be incorporated into the Christian system. Christianity had begun the war against paganism and pagan ideas; it had been carried on by the representatives of that system whose founder professed to be the Light of the world; for more than a thousand years it seemed as if Christianity refused to own that there was a better side to man in his pre-Christian life, and that the same God who gave the fuller light of the incarnation could have given the few gems of thought and rays of light that shone amid the rubbish of an age of atheism, idolatry and superstition; faith had fought against reason and refused to acknowledge that the rational nature of man could be anything but darkness. But now the time has come, in the fulness of the ages, grossly dark though these ages may appear, when faith and reason are to be reconciled when Christian thought and philosophic truth are to be incarnated in one human system, when the God providentially the same in the pagan and Christian wolrds is to manifest Himself as the same God all through time. The body into which that truth is put may be a body of clay, but it must be so, because the body must die in the after ages before the new germ of life can spring up. It was fitting, yea it was a necessity of nature, that Theology and Theologians should accomplish this task. Any other science, purely material or natural, would have destroyed the spiritual and moral, the result would have been a morbid pessimism; whereas the spiritual and religious life of Theology and its aim after immortality gave an elevating and sublimating influence to the natural and political sciences which prevented these from degradation to pure materialism, until they were so matured as sciences that they could stand alone.

It is for this reason that we place such a high value upon Thomas Aquinas and his work, in whom nature and revelation, science and theology, faith and reason find a coitus, that bears fruit nearly five centuries later. Thus though Political Science occupies but a humble place in the Theological system, consummated by Thomas, it still holds a place of honor and it has received through its relations with Theology a new form which cannot be overlooked in the history of politics. Social, political and economic science, as well as Public and International Law appear in a new light after the age of the Summa and the Christian commentators on Aristotle and on sacred Scripture. The institutions, social and civic, of the Middle Ages stand forth in greater grandeur in the light of these writings, because the establishment of these institutions is written in the lives and conflicts of the very men who stood in the heat of the battle. Politics can never forget that John of Salisbury was the most war-like and courageous spirit of h's time, as Cousin well says; that Thomas Aquinas was the most celebrated among reformers and publicists, the ideal of the populace and the oracle of the Church; that

Aegidius Romanus was the preceptor of Philip le Bel and the royalist lawyer of France; that Marsilius was the friend and counsellor of the Imperial cause, the moving spirit in defence of a peaceable nationality; that Dante was the poet and philosopher of universal empire; and Suarez the last publicist of Scholasticism, the progenitor of the new order, and the champion of popular sovereignty. These are the men who in the history of their own times led the van of theoretical acquaintance with science and have given to us the details of that political science which forms a part of the development of the science. Thomas stands head and shoulders above them all, because of his massive genius, because of the position he occupies as fifth Doctor of the Church by the decree of Pope Pius V., because of the place assigned him by the learned world as the Universal and Angelic Doctor, and because of the influence, almost amounting to infallibility as a standard, which his writings exercised during the centuries upon Church decisions as well as political opinions, among laymen and Ecclesiastics alike. A special interest attaches to his works because he wrote, not as a prejudiced partisan, while fully acquainted with the controversies of the times and reflecting the spirit of the age in the calm reflections of his own monastic life upon political problems, but as a dispassionate seeker after truth. He combines general with special political theory, in the essay he wrote upon the government of a kingdom by a prince; and he systematizes and collects into Scientific form the opinions of past writers with an accuracy that may be characterized as independent and faithful. Aquinas is the star of Scholasticism, the highest and best embodiment of its principles, method and spirit. To know his political principles is to be introduced to the general thought of his own age and to understand the guiding ideas that kept alive the same system, that propagated the same spirit with a force and clearness varying during the successive ages for well-nigh a thousand years.

2. Thomas Aquinas was an Italian, of the illustrious family of Aquino, in the Terra di Lavoro, and related to the Hohenstaufen house. He was born in 1224 at the Castle Aquino, near Monte Cassino. He was educated as a child at Monte Cassino, after which he went to the University of Naples. Here he acquired the habits of a retired life, and despite the opposition of his family and the entreaties of his mother, he became a Dominican, entering the order of the preaching Friars. After entering the order he was forcibly conveyed to the Castle at Aquino and there detained for two years by his mother's orders. He escaped by the aid of some Dominicans and took up his residence in Naples. Afterwards he became a pupil of the celebrated theologian and philosopher, Albert the Great. By persistent discipline and patient study, he overcame a natural diffidence and dullness, and very soon outstripped his master. He became a distinguished teacher in Paris, then the University Capital of Christendom. After a few years spent as Doctor of Theology at

Paris, he retired to Naples where he spent the rest of his life lecturing on Theology. He died in 1274 in the Monastery of Fossa Nova in Campania, on the way to the Council at Lyons, to present a refutation of the errors of the Greek Church, prepared by the order of Pope Urban IV. Albert called him "the light of the Church," and the Catholic Church grateful to his memory enrolled his name among her worthies as her greatest theologian and philosopher and canonized him as one of her saints.*

The collected works of Thomas are very extensive, embracing in all over twenty volumes. Several editions have been published at Parma since 1851, and several editions have been published at Rome, under the authority of the Popes from Pius V. in 1557 to Pius IX. and Leo XIII. His chief works are *Summa Theologica*, *Summa Contra Gentiles*, the latter being a defence of Christian doctrine against heathen doctrines of Mohammedanism and the Arabian philosophy, the former being a system of Theology in which philosophy and Christianity are declared, defended, and summarized. He wrote also extensive commentaries upon Aristotle's works, physical, metaphysical and political, also commentaries upon holy Scripture. Great men have spoken of him with admiration. Erasmus regarded Thomas as the most superior genius of any age. Ludovicus Vives speaks of him as the soundest of all the Schoolmen. Charles Werner published his work on "the life and doctrines of St. Thomas" in two volumes Regensburg, in 1858, 59. He characterizes Thomas as "the most thoroughly educated theologian who has arisen in the Church, standing unrivalled,† the most honored teacher of sacred science." Maurice in his "Moral and Metaphysical Philosophy" writes of him, "A time may be coming when it will be possible to derive more good from Aquinas than any age has owed to him because we are free from his trammels...Protestant Europe may even yet do him a justice which cannot be done by those who dread lest he should make them sceptics, or who sit at his feet and receive his words as those of one who understood all knowledge and all mystery."‡ "In the progressive systematizing of truths in philosophy and theology the massive figure of the saint, scholar and monk of Medieval ages holds a foremost place," is perhaps the truest estimate of his merit.§ In the literature of Political Science Thomas has received a more careful con-

* G. de Thoco Vit. Aquin. in Act. S. T. III. p. 655; Oudin. de Script. Eccles. III. p. 239; Launoius, de Fort. Arist. c. 10, p. 215.

† Vol. I. p. 871

‡ Vol. I. p. 616.

§ Lord, Beacon Lights of History, Vol. II. p. 276; see also Stockl. Hist. of the Phil. of the Mid. Ages, Vol. II. p. 422; Main, 1865; Townsend, Great Schoolmen of the Middle Ages; Hampton, Bampton Lectures; Hist. de la vie et des Ecrits de St. Th. d'Aquin.; Abbe Bareille; Lond. Quar. July 1881, Th. Aquin.; Werner's Leben des Heiligen Thos. Von Aquin.; Hampden's Article in Encycl. Metrop. on Thomas and Scholast. Phil. which Hallam regards as the best on the subject in the English language.

sideration within recent years. Forster,* gives some account of the politics of Thomas in an unsatisfactory manner. Blakey devoted three pages to him in the History of Political Literature.† Mohl does not set a high value upon Medieval writers.‡ H. R. Fenger§ gives an extended account of the Politics of Thomas. Frederick Von Raumer‖ gives an account of justice, ethics, human and divine law, the relation of the Church and state, and statesmanship as found in Thomas and considers the question of the authenticity of the *De Reg. Princ.* and *De Eccod. Princ.* Bluntschli¶ mentions Thomas' views in reference to the superiority of the Church over the state. Frohschammer published his Die Philosophie des Thomas Von Aquino in the year 1889 in which he devotes pp. 477-502 to the politics of Thomas, giving a brief summary of his views, specially in relation to the Church, and also a trenchant criticism of his Ecclesiastical politics. Franck,** and Janet†† and Poole‡‡ give us valuable Summaries of the political doctrines of Aquinas. But there are two writers, the one a German and the other an Italian, to whom we are indebted for the most satisfactory and systematic account of the politics of Thomas. Baumann published his Politik Von Thomas Von Aquino, 1873 in which he presents a translation of the *De Reg. Princ.* with supplementary extracts from the rest of the works of Aquinas bearing upon political subjects. Barri presents in his Le Teorie Politiche Tomas Aq., Rome, 1884, a systematic and scientific account of the political doctrines of Thomas in seven chapters: (1) the concept or the nature of the state; (2) the end of the state; (3) the sovereignty in the state; (4) the form of the government; (5) the function of the sovereign power; (6) the limit of the action of the state; (7) the relation of the church and state.

The works in which St. Thomas has treated of politics are: (1) *Theological*, *Summa Theologica*, the *Summa Contra Gentiles* and the *Expositio* of the Book of *Sentential*, with the commentaries on the Bible. (2) *Philosophical*. Treatises on Aristotle's Ethics and Politics. (3) *General works*, which are classified under *opuscula* in the Roman editions, over sixty in number, the chief work being the special treatise on government, *De Regimine Principum*. Three of his works are chiefly of importance on the subject of politics, *the Summa*, the *De Reg. Prin.*, and the commentary on *Aristotle's politics*. In the latter work

---

* Ueber die Staatslehre des Mittelalters. Allg. Monatschrift fur Wissenschaft und Literatur. 1853, pp. 832-62, 922-36.

† Vol. I, pp. 226-229, London, 1855.

‡ Die Geschichte und Literatur des Staatswissenschaften. Vol. III, p. 374.

§ Essai sur les doctrines politiques de St. Th. d'Aquin., Paris, 1857.

‖ Geschichte des Hohenstaufen, Vol. VI, pp. 406-21.

¶ Geschichte des Allgemeines Staatsrechts und der Politik. 1864.

** Reformateurs et Publicistes de l' Europe, Moyen age, pp. 39-69, Paris, 1864.

†† Histoire de la Science polititique dans ses rapports avec la Morale, Vol. I, p. 457 seq.

‡‡ Illustr. of Med. Thought p. 240 seq.

he sets himself to explain, analyze and interpret the genuine work of Aristotle, so as to reproduce with slight modifications the philosophy of his master. The *De Reg. Prin.* is more original than the commentary, being a letter on the origin of royalty and the duties of Kings, in which there is considerable adaptation of political theory to the circumstances of the time. It gives us a picture of the ideal kingdom before the mind of Thomas and brings him into line with the age in which he lived. The last part of the second book, the third and fourth books are no doubt the work of a later Dominican writer and follower of Thomas.† As Baumann points out there are certain lacunae in the *De Reg. Prin.*, e. g., (1) the consideration of the state from the point of view of nature and reason; (2) specially the rational view of the state as modified by divine revelation, and the relation of the state to the church. To fill up these blanks recourse must be had to the miscellaneous works of Aquinas, chiefly his *commentaries* and other *opuscula*. The *Summa Theologica* is the greatest of all his works, in which is presented in its entirety all his doctrines, in a more general way than in the special hand-book, *De Reg. Prin.*, and with more individuality than in his commentaries upon Aristotle. His treatise on Laws in the *Summa* is one of the finest Ethical writings which any age or literature has produced; it is known as the *Prima secundae*. His treatise on virtues and vices is important because of the relation of virtue to justice and the relation of vice to sedition, in the former finding as he does the principle of equality and in the latter the limits upon sovereignty. Among the *Opuscula* there is a writing of considerable merit, *De Eruditione Principum*. It is a treatise on the politics of the times and presents the qualifications and training necessary for princes. It commanded the admiration of Bellarmine and contains an attack on the nobility. Its authenticity however is questioned. Among the other writings may be mentioned *De Emptione et Venditione ad tempus*, *De Usuris in Communi*, but these are both of doubtful authenticity. Another writing *Determinatio quorumdam casuum*, later known as *De Regimine Judaeorum, ad Ducissam Brabantiae*, is a letter to the Duchess of Brabant and it has chiefly reference to the action of the state towards the Jews, containing also an important point on the subject of taxation.

3. The importance of the works of Thomas arises from the fact that he is the embodiment of Scholasticism. The spirit of the Middle Ages was aiming at the realization of an unlimited empire, the means to be used in its realization being an outward form of organization and authority. The state is an enlarged church, and the Church a visible unity exercising the highest

* For the value of his comments and how to use them, see Baumann, p. 103 sq.; Fengeray p. 16; Werner, Vol. I, p. 187.

† Baumann, pp. 556; Riezler, p. 135 sq.; Fengeray, Introd.; Franck, Ref. et Pub., p. 53 sq.; Bernhardt, Mazin de Rubeis, Opera Aquin. Vol. XVI. pp. XV-5, Parma Ed.; Life and labors of St. Th. of Aquin, R. B. Vaughan, 2 Vols. London, 1876.

influence upon all human affairs. With the rise of the principle of nationality this Ecclesiastical-imperial idea became somewhat limited. Scholasticism meant, in opposition to this universality, one grand system, one great science, one all-powerful authority. Gathering all knowledge into one centre, every fresh conquest in the field of thought added one more link to the chain that led up to the *Summa*. The plan of the work coincides with the method used in establishing the conclusion, namely, the reduction of all knowledge to a unity. The whole range of knowledge with all its causes and consequents is reduced to two terms, human and divine philosophy, faith and reason. The reconciliation of these is the *summum bonum*. In the *Summa cont. a Gentiles* of Aquinas these two are distinguished and each one is recognized as a distinct *origo* of knowledge. Revelation is the divine unveiling of mystery through the media of scripture, tradition, the fathers and Church decrees. Human philosophy is the natural system of right, revealed in the human reason, not of persons, but through the various systems which represent the collective wisdom of the heathen, particularly the platonic philosophy and the Aristotelian method. In these two departments there is a higher and a lower kind of truth, the latter alone attainable, both of which however find themselves reconciled in the supernatural being. Thus like streams of thought all other forms of knowledge lead up to this. This illustrates the method of Aquinas. It implied a keen insight into the products of reason and revelation, in man's experience, and a knowledge of the relations which these results sustained to man himself. Revelation produced a mass of doctrines, from the theologians and fathers to the sacred scriptures. The master of sentences formed the first link in the chain; then came the opinions on disputed points in the *Quæstiones Disputatæ*; then the doctrines of the Church fathers and apostles in the commentary on the gospels; the last link being his commentary upon sacred scriptures, the direct supernatural revelation. Passing by the platonic and neo-platonic Philosophy, he grasped the Aristotelian system as the best theoretical and practical manifestation of the light of human reason.

The method of the system he elaborated in his extensive commentaries upon Aristotle's Politics, Physics, Metaphysics and Ethics. These he applied to his great system of formulated human thought in matter and form, in substance and shape in the *Summa*. It is easy from this to gather his method. The method of his whole work is systematic, the aim being to present, first, a scientific plan of all human knowledge; and secondly, to reconcile philosophy and theology. His method as a commentator, his commentaries being lectures delivered as a professor, is the exegetical and explanatory. He began by reading the Latin version of the text; proceeded to give the literal sense with different variations; appended new proofs and reproduced the entire syllogism; lastly, he criticizes the principles, adducing his authorities for these are the important factors in scholastic writing and method. The great characteristic of the stupendous mass of his writings is the reverence for authority, as it is of all the Schoolmen. The method was dialectical and syllogistic. He analyzed, first of all, the statement of a writer, till he discovered his fundamental ideas. He stated the arguments for and against, and formulated a solution out of these antinomies. He got all the authorities and judged from probable evidence which had the greater weight. The general plan of judging is by delicate analysis and fine discrimination in order to resolve different and often opposite solutions into a satisfactory conclusion; afterwards by another series of syllogisms he enforced this conclusion. On account of the weight given to authority the method made use of is wholly deductive; first principles are chosen at will and from these conclusions are drawn. The whole of scholasticism was ruled by authority, the authority of Aristotle and Augustine, the authority of the Church fathers, Canonists and Doctors among the casuists of later scholasticism. There were only two possible ways of dealing with authority, (1) to elude it, or (2) to accept it. In the first case authority is eluded by fine discriminations and delicate distinctions, a good example being found in the case of usury, and the reconciliation of the Church fathers on the doctrine of property with the theory of Aristotle. In the latter case acceptance meant that the validity of any question was determined by the weight of an opinion, whether logical or not, in accordance with or contrary to the truth. This is illustrated in the matter of slavery, as explained by Aquinas. Slavery could not be rejected by Scholasticism without overturning the entire system of civil society established in the philosophy of Aristotle and accepted by the Church fathers. It would have required an entirely new constitution of the social elements.* Scholasticism always marches along with authority. Aquinas recommends the method he uses, the deductive, in connection with his explanation of law, *lex est quoddam dictamen practicae rationis. Similis autem processus est invenitur rationis practicae et speculativae; utraque enim ex quibusdam principiis ad quasdam conclusiones procedit ut superius habitum est. Secundum hoc ergo dicendum est, quod sicut in ratione speculativa ex principiis indemonstrabilibus naturaliter cognitis producuntur conclusiones diversarum scientiarum, quarum cognitio non est nobis naturaliter indita, sed per industriam rationis inventa; ita etiam ex praeceptis legis naturalis, quasi ex quibusdam principiis communibus et indemonstrabilibus, necesse est quod ratio humana procedat ad aliqua magis particulariter disponenda; et istae particulares dispositiones adinventae secundum rationem humanam dicuntur leges humanae, observatis aliis conditionibus quae pertinent ad rationem legis. Unde Tullius dixit quod initium juris est a natura profectum; deinde quaedam in consuetudinem ex utilitatis ratione venerunt.†* The Scholastics have often been accused of confusing ideas in a labyrinth of reasoning. There is nothing, however, that cannot be discerned in their wonderful maze of thought. Whatever idea

* Sum. Theol. I a. qu. 96.

† Sum. Theol. I a. 2 ae. qu. 91. art. 3.

or ideas they wish to present, they present in the garb of logic. It is not difficult to note the point that is made, because each question is set forth by itself, each article is definitely marked. Under each article the affirmative and negative are set forth in the form of antinomies. The scholastic problem is to find a delicate distinction which will form the characteristic intermediate solution. This is the method of all scholastics. It may not be very interesting, but at any rate it is marked by precision and definiteness. The Schoolmen, chiefly Thomas, are not strangers to the semi-historical method. The *De Reg. Prin.* is an essay away from the pure scholastic method in which there is a quasi-historical treatment of the subject of monarchy. We have the germs of the historical argument in the principle of *utility* that is introduced, the adaptation of means to ends in the whole reasoning of the book. In the law of progress from imperfect to perfect we have the basis of an historical development applied to the history of law and to the development of man.*

* Sum. Theol. 2a 2ae. qu. 98, 2.

CHAPTER II.

ETHICAL PRINCIPLES AT THE FOUNDATION OF POLITICS.

1. In the writings of the Master of Theology in the Middle Ages bearing the sanction of the Catholic Church we are not surprised that the relation of Theology and Politics is very close; especially from the fact that Thomas is the reconciler of reason with faith, we naturally expect that the entire basis of his political ideas is to be found in Ethics, the ethics of human reason and the moral philosophy of Divine Wisdom. God is in all things by essence, presence and power this according to Thomas is the ultimate fact in all science and philosophy.* All things are governed immediately by God according to reason although the execution of the government may be by media.† Reason is the first principle of humanity, the foundation of all society.‡ As man is a political animal the four cardinal virtues, justice, prudence, temperance and courage, as they exist in men, corresponding to the condition of his nature, are exercised in the conduct of human affairs. Justice alone directly respects the common good, but the other virtues lead indirectly to the same end. Justice is the most illustrious of the moral virtues.§ Prudence is specially directed towards the good of the multitude, that is political prudence, being allied to virtue, as political justice is to legal justice.‖ Political Ethics may be characterized as individual ethics extended to the political domain; all relations are controlled by ethical principles and all conduct is guided by rational considerations. Political Science, therefore, presupposes the ethical principles of Thomas. When he came to set forth his politics proper he based them entirely on the abstract principles of human nature, having no concern with the facts of the external world. Human senses give only a partial view of the social existence. It is only in the moral and religious consciousness that we get a complete view of social philosophy, and the basis of a perfect governmental system. The ethical elements are the fundamental grounds of political action and evolution. It is in this way man is viewed in his complete being, and in this unity of being he attains his ideal in the social life, for the moral nature of man brings him into direct

* Sum. Th. 1a. qu. 8. 3.
† 1a. qu. 96. 4.
  1a. 2ae. qu. 90. 1
‡ 1a. 2ae. qu. 95. 4
‖ 2a. 2ae. qu. 47. 12

association with the social aggregation of men. In the exercise of the moral attributes or virtues of man's nature he makes progress; yet he never reaches perfection, because he is still capable of fuller development. The powers of man's social nature drive him into society and lead him to the exercise of reason and judgment in the attainment of the highest political wisdom. These powers of reason, moral nature and understanding are utilized in the development of the principles of political justice. While there are rules to guide individuals, societies and nations in their separate relations, these rules all rest upon the great universal law engraven upon the nature of man, having therefore a common foundation in man's being.

The ideas of Thomas upon the place of politics as a science are set forth in his introduction to the Politics of Aristotle. He distinguishes between the speculative and the practical sciences, assigning to the latter the first place, because of the superiority of reason, which is concerned in them. Political Science, *Civilis Scientia*, is a practical science. In the practical sciences reason deals with things and also with human beings; consequently there are two practical sciences, the mechanical arts, *Scientia factiva*, and the sciences which guide the moral action of men, *Scientia activa et moralis*. He also describes the *Scientia factiva*, productive sciences, as *operatione in exteriorem materiam transeunt*; whereas the *Scientia activa et moralis* are *operatione manente in eo qui operatur*, according to the human work which directs in producing an external object. Among the practical sciences, the moral sciences are the highest and most important, because they have the highest aim, since physical sciences have for their object mere things which are inferior to man, the moral dealing with man, leading him up from the simple to the complex or composite of society. Among moral sciences politics occupies the highest place, because the other moral sciences deal with the individual and lesser communities as the family, while politics deals with the highest community, *communitas civitatis*.* In the development of Political Science, he admits the value of experience and utility, the first suggestion we have of the inductive and historical element in politics. In order to make right laws, it is necessary to observe, that one must give attention to the matter of law-making for many years in order to know from experience, whether the laws and ordinances are just. It is especially to be remembered that in the long years of the past, all that it is possible to know of human life has been discovered; but much of the knowledge has not been put into exercise or utilized in execution; much of the knowledge and experience has not been retained in laws because it was seen to be unprofitable; consequently experience teaches what is most beneficial. In religion is found the settlement, by means of Christian doctrine, and in Science by means of human reason.

* Expos. of Arist. Politics. Bk. I. lect. I.

of what is just and useful in leading man to the highest possible ideal.*

One distinction that runs through the whole theory of Thomas, which it is important to mark, is the distinction between the natural and supernatural. The divine order is above the human, while the human is subject to the divine providence, the divine intelligence being revealed in the human reason, natural religion being perfected in revealed Christianity. *Sub providentia* is the condition implied in all the human order.† In Politics the supernatural order comes to the rescue of the natural to raise it up and give it a new character. Hence the doctrine of the Church in its relation to the state, to be examined hereafter, is the culminating point in the political science of Aquinas.

2. *Law*. The doctrine of law is very closely associated with the idea of reason and bears a close relation to the state, because law furnishes the basis as well as the principles of government. Thomas defines law as, *lex est quaedam regula et mensura secundum quam inducitur aliquis ad agendum vel ab agendo retrahitur*. Law is a certain rule and measure according to which any agent is induced to act or restrained from acting.‡ *Ordinatio rationis ad bonum commune ab eo qui curam communitatis habet promulgata*. Law is an ordinance of reason for the common good and promulgated by him who has the care of the community devolving upon him.§ That is a definition of human law. Reason is the essence of law, *dictamen rationis*. It is not, *quod principi placuit*, as the Digest had defined it, because the *vigor legis* does not depend upon the pleasure of an individual. Law is enforced, it is true, by a will, but it is only rightly so, when it is according to reason. The characteristics by which we are to judge law are threefold:—(1) it is ordained for the common good; (2) it should be ordained by some one who has the right to make the order and command obedience; (3) it should be sufficiently promulgated. It is accordingly an order of reason for the common good by one to whom is entrusted the charge of the community, and an order proclaimed to those to whom it is meant to be applied. The reason of the law is the wisdom of it. It is not only a rule binding to the observance of certain conditions, it is a measure of the manner in which obedience is offered to the requirements of the command.‖

In order to explain the nature of law, he distinguishes four kinds of law, (1) eternal, (2) natural, (3) human or positive, (4) Divine or revealed. (1) *Eternal Law* is the Divine or Eternal reason governing the universe, divine wisdom as it exists in the mind of God, formulating the plan of all existence and governing all things. *Lex aeterna est summa ratio cui semper obtemperandum est;*

---

* Expos. Arist. Pol. p. 114; Parras, Vol. XVI; Baumann, pp. 163-4.
† 1a. qu. 96, 3, 4.
‡ 1a. 2ae. qu. 90, 1.
§ 1a. 2ae. qu. 90, 2.
‖ 1a. 2ae. qu. 90, 2, 3, 4.

Eternal law is the supreme reason to which one ought always to be obedient.* This law cannot be known in itself or in its essence; but all obey it, because all are subject to providence, and all have an inward revelation of it in their knowledge of the truth. It is the law of the Divine and general government of the Universe, the model of all mundane relations.†

(2.) *Natural law* is the law of finite beings endowed with reason, *participatio legis æternæ in rationali creatura*, the participation of a rational creature in the eternal law, such is *naturalis lex*. It is the highest possible knowledge man can gain of the Divine plan of all things. Rational creatures participate in providence to which they are subject.‡ The beings destitute of reason participate in eternal law, but it is an irrational kind of law, and does not furnish them with the rule of their actions. They are regulated by a great law of mechanism. Rational creatures being endowed with reason govern themselves. In this originates natural law, and from it flows all legislation and all politics. It is the natural reason or light by which men participate in the Divine intelligence.§ The more intelligent man is, the better he is acquainted with it, although even the perverse are not unacquainted with it.∥ God is the first source of natural law as of grace for he *instruit per legem et juvat per gratiam*.¶ It is a rule of right and wrong established by reason. Man is associated with the Divine providence and is naturally directed to his proper end. The precepts of natural law are to practical reason what first principles are to speculative reason. Speculative reason aims at knowledge, practical reason rules the actions. These are the first principles given by nature. By speculative reason man is guided in reasoning concerning knowledge; by practical reasoning man is guided to those universal conceptions in regard to his moral and physical necessities, as for example, that man lives naturally in society.** Both are self-evident. Good is the first idea which exists under practical reason. We ought to pursue the good and avoid the evil, is the first principle of natural law. These first principles are equally known to all men and are unchangeable. From them we deduce all other principles, for all particular good is subordinate to general good, the body to the soul, and the soul to reason, because the good of reason is truth. From these first principles which are really tendencies and necessities man is led by reasoning to judge of the contingencies and special cases arising in practical life.†† Man should be good by his obedience to natural law. All good acts are conformed to and all bad acts opposed to nature.‡‡ Reason is the same for all beings, therefore there can be but one natural law for all rational beings.§§ It is universal and unchangeable by its relation to the eternal

---

* Augustine, De lib. arbit. bk. II. † Ia. 2ae. qu. 9.
‡ Ia. 2ae. qu. 91, 1, 6; 93, 4. ∥ qu. 93, 1, 2; 91, 3; 91, 2.
§ qu. 91, 2; 93, 4, 5. ** qu. 94, 2.
¶ qu. 91, 2. †† qu. 94, 3.
∥ qu. 93, 6. ‡‡ qu. 94, 3.

law. The tendencies and necessities which propel man to seek the good form natural law. All humanity is subject to this law; by a process of deduction from it all human laws are evolved. There are certain universal applications of this law. Reason teaches to man the special applications of these.¹

2. Natural law requires to be perfected and corrected by *human law*, *lex humana*, which form the application to particular, material facts and things upon earth of natural law. By natural law we participate in the general principles of law, human reason determining the particular practical application of it, supplementing for the general good what natural law has left undetermined. It is impossible to depend on individual men to apply the law to themselves, for some are good and others wicked. Therefore, we look to wise men as legislators to decide in the general circumstances how law is to be applied. This human law must conform to natural law, otherwise it is not obligatory as a human regulation. Those who make laws reflect for a long time upon the conditions of men and are therefore able to decide what laws are applicable, law becoming a dictate of practical reason. Law is to be suitable to the conditions of men in so far as eternal law can be accommodated to man's position; and consequently it may be said there is a law for soldiers, for merchants, etc. All law is according to reason which presides over those who are ruled. Seeing that law directs to the common good it is only the reason of the multitude, or of a prince representing the multitude, which can make law.² The principle of human law is rational constraint. Practical applications of natural law differ according to the character, spirit, and interest of the parties concerned. In order to determine what shall be applicable in a certain case, some one must determine; this determination is left to the legislator and the enactments of such a legislator are *positive law*. Such law as is derived from nature in this way may be called, *jus civile*, or *jus gentium*; or it may be divided according to the classes to whom it is applicable, or according to the variety of circumstances for which such rules are made. Positive law is a necessity of human nature and of social order. Established at first by the necessity of social order and the will of the legislator, it gains force and sanction by habit and use. Accordingly custom has the force of law, is a means of interpreting it, and often abolishes as well as enacts law.³ According as law is derived from the principles of natural law in general as a conclusion, or from the law of nature by particular determinations, it is *jus gentium*, or *jus civile*. There are three species of laws: (1) *leges communes*; (2) *leges privatae*, or *privilegia*, that is,

¹ qu. 14, 5.
² qu. 15, 1.
³ qu. 21, 5, 6.
⁴ qu. 96, 1, 2, 3.

for single persons; (3) *sententiae*, that is, applications of laws to particular acts
He circumscribes the human legislator by certain limits. Positive law does
not aim to suppress all vices, but only as are most dangerous to social
order.* It likewise does not enjoin all virtues, but only such as those most
beneficial to the social order in human relations.† In this way all extremes
are to be avoided. Law is to be interpreted according to the spirit, not according to the letter, for it may be presumed that all law has for its object
justice, equity and common safety; therefore any interpretation contrary to
this principle should not be imputed to the act of a legislator.‡

All human law is derived from natural law in one of two ways, (1) as a
consequence from a principle; (2) as a particular determination of an indeterminate principle. Thou shalt do no evil, is the general principle; the special
application, thou shalt not kill. Law declares punishment will be meted to
him who sins, but the measure of punishment is the special application of a
determinate judgment in the case of evil doing. In the first case law par-
takes of the force of a natural law, it has the force of human law in the
second because human law is an application of natural law.§ The power of
human dispensation suspends what applies in general to all, in the case of
the individual. It often happens that in special cases what applies to the
multitude is not convenient when applied to an individual, because it im-
pedes something better or induces to something worse. He who rules has
the power of dispensing. He is not faithful, however, if he acts
according to his own will or not for the common good.‖

(4) *Revealed* or *Divine Law* properly belongs to Theology. Human and natural law are not sufficient because the supernatural end of man is eternal
happiness and human reason is not adequate to direct man to this end. Human judgment is uncertain and can only be applied to external acts;
therefore divine reason which is certain and takes cognizance of internal
acts, reveals another law equally positive, but divine. It is therefore a correction of all human law and a means of raising man to his eternal destiny.
It is contained in the sacred Scriptures. Wherever positive laws come into
conflict with the word of God or *lex naturalis* they are not binding on the
conscience.¶ Natural law and human law are concerned only with things
which belong to the natural social order, which fall under our natural faculties. Divine law regards the soul and eternal salvation, and emanating from
God completes natural law.** The precepts of the moral law are derived
from the law of nature, some being deduced *per se*, as commands to do or not
to do; others by a more subtle process of reasoning, as reverence to superiors.

* qu. 96, 1, 2.   § qu. 96, 1.
† qu. 96, 2.   ‖ qu. 97, 1.
‡ qu. 96, 6.   ¶ qu. 96, 5.
** qu. 94, 5.

and others from human judgment, instructed by divine reason, by which we are taught of God.* The consequence of this would be that religious law deals with man's relations outside of and above the domain of civil society, and that therefore conscience and the religious life are not subject to the restraints of human law. Thomas should have gone further and said as the two laws are distinct and have their proper spheres, so the two societies which are subject to these laws, civil society and the Church, are also distinct and independent. This was the logical result of his first principles, but we shall see that he does not accept it.†

The *law of nature* has played an important rôle in the history of Political Science, especially in the controversy concerning the rights of man and the popular sovereignty. In Aristotle it was the technical term used to denote Divine and universal law as opposed to human and special law. Plato makes eternal law the ideal of all human law, the eternal law in conformity with nature producing harmony. Among the Stoics nature is the term which sets forth the harmonious spirit of the world, the varying manifestations of which are united under a common law of reason. The law of nature therefore is the unconditional and eternal rule of reason which regulates the natural association of creatures. It is the harmony of the spirit of the world and human justice, produced by the union of natural and moral interests, apart from any positive institutions. Natural law is thus merged in the standard of right conform to human consciousness. It became the foundation of the Roman law of nature. Cicero added the idea of equity, founded upon the Aristotelian idea of distributive justice and equality. In the Roman law the *jus gentium*, originally the universal world-idea of justice collected from different nations, becomes identified with natural law. In the later Roman jurisprudence natural law is presented as the original from which and the standard by which positive law is determined. In the writings of Aquinas, as we have seen, natural law is distinguished from Divine supernatural law revealed in the Scriptures; from Eternal law, the divine plan of the universe in creation and government; and from positive human law, (1) as a rule of right reason, distinguishing between good and evil, conscience directing to follow the good and avoid the evil, this being the primary natural law; (2) as the law of human nature, in the secondary sense, imperfect because nature is corrupted and therefore needing correction and completion by Divine law. Thomas calls this the secondary law of nature, as distinguished from the primary participation in eternal law. There is a natural process of evolution in his idea of law. The eternal is the Divine reason, with the plan of relations; the natural is what is known of eternal law by human reason; the human is man's application of the natural to finite conditions and affairs; while the divine is the application of the eternal to elevate man above the condition of knowledge and life possible to reason, the cor-

* qu. 100, 1.
† See Chapter IX.

rection of what is subject to vitiation in all human judgments, the salvation of man in an eternal and supernatural order of life. From this idea of natural law of human reason sprung the first germs of International law, as applied to the idea of community among states and developed among nations in connection with the Ecclesiastical imperialism of Aquinas.*

3. *Justice.* Thomas next proceeds to consider the conditions of social human existence in so far as these are not solely concerned with the rights of man as an individual. All these conditions he embraces under the term *natural law.* He means by it justice, equality and all other social principles. In his conception of society he does not regard individual liberty or personal rights, but is engaged with the social idea. In this social life the grand governing principle is justice. *Jus* or what is just is the special object attributed to the virtue of justice, *justitia.*† A thing may be just from its nature, in which case it is *jus naturale*. For example, in the case in which some one gives just as much as he receives.‡ Justice rules the actions of men in their relations with others, *ordinet hominem in his quae sunt ad alterutrum*. The essence of justice is equality. In the other virtues good is measured by the individual but in justice it is judged by his relations to others. That is just which is according to the law of equality as in the case of payment made for something received. There is an equality between the money paid and the thing received, therefore it is just. This exact proportion between the two things is an abstraction from the will of the agent and what we call *jus* or right.§ *Jus* is of two kinds, natural and positive. Right spoken of in itself is *naturale, secundum naturam*, giving rise to what are known as natural rights; regarded as a common agreement, right is positive. According to the agreement which determines the right it may be private or public, the latter representing the case of a contract between the people and their prince. Some distinguish between *jus naturale, jus gentium* and *jus civile*. *Jus naturale* is common to men and animals, as the union of the sexes; *jus gentium* is peculiar to men; whereas *jus civile* is peculiar to a special community of men. To *jus civile* belongs the special laws made by a special state to suit their necessities and to satisfy utility. To *jus gentium* belongs every right which is deduced from the first principles of natural right as a natural and necessary result. Justice like *jus* is either in the nature of things or according to agreement or consent.‖

Thomas distinguishes between commutative and distributive justice; the

* Pulszky, Theory of Law and Civil Society, pp. 78 sq. London, 1888; Maurice, Hist. of Phil. I. p. 606 sq. Lorimer, Inst. of Law, p. 3; Blakey, Pol. Liter. I. p. 28-9; Janet, Hist. de Pol. Sc. I. 320-71; Heron, Hist. of Jurisp. p. 59; Feugeray, Essai etc., p. 11 sq.; Franck, Ref. et Pub. Moy. age, p. 39-53.

† 2a. 2ae. qu. 57. 1.

‡ 57. 2. 3. 4.

§ 57. 1.

‖ 57. 2. 3. 4.

first has for its object the relation of individuals to one another, while the second has for its object the relation of all the parts to the entire whole. Distributive justice divides the common good, such as honors, power, and the privileges of the State among the individuals who constitute the social body; it also distributes the public charges on a similar basis. In commutative justice the rule is absolute equality, each person having the same value, on the principle of Arithmetical proportion. In distributive justice the rule is that which considers separately the persons among whom things are distributed and the things which are distributed, according to a kind of geometrical proportion. Account is taken of personal position and social rank in the society, a special value being placed upon each individual in the distribution of common good.* To give to each one his due is the principle of all justice. This rule is applied to men in all their private relations and also in their social relations. In the former case each man is entitled to be regarded on an absolute equality with every other; but in the latter when a man is socially united with men a distinction is drawn that is based upon social merit. Thus there is a kind of inequality in justice as well as an equality. To treat those who are upon an equality as if an inequality existed among them would involve injustice; and to regard those who are unequal as entitled to be considered on an equality would be similarly an injustice.† This doctrine is applied by Aquinas to the difference in rank and position occupied by different citizens in the state, not necessarily involving a hereditary or Aristocratic idea. With Aristotle the distinguishing features among the different classes of citizens are of an intellectual and moral type, and these qualities are looked upon as hereditarily descending, in part at least, in the same race of men, and among the members of the same family, the result of rank and the product of nature rather than of personal value or merit.‡ Aquinas is content to explain the doctrine of Aristotle without giving it the Christian basis of community and equality except on the principle of personal merit. Virtue is that which makes a man good and makes *bonum* that which he does. So political virtue makes a good citizen and renders his civic work good; that is, it qualifies men to rule and to render obedience in their own proper sphere. Thus good citizenship and good rulership depend on two thing, (1) the possession of the moral virtues; and (2) capacity to use these to the common welfare; for the moral virtues lead up to the political, prudence, temperance, being the essentials of all whether they are rulers or subjects.§ It is on this principle that Aquinas sets up the legitimate royalty and nobility. At creation mankind was not only unequal in sex, but in some there was

* qu. 61. 1, 2.
† Expos. Arist. Pol. III. lect. 9; V. lect. 4.
‡ Arist. Pol. III. 5 and 6.
§ 2a. 2ae. qu. 47. 10 and 12; 50. 1, 2.

a super-eminence of knowledge and justice over and above others."

Among men who possess the political virtues there are different degrees of relative perfection. Chiefly in the exercise of justice and prudence do men become entitled to higher consideration in the enjoyment of social honors. The more one labors for the good of the state, the more does he increase his influence and raise himself above those who are otherwise his equals in the enjoyment of freedom or wealth, he being superior in political virtue. It is not only justice to give pre-eminence to those who merit it, it is an injustice to deny it to one who has real Superiority in Political virtue. It becomes in fact the basis of his doctrine of sovereignty in government.† According to Aristotle there are different kinds of government according to the principle of distributing power. In some cases power is given on the ground of wealth, in others on the ground of hereditary relationship, and in others distribution takes place on the principle of equality. These are, as the Scholastics say, *justum secundum quid*, that is justice is relative to a certain arbitrary standard. In the ideal state the distribution of power is according to absolute justice and is therefore *justum simpliciter*. Men are judged according to their efforts to promote the virtue and happiness of the state, enjoying higher honor and greater power the more they do to promote this social end. That is, there is a twofold standard by which capacity for power is judged, namely *utilitas* in securing the common good and *virtus* which fits for the service of *utilitas*. Distribution of power on such a basis is *justum*.‡ Aquinas is content to put this doctrine in scholastic language. The conception of justice and righteousness says Thomas is determined according to the nature of the state-constitution. Righteousness chiefly respects the state, for it is the continuing characteristic of the state which has power to do right and wills to effect right.§ The subjects must have virtue and righteousness according to the standard which the states have. For in every state-constitution there is an equality according to its idea of *dignitas* to which righteousness and justice must correspond. To say that anything is just in the state is to assert that justice is an adequate means to attain the end of the state. Right is the true object of justice. Right is both natural and positive, viewed in their utilitarian aspect. Justice is the constant will, determination and habit to give to each one what is his due. Justice also refers to the dealings of one man with another or with others, the proper organ and residence of justice is not the understanding but the human will. Justice in its general sense may be said to embrace within it all other virtues, in its more special sense it is a distinct virtue dealing with the external acts of men having nothing to do with the passions

* Ia. qu. 96, 3, 4.
† Expos. Hist. III. lect. 7; V. lect. 1.
‡ Expos. Polit. Arist. V. 1
§ Com. Pol. Arist. Vol. XXI. p. 482. Parma.

of the intellect of men. The other virtues are based on justice, because they are attempts to realize in a measure the right. The religious virtues, the family virtues, the social virtues—all these tend to fulfil the end of justice which is that of giving to each one his due.*

* Baumann, Politik von Thomas von Aquino, p. 141.

CHAPTER III.

Civil Society and its Social Elements.

1. The powers of the Soul are associated together as a unity and in subjection to reason; the different parts of the world are united to form what we call nature, and these are placed in subjection to the divine being; likewise men are associated together as social beings and in subjection to one Superior which is the embodiment of power. Man's helplessness, his social instinct and the power of speech possessed by human beings indicate that he is capable of and can only reach perfection in a society of the state. Thomas accepts the definition of Society taken by Augustine from Cicero, "every aggregation of men is not a people, *populus*, but that only which is collected in such a way that there is associated a large number of persons on the basis of a common bond of law and community of interest." *Coetus multitudinis juris consensu et utilitatis communione sociatus.** Cicero adds, *Civitas est constitutio populi.*† That is practically a two-fold basis of the conception of civil society. It is not only an institution which subjects the members of it to a common justice which is equally binding upon all, but it is a union in which the interest of each one is best attended to in the common interest of all. It is not only a judicial combination, it is a utilitarian union of men for social interest and welfare. These two ideas are at the bottom of this association, *Community of interest* and *right or justice*. This carries out the ethical principles of law and justice upon which Thomas bases his politics. These are the social elements in the concept of the state. Society comes to be organized and maintains its organization on the basis of right and justice.‡ It is the appearance of social conditions which gives rise to his conception of natural law. Reason and understanding unite in impelling man to develop the principles of political justice as these are engraven upon his nature; this brings man into the state-society, for civil society embraces all other communities, that is, associations of men, as families, etc., uniting them for the common good and in the interests of justice.§

The development of the state-idea is interesting. Plato's state is that of a great person uniting all the virtues in its own being, emphasizing state per-

* Cic. de Repub. I. 25.
† De Repub. I. 26.
‡ De Reg. Prin. I. c. I.
§ Expos. Aris. I. lect. I.

sonality. Aristotle on the other hand views the complex natural structure of the state in which there is an association of kinships and communes to develop the perfect life. Cicero's state is an association of men combined by the bond of law, the natural law furnishing the bond of union among individuals and leading them up to the unity of reason and community of interest. Augustine applies Cicero's conception of the state to the divine society, because the human state is imperfect in nature and the law of justice, and it occupies the place of a temporary peace-preserver in preparation for the divine. In Thomas the divine state is identified with the Church which is of heavenly origin, whereas the earthly state is of human institution, and bearing the highest character as a human community it tends to the satisfaction of human life in all its necessities and therefore surpasses all other communities in dignity, force of character and in the influence it exerts upon all other communities or combinations of men.*

The theological conception of the essential principle of law, right and community bases it upon the reason or will of God, as its final and ultimate resting place. Thus the tendency to associate the human order with the divine, human law with the eternal order of the universe, first noticed in Augustine's idea of *lex æterna* finds its place in Thomas as we have seen; for law and right rest upon a rational order and a rational principle of order which gives force to the socialistic conception of the state as opposed to the individualistic. Man is led to pursue his proper end by the light of reason within him. He would need no other guide, were it his destiny to spend his entire life in isolation. But man is a creature of society, for it is only in society that he can preserve his life, protect himself and his share of the gifts of his beneficent maker; it is only in society that he is brought into contact with those educative influences that fit him to be an intelligent and moral being; it is only such a state of society that can utilize for man his language, given to him as a sign of speech to distinguish him from the animal creatures.†

There are three ideas involved in the concept of civil society, all of which are natural. (1) *The idea of association in society.* Thomas rejected the theory known as the spiritual theory of society, which attributed civil association to the fall of man. In man's innocence the instincts of his nature towards society are a part of his human constitution. Man is unlike the animals of the lower creation, he cannot live alone, and he cannot like them provide for the necessary supplies of life. His life and the preservation of it depend upon co-operation and association. The necessity of such association gives rise to the idea of the state.‡ Men are naturally constituted to live together. If man had been made to live alone he should have been able to supply him-

* Pulszky, pp. 231-3.
† De Reg. Prin. I. I. 14.
‡ Ia. qu. 96. 4.

self with all the necessaries of physical life. Animals are different; for they are supplied by nature with food for which they work not, fur for their clothing, teeth and natural weapons with which to defend themselves. If man were left to himself he could scarcely raise himself to the perfect use of his intellectual, moral and spiritual faculties.

Man is a social and political animal living in the mass, *homo est animal sociale et politicum in multitudine vivens*.* The addition of the word *sociale* to that of *politicum* indicates the difference of view entertained by Thomas in regard to the state from that of Aristotle. Aristotle regarded man as by nature a political animal, that is, an animal for *politia*. In his system of philosophy he considered slavery, property and labor as part of the preparatory system of Economics leading up to the higher science of politics.† Aristotle distinguished between certain communities and constitutions which are economic, and certain which are political, economics being the science of household affairs, politics the science of the civil state. Yet Aristotle's political system is mainly occupied with questions of social science, in which the physical rights of men alone are concerned. In the time of Aquinas we must take into account the fact that by the Roman idea of universal citizenship the old states had been destroyed and now society embraces the civilized world of many states. Political citizenship in the Roman Empire implied only the enjoyment of certain social privileges and distinctions. Society is composed of several states, the state existing for the preservation of the society and the various feudal classes in the communities being marked off from one another by strong points of difference. By the influence of the Church and through the growing rivalry created by commerce and the contests for temporal possessions, the spirit of nationality encouraged by Aquinas and commented on as desirable in a kingdom is fostered, and social questions become political, man being associated with man not merely for political privileges but in the enjoyment of social rights. These two words, *politicum* and *sociale*, describe adequately man's position in society, as a member of the *polis* (state) and yet having a community with others that identifies him with the principle of sociability. Man's nature requires association and we cannot think of man except as associated with those of his own kind.‡

(2.) *The idea of power.* There are two senses in which the word *dominium* is used, (a) a *dominus* of *servi*, and (b) *dominus* of *liberi*. Of the first there is no trace before the fall; the second is natural, even in innocency. He who directs others with a force that is directed to the common good or his own good is *dominus*. Such a *dominium* is possible in the natural condition of man,—(a) because man is a *sociale animal*. Social life cannot be unless some

* De Reg. Prin. I. 1.
† Ar. Pol. I. 2.
‡ Principles of State interference, D. G. Ritchie. Appendix A, pp. 157-9.

one presides over the others, directing to the common good, because many minds do direct to many ends, while one mind directs to a single end. (b) Because if one man possesses preëminence in knowledge and justice, in scientific attainments and uprightness of character it would be improper that these gifts should not be utilized for the common good; for, as Augustine says, the upright do not exercise power from the desire to rule but from a sense of duty to give counsel and protection. There is a *dominium* over others as free men, when one leads them in a way that is for his own interest or for that of the community.* Political power and government are of human law, *dominium et praelatio introducta sunt a jure humano*.† Human law springs from and is conformed to natural law and natural law in turn is the reflection of eternal law, and so by this chain of association power and human government are attached to God. But this is not the same as if the power immediately originated with God. Properly speaking it is an institution of human will, depending for its special form on circumstances of time and place. Paul presents his doctrine in the saying of his, *omnis potestas a Deo*, according to which the power is of Divine right, in which case all powers righteous and unrighteous are *a Deo*.

Thomas gives us an analysis of power,—(a) power, denoting the relation of superior to inferior, *dominium* and *subjectio*; (b) the means used to attain the power; (c) the manner of exercising power. He draws a distinction between power, *forma praelationis*, that is the abstract nature of the power exercised in relation to the beings governed, *ordo alterius tanquam regentis, et alterius tanquam subjacentis*. He distinguishes between the power as exercised and the means by which it is secured. The power in itself, abstractly, comes from God, the principle of power, the essential element of authority; yet it does not follow that by Divine right the particular form of the power or the person who exercises it has any appointment from God. The human side of the power therefore is found in the particular institution and the use that is made of the power. Therefore the formal principle of the power alone in civil society is especially instituted of eternal law. The question of the origin of the power in society and the exercise of it in the state in accomplishing its end is left indeterminate.‡ The power considered in itself is a necessary consequence of our nature, because men being social-political animals must be kept together and live under a ruler. Therefore the power of the ruler of society is from nature and from the God of nature. The way in which the power is secured and its use are not absolutely from God. On these two points man is left free to act. When the rulers get this power in accordance with justice, it comes from God and all that is done in exercising it is under heaven's sanction; if it is unjustly gotten and used in opposition to natural justice it is not from God. *Ad hoc dicendum est quod regia potestas ad cujus cumque alterius dignitatis potest considerari quantum ad rem. Unoqui dummodo quantum ad ipsam potestatem ... Christum ejus.*

Neglect to consider the distinction drawn between the principle of the power and its use as well as the means of obtaining it have led many to adopt the doctrine of the Divine right of kings. Thomas made it very plain in his theory of civil society that what was necessary in every human society by the law of nature was the power itself, in principle; whereas the means of obtaining and the manner of exercising this power is left open to man's free choice. An individual or a form of government, or a special family in whom power is vested,—these do not come from God, but simply power itself. God implants the principle in human nature, man in obedience to the voice of reason is to organize and particularize it by giving it to some person or persons. It is man's nature, as it were, to be drawn by the electric influence of association under power and in subjection to it.†

(3) *Community of interest.* Man is a social-political animal by nature and this implies a community *ad commune bonum*. This determines the conception of civil society. If it is natural for a man to live with a multitude in society there must of necessity be something to lead men into society. If men were living in society and each one cared only for himself and his own pleasure, then society would be broken up, because no one would interest himself in the common welfare. "Where there is no counsellor the people perish," said Solomon.‡ This idea is rational for what belongs to the individual does not exhaust the social idea. The principle of individualism is diversity, that of the common is unity. Whatever one does for one's own good tends to promote the good of the community. In order to guide to this there is a common principle of reason in all human constitutions. As in the heavenly bodies all are governed by the Creator with an order of providence, so among creatures they are all governed under the guidance of nature.§ Thomas's ideas of justice and equality give to his conception of the state a peculiar sense. He does not emphasize or indicate the importance of individual rights or liberty. His ideas are fully associated with the society itself and the prevailing principle is the social one of community. The necessity of society finds its relation in the idea of a social community with all the social organization necessary to maintain its composite being. The social body is an organism consisting of certain organs, the one in necessary relation to the other, all in union accomplishing the ends of human life. Overlooking, practically ignoring individual rights, man in his necessities and interests is only viewed in society. The words *communis* and *communitas*

* Aquinas on Rom. XIII.
† De Reg. Prin. 1. 13.
‡ Prov. XI. 14.
§ Ia. 2ae. qu. 91.

a., repeatedly used to set forth this idea.* In his metaphysical conceptions we have the foundation of this principle, for with him all being is simply the absolute being and the individuals are only particular parts or shadows of the supreme being. Hence the human individuality of the soul did not according to him spring from a spiritual personality unique and peculiar to every human being; but arises from the relationship of each being with the whole organism which differentiates and distinguishes individuality. Hence individuality and community spring from a psychological idea in which the organism is all in all and the individual is sacrificed. The great prevailing principle of sociability only brings man into the organic community; when he has been introduced into it and merged in the society justice is the all prevailing and ruling principle, distributive justice, that is, which accords to each one what is his due in the social community.†

Another evidence of the strength of community is found in the permanence attaching to natural law as against human law chiefly in cases of urgency. Non-observance of human law is justified in certain cases. In ordinary cases every one subject to the law must observe it in the literal sense; but if its observance would entail danger upon the community, especially in the case of a sudden emergency when there is no time for taking advice or providing for the circumstances an individual may disregard the human law and act according to natural law *ad commune bonum*. In the case of the rulers as in the subjects there is the same exemption from the operation of human law in urgent and extraordinary circumstances and when there is just cause for the exercise of the power of dispensation.‡

2. *Right of property.* Natural right may exist, (a) in virtue of the essential nature of two things, or (b) in virtue of some utility or question of expediency involved in the relation of things. Anything may be therefore of natural right for one of two reasons, (a) on the basis of a natural and absolute agreement between two things; in which case one cannot be the property of another and one cannot be absolutely controlled by another; or (b) in relation to a definite result or as considered of value for a certain utility; in which case one must control the other to secure the utility and to obtain the desired result. Absolutely, for example, a field cannot be said to belong to anyone by natural right, excepting to the creator and sovereign owner; but in relation to an individual as an article of use there are certain natural reasons which point to the fact that it ought to be attached to a certain person. In order to cultivate land, in order to establish a relation between the land and the worker there must be a certain right of property. The relation therefore between a field and the idea of property is not immediate, but indirect and derived from utility and from the results which follow from

* De Reg. Prin. I. 1.
† 2a, 2ae, qu. 61, 2.
‡ 1a, 2ae, Vol. 11, p. 354 and 355, qu. 97, 4. Parma.

such property.* Things in their essence and of themselves do not belong to man, nor are they subject to his power, but are subject to divine power because they belong absolutely only to God. The divine absolute being, therefore, in this sense is sole owner and proprietor. But in the sense of utility man does possess a natural right of dominion over material things in so far as he can by his reason and will possess them and use them for himself. God's absolute right of property is transferred to man in so far as it is a relative right to his necessities. Man's relation to material things is, either, (a) the possession of them by expending labor upon them; or (b) the possession of them by the use of them. In expending individual labor upon material objects man particularizes them in relation to his work, for three reasons, (a) because an individual expends more toil upon and takes greater care of what is individual than of what is general; (b) human society would be much more easily controlled were each one to concentrate his attentions and labors upon his own, *sua*; (c) common peace would be preserved better if each one was satisfied with his own portion and abstained from the lust for what is another's, *aliena*; and consequently dissensions would be avoided because order would be more firmly established.

In this way the idea of personal property springs not from absolute natural right but from considerations of personal interest, public utility and general welfare. Men have a natural right to things not in the sense that they belong to them in themselves, but that they have a right to use them for their good as things made and also destined for their use. This right is common to all men. It comprehends, *potestas procurandi et dispensandi*, the right of possessing and dispensing; and *usus*, the right of user. In regard to the first, human positive law attends to the distribution among men, establishing private property in place of the ancient common lands. This institution of private property has done good among men, in establishing state security and peace, and uniting men in the bonds of society. This division of goods according to human law concerns only the right of possessing, in regard to their use things ought to be common. They remain in the possession of the private owner and the use is divided among those who need them with the consent and will of the possessor, according to Scripture, "the rich shall share their goods with the poor." This consent is necessary to prevent the destruction of virtue and charity.† The distinction he makes between the right of possession and disposition and the right of use shews the change in medieval property as contrasted with ancient property. The former is the basis of private property and has been changed because the ancient conditions of society in which everything was common have been changed; the latter maintains its original form as common to all. This is the fundamental point of his theory. He lays great stress upon the right of property in

* 2a. 2ae. qu. 57. 3.
† 2a. 2ae. qu. 66. 1. 2.

possession and disposition; and reconciles or tries to reconcile many contrary passages in the writings of the Church fathers on this point. Basil compares the wealthy man who possesses the common good of humanity to a man who has taken possession of some house and refuses to let the others enter into it. But, says Thomas, it is not the fact of his having taken possession that is or ought to be condemned, it is because the one prevents the rest from entering and the other prevents them from using his goods in their time of need. Basil condemns, therefore, not private possession, but privacy in use. All the goods ought to be common in use.

But Thomas does not explain in what way or by what principle this common use will be applied. It is a moral right, a natural right, but whether that moral right is to be carried out by civil law he does not say. The only explanation he gives on this point is, that to distribute the use of these common goods is not simply an act of charity, it is also and primarily an act of virtue, that is of justice. Yea more, it is the extinction of a debt due to others, so much so that the injustice would be less in the case of him who took the goods possessed by others under the demand of necessity than in the case of him who refused to give them.* It would be a simple matter to infer from this that, when we add, that rulers are entrusted with the execution of justice, which is a first principle with Aquinas these common goods in use ought to be legally divided in order to conform to strict natural and human law. Thomas does not draw this conclusion. He gives however to those in urgent necessity the right to take for the satisfaction of pressing needs from what is in excess in the hands of others. Human right ought not to take precedence over natural or divine right. In the natural order of divine providence material goods were created for serving human necessities; therefore in virtue of natural law, what is superabundant among the rich should supply the needs of the poor.† The general rule implies that the possessor himself dispenses his superfluous goods but in such cases of necessity as danger of death, all men in such hazard have a natural right to take the goods at his hands to prevent starvation. He ought to take them openly and in such a case his action would not amount to rapine or plunder; for necessity gives him right confirmed by the divine order. It is allowable even to help another to supply his necessities in this way.‡

In the *Secunda Secunda* all this doctrine is set forth at length. Thomas is filled with a deep reverence for justice and charitable feeling towards the needy and is led into these socialistic ideas out of a profound regard for those who are in miserable destitution. He entertains a high regard for human industry; but he is carried away by the theological conception of all material goods as the direct gift of the benefactor of mankind to men, for the purpose

* qu. 66, 2.
† qu. 66, 7.
‡ qu. 66, 7.

of supplying all the necessities of human creatures. He does not apply his own principle: animals he says, have all good things provided for them, but man gets his wants supplied only in society with other men, by means of which society his life is preserved. Community of all in possession and use is only a principle of unorganized society; organized society protects human industry and labor. To the Divine first cause of all things we only need to add the second cause of human work and agency. This he has acknowledged in the right of possessing and dispensing.* The doctrine of human riches propounded by the Church fathers and fostered by the Church in its application to the individual helped to vitiate the system. To appropriate wealth to the individual is an unjust usurpation by a person of what God has given to all men.

Aquinas reconciles the doctrine of Aristotle and that of the Church fathers. Aristotle advocated individual property on the ground of public and private interest.† But the church doctrine of community had been introduced since Aristotle. The Church fathers accepted the distinction of private and public property but on the condition that the rich attend to the needs of the poor, the name given to the rich being, *dispensatores.* Aquinas accepts from Aristotle the fact that human labor demands private property and social peace depends upon its establishment; but community is demanded in the use. He reaches this by a fine distinction. Natural law demands that all things should be possessed in common. Property is not contrary to material right; it is a human invention, *per adinventionem rationis humanae.*‡ The common possession of goods is a natural right in a secondary sense, because nothing has been established contrary to such a community of goods. But as man born in a natural state of nudity has a human right to clothe himself, so society has the right to institute private property because of its utility to the social human life.§ The primitive community of goods is not positive but negative, that is there is no *a priori* reason why it should remain so always. Human invention, according to Thomas, breaks this primal community. This idea he does not work out. Human law does not act upon the basis of the nature of property but upon the fact of its relation to human beings. Natural law gives no right to possession of the property, but only to the use of what is necessary. And it is this which becomes the foundation of his idea of the possession of the use, the necessities of individuals. It is personality then that makes property private in possession and common in use, a principle which contains in it the modern theory of the right of private property. Thomas alludes to the Mosaic institution in reference to property, in which the poor get a share of the fruits on the ground of com-

* qu. 66, 1.
† Pol. II. 5.
‡ 2a. 2ae. qu. 55, and 56, 2.
§ 1a. 2ae. qu. 95, 5.

mon use. It also sanctions the division of property according to families, each family receiving a portion, however small. Thomas regards the consolidation of large estates in the hands of a few as one of the greatest dangers to a country, tending to depopulate the territory and making men avaricious and jealous of their own claims to power and honor. A system of peasant proprietorship in the Mosaic sense would be the best for the good of all, the public peace and individual interest as well as for the cause of religion.*

The idea of community *versus* individuality is so strong that not to the individual but to the community does absolute right belong, and the individual from the point of view of the natural right to property can appropriate what necessity demands. He asserts that one in actual, undoubted necessity may either openly or secretly appropriate goods *aliena* for immediate use. If one looks at a particular field there is no reason why it belongs to one and not to another; when the *opportunitas*, opportunity to cultivate it, and the use of it are considered, then one feels that it belongs to one and not to the other by this right *uti et frui*.† In another place he states that good care and stewardship rendered necessary private property. In regard to the use of material things a man should have them as his own, *sua*, but as common so that he may without difficulty communicate (*communicet*) in case of the necessities of others.‡ He concludes from this general principle, to appropriate what belongs to another cannot be characterized as a theft or robbery. He asks whether it is lawful to steal in a case of necessity. His answer is on the basis of the natural right of community. The order of human right cannot nullify the natural and divine arrangements of right; in accordance with natural law under the divine providence arrangements are made in reference to material things so as to provide for the relief of necessities. Therefore the division and appropriation of human things cannot be interfered with by human right *versus* natural right. In order to relieve the necessities of man those things which men have in excess ought by natural law (*debentur*) to go to the poor for their support. Since there are many needy and dependent, and since one cannot give to each one the same thing it is right for each one to make over his property that the needy may be relieved. If the necessity is pressing it must be immediately relieved by whatever is at hand; the taking of what is not one's own but another's under such circumstances, either secretly or openly, does not fall within the compass of robbery or theft. To justify such appropriation impending dangers must threaten the person when help cannot be obtained in any other way.§ This amounts to a restatement of the principle of Aristotle that private property is necessary but that the use should be common. He enjoins the right of property on general moral grounds because if there was absolute community it would destroy virtue and charity.‖

*2a. 2ae. qu. 105, 2, 3. ‡ 2a, 2ae. Vol. III, p. 247. Parma.
† Aris. Pol. II 3.   ‖ Ibid. 256.
  ‖ Pol. Ar. II, 5.

3. *Political disabilities.—Slavery.* This is a subject of considerable importance because the verdict of Aquinas affects the entire Scholastic history and upon its solution depends his attitude toward free institutions and liberty. Does he accept of slavery? Yes, because the principle of Scholasticism compelled him. Aristotle and Augustine, the two pillars of the system, admitted the legitimacy of slavery, although on very different grounds. Aristotle based slavery on the principle of natural inequality. Some men are impotent to reason and naturally in subjection to others.* Augustine bases slavery on the fact of the fall. In a state of innocency there is an inequality among men, but not the same as servitude; thus it is a punishment for sin and we cannot hope to be freed from it till we enter the kingdom of heaven. Aquinas could not escape the conclusion of these thinkers. Hence he does not oppose slavery, but gives it a place in his system.

In the ancient state the majority of human beings enjoyed no civic rights and shared no civic duties. Females and children were excluded from the membership in the state. They were members of the small household community and they participated in the state privileges only through the male members who were themselves parents or husbands. Among the rest of the population laborers, commercial men and agricultural farmers were placed in a semi-servile position which in the greater number of cases soon became servile. In Plato political power and privileges belonged to the priests and warriors, others being condemned to the deprivation of civil rights. In Aristotle's ideal rupublic the population is divided into two classes, the first being composed of those who act as warriors, perform the functions of priesthood, and exercise the offices of government, administration of justice and enjoy an exclusive monopoly in possessing land; the second class embracing artisans, traders and servants who occupy a semi-servile position. Thomas carries out the social principles of antiquity in regard to the elements of population. In the same treatise in which he discusses justice and elaborates the ideas of equality, the wife and daughter and slave are not acknowledged as having any legal life which can be called individual; their only relation with the community as a whole and with the civil rulers is through the husband, parent and master. The position of the child and slave is that of dependence on the parent and master who is a member of the state. *aliquid patris et dominii*; the child is an element in the parent's civic life and the slave a chattel of the master. The standard of right which regulates the relations of parent and child, master and slave, differs from the justice which regulates the relations of citizens, in that it is an inferior justice suitable to the particular lot of each, known as paternal and dominical justice. The child and slave are not only barred from the enjoyment and use of property, they can only enjoy civic justice through the judiciary at the will of and by the pleasure of the parent. Domestic society recognizes a head just as civil so-

*Pol. 1, 5, 6.

ciety; he alone is responsible to the civil ruler who is its head and he only can be the intermediary of all rights and privileges.*

Thomas looks on all the laboring classes, the class of traders and professional artisans as lower class persons (*vils*); the form of life they live is contrary to virtue and right reason and as a consequence their works are to be regarded as despicable. In his estimate these occupations are derogatory to the dignity of one who esteems justice and prudence, for manual labor and trading are inconsistent with the virtues of a social and civic life that would lead man to attain his ideal in life. No man engaged in trade, labor or industry is competent to exercise political rights in the state and anyone who does menial service lacks knowledge as well as virtue, and consequently is below the average standard fixed for the enjoyment of social privileges.†

All other political and social disabilities circle around slavery and the conception of slaves in servitude. The ideas of knowledge, power, charity, justice as found in Aquinas are limited by the distinctions of inequality, lack of capacity, and absence of individuality. In the idea of servitude we trace the same principles. Aristotle had distinguished between natural and legal slavery. The former he held to be just because based on differences in personal endowments, and on the necessity of the pre-eminence of the capable over the incapable; the latter, founded on the right of war, he thought conformed to a relative justice that regulates the relations of conqueror and conquered, by means of which the justice of victory on the part of the conquerors is mingled with charity in preserving the life of the vanquished. Legal slavery is therefore a state institution because war is a valuable source of utility and strength to nations and it also advances the public welfare. Thomas accepts without demur the specious defence of slavery by the master genius of antiquity.‡

According to Thomas the world's inhabitants may be divided into two classes, those who rule and those who are ruled, forming a natural hierachy, extending over all creatures, finding its model in God, the world-ruler, and men the subjects; in the soul, the body ruler, and the body its subject; and in the reason which governs the appetites and desires. Among men there are inferiors who can only obey and superiors who are capable of commanding. So is slavery; for a slave is *ordinatue ad alium*.§ This superiority extends to one race or certain races over others, and to certain nations which are superior in the scale of sovereignty, the others being subject.‖ He also accepts legal slavery as an institution for the social welfare, chiefly because it accords with his theory of dominium and with his view of justice and charity

---

* 2a, 2ae, qu. 57, 4; Expos, Aris. VI. lect. 5.
* Expos. Ar. VII. lect. 7, lect. 3, g. and 4, o.
‡ Pol. I. 5, 6, 7.
‡ Ia. 2a. 96, 3, 4; Expos. Aris. I. lect. 3, 4.
‖ Expos. Arist. V. I. I. lect. 2, W.

to promoting the interest of relative justice and good among men."

Some think that Aquinas only commented on Aristotle without accepting these theories. It is to be premised that he would have stated if Aristotle's theory had been in his view opposed to Christianity, just as he repudiates distinctly polytheism. This view is confirmed by the statements in the *Summa Theologiae*. Natural law he asserts is the same as the law of nations; in supporting this, he says, servitude among men is natural for some are naturally slaves; but servitude is from the law of nations, therefore natural law is the same as the law of nations. The reason of slavery is not to be found in nature absolutely, but in utility, that is, he qualifies Aristotle's view of slavery maintaining that utility demands that the feeble be placed under the strong and wise.† He sets forth the essential elements of Dominical power over the slave ‡ He discusses the Mosaic law on slavery.§ Thomas eulogizes its moderation as more liberal than the pagan. Yet he does not follow it, nor does he regard it as better than the Roman system. The Mosaic was simply an adaptation to the peculiar circumstances of the people of Israel in which God liberates them from servitude to their oppressors and places them in servitude to Himself. The liberation of the slave every 70 years he regards as an exceptional measure conformed to the special rule of justice in vogue among the people of Israel, so that it is no exception to slavery itself. Slavery like property belongs to a relative kind of natural right. It is not in the absolute nature of things but depends on expediency.

This inequality of *dominus* and *servus* is born of sin. Is it then a political inferiority? There are two senses in which we use power, (a) in so far as we oppose *dominium* to servitude, the *dominus* to *servus*; and (b) in so far as we place power over against subjection or obedience. In this latter sense the government of free persons is embodied in a master-ruler. According to Aristotle the two powers are political and dominical or despotic. The slave is different from the free man because he is *causa sui*, while the slave reckons himself another than himself. The *dominus* therefore commands the slave for his good and exercises a power which is disciplinary in character. It did not exist in a state of innocence. Political power of a free man over free men existed before the fall. Therefore the only inequality which would have been absent if sin had remained away, and which is present as a consequent of sin, is that of master over slave.∥ Thomas reconciles slavery and natural law. The primary principles of natural law are changeless. But the secondary principles which depend upon utility and human law are not. It is objected that the liberty of all is a natural right. Thomas says that at the first liberty was of natural right, that is, there was nothing contrary to liberty in natural right. Man was created naked, but he had a right to clothe

* Expos. Ar. 1. lect. 4. c; V. lect. 3. 4.   † qu. 57. 4.
§ 2a. 2ae. qu. 57. 3.   ‡ 1a. 2ae. qu. 107. 1
∥ Com. Sent. 45 disq. 1. 4; 1a. qu. 95. 3. 4

himself. In the same way the state has a right to add slavery to natural right because it is useful to man's life, slavery therefore is legitimate.*

Slavery is supported by two arguments, a psychological and a theological, the one Aristotelian the other Augustinian. (a) It is really upon *psychological grounds* that he advocates slavery. Aristotle builds his psychology upon imaginary differences among men, ranging from wisdom to ignorance, from sanity to folly, and from strength to weakness. Thomas' conception of the human soul accounts for his doctrines of liberty and slavery. Soul is the presiding genius over every form of life; even the human physical system cannot be said to possess vitalizing life apart from the soul. It is the sovereign in the human life, in physical action, in mental and moral activity, the form of unity amid the complex and diverse functions which are performed by the various organs, the one principle which pervades all human being. All the faculties of being are fused in the soul and consequently the differentiating principle in human beings is found in the soul, according to sex, intelligence, etc., the energy of the soul being proportionate to the capacity of nature in each individual.† It is in this way that human individuality and liberty are lost sight of, because personality is closely related to materiality and there are different grades of perfection among human souls, giving rise to the inequality among individuals reaching from wise to foolish. From such a conception it is natural to infer that those who are superior will control and direct those who are inferior.

(b) *A Theological basis for slavery.* In a condition of innocence there was no servitude. There existed certain natural inequalities; there existed also a social power which divided mankind into ruling and subject. By reason of the fall of the first human beings humanity was placed in circumstances which gave rise to the condition of master and slave. Slavery is a punishment for sin, at least for those men who are in the condition of fallen nature, not those who are in the condition of the supernatural, that is, in the fellowship of the Church. This last condition lies at the foundation of the policy of the Church whose Head on several occasions condemned excommunicated persons to slavery,—for example, the Venetians—permission being given to anyone to make them slaves. This is made use of to support the idea that the Church of Rome was not opposed to slavery. So Thomas regards the slavery of the Jews to Christians as legitimate, and he gives the Christians the right to the property of those set free without compensation. He justifies this on the ground of the murder of the Son of God in Jewish unbelief, and their wilful rejection of the divine law made known to them in the Christian system.‡ This does not imply that slavery was in any sense opposed to human nature, but rather that it was suitable to the altered

* Ia. 2ae. qu. 94, 5; 95, 5.
† Ia. qu. 85, 7.
‡ Frohschammer, p. 481

condition of man's life. As a penalty for sin man lost original rectitude and by reason of its departure from the communion of God which was the foundation of his likeness to the divine, he was bereft of his birthright and cast out into an estate and condition contrary to his original condition. The penalty incurred was the loss of that divine *dominium* which was his original right.

Mitigation of slavery. Slavery is not unlimited, its evils are not unmitigated. Slaves are not subject to their masters in servile work and in obedience to the orders that fall within the limits of the dominical power. Beyond these limits the slave is naturally free. Obedience in all things, that is absolute obedience, would be of a questionable character on the pretext of acting as an intermediary between the subject and God. Above the limits of servile obedience the slave is subject to God directly, through natural and revealed law; hence Thomas does not recognize the despotic powers of life and death which are found in the old Roman conception.* In marriage the slave is free from the controlling power of his master. A slave ought not to be sold separately and so be separated from his wife and family. He distinguishes therefore between certain acts done as a slave in obedience to dominical law and certain acts in which a slave possesses the rights of a man. Christianity tempered the hardships of slavery by counselling slaves to accept their position as a discipline in preparation for a higher freedom hereafter.†

* 2a. 2ae. qu. 102. 5.
† 3a. qu. 52; Fougeray. pp. 69-81; p. 178 sq.; Janet. I. pp. 374-380; Pope, Prince and People, Pius Melia, 1869.

CHAPTER IV.

THE ORIGIN AND NATURE OF THE STATE.

1. *Origin of the state.* According to Thomas the state is only indirectly of Divine origin. The people must be recognized as the instrument or means by which God has called the state actually into existence. Likewise the constitution of the state springs from the people exactly in the way in which the power of government springs principally from the people in whom is reserved the right of revolt against the abuse of such power as is conferred, and in all cases the alteration and changes in the state constitution depend upon the people, according to their circumstances and requirements.

Plato's ideal state is of divine origin: his historical state arises in sudden changes which take place among men, altering the primary conditions of humanity, giving rise to different kinds of states from the patriarchal to the contractual and historical. Aristotle associates the origin of the state with the natural and necessary growth of the family and commune, resulting in a higher and larger organization in the community. Association is the real originating cause in all society, natural association giving rise to the family and voluntary association to the state. Cicero ascribes the primary origin to man's social nature adding as a secondary cause the principle of utility in the preservation of life and the protection of property. Augustine under the influence of theology ascribes the human origin of the state to the imperfections of man due to the fall, but the divine origin is to be found in the divine will. Feudalism in its perpetual strife of partisanship, gave rise to the principle of unity in the community embodied in the feudal lord, as the natural foundation of government, from which point Aquinas starts in following Aristotle, going back to the idea of natural *dominium*, on the principle of inequality in the extent and power of sociability.*

If we might interpret the Aristotelian idea of origin as expounded by Aquinas, we would distinguish between the origin *philosophical* and *actual*. The *origin philosophical* or in principle is to be found in the nature of man, that is, the state principle or ideal is founded upon human sociability and hidden beneath the forms of association as a conception of human reason. Whereas the *actual origin* in the definite appearance of the state is more arbitrary depending upon human will and accomplished in fact under the

* I-a. qu. 96, 3, 4.

direction of the people or of a governor. The idea or conception of the state in the mind of man is precedent to the idea of individuality. But the state, which before is intelligible only as a principle, becomes an actual fact only when an alliance is demanded, offensive and defensive, against all external perils and in favor of temporal well-being, as well as for ethical and spiritual progress. Thus according to Thomas, it appears as if the state was created by a formal agreement between men. A distinction must therefore be drawn: the community can and does assume shape in the course of historical evolution according to the will of the people, but the state does not originate in that way, neither does the original power of governing, nor the original constitution of the state arise from the people. The state did not originate arbitrarily or by agreement; but it sprang up naturally from the fact of the existence of men by generation, out of the family and family relations, which gradually extended to and embraced the race, and comprehended the entire people under the supreme power of the rulers of the different families. In order to the establishment of powerful states, various arbitrary changes were wrought, different forms of state, and kinds of government being instituted by human law in the hands of the people themselves through their representatives or by a single autocratic ruler. It is this secondary origin and consolidation which is effected by the means of contract.*

Thomas suggests the idea of *contract* as a prominent principle in the formation of the state. When he introduced the doctrine of natural law and the social principle in man as a political animal, he gave scope to the theory of the social contract which grew up in the minds of the people and embodied itself in the writings of the Churchmen, the idea of a contract between the people and the government. The first introduction of this theory is due to the consideration that was given to the mutual obligations of rulers and ruled in the writings of men before Aquinas. This was enforced by the conception which was added of the responsibility of kings to God and their duty to the people, to rule among them so as to promote the highest virtue. It became common to speak of natural law as the limit placed upon the prince and given into the hands of the people, so that natural law is viewed in itself as a form of contract between rulers and ruled which is always presupposed. This, when combined with the doctrine of the sovereignty of the people, that princes derive their power from the people, gave full sway to the idea of contract in this medieval form. "To order anything for the common good belongs either to the whole multitude or to some one acting in place of the whole multitude."† Political society is founded upon human nature and those who form the political society are sovereign.

Such is the form of the contract theory found in Aquinas. It differs from the contract theory found in Rousseau in this, that according to the latter,

* De Reg. Princ. I. 1, 4, 14; Expos. Ar. Pol. I. 2.
† Ia. 2ae. qu. 90. 3.

man in a state of nature is not in society, his rights as man in a natural state are all individual; and that he enters society in ending the state of war of each against all, by making a formal post-natural contract with his fellows by which the state is originated and authority is established over the society entering into the contract. According to Aquinas there is a two-fold basis for the state, and accordingly a two-fold origin, the submission of all the members to a common law of justice which is over them all in common, and the advantage everyone gains in the common union of all." Society originates in human nature, its principle is implanted in the human breast and it manifests itself in the human life. A condition of savagery and isolation is foreign to man's moral and physical being, and unnatural to his life. Human association is coeval with man's existence and develops with human generation.

Man is the most social of all the animals. The other animals are supplied by nature with what they require for protection, sustenance and continued existence. They have natural weapons by which to defend themselves, or the power of flight to escape from danger. But man has none of these natural resources. He has only his reason to guide his hands and to enable him to devise means of supplying all his wants. Man in isolation cannot look after himself and his wants. The other animals are guided by instinct in following after what tends to their advantage and avoiding what is hurtful to them; man has only his understanding to enable him to judge what actions are suitable in special cases. It would be impossible for an individual to gain a knowledge of all possible circumstances that may arise, hence the collective society is required with its distribution of function, so that individual men may have the benefit of the wisdom and skill of the collective body, and power to carry it into execution. Man likewise is endowed with speech to enable him to express his desires and communicate his thoughts to his fellow men which is impossible in the case of the animals, who express their ideas only in a general way to other animals.†

We have seen that he distinguishes between power itself in its abstract nature and the means by which the power is obtained. Just in the same way he distinguishes between the natural principle of association which is found in man's nature, and the particular application of it in the combinations that depend upon circumstances of time, place, fortune, which are all guided by human will.‡ There is no idea of divine right in the application of this principle of association to the particular form of the state, at least in the sense in which Divine Right of Kings was used in the 17th century. By natural right the power is in the hands of all originally and any change is brought about by human law, and depends upon utility, advantage or expediency.§

The origin of the state is the establishment of a government. Society is

* De Reg. Pr. I. 1. † 2a. 2ae. qu. 10, 10.
‡ De Reg. Pr. I. 1. § 1a. 2ae. qu. 90, 3.

natural to man as a multitude, but every aggregation of men has need of being governed; therefore the society requires a government and for this purpose it is organized and the power is given into the hands of one or some. The soul governs and keeps in unity the body, the sun commands and leads all the planets, the intelligent being guides all creatures, and the providence of God controls the entire universe. The appointment of that government or governing body is of human will and law.*

In the introduction to the *De Regimine Principum*, he says that his design is to set forth the fountain of kingly power and the calling of a king according to Scripture, the doctrines of the philosophers and the examples of much-praised princes. In the beginning, progress and completing of the work he says he expects to enjoy the assistance of Him who is the King of Kings and Lord of Lords from whom all Kings have their Kingdoms, God the great King and Lord over all Gods. Evidently the ultimate origin of the government of a Kingdom comes from God as the first source. In saying *omnis potestas a Deo* he does not say *justa*. Paul, therefore, enjoins absolute obedience, although there are certain reserves. All power in itself, in its essence comes from God; but relatively it does not come from God, if the means of acquiring it are unjust and the use that is made of it is unjust. Yet all power just and unjust depends upon the permission of God and therefore is permissive. Often the unjust power is used by God as a means of punishment.† It would seem then that in principle the origin of the state, or which is the same thing in Aquinas, the power set up in Society, is from God, but the application of that power to a special state is from God only in the sense in which it is permissive, and consequently it is of human law.

Thomas does not consider temporal authority as a necessary evil as many Ecclesiastical writers and even Popes have done, nor does he regard it as a direct work of the devil. The state with its ruler is the natural and necessary foundation for the preservation and development of the temporal existence and well-being of humanity. The state is a necessity growing up out of the strivings of men to satisfy their wants, natural inasmuch as it is the embodiment of the social impulses in man, originating primarily in human nature, receiving confirmation in the association of men.‡

2. *Nature of the state*. It is difficult to distinguish the nature from the end of the state as treated by Thomas, because the nature according to him depends upon the end. Several points however may be established in this connection. (a) *The state is an order of social life*. Thomas defines man as an *animal sociale et politicum*. By natural and necessary association the community of the state is formed. Human society in general is, *in diversa dispergeretur*....

* Deg. Reg. Princ. I. 1.
† Com. Sent. 45, qu. I. 2; qu. IV. 2.
‡ Feugeray, p. 32–37; Pulszky, pp. 215-55; Social contract theory in Pol. Sc. Quart. VI. 66 sq. D. G. Ritchie; Annals of Amer. Acad. of Pol. and Soc. Science, Vol. III, 23; Frohschammer, pp. 478-9; Frohschammer, Origin and Culture of Society, p. 75 sq. 1885.

sicut et corpus hominis et cujuslibet animalis deflueret, nisi esset aliqua vis regitiva communis in corpore, quae ad bonum commune omnium membrorum intenderet.* The nature of the state depends upon the proper relations of the rulers and ruled; some are naturally fitted to rule, others to be ruled,— when these two classes in the social community are organized into a *corpus* or body, they form the basis of the state. Man is an animal, *sociale* in regard to the material element; *politicum* in regard to the formal element of Society, that is, in form the life of man is political, in matter it is social. Thomas distinguishes in the social order three different societies, *domus*, *civitas*, and *regnum*. *Domus* is the family consisting of matter and servants, husband and wife, parents and children; *civitas* is the *communitas civitatis* or city state; *regnum* is the state or kingdom or province state, larger and more perfect than the other *societates*. *Domus est communitas consistens in his perquos fiunt communes actus, et idea consistit in triplici congregatione, ex patre et filio, ex marito et uxore, ex domino et servo. Communitas Civitatis omnia continet quae ad vitam hominis sunt necessaria, unde est perfecta communitas quoatum ad mere necessaria. Tertia communitas est regni, quae est communitas consummationis. Ubi enim esset timor hostium, non posset una civitas per se subsistere; ideo propter timorem hostium necessaria est communitas civitatum plurium quae faciunt unum regnum.†* As it is a characteristic of man to live in society because he is not sufficient for the requirements of life when living in isolation, so the community must become more perfect in society (*societas*) the more adequate it becomes for the necessities of life; it is true there is a certain sufficiency in the family association that is not found in the individual, in respect of the production and support of posterity and matters of such a character. One thing may be said in regard to the requisite of an art or trade or handicraft. In a state (*civitas*) which is a complete community one has this trade or handicraft in reference to all the requirements of life; still more is this the case in a province or kingdom on account of the necessities of a common condition of war and common helpfulness against an enemy. For this reason one who governs a perfect community, that is a Kingdom, is called a King. He who governs a house is called a *paterfamilias*, head of a family; he has however a certain similarity to a King, because Kings are often styled Fathers of a nation. In nature the state is the highest form of social order.‡

(b) *The state is a natural order of social life.* The formal element in the state depends upon the principle of authority or power. It is from this principle of authority the natural state springs. The definition of a state according to Thomas is *multitudo hominum in una societatis vinculo colligata*, as taken from Augustine. The necessity of the state and of government among men through state-power did not arise through man's fall; but before the

* De Reg. Princ. I. 1.
† Evang. Matt. c. XIV.
‡ De Reg. Pr. I. 1.

fall in paradise there existed the distinction between rulers and governed, and therefore a governing and a guiding of the people was a natural necessity. Just as law is an emanation of reason, not of human will or caprice or power, so it was not the idea among men in paradise that they should live in perfectly equal freedom, in equality and fraternal relations. Their lives did not conform to one unvarying standard. Hence rulers or the authoritative power in society was entitled to demand obedience from the subjects. The variety of human strivings and activities shows the need of directing man, and therefore he requires some one to lead him to his goal in life. In man the light of the understanding is implanted by nature, by means of which in his actions he may be led towards the end of life. If it pertained to man to live alone as is the case with several animals, he would need no other guide, each individual would then be his own King, under God the supreme governor. It is peculiar however to man that he should be a living being of importance to society and the state, and to live in society (*multitudine*) he must live on the higher level of living creatures. This shows man's natural poverty as an individual.*

By nature he is a leader and ruler who is able to foresee by his reason what tends to well-being, he who, for example, employs the useful and rejects the injurious in social life. On the other hand he who by bodily strength can produce the thing which the wise man has planned is by nature a subject. It is in the nature of both and for their common good that the one be over the other as ruler, and the other in subjection as a subject. For he who has genius to plan and wisdom to foresee would often fail through lack of physical strength, and he who has bodily force could not act for himself did he not enjoy the discernment and guidance of another.† The character of the state is then determined by nature and the distribution or division of labor takes place according to natural principles. Wherein consists the nature of state-community? Thomas rejects the ideas of Plato, Aristotle and Socrates in regard to an extrinsic bond as the sole bond of community. He bases the community upon natural law depending upon a common social nature.‡ The bond of community consists of an extrinsic and intrinsic element, the latter being the ethical, the former the physical. Individuals are united in society by love and the true nature of the social bond among the members of the political community is virtue.§ These individuals in association form a unity by means of peace. *bonum et salus consociatae multitudinis est ut ejus unitas conservetur quae dicitur pax*.‖ Peace as here described consists in *tranquilitas ordinis*,¶ and also *pax ergo in hoc est quod omnes sua tuta teneat*.** The form in which social love appears is *amicitia*, friendship, and this principle of natural asso-

* De Reg. Prin. I. 1. ‡ Verit. qu. I. 10. c; 2. 2. c.
† Com. Pol. Vol. XXI. p. 438. Parma. ‖ De Reg. Prin. I. 2.
‡ Ia. 2ae. qu. 57. 3; qu. 66. 2. ¶ Ia. 2ae. qu. 70. 3.
** 2a. 2ae. qu. 29. 3. 4.

ciation gives rise to four different communities, the natural, domestic, civil and divine.* Thus the natural association takes place under the authority which is intrinsic, friendship and virtue, and is then reduced to social unity in the society which is placed under extrinsic authority or government, in other words the state is a natural order of social life.

(e) *The state is an organism.* The individuals who form the community are all members of one great body.† The soul by nature rules over the body; so do all who are placed over others. The result is that those who have a predominance of intelligence rule over others and those who lack intelligence are in subjection. Solomon says the fool shall serve the wise.‡ There are various degrees in human society but the highest community is found in the state. It is so constructed that human life may have satisfaction in itself as an organized unity. It therefore stands higher than all other communities which human intelligence can devise. It belongs to this state as an organism to unite in itself all other lesser societies.§ In every plurality there must be something which unites and governs. The understanding unites all the faculties of the soul and controls all the members of the body, each member and faculty contributing to the formation of the organic unity. In the state the natural differentiation of rulers and ruled embraces the entire range of the state, including those who have no rights, or only rights through others, as well as those who have rights. That which determines however the nature of the state is the fact that it is a moral organism. It is not an organization for the play of mere force or authority, but is an ethical organization *potius agantur quam agant.*∥ The moral force in the organism of the state is unity of thought and unity of action, as these tend to ethical ends and are guided to such ends by rationalism in the organism of state.¶ There are different elements or members in the state, these are all united by the bond of *communitas.*** Each member holds its own place in the organism and performs its own functions, producing harmony or peace,†† peace on the other hand being regarded as *effectus caritatis* in the organized life.‡‡ The lesser communities the *familia* or *domus,* and the *civitas,* are likewise organic in structure; but they develop upwards into the grand organic structure of the *regnum* or state. The different elements which form constituent members of the *regnum* are individuals, families, cities; and as these are all ethical in their nature, they constitute a state which has a moral nature. Thus

---

* Sent. Com. III. disq. 37. qu. 2. 2. c.
† 1a. 2ae. qu. 1. 8.
‡ Com. Pol. Vol. XXI. p. 377.
§ ibid. p. 366, 7.
∥ 1a. 2ae. qu. 1. 2.
¶ Barri, p. 23; Taparelli, Sagio di Dir. Nat. Diss. II. 1. no. 304.
** 2a. 2ae. qu. 58. 9; qu. 47. 10.
†† 1a. 2ae. qu. 70. 3.
‡‡ 2a. 2ae. qu. 29. 3. 4.

the political *communitas* of the state may be characterized as a moral organism by means of which the end of human life in its highest form is attained."

The principal element in the nature of the state as an organism is found in the idea of self-rule. Thomas takes his theory from Aristotle who defends the principle of autarchy, based upon the ideal that the virtue of a good man and of a good citizen is identical. Goodness determines not only the principle of authority, but those who are to exercise it; consequently it influences the form of government. Where one is good by eminence above others, he ought to rule; where a few are good and no one pre-eminent, they are the aristocracy of rulers; where all are good we have a Democratic polity.† The principle of union is the sovereign power, deposited somewhere and exercised by some person or persons in the social body. It is the formal element in the nature of the state and determines the state organization.

3. *Psycho-physical character of the state.* The *communitas* of the state is made up of moral and physical elements. It is a social order tending to the organization of human society so as to attain the highest ends. It is an organism in which the exercise of human intelligence is the ruling principle; but for the satisfaction of the requirements of human life and for the preservation of life there is required a physical basis for the community. This material basis provides for the sustenance of life and furnishes a sphere of activity for the weaker members, who are unable to rule by lack of wisdom. Even the working population depend upon the wise and forseeing, for only as workers are guided by the wisdom of superior guides, can they employ their energies aright. The psychic principle of reason then determines the relations of the elements of population to one another and their spheres of activity, as well as their relations to the land.

External possessions which really lie outside of the true spirit of virtue he refuses to regard as the highest aim either of man or of the state. Many say that little virtue is sufficient to give complete happiness, and that not too much wealth, fame, honor and power can belong to it; therefore it is said that happiness consists chiefly in securing external possessions. Some regard wealth, some fame as the highest of earthly possessions. They desire virtue first and then say that it is related to these possessions.‡ Thomas rejects this theory and declares that happiness consists chiefly in virtue, that is, in the habits of our usual activities as these are guided by reason, and especially a perfect activity of mind along with a moderate possession of external goods. Happiness consists in the possession of what we have acquired and rightly can regulate, for that through which something is guided and measured seems the principal thing. External possessions are acquired and applied according to right reason by the activity of virtue and discernment.

* Burri, 22, 23.
† Arist. Pol. III, 4 and 7.
‡ Com. Arist. Vol. XXI, p. 631.

and as such are not perverted. Virtue and its activity are the chief elements of happiness. Virtue in itself, in the state, and in the individual, is of the same character and in reference to its efficiency as well. It is distinguished only as the whole is from a part. The ethical virtue of the state, or its moral basis, is made up of the virtues of the citizens as the parts of the state.* The best activity is that of theoretical reason or scientific contemplation.† The possession of land therefore by the state as by the individual is subordinated to reason and regarded as of value in so far as it promotes the virtues of the citizens.

Physical basis of the state. Thomas is very familiar with all the material necessities of a state. He prefers for the material provision of the community agriculture to commerce, because by the latter arises selfishness and a mercenary spirit. It is to be remembered that if a city or kingdom had not been founded there would be nothing to govern. In the office of a governor the establishment of a city and kingdom is comprised. Many have founded cities which they governed themselves as Ninus, Nineveh, and Romulus Rome. One cannot perfectly know the office of a ruler if one does not know the foundation principles of the establishment. This is to be drawn from the prototype, in the establishment of the world. In this there comes first the production of the things themselves, and then the orderly division of the world. The different parts of the world are different kinds of things, stars of the sky, birds of the air, fish of the water, and other animals of the earth, and at last God provides in abundance what is needed by individuals. He refers to the Mosaic account of creation in which step by step the world is prepared, and last of all man the lord of earth and animals is created. If anyone plants a kingdom he cannot produce new living beings, or another place of abode, nor a new means of livelihood; but he must make use of what already exists in nature as the workman uses the materials which he receives from nature. It is therefore necessary for the founders of a city or kingdom to seek first for a suitable place which will be healthy for the people, whose fertility will suffice to support them, whose beauty will charm and which will also be secure from foes. The more it has of these qualities, of such at least as are necessary, the more suitable it will be. It is necessary that the founder of a city select a site that will meet the wants of the inhabitants when the city or kingdom reaches perfection. When a Kingdom is to be founded we must consider which territory will be suitable for laying out cities, villages, fortresses, universities and schools, (*studia literarum*,) where soldiers should receive military instruction, where markets are to be held, and meeting places (*conventus, colloquia,*) for the merchants and others, and everything necessary for a perfect Kingdom. If a city is to be founded it must be considered where the Churches (*sacra*) are to be, where

* Ibid. 635.
† Ibid. 641.

the courts of justice should be located and where trades are to be carried on. The men must be brought together whose business or calling is suitable for common residence, that there may be a difference in the residence part and in the business part, and different classes of people associated together. Care must also be taken that each one is satisfied according to his position and circumstances; for otherwise the Kingdom or city cannot long endure. The important point is that there is a matter of choice in locality, situation, and that it depends upon many circumstances and very much on the pleasure of the parties concerned. It looks very much as if the social contract was not indistinctly seen in the matter of selection of a site.*

In the conduct of a good life in an individual it is necessary that there should be virtuous effort, for it is in virtue that good living consists. But as a means to this end there is a second necessity, namely, the existence of material possessions the use of which is necessary to effective virtue. The unity of men in society as individuals is secured by nature and this unity prepares for the unity of society, called peace. For the good of society requisite material things are demanded.†

He goes on to the founding of new states or enlarging existing ones. The mightiest nations and princes whose names have been most famous have sought either to found new cities or to enlarge those already in existence, which have been named after their founders. The name of Romulus would be unknown had he not founded Rome.

In establishing a state, the king should choose a suitable location, for the inhabitants gain many advantages by a suitable climate. In a comfortable climate there is better health of body and more prospect of long life. If there is an excess of warmth or cold it becomes necessary in the changed condition of the air to change the condition of the body. Hence many animals by natural instinct resort to a warmer region in time of cold and to a colder in time of great heat, in order to enjoy comfortable circumstances during undesirable weather. Living beings who live through the warmth and cold, in case the heat is great become languid, and life is shortened. In some of the warmer regions of Ethiopia men do not live to be more than thirty years of age. In extremely cold regions life is exposed to many perils. A mild climate has favorable influences upon the carrying on of war, by means of which, he says incidentally, human society becomes firmly established. People who live near the equator are weakened by the heat; they have really more wisdom but little vitality and therefore have little perseverance, lack confidence in a warlike encounter. They fear being wounded because they are timid. On the other hand, Northern peoples do not fear war, because they have courage and are skilful in war. Those who live in temperate regions do not fear to be wounded; they have also more practical intelli-

* De Reg. Princ. I, 14.
† I, 14.

gence *prudentia*) which enables them to discern the value of temperance in camp life, and guide them in the conduct of war. A temperate climate has a great influence upon the conduct of state life. The people who live in cold regions are courageous, but intelligence and skill in the arts. They remain free but attain no perfection in state-life, because they have not practical prudence to enable them to become better than their neighbors. People who live in warm countries have bright intelligence and great skill, but they lack courage. The result is they are subjected to other nations. Those who live in the middle regions have both of these qualities, enjoy freedom, attain a higher standard of state-life and have practical knowledge of how to govern others.*

In selecting a location it should be remembered that living together as a nation is based upon natural life. Natural life is preserved by means of healthful air. The most healthy site is one that lies high, because the air moves freely and so is not misty, where neither the extreme of heat nor the extreme of cold prevails. It must not be in the neighborhood of marshes. The sun striking the earth and water sets free a variety of gases found more in valleys and low-lying districts than in the high-lying parts. From marshy places there arise vapors which unite with animal bacilli and create a pestilence. In sea board states he speaks of the value of walls which form a protection, the sea cleansing it from impurities, and destroying disease germs and other nuisances which cause an unsanitary condition in cities and states. The laying out of the city or of the state should be attended to so that full advantage may be taken of the genial warmth of the sun and the cool, refreshing breezes which tend to promote health among the inhabitants. It is not conducive to health to be transferred to a warmer atmosphere than that in which one has lived heretofore.

As it is necessary also to have suitable food the choice of a location should be made with a knowledge of the nature of the food that is grown in the district. The ancients got this knowledge by investigating the nutritive animals. For the nourishment of men and animals springs from the ground, and if animals thrive upon the fruits produced in a certain district so will man. If the animals that are found in the place are unhealthy, then man naturally would be unhealthy also. Good water must be sought for, for the health of the body depends upon water of which man uses so much. We inhale air into our bodies, hence it is the first essential of life; we use water not only to quench thirst but also as a part of food, therefore nothing is so conducive to health as good water. Another sign of the healthfulness of a region is to be found in the complexion of the people who live there, whether their bodies are strong, their limbs well developed, whether the children are numerous and vigorous and whether many old people are found in the place.

* De Reg. Princ. I. 1.

Such are the climatic and public sanitary arrangements considered necessary by Thomas in a well regulated state.*

The agricultural state. The location of a state must be in a place that is fruitful and such as will provide sufficient food. A society of men cannot live where there is not plenty of food. Aristotle says that it is imprudent to build a city in a mountain where sufficient arable land does not exist to provide food. A state cannot have a strong population without sufficient means of livelihood. A state can command its food supply in two ways, (a) by selecting a fruitful district that produces enough to support it; or, (b) by the use of trade, by means of which from every quarter the necessaries of life are brought in. The first means is the more suitable and worthy, because where there is a scarcity it is known as soon as the want is felt. A state has greater self-sufficiency when the products of the country immediately around it suffice for the sustenance of life, than when recourse is had to other provinces by trading. A state is the more worthy if it can supply its own needs without having recourse to the merchants. It presents greater security to its people for in case of war or not importation of supplies can easily be suspended and the state may perish. It is more suitable also for state-life, for the state which depends on merchants for its food must live a common life with, commingling with foreigners. Life with foreigners tends to destroy the good habits of the citizens, for foreigners trained under different laws and customs act differently from the citizens. The civil life becomes corrupt by citizens following the example of the foreigners. If citizens themselves engage in business as traders there are many gateways opened to vice, for merchants strive chiefly for gain and so a desire would be created in the citizens' mind that everything should be merchantable in the state, and all kinds of impositions and frauds would be practised in reference to the products of the fields, and the welfare of the community would be lightly esteemed, each one seeking his own interest, and the effort to be virtuous would cease. Commerce is also opposed to the bearing of arms. Traders are not used to hardships because they live in rooms and warehouses, not in the open air; they also need delicacies, and so tend to become effeminate, their bodies being weak and unfit for the hardships of war. Hence commerce is forbidden by state law in time of war (*jus civile*). The state whose population is assembled is more likely to be peaceable. In the association with men outside an opportunity arises for strife, and conditions arise which produce unrest. If the state is given to commerce the citizens must remain inside the walls to carry on their trade, therefore it is better that a state should have the satisfaction of providing its means of living from its own lands rather than that it should trade for a living. Yet it would not do to exclude entirely the merchants from the state, because it is difficult to find a place where there is a superfluity of the means of livelihood and no need to

* De Reg. Princ. II, 2.

import anything from the outside. There would then be an excess of provisions in one place that would go to waste, which by the merchants might be carried to other regions and utilized where there is a scarcity. A complete state therefore must have traders, but trade must be conducted in moderation."

Beauty of landscape. In founding states the location should by reason of its agreeable characteristics give pleasure to the people. A charming country will be hard to forsake, and many people will not go where there is an absence of the beautiful in nature. Without the pleasing and enjoyable man's life cannot long last. This sense of beauty will be satisfied if the district is a broad plain, if it has fruit trees, a view of mountains near by, beautiful woods and flowing streams. These must only be enjoyed in moderation, because overpowering beauty allures men into unrestrained pleasure and that is hurtful to the state. Men who live only for pleasure are dull in spirit; the sweetness of pleasure sinks the soul into sensuousness, so that they cannot exercise sound judgment. Those who give themselves to excessive pleasure become timid and faint-hearted, and become slothful in business, neglecting necessary exertions for the good of the state. Therefore it is injurious to the state to give excessive pleasure to the people in the situation of the kingdom.†

States on the sea. There is danger to a state that is located on the coast. It is better, as Aristotle says, that a state should not be too near the sea, because very many enter who have been brought up under different laws and accustomed to strange habits and manners as is seen in all states and cities beside the sea. Strangers detract citizens from the observance of their own laws.‡ It is not fitting that a state should be bounded by the sea because the location is also liable to be unhealthy as well as dangerous. Yet it is not well to be too far from the sea for the state derives from the sea many advantages. It is better therefore that the location be a middle one so that the state may gain the advantages and avoid the disadvantages of the sea.§ Choice of location, agricultural condition and the nature of the climate are all applied to the end to be realized by the state and therefore to be judged in their relation to reason and virtue.

4. *People.* The state must if possible, by preference (*potius*) consist of one people or nationality, because the similarity of people in customs, habits and manners creates a relation of friendship among the citizens. States that have been formed out of various nationalities have perished in consequence of lack of unity and difference in customs never unified, leaving one portion of the state in antagonism to another.‖ Aristotle alleges that it is because of differences that innovations are brought into states, for when men are

* II. 3.
† II. 4.

‡ Ar. Pol. XXI. p. 649.
§ p. 650.
‖ Ar. Pol. XXI. p. 454.

found in states which manifest diversity of customs there is every likelihood of a war of customs, if the peoples have lived a long time together without becoming blended into one people. Those who have different manners of life tend to different ends and use different means in attaining them; there springs up a diversity of interest which produces confusion. Among those who have different customs and have lived long together, it generally happens that one people gives place to the other, the stronger prevailing. In this case no great changes take place in the state. Those who live long together and still continue to have different customs will finally come into conflict with one another. Statehood then Thomas, following Aristotle, thinks should be based on nationality, the principal idea of a nation being a community of customs and manners in a single people.*

Scientific contemplation is the highest occupation for the individual. It can only be realized however by individuals in a state, and man only reaches his highest condition in a society which is the national state, whether that nationality is natural or historical.† It is by the power of reason that men in a state are governed under the authority of rational laws; it is by the same intelligence they are led to cultivate science. That policy is scientific and rational which provides a written language in the vernacular of the people, *habere literalem locutionem in suo vulgari idiomate*. Those people who do not possess such a vernacular speech and rationality in thought are accounted barbarians. A cultured people on the other hand is distinguished by two characteristics, (a) possessing a literature in the popular language; (b) having the rational regulations to regulate life embodied in the form of the state and its legal requirements.‡

Some nations are more fitted to rule than others, Aristotle says. For example, Greece, naturally and by its geographical position united the courage of the Northern peoples with the intelligence of the Southern, and it is called accordingly to a state life of a higher order and to the government of others. To this doctrine of Aristotle Thomas objects, that if it were true of the Greeks on natural grounds, they would always have had the same dominion over others and never have lost it. History is against this, for the Persians and Romans have controlled the Greeks and have had in turn the empire of the world, that of the Romans being much wider and of longer duration. Thomas explains the view of Aristotle. He explains it on the ground of the natural position of the country which gave it an advantage over other countries. In this way the Greeks, midway between cold and heat were intelligent and brave, their bravery being inspired by the patriotic spirit cultivated on her plains and hills. The position of the kingdom according to the location of the planets and fixed stars also had an influence

* p. 530.
† Baumann, p. 40.
‡ p. 529.

upon it. This position varies. Whenever her position changed relative to the heavenly bodies her qualification for empire would cease and the empire would pass to others.

But the influence of the heavens and heavenly bodies cannot affect the understanding or the will of man. Gifted people attain to the government of the world through moral and intellectual genius, and likewise the governing power is lost by sloth and misdoing. This is one reason why the empire of the world was lost by the Greeks and Romans. When they had the empire they were luxurious and covetous, and thereby the rule of the world passed to others.* This forms an approach in idea to a universal empire, under the control and authority of the best nation, in culture, situation and laws.

Elements of state population. The state must of necessity consist of men occupying different positions and in different circumstances. If all the men in a state followed the same business and dwelt under the same roof it would be a domestic or family society, not a state. In a state there must exist a variety among the population, each one or each class following its own profession; yet this variety of population elements must be united together to form a state unit by the discipline (*disciplino*) of good laws properly administered.

There are several constituent parts in the population of the state. In the *first class* we find farmers, common laborers, (called *viles* because they soil their bodies with their labor) as tanners, weavers, laundresses, and musicians; trading and peddling merchants; lastly those who work for wages, called *operae*, because they lease or let their work. The *second class* embraces all who occupy a middle position, intermediate between the highest and the lowest classes of the people. It includes five different grades, soldiers, knights, stewards, advisers, the rich and the popular leaders. These are called defenders of the people and are a necessity in the state to preserve it from falling into a servile condition; and since it is contrary to nature that the state should be unfree, the state must possess self-sufficiency, having freedom of action to direct its own progress. If the state did not have defenders then it would have to be dependent on some other state and consequently be in a feudal position. The principal part in this class consists of those who fulfil the offices of the state under the governors. The *highest class* consists of those who possess the governing power in the state and occupy therefore the position of heads.†

All who are embraced in these three classes do not hold the rank of citizenship. A citizen is one who has held an administrative office, or some other office of authority in the state, or is capable of holding such office. Those who do not enjoy the privilege of such official dignity do not take part in the state-life as such and are not citizens of the

* p. 632.
† Ar. Com. XXI. p. 512-14.

politia.* Slaves also who are necessary to complete the work of the state by menial service are not citizens.† In reference to the position of women and children Thomas follows Aristotle. Care for what belongs to many in common is of little importance; every one cares for what belongs peculiarly to himself. Two things produce what men care for and love, (a) what is their own and belongs to no one else; (b) and the special love which one has for a certain thing. Love is lessened by its division among many. Parents love one child more than they do many. Hence children and women do not belong to the general citizen-society of the state, but are embraced in the *familia*.‡ The position of women is somewhat higher than that of children. They are free and may have an advisory part in state affairs, but have no deciding power in its management, *potestatem consiliandi sed consilium ejus est invalidum*, their influence being exerted through the husband in their domiciliary position. The nature of women is weaker than that of men, and her opinions are not staid, but are easily changed by her passions,—hence she is a creature of desire or feeling, while man is a being of intelligence and reason.§ The duty of women is to attend to domestic affairs which suit her nature; to these she ought to give her undivided attention and leave state affairs to men.‖

True nobility among men is excellence of race, that is, it is a pre-disposition towards virtue descending from father to son. Nobility of race and of wealth are of the same kind; not that among the poor there is no nobility or inclination to excellence; but since wealth necessarily tends to promote virtue the inheritance of property by a child from his father is as much an inheritance of nobleness as is virtue. Hence the aristocracy of virtuous excellence is generally that of wealth.¶ But such a position of wealth is not unqualifiedly approved, because wealth promotes greed of gain and selfishness. The middle position is the best, comprising those who are neither too rich nor too poor, they are the true aristocracy of a state. They are the most obedient, for those who excel in wealth, nobility, military skill or beauty scorn others and become haughty, and by reason of their elevation above others tend to yield to unlawful desires. Such a pre-eminence subjects them to passion and leads away from reason. On the other hand the needy become unreasonable in their demands and give way to selfishness and force, to get what they desire from others. If the legislator would act in the best interests of the state he would promote the middle class in the state and establish by means of a constitution such men in the government. The more the middle class is set up in the state to keep in check the rich and poor the more permanence will attach to it, because they are more evenly in their performance of duty and more steady as defenders of the

* p. 452. ‡ p. 398.
† p. 400. § p. 415.
‡ 408, 409. ¶ p. 535.

state.* The state must consist of those who have not only reason and a competent portion of goods, as well as weapons of warfare, but of such as have previously used these, that not the unskilful, not the self-sufficient and independent, but the middle class who know how to use themselves and their weapons in defence of the state.† Thomas, therefore, would elevate what he calls the middle class, that is, the moderately rich and noble class who hold military and other offices by succession, not those who in modern times would be spoken of as the ordinary citizen class of farmers and merchants, for those engaged in handicraft and those occupied with farming he debars from a share in the state.

Land in relation to the people. The state must be so large and only so large as to secure that the land can support the people, and that they may have ability to defend the territory and the state from the attacks of enemies. But it is necessary to remember that good laws and proper discipline tend to the promotion of the welfare of the state more than anything else; therefore the citizens of the state ought to be many (*plures*, the quality of them making up for the lack of quantity.‡ Too large a state it is impossible to govern by means of laws and customs, when few are intelligent, difficult to govern when many are intelligent. Therefore Thomas advocates a moderately small state. The numbers of the people must however be so large that the rulers do not know them personally, although he contradicts this in reference to the rendering of just judgment and apportioning to each the property according to his merits.§ Larger states are less liable to civil dissensions, because there are more people of the middle class and hence the medium size state is the best.‖ There should, he thinks, be little property held in common possession. Those who have common property quarrel over the division in regard to expenses of food and labor, and often a small matter creates a tumult. Those who have separate possessions are more likely to enjoy peace. Hence the state should not hold mutual possessions of property, for this would raise constant strife.¶ It is better for each one to have a moderate portion for enjoyment and the support of life.**

Citizenship. The idea of free citizenship in the state is that of living in accordance with the state end. One is not free when he follows his own pleasure; neither is one a slave when he lives according to the idea of the state, for man attains to his freedom and enjoys prosperity in state-life. According to Aristotle, to enjoy freedom man must regard the *causa sui* as well as the effect of it. Reason is the predominant thing in man, therefore a free man who is most free is rational, and it his best interest to act according to reason. To live in the state is to live according to reason and to be

* pp. 331–36. ‡ p. 647.
† p. 338.   p. 645.
‡ p. 568.   ¶ pp. 411, 412.
               ** pp. 388, 389.

guided by understanding, therefore such life is freedom.* To be free in the sense of Aristotle is to be *sui ipsius causa*, that is, the agent is the cause of his own action, or he is guided by his own reason. This does not mean that there is a cause in itself, but that is free which has a special reason for its activity.† A man is free because his existence is determined by reason and he lives in reason.‡ He is more free who is strong in understanding than he who is strong in body.§ Therefore free citizenship belongs not to those who exercise their bodies in their employments, but to those who use their understanding in living the state-life.

Among free citizens age is principally the determining element in fixing the position in the state-activity. Young men have an imperfect practical knowledge and apprehension by reason of the strong influence and excitable nature of passion in them. They have bodily strength on account of their youth, however, which makes them suitable for war. When they have grown in years passion becomes moderated, and with diminished passion their bodily force is abated and courage is less prominent, reason and practical judgment however being stronger; for by fidelity and perseverance the soul reaches intelligence. In this condition they are suitable for advisory and judicial functions in the state. When men ripen in years they become cool in passion and reason becomes very strong. In such a stage of development they are fit to fulfil the functions of the priesthood, in the service of God. Men engaged in such a calling must retire from all secular avocations and spend their time in the contemplation of divine things. So aged men are suitable for divine service. Life then has three stages,—*first*, it is devoted to the war-like profession; *secondly*, to the practical duties of the state-life; and *lastly*, to the divine life in which man attains his perfection.‖ This was the trend of the Athenian philosophy and Thomas conceives of it as the process reaching from the men of the world to the men of the state and finally to the church life.¶ A good citizen and a good man are synonymous terms; a virtuous man and a good prince are likewise identical.**

5. *Nature of the ideal state.* The citizens of the most perfect state have as their aim, to be virtuous and happy and they are guided by rational principles in all their actions. The social virtue (*civilis virtus*) is to live according to the direction of intelligence in doing what is right, and those who are true citizens of the state must be perfectly virtuous, *virtuosi cives*. In distinction from this highest class of men, the wage laborers and the market-traders are *virtuosi*; the life they live is of a lower order, and by reason of the occupations they follow they are incapable of practising the higher virtues and cannot be admitted to citizenship in the best state. So likewise farmers

* p. 584.
† p. 610.
‡ p. 641.
§ p. 679.
‖ p. 679.
¶ p. 435.
** p. 450.

and peasant-workers are excluded from the citizenship, because in order to be citizens and to exercise the functions of members of the state, they must have time and opportunity, as well as facility in studying that which is scientific, and must engage in the noble avocations of life, *liberales*, as opposed to the lower and lowering employments of the men who can only work with their bodies (*ribis*). Virtue engages itself in the higher activities of life, while those who have no leisure keep themselves constantly in relation with the land, and in their earthly occupations are unfit to be citizens.

In the ideal state the citizens are of two classes, those who follow the military profession and the leaders, advisers, and counsellors of the people. The military class are chosen from the younger and the advisory counsellors from the older men. These men compose the citizens of the state and are entrusted with the conduct of state-life. The property of the state as well as the control and preservation of the state must be in the hands of the same class of men. These wise and active men alone can be entrusted with property stewardship. The peasants ought to be servants, and they ought to be taken from the class of foreigners who come in from strange countries or from the servile class among the natives (*ministri*), *barbari aut vernaculi*, either brought from foreign lands or else born as slaves in the family. Thomas prefers the latter class, the former class being hurtful to the customs and manners of a state. Peasants and laborers for wages are a necessary element in the state, but not a part of the state. Soldiers, counsellors, priests, these are the necessary parts of the state, the citizens of the state, at different periods of life being called to do service for the state.*

Property should be held in private possession by individuals of the class of *virtuosi*, but the use should be regarded as common with others, by the provision for the wants of the laboring classes, and by active liberality towards the poor. It is not in the interest of the state that any citizen should suffer want, because the citizens being regarded as part of the state, it is the interest and duty of the state to make appropriations for their nourishment and and for the supply of the necessaries of life.† In the ideal state it is for the benefit of the state that the entire property be divided into two equal portions, the one portion of the common possession being held as state property in order to defray the expenses connected with government; the other portion being divided among the individual citizens to be used for their own and their family's needs. Each of these two portions is to be again divided into equal parts. The one half of the state property is to be appropriated as an offering to the service of God, the other half to the state expenses. One portion of the part belonging to the citizens is to be for the individual use, the other portion to be devoted to the state in payment of expenses of defence,

* p. 658–60.
† p. 661.

fortification and adornment.* In the ideal state the slaves cultivate the land. The characteristic of a slave is strength of body, weakness of understanding, lack of courage and difference of race or nationality; for if they are such they will be more likely to be subject, to do their work, and to abstain from secret plots against the state.† Wealth or the enjoyment of external possessions is necessary for the individual, family and state-life. Wealth conduces to happiness as the means to an end. Therefore wealth must be sought and obtained only in proportion as it can promote the state-end. Greater wealth is required for the public social life than for the private contemplative life, for in the social life more wealth is needed to accomplish the end of the state. Reason must dictate the measure or proportion which must not be in excess.‡

* p. 652.
† p. 662.
‡ p. 671. Expos. Arist. Bk. VII. c. 4-8; De Reg. Princ. I. c. 11-13; II. 1-7; Barri. c. 1; Baumann. p. 72 sq., 112 sq.

CHAPTER V.

THE END OF THE STATE.

1. *The end in general.* The state is the highest social community. It is however not an end in itself but the means to a still higher end. In the third book of his *De Verit. Cath.* Thomas discusses God's government of the world, that is, the complex of temporal things. The ultimate end to which everything tends is God. God is the ultimate worker in all human affairs, but he uses the free agency of man in accomplishing his will. To man laws are given, and man in a sense is an end in himself, because the end of his being is revealed in natural law. The state being according to Augustine the direct work of God, its aim is fixed by him as that of setting up and showing forth God's glory in us. Thomas rises to a higher idea in setting forth the highest aim of the state, not merely as the good of society, but as the establishment, in a more or less perfect degree, of peace over the entire world. In another sense it becomes the means in the power of a higher organism, the Church, of establishing religion and virtue, the Church alone having ability and power to determine what is the chief good for man's life.*

The idea of the end of the state occupies a large place in the writings of Thomas because every other question in politics is treated in connection with the end of society, so as to bring the theory of the state into harmony with the social design. In his *Summa*, after discussing theology as it relates to God, he speaks of man, and declares that man always acts with a certain end in view, the acts of a rational human being are always guided by the idea of design.† What is the end of the state? The individual and society have the same end, namely, happiness. The individual man finds this happiness, not in wealth, fame, power, bodily pleasure, or worldly enjoyment, but in his union with God which takes place upon the foundation of an intimate acquaintance with and knowledge of the Divine, which gives to the human understanding satisfaction and stability. It is impossible to attain to the perfection of happiness in the natural life, therefore the natural man attains only an imperfect blessedness in this life. It is this last imperfect happiness which man as an individual and man in political society secures in the present order of things.‡

---

* Pulszky, Theory of Law and Civil Society, p. 283; Erdmann, Hist. of Phil. I. C. 284.

† 1a. 2ae. qu. 1.

‡ 1a. 2ae. qu. 4, 5; Expos. Arist. VII. lect. 2. 66.

With Aristotle he distinguishes three kinds of good, the good of the soul, of the body and purely external good, which man uses for the perfection of of his soul and body. The combination or union of these three kinds of good in the virtuous life produces the condition of imperfect blessedness. To attain it there is required a certain perfection of the body in health and strength, a proper disposition of soul and rational faculties, and also the external necessaries to sustain the physical system. The proper play of these elements in a life of activity, in which a rational being is brought into relation with the divine by a knowledge of God and obedience to his laws, is the best means of securing the end of life. It is only when the external goods and the health of body are used in the exercises of the soul that they become instruments in attaining the measure of blessedness possible in this life.* Thomas makes friendship, *amicitia*, the condition by which man realizes this happiness in the state-society, for by means of unity man enjoys the social good and makes use of himself in promoting the good of others, and the common good of society. Blessedness consists in a man filling his place in the social order according to the directions of natural law and the will of God.†

The design of society may be embraced in two things in general, (a) that men should live together; (b) that they live together virtuously, or that they live according to human nature and reason. The result is happiness for the individual, blessedness and prosperity for the state, for the perfect life is the final cause of the state. The common good is attained by means of virtue and by means of virtue the society becomes an end in itself and to the individual members.‡ The ethical nature of the state as a moral organism implies the element of intelligence *agens per intellectum cujus est manifeste propter finem operari*.§

The state has an ethical force and acts just as a complete man. The end of the state may be described as Burri describes it, philosophical-political-christian, in which the political is subordinate or secondary.‖ The individual is completely sacrificed to the state, or rather the end of the individual and the end of the state are identical.* There is a primary and a secondary or subordinate end, the one superior to the earthly, for the Godlike on earth are akin to the divine essence. The secondary or subordinate end has for its object the good of society.** In the state as in individual man the *bona vita* is *vivere secundum virtutem*; and *operari secundum virtutem* implies among other things *corporalium bonorum sufficientia*. To this end men are congregated

* Ar. Expos. VII. lect. 1. 6.
† Ia. 2ae. qu. 4. 5. 8.
‡ Expos. Ar. III. lect. 7. 12.
§ De Reg. Prin. I. 1.
‖ Burri. p. 27.
* Ia. 2ae. qu. 1. 4. 2m.
** Ia. qu. 116; Verit. qu. 24. 1. 1m; Ia. 2ae. qu. 109. 6. c.; qu. 3. 4. c; 2a. 2ae s. qu. 151. 1. 1m

together to live according to virtue which Thomas calls the *divina fruitio*. Therefore the end of the state is not an end subordinate to that of the individual but it is an end of the same kind.* In that *communitas* of the state which can be described as *perfecta* it is necessary that there should be a settled harmony among the members, this unity of the multitude is accomplished *pax*.† The general end to which society tends is *bonum commune* and it is this which determines all state activity.‡ The final end of man is *pervirtuosam vitam pervenire ad fruitionem divinam*.§ The association of the state, *regnum* is described as *communitas civitatis omnia continet quae ad vitam hominis sunt necessaria, . . . propter timorem hostium necessaria est communitas civitatum plurium quae faciunt unum regnum*.‖ The special virtue in the state is citizenship and to accomplish its end free citizenship as explained above is in full exercise.¶ The end is determined either as primary or secondary, *assoluta aut relativa*, according to the law human or divine which directs it, the end of divine law being eternal happiness and the end of human law being the tranquility and peace of the city or state.** Human law directs in state-life *quod ordinantur homines inter se*, the result of which is peace.†† The end of state society therefore in general is an individual one, the individual and the state tending to the same end, *virtuosa igitur vita est congregationis humanae finis*.‡‡

2. *Twofold end in the state.* Following after Aristotle Thomas gives to the state a twofold end, (a) the end of placing man who is a social being in union with his fellow men, especially to render possible the fulfilment of his lifework in its physical aspect, and to protect and continue his existence; (b) an ethical task in making men good citizens and virtuous men, and to promote their virtue and happiness, that is, their earthly happiness; but as spiritual and eternal happiness is the goal of man's efforts and the final end of his being, the Church alone can perfectly promote this end, because the state is not concerned directly with spiritual affairs. In harmony with his ecclesiastical position he places the Church back of the state and regards the state as simply an instrument directing towards the spiritual end of the Church.§§ There is a great difference between the earthly aim of man which he recognizes by the human intelligence and by natural powers, and the spiritual aim which can only be apprehended by faith, which depends upon free will.‖‖

 * De Reg. Prine. I. 14.
 † De Reg. Prine. I. 2.
 ‡ Verit. qu. I. 10, c; 1a. 2ae. qu. 92. 1.
 § De Reg. Prine. I. 14.
   Com. Matt. c. XII.
 ¶ Verit. qu. I. 10; qu. 2. 2, c.
 ** 1a. 2ae. qu. 98. 1, c; qu. 100, 2, 5, c; II. Sent. disq. 9. 3. c; 1a. 2ae. qu. 90. 2. 3; qu. 92. 1.
 †† Opusc. 73. c. 3; 2a. 2ae. qu. 29. 3. 4.
 ‡‡ De Reg. Prine. I. 14.
 §§ Frohschammer, p. 477, 478.
    Ar. Exp. s. XI. p. 659.

The state can take action upon the natural aim, because it rests upon human understanding; the second design is above understanding, except in so far as it depends upon the activity of human freedom, and this individual liberty raises it above state regulation. There is the distinction in aim between common understanding and individual voluntary will. Since the state is an emanation from the common reason it is debarred from everything which depends upon the individual free will. Hence the state has nothing to do with the Church by interference, because her aim is higher than that of the state, being to complete the individual members in eternal blessedness. To the Church is entrusted the cause of individual freedom, to the state the interests of common understanding and common humanity.* Thomas often changes his expression of opinion regarding the real aim of the constitution of the state. He uses such formulas as these, the aim of the state is the peace and unity of society, the declaration of the rights and privileges of princes, human laws can only prohibit what the condition of society demands. The state in other words only has a practical aim.† The calling of the king is described as that of guardian of justice and the living practical righteousness. The aim of human law-making is to make virtuous citizens, and the failure to interdict the wrong conduces to the destruction of society. The end of the state-unity is to live virtuously, this virtue being what is called ethical and scientific contemplation, or in other words the activity of the state is always directed to a higher end than the physical or social good, namely, the supernatural. In subjecting human beings in society to the state and the whole order of society, you say to them, "honor, wealth, power should not be the desire of thy life, but a moral activity which takes in contemplation of the divine order; in this way alone can life be happy." This springs from the idea of natural right and justice as ethical elements of the social life. Consequently for the state to attain its real end there is required, not simply right but also religion, for religion crowns the edifice with glory.

Thomas's view of the Church and state bears very directly upon the aim of the state, for while the Church may restrict and limit the activity of the state, the state cannot dictate to the Church in regard to her end. The state is a necessity for social order, but this is only the lower form of life; man to reach a measure of perfection and happiness must rise into the supernatural sphere of the Church. Hence religion gives an ethical direction to every aim in the state-life.‡ This will be treated more fully in the chapter on the relation of the Church and the state. In general the state is subordinate to the Church in all cases where the aim of the Church and the authority it claims comes in conflict with that of the state. This fact is founded upon the aim of both institutions and the means used to attain their aims. The

* Baumann, p. 16-21.
† De Reg. Prin. 1, 2.
‡ Baumann, p. 16-24.

state is fitted for the promotion of the earthly, temporal welfare of the nation and of individuals, and to preserve human life as well as protect human possessions, and to direct in the obtaining and retaining of all earthly possessions. The Church is qualified to aid man in securing his eternal and supernatural aim, namely, everlasting blessedness, which the state cannot do. The Church has a higher work and a more glorious aim. And as the supernatural aim of man is of greater importance than anything earthly it is the ultimate end of his existence to which the state must contribute in guiding him under the direction and according to the counsel of the Church.* The temporal government must help earthly citizens to become heavenly citizens. This assistance is rendered chiefly in the state protecting with its legislation and political power the Ecclesiastical community and defending her doctrines against enemies, as well as punishing apostates, executing by the secular arm the Ecclesiastical sentence (*brachium seculare*).

3. *Temporal aim of the state, unity and peace.* The intention of every ruler must be directed towards the preservation of that which he has undertaken to govern. Thus it is the duty of the helmsman to preserve the ship for the voyagers and to bring it unharmed into a safe haven. The welfare and prosperity of a united people implies the preservation of their unity which is called freedom, for when this is absent the usefulness of life in society falls to the ground. Certainly a disunited people is a burden to itself. Therefore the ruler of a community must direct his chief aim to caring for the unity and peace of the community, and it is right for him to consider how to restore peace among his subjects; for so far as the aim for which he should strive is concerned there should be no deliberating except in regard to the means of attaining the end. With this view speaks the apostle when he commands unity in the case of believers "endeavoring to keep the unity of the spirit in the bond of peace." The more active a government is to preserve unity and peace, the more suitable it is. We call that most fitting which best leads to the realization of the aim. It is apparent that what is in itself a unit can better effect unity than several units.†

Aim of the state in so far as the rulers are concerned. Share of the king in the good. The aim is not self. It is the duty of a king or other ruler to seek the welfare of society, yet his vocation would be very hard were it not that something of a personal nature comes to himself. This is expressed in the usual reward of a good king. Many are of opinion that honor and fame are the only reward. For this reason Cicero in his political teaching states that the leader of the state must be satisfied with fame. As a reason for this Aristotle states in his Ethics that the prince who is not content with fame would become a tyrant. It seems to be an innate principle that each one seeks a personal good for himself. If then the prince is not satisfied with fame and honor he will

* Frohschammer, p. 485 sq.
† De Reg. Prin. I. 2.

seek pleasure and wealth and turn even to robbing and oppressing his subjects. If we accept these views many evil results will follow. If it were the portion of kings to bear so much trouble and pain for a perishable prize, kingship would have little reward. There is nothing in human affairs that appears so transitory as fame and honor and the favor of men. It all depends upon the opinion of men which is most changeable in human life. To please men he will become a slave of opinion. The desire for fame robs even of present freedom, on which independent men will expend all their exertions. Nothing is more seemly for a ruler who is trying to promote good than independence of spirit. The prize of fame is an inadequate recompense for a king. It is also injurious to society when such a prize is set up. Though fame follows virtuous actions, yet fame for the sake of virtue is regarded as of little consequence, and a man through small esteem of fame acquires fame. The disciples of Christ showed this as servants of God, whether in fame or in disgrace, in ignominy or in good repute. Therefore fame such as the worthy despise is not a suitable reward for a worthy man. Were this the only reward that lay before a ruler the result would be that brave men would not accept the dignity of the office, or if they did they would go without reward. Out of the ambition for fame spring many dangerous evils. For many in their boundless strivings for war-fame have caused themselves and their armies to perish, and brought their fatherland into the power of the enemy.

Ambition for fame has another closely related evil, namely, desire for show (*simulatio*). As it is difficult to acquire, and few succeed in acquiring true virtue to which alone honor pertains, many men out of desire for fame have merely the appearance of virtue. Therefore, as Sallust says, avarice has made many men false, some in heart and others in speech. Our Saviour called those who did good works to be seen of men, hypocrites, that is men of pretence. When the prince seeks pleasure and wealth as his reward, there is danger to society that he will become a robber and a defamer, there is danger that when the prize enchains the soul he will become full of self-conceit and pretence. It is clear however from the opinion of the wise that they do not esteem honor and fame as a reward for the ruler, as though his mind were set on them as the principal aim; but when a king does seek fame he is more worthy of toleration than when he is avaricious or goes after self-pleasure. Each vice stands near to a virtue. The fame which men desire is, according to Augustine, simply the favorable opinion of men, and the desire of fame has in it a trace of virtue, in that it seeks the approval of the good and does not wish to displease them. As few succeed in being truly virtuous, it is preferable to take those for rulers who at least respect the judgment of men and so are held back from open wickedness; for one who is desirous of fame goes either in the true way through virtuous actions to the goal of approval by men, or he strives to attain his end by means of cunning and deceit. On the contrary, he who has an inordinate desire for power, but is without desire for fame and is indifferent to the judgment of the wise (*bene judicantes*) will seek to reach his aim generally by wrongful methods. In this he will outdo even the animals in his vicious life, as it was with the Emperor Nero, whose gluttony was such that we cannot believe anything manly could find a place in him, and whose cruelty was such that he could do nothing gently or kindly. Aristotle says, independence of spirit seeks honor and fame, not as something great or as a sufficient reward for virtue, for this is the best of all earthly good, that a man have testimony from his fellow-men concerning his virtue.*

As earthly fame and honor are not sufficient for a ruler's reward, it is becoming that the prince should look for his reward from God. The servant expects his reward from his master. The king is as ruler of the people the servant of God, as the apostle says, all authority is from the Lord, and he is a minister of God taking vengeance on those that do evil. God often rewards kings for their services with temporal goods. God says of Nebuchadnezzar, "Behold I will give the land of Egypt to Nebuchadnezzar the king of Babylon: and he shall take her prey and it shall be the wages for his army. I have given him the land of Egypt for his hire wherewith he served against it.†" The Lord rewarded even unrighteous kings who fought against his enemies, —of course they did not intend to serve God but to satisfy their own hate and lust—in that He gave them victory over their enemies, cast down kingdoms and allowed them to have the prey and spoil. What will he do to good kings who with devout mind rule the people of God and make war on his enemies? He promises them not an earthly but a heavenly reward. So Peter says to the shepherds of God's people, "Feed the flock of God which is among you.... and when the chief shepherd shall appear," that is, Christ the King of Kings, "ye shall receive a crown of glory unfading." This is also proved from reason. In all who have the use of understanding there is implanted the conciousness that the reward of virtue is happiness. The virtue of each action may be described as, "what is done is good and the doing of it tends towards good." Every one strives to acquire through good works that which he longs for, namely, to be happy: therefore the reward of virtue, that which makes men happy, is expected with good reason. If it is the ministry of virtue to be actively engaged at work, it is the king's ministry to rule his subjects well, so that the king's reward shall be happiness. It remains to be seen what that is. Happiness is the ultimate yearning of the soul; this longing does not reach into the infinite, because the desire implanted by nature would then be void as the infinite cannot be taken in. The further the yearning of an intelligent being goes out toward universal good, the more does that kind of good really produce happiness, after the attainment

* De Reg. Pr. I. 7.
† Ezek. 29. 19, 20.

of which no other good remains to be desired. For this reason happiness is called a perfect good, because it possesses in itself all that is desirable. This is not found in any single earthly good, for he who has wealth wishes more, and so with all other earthly possessions. There is no permanency in earthly things, therefore nothing earthly can satisfy and form the aim of a king. Again every perfect and complete good depends upon a higher one. Even material things become better by union with something better and higher, as they become worse by mingling with what is bad. All earthly things are inferior to the human spirit, and hence nothing earthly can make man happy. Augustine says, "we do not call earthly Christian princes happy because they have reigned longer or have died more peacefully than others, or because their sons have preceeded them, or because they have conquered their enemies and obtained wealth, or have defended themselves against rebellious citizens whom they have subjected; but we call them happy if they rule justly, if they prefer to master their own passions rather than rule over a people, and if they do nothing out of mere regard for empty fame but from a desire of eternal happiness. Such Christian rulers as we call happy, because they hope for that which later will be a reality in their experience."*

The cause of the human spirit was God, therefore God alone can be its befitting aim. The human spirit recognizes a universal good, and desires it through its will. Universal good finds its realization only in God. The answer of the Psalmist is, "It is my good to draw near to God; I have set my trust in God the Lord."† He it is certainly that gives prosperity to the king, not only for the present but forever. The reward of a king then is honor and fame, not earthly but heavenly. For what transitory glory can be compared to the honor of being a citizen of heaven and a companion of God, as a son of God and heir of heaven with Christ. What human praise can be compared with God's, not the deceitful tongue of flattery nor the delusive opinion of men, but the testimony of the inmost consciousness confirmed by the testimony of God. Those who seek this honor acquire with it the fame of those whose opinion they seek not.‡

Aim of the state in so far as the subjects are concerned. Government is the directing of the governed in a proper manner towards the desired goal. A ship is managed when it is, through the activity of the ship-master, brought safely and directly to the haven. It devolves not only upon the master to keep it from damage on its voyage but also to bring it to the haven. How much more fitting is it in matters pertaining to God and men that pains should be taken to reach the highest end.§ Thomas shows the relation of individuals

* De Civit. Dei, I. 5.
† Psalm 73, 28.
‡ De Reg. Pr. I. 8.
§ De Reg. Princ. I. 14.

to the whole organism and its aim. One individual is probably anxious that what relates to him should be left to his own will, another that he should succeed in obtaining a higher degree of perfection than others. In the management of the ship the carpenter repairs whatever has been damaged on board, the shipmaster however attends to the bringing of the ship into harbor. Among men in society the physicians attend to the health of the people, the steward supplies the necessaries of life, the teacher of science educates in the truth and the moralist (*instilutor morum*) directs according to reason. If man were not destined for a higher end he would be self-sufficient. But there is another possession for man, outside of himself, the highest happiness which is hoped for in the enjoyment of God after death. These requirements are provided for through the servants of the Church. We must regard the final aim of society as a whole as well as that of the individual members. If the ultimate aim of individual man were some possession lying within himself, the final aim in the government of society would be, that society had the right to this possession in him. Hence if the final end of individual man were physical health and life, the task of securing it should devolve upon the physician; were it to obtain an excess of property, the economist (*œconomus*) would be the king of society; were it to secure such a knowledge of truth as society could attain, the king would be a master of knowledge; but the aim of uniting a mass of men in a state is, that they may live in accordance with virtue, for men form themselves into unions to live a good life (*bene vivere*), to which the individual could not attain of himself. Therefore the virtuous life is the aim of human association. An evidence of this is found in the fact that only those who have a mutual interest in helping one another unite in such an association. For if men formed a society simply to live, animals and slaves would form a part of the state. If men simply wanted by union to acquire property, then all who carry on business and trade must necessarily form part of the state. But only those are members of society who are under the same laws and the same government, tending to develop a well regulated life. Man living virtuously is destined to a higher aim because through virtuous living he reaches the enjoyment of God. If this could be attained by the powers of human nature the king would guide to this ultimate end, for the king is the most important element in human affairs (*summa regiminis*). But it belongs to those who teach the ultimate aim (*ad quem pertinet ultimus finis*) to guide those who are aiming after it. This is a divine guidance and belongs to that king who is not only man but God, the Lord Jesus Christ, who acts through his Church and priesthood on earth.*

The state then has an ethical task to perform. Originally it was formed that human beings might get sufficient means of livelihood, and not simply that man might live, but live aright in so far as human life is directed

* De Reg. Prin. I. 14.

towards virtue by the laws. A man who by nature is not fitted for such a state-life must either become worse than other men through perversity, or better than other men through perfection. Thus the extraordinary man has an end in himself. John the Baptist and Antonius the hermit were of this extraordinary class, being above the ordinary class of men.* The state has also an economic end.† The end of legislation is of a similar character. All who are concerned with legislation regard virtue as something to which citizens should be led and wickedness as something from which they should be restrained. This is the purpose of good legislation as it is of the existence of a state that citizens be virtuous through laws and customs.‡ In the commentary on Aristotle's Ethics§ it is stated, that man by nature is a social being and cannot provide for all his needs; he is naturally a member of society (*multitudo*), that through the aid of others he may live a regular life, which would be devoid of perfection without such society. This life he lives in two societies of which he is a member. (a) Man is helped by domestic society to provide himself with the requirements of the present life. Every human creature receives from his parents being, support and training. (b) The society of the state furnishes him with what is necessary in order that he may live an upright life. This state-society supplies him with certain material things, for there are arts and trades which are found in the state such as cannot be provided by a domestic society; but by the exercise of moral control the power of the state brings him into subjection, and in the case of the intractable who have failed to benefit by the parental admonitions the power of the state checks them through the fear of punishment.

4. *Summary.* The moral work of the state is the same as is that of the individual. Man as man on account of the unity of human nature has one ultimate aim. For the accomplishment of this end all things must be done in the social and state-life, as well as in the individual life. Life appears under three forms, (a) the life of desire; (b) the life of the state or political life; (c) the life of scientific contemplation. The aim of man in these forms of life is different. In the first, the aim is earthly material goods; in the second, the exercise of practical reason in the pursuit of virtue; and in the third, the possession and use of theoretical reason or of speculative knowledge. The first is a sensuous life which prefers material things and finds its pleasure in the enjoyment of them. To this life belong many not only of the common people but large numbers whose sole aim is the happiness of the present. These members have not the proper use of reason and are content to live an animal life, of immoderate eating, drinking and revelling, resulting in vices that lead to imprisonment and punishment under the regime of social order.

* Ar. Com. Vol. XXI. p. 367 sq.
† see Chapter X.
‡ ibid. p. 620, 678.
§ p. 2.

The other two forms are lives of intelligence, and only the life of reason in its practical and theoretical forms can be called truly human. The political or practical life in which the activity of the state society relates to the community is a preparation for the activity of pure reason, unannoyed by the unrest of political life, such a life of pure reason being realized in contemplative study.* The aim of desire regards the state as the best society in which to secure wealth, honor, pleasure or power; the aim of human life which seeks possessions as a reward of virtue regards the state as the best society in which to enjoy social peace and to attain to social virtue; virtue in the individual and in the state are of the same character, the only difference between the two being that of the whole in relation to a part.

The best activity for man is that which leads him to the superior being who is above himself. Means must be utilized to attain the ultimate end of recognizing the supreme being. This is done by reason in its perfect exercise so as to bring it under the notice of the Supreme being. In order to accomplish this four things are necessary in the individual and in the state, (a) a perfect condition of reason; (b) an imperfect condition of reason; (c) the condition of soul such as leads desire away from the natural and centres it upon the supernatural; (d) certain virtues by means of which external things are utilized.† As the upright life on earth is intimately connected with the happy life in heaven, so it is in regard to the welfare of human society. All the peculiar possessions procured by human effort, wealth, trade, health, civilization are connected together. Those who have a regard for the ultimate aim must control those who have the care of the goods of the earth, the king in final issue must be subject to the government exercised through the priesthood to realize this higher aim.‡

* Com. on Ethics, pp. 11, 20, 22; on Politics pp. 638, 678.
† p. 679.
‡ De Reg. Princ. I. 15.

CHAPTER VI.

ACTIVITY OF THE STATE. SOVEREIGNTY. THE FUNCTIONS OF THE STATE.

1. *Activity.* The possession of power implies its exercise and the exercise of power implies activity. Man is a social and political animal *in multitudine vivens*, such implying human activity.* A multitude without order cannot enjoy peace or prosperity. Order in a multitude cannot be preserved without the moral consent and the unity of all the parts and members in performing the functions necessary to life. This unity of all the organic members can be obtained only by means of some moral head; consequently man was made to live in the society of other men, and by the very same law of nature he is directed to live under authority. Power is a necessary consequence of our nature in order to the attainment of the social end of life. The act of association is natural; it may be reckoned the first step in the active life of the state; following this association is the establishment of a governing body, by the consent of the people, or by the authority of a strong ruler who establishes himself in the seat of power; then follows the activity of the governor or governors in securing peace to the state, the best form of which is found where all the members have a share in it. The activity of the state *par excellence* is the activity of government, controlling the society for its best interest.* The general embodiment of this activity is found in the chief ruler: as the shipmaster to whom belongs the ordering of the voyage, directs those who repair and fit the ship, as the man who uses the weapons directs the smith what kind of weapons he is to prepare, so the chief ruler is the head of activity in the state. As what is seen in art is an imitation of what takes place in nature, we learn from nature by our understanding to be active and also the manner in which that activity shows and conducts itself.‡

It is the characteristic of virtue that good comes through the activity of men; it is also the greater virtue that through activity a greater good is wrought. The welfare and the good of society are greater and more divine than that of the individual, therefore the activity of society is the sovereign or supreme activity. For this reason an evil is endured (*sustinetur*) by an individual, which is contrary to the individual good, when it is for the welfare

---
* De Reg. Princ. l. 1.
† 1a. 2ae. qu. 105. 1; De Reg. Princ. l. 1. 12. 14
‡ De Reg. Princ. l. 12.

of society. Such an institution as ostracism among the Greeks illustrates this sacrifice of the individual for the state good. Likewise robbers are killed in order that society may have peace from their depredations. God would certainly not allow evil to exist in the world if he did not know how to bring good out of it, to the benefit and welfare of all. It belongs then to the office of the highest ruler to care jealously for the welfare of society and the activity which has charge of this supreme concern is regarded as sovereign.*

Since then the Supreme activity of the state centres in the government, we ask, what does Thomas mean by government, and in what way does he conceive the idea of government? He sets forth in the *De Regimine Principum* his ideas upon this subject. Thomas traces everything to, and proves every position by, the principle of government which to him is the grand topic in politics. He first establishes the proposition that man living in society needs a government. To establish this principle he premises that there is need of direction in order to attain the end destined, in everything that is so constituted that it has a variety of elements. Man has always a certain end in life according to which he acts, because he is an intelligent being and in the attainment of the end he has need of guidance. What is needed direction? Man has the natural light of intelligence. To a man living a life of isolation this is sufficient, each one being a king of and to himself under the sovereignty of God, ruling his own life by the light within him. But man is naturally a social being. Individuals are members of a social body, and this social organism requires a uniting force or power in order to prevent its general dissolution. This uniting social force which guides to the common good he calls *aliqua vis regitiva communis*. It gives constitution to the social body and is the means of realizing the state activity.

The state is the larger body for it includes those who hold office and perform the functions of *vis regitiva*. By this latter term Thomas designates the government as that social force which has the ruling power for the common good. It is the moving cause for the good of the society. Wherever there is a unity there is some governing power or person, securing this unity. The soul rules the body of man; and in the complex faculties of the soul the reason is the ruling principle. So in every multitude there is a regulative power *regitivum*, that is a government. Government occupies a large place in the theory of Thomas. The citizen of the state attends to his own private affairs, the government takes the sole charge of common affairs and administers all the offices which pertain to the common welfare. The people in general lack reason and need guidance in order to do what is right.† Thomas compares the recourse which a people have to an intelligent governor to the dependence of a mariner upon the pilot or the workman upon an architect.‡ It is

* De Reg. Princ. 1, 9.
† Arist. Expos. IV. lect. 3, 4.
‡ 2a, 2ae. qu. 47, 12.

in the royal office that he finds the concentration of governmental power and activity. He exaggerates in a sense the attributes of regal authority. Royalty arises from nature, because art always imitates nature. In the universe at large God is sole governor, in the individual man reason is the king ruling the body and the other forces of the soul. Royalty, activity *par excellence*, is the reflex of these natural governments, *sicut anima in corpore et Deus in mundo*, so likewise is the king in his kingdom.* We shall see that sovereignty ultimately belongs to the state. The state institutes the power of government and makes it legitimate by its authorization and consent. But after its institution the government performs its functions without consulting the society, so long as its activity keeps within natural law. The foundation of popular government is to be seen in Thomas, its primary conception being derived from the constitution of the Church perfected before the time of Thomas. Government is natural to society, its chief activity is expressed in the duty of providing for social necessities and guiding the social community to its end. But this does not imply that it is beyond control, or independent, or that the direction of the governing body is the supreme cause of unity, for the common good is the directing cause, to be interpreted by the intelligence of the government. The government is an institution, as Thomas points out, distinct from the principle of power,† resting upon human law and in which the people have certain rights that enable them to express their minds. Government is a means of realizing the social principles embodied in society and therefore in the use of its activity the government is limited, although it is the supreme power in the state, as the rational organ of authority. This is the grand mistake which Thomas makes. He does not make and keep clear the distinction which he has already pointed out and to which he often refers, between the principle of power and the form it assumes in any particular country, at any given time, as well as the person in whom it is placed.‡

2. *Sovereignty in the state.* Absolute sovereignty belongs only to God for He alone has power to do with man and with the world as he pleases without appeal. Man has no absolute right to command or do with man according to his will. Hence the sovereignty which we speak of as residing in the human state is relative, not absolute, and is founded upon the will of God. Human sovereignty depends for its sanction upon divine sovereignty. God's sovereignty is unlimited in its nature and extent; human sovereignty is limited both in its nature and extent.§

In regard to the state the questions arise to whom does sovereignty appertain? Upon what basis does it rest? How far does it extend? These

* De Reg. Prin. I, 12.
† Com. Sent. Super. 45; Com. Rom. XIII.
‡ Ia. 2ae. qu. 90, 3.
§ 4 Sent. disp. 42. qu. 1 and 2; Ia. 2ae. qu. 13 and 109.

questions have been discussed by Thomas from the point of view of Paul, "all power is from God," *omnis potestas a Deo.*[*] Thomas refuses to recognize that every power of fact is a power of right, distinguishing the powers *de facto* and *de jure*. In his commentary on Rom. XIII. he considers power (*potestas*) in three senses, (a) power in itself, in which case it is from God; (b) power in its origin,—if it is just, it comes from God; but if unjust, originating in the wicked perversity of man, it is not from God; (c) power in its use. In this case it is from God, if it conforms to, it is not from God, if it opposes, the principles of justice. According to this there is a divine right of the power, not of the prince or ruler, a divine right of authority, not of kings.

Where does Thomas wish sovereignty to rest and what title gives a right to it? We have seen already that he sets up the sovereignty of political virtue. The foundation of this virtue is reason or intelligence, and its guide is utility. In his ideal state the citizen is one possessed of such virtue, whose standard of reason and activity is divine justice. Upon those who are endowed with such political virtue a full sovereignty rests, *melius est principari quod melius est et studiosus*, it is right that the best and virtuous command.[†] On the other hand *naturale est quod deficiens supponatur perfecti in unoquoque genere*,[‡] it is natural that the imperfect be in subordination to the perfect. It is according to nature that he who is conspicuous for virtue, surpassing all other citizens should be lord of all; if there is a collective number who share this virtue in an equally eminent degree they have a collective right to the supreme power. The eminently virtuous man or body of men have a right to rule the society in the state, just as God rules the world and the heart the human body. This right of sovereign authority belongs to them as rulers in such a degree that they have power to quell rebellions and to oppose all seditious movements, *rationabiliter et peccaren si non moverent seditionem*.[§] In the same way one of very great eminence above the others and of superior merit may have reasonable cause to stir up a seditious movement against any person not acting in such sovereign capacity, *rationabiliter*.[‖] Where the members of the society are all of one race or class the principle of eminence is utilized, because they are all judged by the same standard. But when the community is large there is seldom an incontestable superiority in one or even in some, and in such a case the sovereignty of all the people comes in as a natural right. Where there are different classes and different races among a people, when the industrial and laboring classes have been excluded, it is difficult to take account of the many and judge the superiority of the few. In this case the standard or principle is changed from that of the sovereign-

[*] Rom. XIII.
[†] Expos. Ar. III. lect. 8. m.
[‡] VIII. lect 2. y.
[§] Expos. Arist. III. lect. 12. o.
[‖] Expos. Ar. V. lect. 1. d.

ty of virtue to the sovereignty of the multitude, or of the people. Thomas thus arrives at those who are the possessors of supreme power in the state by the principle of *exclusion*, excluding all those who do not come up to the standard of virtue found in one or a few, and failing such persons of exclusive virtue, he throws the sovereignty into the people as a whole. In all large societies such as the *regnum* this principle is the determining one. Hence he reduces the abstract theory of sovereignty to this practical rule, *in omnibus ordinare in finem est ejus cujus est proprius ille finis*, in all things it is the office of him who has an end to rule with a view to that end. And as the multitude has for its end the common good, when it is united, then it belongs to the multitude or to some one acting for it to rule for the common good. *Ordinare aliquid in bonum commune est vel totius multitudinis, vel alicujus gerentis vicem totius multitudinis.* It belongs to it to make laws, to appoint magistrates, to check the current of tyranny,—in a word the *multitudo* in society is sovereign, the prince holding his place and the magistrate acting in its name, *vicem totius gerens*.*

Thus out of the theory of the sovereignty of political virtue Thomas evolves the sovereignty of the people. It rests upon natural law, and the principle of adequate means to attain an end, in this case the end of the state. Since there is no one in a large or complex community who can judge or rule for all, by reason of conspicuous virtue, the collective wisdom of the mass determines the end and the means that are adequate to its attainment. He supports this general theory by many secondary considerations. He accepts the saying of Aristotle, that the multitude in its totality is more independent and impartial than one or a number of persons, it is less subject to corruption, and it preserves more pure and uncorrupted wisdom on account of the collective reason.† In it we find riches, virtues, nobility and the entire power of the people,—individual citizens would have little virtue, less wealth and still less power—in union the defects and wants of one are made up by the merits of others. This collective society would be comparable to a perfect man, endowed with all nature's gifts and qualities and able by its united strength to utilize everything that belongs to the whole in wisdom and power and resources for the public good. In the general case then, where there is no pre-eminent qualification in the individual or a few to rule in the state, and even in this case the multitude are the persons whom they represent and in whose name they act, the aggregation of citizens in the state possesses the sovereignty. Even in the case of a kingdom, the king rules over subjects who desire him to rule over them.‡

But there is a condition attached to the sovereignty of the people. The rule of the individual is an illustration of the sovereignty of virtue, which in

* Ia. 2ae. qu. 90. 3.
† Expos. Ar. III. lect. 8.
‡ Com. Arist. Vol. XXI. p. 393-6.

the abstract is the only real sovereignty. The power of the multitude is an example of the practical sovereignty of virtue, for the multitude derives its power from the virtue to which attaches sovereignty, it administers as well as enacts laws, it performs the judicial functions, distributes the state offices among its members on the basis of political virtue. If virtue is absent from the multitude it has no sovereign power. The old distinction between *de jure* and *de facto* which he applied to power, he now applies to sovereign power. Hence he distinguishes between two multitudes. There is a multitude which willingly accepts and obeys the voice of reason, tending naturally towards virtue. Each individual is not only virtuous but the mass of citizens can be characterized as such and acts with a view to show its virtue. Such a multitude is sovereign *de facto*.* The other mass disregards reason, despises virtue and follows after the aims dictated by the animal nature of desire and passion. To this multitude belongs no sovereignty; it has no right to a place in the social community, because it does not live a political life of reason.† The sovereignty of the state manifests itself in the activity towards its end, *bonum commune*. This action is political, that is, furnishes the formal element in the state which is its constitution. In the constitution of the states, sovereignty is determined, for it is a necessity that it reside somewhere to the attainment of the state end. The state is a plurality and it implies concentration and unity. Hence the *vis regitiva* directs the totality to the common good of the members.‡ The sovereign is God's minister in the world as a second cause.§

3. *Functions of the government.* As the sovereign power has been located in the state, we pass to survey the functions of the government to whom is entrusted the supreme power in the state. In Thomas the typical form of government is the monarchy, therefore the activity of the prince forms the chief part of his discussion of the right and function of the ruler's power. The function of the *rex* is implied in the term *regere, rex dicitur cui committitur universalis gubernatio*; the function of the king then is that of governing the state universally, that is, in all its departments. It is best to obtain from nature the manner in which a king should conduct himself. In nature there is a double government,—a universal and a special one. The universal is that which is kept under God's direction and is governed by His providence. The special government is similar to the divine direction. It is found in man who for this reason is called the little world, because in him is found the method and manner of universal direction. For as common corporeal nature and all spiritual beings are under divine direction, so also the mem-

* Expos. Ar. III, lect. 11.
† lects. 8 and 9.
‡ De Reg. Princ. I, 1.
§ De Reg. Princ. I, 8; 2 sent. disp. 44.
⸗ Expos. Psalm II

bers of the body and the powers of the soul are governed by the understanding; and so in a certain way the understanding in man is what God is in the world. Because man is a social being who lives with others, there is not only a copy of the divine government in man who as an individual is governed by the understanding; but through the understanding of an individual society is governed. This direction of society pertains chiefly to the office of the king. The king should be conscious that he has undertaken an office which makes him in his kingdom, what the soul is in the body and what God is in the world.*

If one considers what God does in the world, it will be clear what the king will have to do. There are in general two agencies in God's world to be noticed, one through which the world was established (*instituit*), the other through which the established world is governed (*gubernatur*). First, the body was fashioned by the power of the soul (*informatur*); after the body is governed and moved by the soul. Of these two agencies the second belongs in a peculiar manner to the king's office. In this way governing pertains to kings (*regimine*) and from the fact of ruling they receive the name kings (*reges*).† The king must superintend all human affairs *officio*, and direct them by means of his government. On whomsoever the obligation rests of developing fully what is ordered to be done by another, on him must also rest the duty of seeing that the efforts put forth are calculated to attain the end. The smith makes a sword that serves for fighting, and the builder erects a house that is suitable for a dwelling. As therefore the aim of the present well-ordered life is heavenly happiness it belongs to the king's office to lead a good life, by way of showing to society what he desires, in so far as it is suited to the attainment of heavenly happiness, that he should command what will be helpful and forbid what will be injurious. But as the best way to learn the path to true happiness is the word of God, he should apply to the priest for direction. "The lips of the priest should keep knowledge, and they should seek the law at his mouth."‡

The unity of society which is called peace is effected by the efforts of the rulers. Consequently, to the ordering of a good way of living for society, three things are necessary, (a) that society be placed in the unity of peace; (b) that through the bond of peace, society shall be led to a good way of living; for human society is hindered in right doing, if it is deprived of the unity of peace, and there is fighting among the members; (c) that through the efforts of the ruler there is a sufficiency of what is essential to leading a good life. (a) The good way of living is set forth to society through the activity of the king, and may be said to correspond with legislation on the king's part; (b) the next thing is that his attention be given to securing the

* De Reg. Princ. I. 12.
† De Reg. Princ. I. 13.
‡ Mal. 2, 7. De Reg. Princ. I. 15.

observance of this good way of living, corresponding with executive administration.

There is a threefold hindrance to the stability of the public society (*bonum publicum*). (i) One arises from its nature. The public good cannot be arranged for a time, but must be continuous. Men as mortals cannot live forever: even while they live they do not continue in the same efficiency, because human life has many changes. (ii) Another hindrance in promoting the welfare of the society proceeds from within and consists in the perversity of the will of the members, when they are too slothful or careless to do what the state requires, or when they become injurious to the peace of society by transgressing the laws and disturbing the peace of others. (iii) The third hindrance is an external cause, when an attack is made by the enemies of peace; often the result is, that the kingdom or city is dissolved. To meet these three hindrances to state peace and stability, there devolves upon the king a threefold task. (i) The first relates to the fact that men have successors, and that different individuals have special capacities in different activities. Just as God does in the government of the world with affairs of a transitory nature, because they cannot endure forever, taking care that through the existence of others their places may be filled and so the integrity of the universe is preserved; so the king takes care to fill the places of those who die. The vacant places are filled by appointments in the succession of office. (ii) The king should by means of laws and ordinances, punishments and rewards keep his subjects from unrighteousness and lead them to virtuous actions. For this he has the example of God who has given to men his law and to those who observe it promises rewards, threatening to punish transgressors. (iii) The king is to preserve his subjects safe from enemies. It would be useless to avoid dangers from within if there were no defence from dangers that are without.

c) In order to the good arrangement and the preservation of society the king should be careful to promote good order and to preserve the state. He must try to improve what is ill adapted to the state (*inordinatum*), to supply what is lacking and to strive to perfect what is capable of perfection.* A perfect ruler must have three characteristics. (a) Love of ruling. He cannot be a perfect ruler who lacks this, because he must have practical insight (*prudentia*) which is right reason, in knowing what he ought to do and not to do. As he must guide others, he must exercise judgment and this he cannot have unless he love the aim and the means to attain it. He must have a love of ruling and an affection for the state. (b) He must have power adequate to the performance of the important functions of his office. The ruler has to guide his subjects to the state-end. Among subjects there are some easily persuaded by reason; these do not need any chastisements. Others cannot be reached by reason, being disobedient and intractable; in the case

* De Reg. Princ. I, 15.

of these force must be used. The king cannot use force to punish without power. (c) He must have virtue. The ruler must have practical sagacity and this is not possible apart from the right desire which comes through virtue.*

The ruler must not only have power, he must have more power than any other individual; for if he does not have it he cannot punish those who will not obey him. He must have more power than several persons together, otherwise he could not keep them in check or punish them if necessary. But he must have less power than the state as a whole (*civitas*), for if he had greater power than the state he would be oppressive and turn the government of the kingdom into a tyranny. Here we have a distinct assertion of the sovereignty of the state to which the governmental functions must be subject.† The kingly office would seem to be a kind of professional occupation which one enters out of love for the work and which one exercises in subordination to the supreme power in the state.

Thomas not only ascribes excellence to the king but a very extensive power and he gives him the power on account of the excellence. It is the duty of a king to be the guardian of righteousness. To go to the king for refuge should be the same as going to a living embodiment of power for refuge, because it is the purpose of the king to guard and care for the welfare of the community (*bonum communae*). This he cannot do unless he is the guardian of justice. This office he must exercise so that those who have property and wealth may not suffer wrong from those who are destitute of property and that these in turn may not be oppressed by the rich. He must therefore be a just judge. In fine he is a king who aims at the good of all society. He must be virtuous and therefore wrong none of his subjects; he must be rich so that he may not oppress his subjects; he must have honor, for eminence in virtue pertains to a high-souled-honor. His body guard consists of citizens, for a king rules his subjects for their benefit. Therefore he can rely upon them to help him in performing his functions and confide in their guardianship.‡

Thus all the essential functions of government have been presented in connection with kingship. To govern is *regere*, including *habere alios sub sua providentia*.§ To govern is to execute providence,‖ and providence itself is order.¶ In the execution of this order of providence the mode of activity corresponds with the form of the agency, *oportet modum actionis esse secundum modum formae agentis*.** To govern may be described as the function *rem ad debitum finem producere*, of which primary function there are three secondary

* Arist. Expos. Vol. XXI. p. 484.
* Ibid. p. 495.
† Ibid. p. 586.
‡ 4 sent. disq. 49. qu. 1; qu. 5; 2a. 2ae. qu. 49. 6
† Ia. qu. 23. 1; 4 sent. disq. 39. qu. 2. 1.
* Ia. qu. 22. 1; qu. 23. 1.
** 3 sent. disq. 27. qu. 1. 4; Cg. 2. c. 21. 22.

functions, *consilium*, *judicium*, and *praeceptum*.* The general name by which the political virtue of government is known is *prudentia*.† Of this political prudence there are three kinds, *individualis*, *domestica* or *politica*, *militaris* or *aquatica*.‡ The *politica prudentia* applies to the rule in political society. The supreme office of the sovereign is *curam habere communitatis*,§ and this office is fulfilled by the threefold function of power, *dirigere* corresponding to *consilium*, *corrigere* to *judicium* and *cogere* to *praeceptum*.

In the ideas of Thomas there is the abstract distribution of the power, and the concrete distribution of the distinct elements of the power, these being bound up in the person of the prince. In his zeal for royalty the state activity is identified with the activity of the prince. Consequently the supreme ruler is *potestas summa*, or *majestas*, or *potestas activa cum aliqua praeeminentia*,∥ in which the state becomes personified in its ruler. The special characteristic function of *consilium* is *inventio aequalorum*;¶ of *judicium* it is *actus judicis in quantum est judicis; idest actus justitiae*;** *praeceptum* is *applicatio in legis ad ea quae ex lege regulantur*,†† law being described as *dirigere intentionem ostendendo qualis debet esse actus proportionatus fini ultimo*.‡‡ The necessity of this *praeceptum* is *quod importet ordinem ad finem in quantum praecipitur id quod est necessarium et expediens ad finem* . . . *ab eo qui communitatis curam habet promulgata*.§§ Thus the executive, legislative and judicial functions are ascribed to the ruling power in the state. To the judicial and legislative functions a high place is assigned. *Justitia* is said to exercise judgment in the place of God in the kingdom, *ut loco Dei judicium in regno exerceat*.∥∥ This justice includes the *jusdicere* and the *jus punire*,¶¶ and when it is spoken of as a corrective power it implies *cogere ad emendationem per poenas*.*** Thus *judicium* embraces the right of summoning before a court of justice, of punishing for a crime and by penalties seeking to lead to reformation. In legislation there is exercised a fourfold power, *imperare seu praecipere, vetare seu prohibere, permittere et punire*.†††

Legislation and execution. The essential function of supreme power is the legislative, the power of making laws, in its wide sense. It is the chief characteristic of sovereignty. This power of legislation belongs to the whole multitude or to some person representing them. Originally it rests with the whole, but it is vested in the hands of one or more persons who represent the state.‡‡‡ It is for the good of the whole that the prince or rulers ought to make laws. We have seen that sovereign power resides in the same mul-

---

* 2a. 2ae. qu. 51. 2; 3 sent. disq. 33. qu. 1. ** 1a. 2ae. qu. 90. 2.
† 2a. 2ae. qu. 49. 6. †† 2 sent. disq. 41. qu. 1. 1.
‡ 1a. 2ae. qu. 55. 6; 2a. 2ae. qu. 47. 11. ‡‡ 1a. 2ae. qu. 99. 4.
§ 4 sent. disq. 19. qu. 2. 1. §§ De Reg. Prin. I. 12.
∥ 4 sent. disq. 24. qu. 1. 1 ∥∥ I. 15.
¶ 2a. 2ae. qu. 51. 2. ¶¶ 4 sent. disq. 19. qu. 2. 1.
*** qu. 60. 1. *** 1a. 2ae. qu. 92. 2.
††† 1a. 2ae. qu. 90. 4.

titude and that the good government is that in which all have a share."* There is thus a primary and a secondary sovereignty, that of the people and that of the government, the latter derived from the former. The sovereignty of the former is maintained, (a) in the matter of choice and desire, in selecting a governor; (b) in the limitations placed upon rulers to prevent them degenerating into tyrants; (c) because they may deprive a tyrant or unjust ruler of his power, so that the power not only originates with them but returns to them in case of abuse.† The ruler or rulers are representative in legislation. Even in the case of the distinction he draws between royal power and political power, the former ruling after the model of providence by its own wise discernment of right and wrong, the latter governing according to the law, the ultimate point of interest in both is that all human laws are an emanation of human reason,—in the case of the royal power equally with the political, government by law must conform to the standard of reason. The true law whether enacted by the authority of one or many is an expression of reason, not of will or caprice or power, from which tyranny and unjust government proceed. Laws are given simply as an assistance in carrying out the state-end. If the aim of the state is right so will be the constitution and laws that are used as a means to attain the end. The law must govern and guide in all that which it was appointed to do.

The ruler must govern in all that cannot be definitely reduced to law, for the law is made for general application, but it permits of exceptions in special cases (*instantiam*). The lawgiver cannot foresee all the peculiar circumstances in which a law will be faulty. In such cases the ruler steps in. This distinguishes the executive or administrative character of the ruler from the legislative character. It may even be said to apply to the judicial, because it is by the *judicium* that a judgment is given as to the application of the general law to the special case.‡ The formula therefore may be put thus, the law rules in ordinary, the ruler in peculiar cases using his wisdom and discretion. The reason for the indisputable authority of law is that law is free from passion, through which the decision of the understanding is destroyed. These laws are not necessarily written. In every properly constituted state the ruler governs according to the laws, for in every state some one governs according to a rule which is equivalent to law. Some of the laws are internal, in the will and understanding of the monarch, others are external and written. In government by a king the rule is the will and understanding; it is the peculiar virtue of the king to possess the insight which qualifies him to govern. Government is a profession and professional skill is the guide. The other moral virtues are common to rulers and subjects alike. This peculiar quality may be called discretion. It is what monarchy in more modern times has called prerogative.§

* qu. 105, 1.   ‡ Aris. Expos. Vol. XXI. pp. 477-8.
† De Reg. Princ. I. 6, 7.   § pp. 499, 518.

Human laws are special regulations in conformity with natural law, in which man arranges in detail what in principle is in natural law.* Human laws are given to the whole of society, of which the greater number are not perfect in virtue. Therefore human legislation does not prohibit all moral transgressions, but it enjoins the more difficult virtues, to keep which voluntarily is not possible for the greater part of society, especially those which tend to the injury of others and which could not be kept without obstructing the progress of human society. So human legislation forbids murder, theft, etc.; in a word human legislation only controls those actions of virtue by which men come in contact with society. The formula to guide in the legislative function is, "the peace and unity of the society is the guide of the ruler."† This amounts almost to saying that legislation has only to do with the particular social virtues and duties; all others being left to the individuals and even to religion as distinct from the state. Human legislation then is reasonable regulation with a view to the common good, promulgated by public authority. Its validity depends upon three conditions. (a) adequate public authority, *promulgata ab eo qui curam communitatis habet;* (b) conformity with reason, *lex est dictamen aut ordinatio rationis;* (c) tending to the public welfare, *ad bonum commune*. The special design of legislation is to assure the peace of society, the repression of unjust intrigues, and the mutual unity of men. It is not only to punish the violation of public peace and to see that private engagements are kept, but in general to promote the interests of the social community. It does not punish and interdict all evil and mischief, but only those things which are contrary to the preservation of society; it does not ordain all virtue but it accommodates itself and its commands to the majority of men in society.

Thomas prefers what he calls inanimate justice to animate justice, that is, he prefers a law which is general and clear to a judge who can judge according to his own discretion, because, (a) it is easier to get a general rule of justice according to which one may decide special cases than to decide every case on its own merits; (b) it is easier to find a legislator capable of making good laws than many good judges to supply the laws as they go along; (c) a legislator makes his laws upon general principles and is more free from passion than the judge who pronounces special judgments on special occasions. Thus he prefers general legislation to judge-made law. The legislator should derive from the general principles of practical reason his particular determinations in regard to the cases in hand, legislating on the basis of natural right, to the end that he may ameliorate human life, *utilitas vitae humanae*. He must modify and add to the principles of natural law under the guidance of Divine law so as to adapt his legislation to the human condition. Of this sort we have seen is the law of property and slavery. These variations are

* Ia. 2ae. Vol. II. p. 354. Parma.
† Ibid. p. 351; Sum. Contra Gent. Vol. V. p. 367. Parma.

guided by the standard of morals, the political principles of government for the civil and domestic orders must be guided by the political standard.* These variations also follow the progress of man in science and art and civilization, so that there is a progress in legislation to suit the status of the people. It is a human law that man progresses from the imperfect to the perfect. In the speculative and practical sciences much good may be derived from the community at large, but these changes ought to be wrought only with great care and skillful management. This would amount to making it part of the legislative function to encourage science, and art, and education by its fostering care.†

Legislation is thus the all important function of the supreme power of the state, for it acts in three ways, (a) by commanding, (b) by prohibiting, and (c) by permitting.‡ It includes the executive act of administering law, the legislative act of promulgating and declaring law, and the judicial act of punishing the offender and judging what is right and wrong in the actions of members in the state, as well as the act of prerogative by which internal peace is preserved by the exclusion and punishment of enemies of the state in international relations with other states.

* Aris. Expos. IV. lect. I. g.
† 1a. 2ae. qu. 97. 1. 2.
‡ 1a. 2ae. qu. 93. 3.

CHAPTER VII.

FORMS OF GOVERNMENT.

1. *Form of government, not of state.* The common welfare which is the end of the state, requires a directing power, the state government. The question of form is one of the crucial questions of politics, around which centres much political discussion. The classification of Aristotle to Thomas was the best. If government is of the right kind it must seek the good of the community. Aristocracy and polity are true and proper state-constitutions, but monarchy is much preferable, for the unity of government and the peace of the state are best secured in it. Understanding and history both teach this. There is only one difficulty that of the king becoming a tyrant. History shows among people the change from monarchy to other forms, and from these to monarchy with the risk of tyranny. In all arrangements directed to an end which may reached be by different ways there is needed guidance. Hence it is that man being a creature of reason can be guided aright and may also go astray, in several ways. One can proceed in arranging for the attainment of an end, rightly and wrongly. Therefore one finds in society a right and a wrong way. The aim of a society of freemen is different from that of a society of slaves. Hence the distinction of different forms in the government. Governments may, *first of all*, be classified as *just* and *unjust; secondly*, they may classified according to the number of persons in the government or governing body. These three classifications are intermingled.*

Just or unjust governments. The fundamental difference between the good and bad government is that the good is in the interest of the governed, the bad in the interest of the governing. Governments of the first kind are *recti* and of the second *non recti*. The first is a government over free men, the other over slaves. When a government governs for self its subjects are slaves; it is free when there is liberty of action for all. Selfishness is the chief vice of all bad governments and by this test they descend from the category of good into that of bad. The just and the unjust have a threefold scale according to the numbers in each, each corresponding good having its counterpart in the corresponding bad form, Monarchy and tyranny. Aristocracy and oligarchy. Republic (*politia*) and democracy. Aristocratic or republican government is quite legitimate, although it may not be so well fitted to the state. It is not the actual form but the character of the state-constitution which gives it the character of good or bad.*

Whenever the government is conducted for the private benefit of the rulers it is *unrighteous*. When such a perverted government is conducted by one, who seeks his own good and not the good of others, he is named a tyrant, which is derived from the fact that he uses his strength to oppress. The ancients called all mighty ones tyrants. If an unrighteous government is carried on by a few, not by one, it is an oligarchy, that is, when a few keep the people in oppression and raise themselves above the people by tyrannical rule. These are tyrants. If an unrighteous government is conducted by many, it is called democracy; that is, government by the people when the lower classes, *populus plebeiorum*, powerfully oppress the richer people. In this case the collective people would be a tyrant. Tyrant expresses the character of all bad governments, *per tale regimen fit injustus quod spectat bono communi multitudinis, quaeritur bonum privatum regentis*.†

Just governments are similarly classified. (a) if conducted by means of a multitude it is called polity; (b) if conducted by a few or by desirable men, it is Aristocratic, that is, the best government or government of the best, *optimates*; (c) if the government depends on one then it is designated kingly.

Thomas reduces in ultimate issue the forms of government to those conducted by *one* and *not one*.‡ Here the king who is *the one* seeks the good of society, not his own private interest.§ The proper constitutions of state then are the *kingdom*, *aristocracy* and *polity*. Of these the kingdom is the best, then comes the aristocracy, the polity being least just of all.‖

There is a twofold division of kingdoms, (a) an improper kingship, the Lacedemonian, in which the ruler governs according to the laws and does not lord it over the subjects; (b) the regular kingdom in which the king governs according to virtue and is lord of all. He only has a right to the title of king who holds an absolute government subject only to virtue, just as John of Salisbury set up the king in a position external to the law.¶ In the ordinary kingdom it is not proper for the society to have power to elect or control (*corrigere aut dijcere*) as in a republic; in a kingdom in which an individual has absolute power in governing and the others obey him just as slaves do their master (*quasi dominativo principatu*), it is not proper that society have this power as is the case in a republic where all the members of society are of equal standing.**

What course should be taken if an individual citizen in a republic should be

* De Regim. Prin. I. 3.
† De Reg. Princ. I. 3.
‡ Taparelli, Dissert. II. 9, note 65.
§ De Reg. Prin. I. 1.
‖ Ar. Expos. Vol. XXI. pp. 506-7; De Reg. Princ. I. 12; Expos. Psalm II.
¶ Expos. Aris. III. lect. 8.
** Expos. Aris. Vol. XXI. p. 476.

found qualified for the kingship? It is not a question of his superiority in wealth, bodily strength or friendships, but of one exceptional in political virtue. It cannot be said that he should be driven out of the state and located elsewhere for that is contrary to reason, because he is the best citizen. He cannot be asked to rule for a time, for that would be like asking Jupiter to reign awhile and then desist. It is right that the best qualified should be cheerfully obeyed and that he be made king. Aristotle contradicts this, because he says it is better that a number should rule rather than a few, and when one reigns alone the others are without honor, which is to be avoided. He who excels others is no citizen and he who is no citizen cannot be a ruler. To offset this, when an individual is found who excels all others in political virtue he must be ruler. The more one is qualified to rule, the better he will rule; and if one excel all the rest he should be the state ruler. In the state a government is like that in nature and in the world. It would be better if there were but a single ruler and he the best. Thomas answers Aristotle's objections. (a) *It is more fitting for a number to rule*. This is applicable only in a republic where the virtue of all is equal. (b) *All others are without honor when one or a few reign*. In a properly constituted state each one loves his own rank and degree and that of others, and so will receive the honor belonging to him and give the honor that is due to others to them, not coveting his neighbor's honor. No one will be without honor. (c) *One who excels others is not a citizen*. That is only so far true as he rules because of possessing excellent virtue, for any one is a citizen who keeps the laws.* Law given in the state is necessary for all who are equal in power and degree, and it belongs to the means which the state uses to attain its end. All are not in circumstances to be guided by themselves and require the law to lead them in what they ought and ought not to do. The law is given to those who are equal in power and rank and these are termed citizens. To those who excel in virtue there is no need of law for they are a law to themselves. The law is an ordinance which the state employs to attain its end and as such is a means. Consequently prominent men, conspicuous in virtue, are not citizens but *rulers*.

It is evident from this that Thomas distinguishes state and government, and *the form is not of state but of government*. The supreme power embodied in the government manifests itself in different forms and different constitutions. He does not base on divine right the preference he has for the kingly form, but on reason and social interest. In general all government is just which accomplishes the end for which it was instituted, namely, the good of society, and all government is bad and perverse which sacrifices the social good, the common welfare to particular private interest.† The most common forms of human society are, monarchy in which one man rules, aristocracy in which a limited number of the best men rule, and democracy in which all

* Ibid. p. 487.
† De Reg. Princ. II. 1.

the members of the community are rulers, provided they have full use of their capacities. There is another form which is the combination of these three, constitutional government. In every form the essential point is that the ruler or rulers act for the public good, *rex est qui unius multitudinem civitatis vel provinciae propter bonum commune regit*.* All other forms are unnatural and unlawful. Thomas approaches the subject without any prejudice in favor of any special form of government.†

2. *Actual forms.* (a) Monarchy is the form of which he treats with full details in the *De Reg. Princip.* He sets up an a priori argument in favor of monarchy on the general grounds of the unity of society and that the chief end of the state is best secured by its subjection to a single ruler.‡ He gives monarchy the highest place. He intended to use monarchy in the etymological sense as the government of one, the form in which the supreme power is in one person. In modern language Monarchy is the government of the state by a hereditary dynasty. With Thomas it is different. Dynastic government is a type of monarchy, but not the best. Monarchy is that type in which one unique governor owes his position to superior virtue, and to his election by the people, which is one way of proving the possession of this virtue. Thomas compares the elective and hereditary monarchy, and decides that the elective is the best form, chiefly because reason has free play in choosing the worthy and this adds worth to the crown of the king. Election is free *per se*, but heredity comes to be *per accidens*. It is of special value to adhere to heredity to avoid dissension among the electors and to prevent the choice of a bad prince, but heredity is the exception to the general rule of election to office.§ In general monarchy is elective on the basis of pre-eminent virtue, therefore the elective principle is the first characteristic of monarchy.

But what is the power of the chief or monarch? Was this authority absolute or limited? Thomas differs from many of the theologians of the middle ages who founded a royal despotism upon the kingship of the Hebrews as set forth in I. Kings VIII. 11. Thomas repudiates such an absolute despotism and rather finds in the passage a prediction of the usurpation of tyrants.‖ Monarchy is limited and ought to respect the rights of citizens. To treat them as slaves would be to make royal power dominical and despotic. Citizens must be treated as members of the state and if they are not so treated royalty, as all governments do, becomes tyranny. The duty of the supreme ruler is to regard not his own interest but that of the ruled. Yet the monarch in theory is absolute, and to this there are no legal limits. Power is to him the sum of government and it is not shared by any one else. Its office is to institute, preserve and perfect the state, but it is not bound by

* De Reg. Princ. I. 1.   ‡ Sum. Contra Gent. IV. 76.
† De Reg. Princ. I. 2.   § Ar. Expos. III. lect. 14.
‖ Ia. 2ae. qu. 105. 1-5.

any law save reason, according to which the will of the rational monarch is law. The king is the source of law; he has full power, he is the embodiment of all state authority.* This royal power is a despotism of virtue and reason, *cuius praeficitur secundum virtutem*.† In the *De Reg. Princ.* in which he applies the monarchic principle to his own age he expressly advises the exercise of the power to the avoidance of tyranny and hence he says that the power is tempered, *temperatur potestas ejus*. These precautions are all in the interest of the state and of the future reward of the prince himself. Monarchy then is absolute power in the hands of one, and it is superior to every other form because in it the governmental hierarchy is most natural and the social body is most perfect as a natural organism, *unitatem magis efficere potest quod est per se unum*.‡ It is the best form of government, *optima et rectissima*, and he uses it as the standard by which to measure all the rest§ because in it is the social order more like the universal order in which the entire universe is subject to God as King.

The opposite of Monarchy is Tyranny. The characteristic of tyranny is that the tyrant acts for his own interest. As soon as the monarch forgets that he acts for the public interest he degenerates into tyranny. The tyrant is also characterized by his rule of constraint; the monarch ruling by natural consent he preserves the power of the state with the assent of the people.¶ If monarchy is the best form tyranny is the worst form, *corruptio optimi pessima*. The tyrant uses all the state force for his own own good and being armed with more despotic power than any other bad government it is the worst form.* Tyranny means the absence of all security, guidance by the passion and caprice of the tyrant, resulting in oppression of body and soul.

Aristocracy and oligarchy. Aristocracy like monarchy is used in the etymological sense, the government of the best. If in a state there are good citizens eminent above the others in political virtue, and if these govern, their power is that of the aristocracy. *Aristocratia est potestas optimorum in qua aliqui principantur secundum virtutem*, according to Aristotle.** Oligarchy on the other hand is the government of the few who are also the richer; it rests not upon eminence in virtue, but abundance of wealth. The true Aristocratic rulers command in accordance with virtue, obeying natural law, and their power is exercised for the common good. Oligarchy governs for personal advantage, and obeys only passion and personal interest. Aristocracy presents in a lesser degree the advantages and merits of

---

* De Reg. Princ. I. 11; Ar. Expos. III. lect. 13 and 15; IV. lect. 4.
† Ia. 2ae, qu. 105, 1.
‡ De Reg. Princ. I. 2 and 3.
§ Expos. Arist. III. lect. 3.
    Polit. IV. 2, 2.
* De Reg. Princ. I. 3.
** Pol. III. 6.

monarchy; oligarchy is full of the dangers of tyranny. In the language of Thomas, all aristocracy is elective for its end is to give a share of the government to the more virtuous, that is, to form a government of the betters.* There is in aristocracy more of a personal merit recognized in election. The aristocratic governors are *ab omnibus eliguntur, . . . et ad populum pertinet electio principum*.† It is more natural to find the best among the nobles and rich persons than among the poor, because they have more facilities to enable them to become good and fewer temptations.

(c) *Republic and democracy*. The essence of republic is the sharing of the power equally among the citizens, who exercise the judicial, political and other offices in turn. The right of judging and deciding in all matters of state pertains to the assembly of the people theoretically, it alone makes laws to which the magistrates and people conform. Of this assembly all citizens form a part. The designation of the magistrate by means of the lot is decidedly republican, because it gives an equal right to all citizens, as distinguished from the election of magistrates in aristocracy. Democracy is the perversion of republicanism and the perversion of liberty. All morality and government disappear, each one living for himself, regardless of rules and customs; family rights are disregarded; the slaves no longer obey their masters and the people, forgetful of natural law, give place to the demagogue, and they become entangled in the schemes of passionate men. The worst of all democracies is that in which the power belongs to the industrial classes. The tyranny of the many is less evil than the tyranny of one or of the oligarchy, because the greater number have an interest in it, and the advantage is more general. If the democracy is least evil of bad governments, republic is the least good of good ones, because in it there is the smallest realization of the government of virtue, and the natural hierarchy is less complete because the state is less organized.‡ Thus, considering the forms of government in themselves, apart from their application to existing conditions, there exists a twofold series of governments, the good and the bad of which there are three grades. The best of the good is monarchy and the worst tyranny, the medium of the good is aristocracy and the bad oligarchy, the least of the good is republic and the best of the bad democracy. We come now to the question which Thomas treats at length, which of the governments is preferable in principle and practice? He says in answering the question that people are called upon to solve it according to their needs, ideas and genius.

3. *The best form of government*. Aquinas distinguishes between the best government theoretically and the best in practical application. (a) In principle, by comparing the one form of government with the other, we have

---
* Expos. Ar. II. lect. 17.
† Spedolari, Dir. dell'uomo, I. 6, appendix 4; De Reg. Princ. I. 5.
‡ Expos. Aris. IV. lect. 2; De Reg. Prin. I. 2.

his first solution. By applying the principle of government to the state we have his second solution.

In the commentary upon Aristotle, following the Greek, Thomas defends the choice of a government on the grand consideration of equality or inequality in political virtue among the citizens. The question is, is there any citizen of surpassing excellence? If so, there is a perpetual royalty lasting as long as preeminence lasts. The monarchy in such a case is the result of the sovereignty of virtue. Similarly if in a certain community a number of individuals possess preeminence above all the others, they are entitled to exercise the sovereignty and we have an aristocracy of virtue. If there is no such preeminence of one or some, then there is an equality of virtue among the citizens, and the power ought to be divided among them and a republican form of government adopted.*

Thomas inclines to the idea that for the kingly government there is necessary an inclination towards that form. The system of government by a king subjects the state which by nature is arranged (*nata est*) for its subjugation to one of excellent virtue in order that he may conduct a citizen's or king's government *ad principatum politicum seu regalem*. The government by citizens is defined as that in which some one rules over those who are equal and free according to virtue and for the welfare of the subjects. If it happens that an entire race is conspicuous for virtue it is right that this race be the race of kings.† Next to this government by citizens is one he designates government by masters, *principatus dominativus*, and he explains it in accordance with the dominical kind of rule, that is, the control of masters over slaves.‡ As an historical example this is given, in certain states of non-Greeks, *barbari*, one was made a monarch who ruled according to the laws and traditions. As such kings governed according to law and with the consent of the subjects, these monarchies were king-governments.§ They subjected themselves willingly to the autocrat, because they were inclined to subject themselves to this kind of government.‖ The royal kingdom is also found to exist under peculiar historical conditions. It has arisen by reason of the assistance offered by the good against the crowd, in order that the multitude might not tyrannize over those who aspired to a higher life. For the king is selected according to virtue, in character or action, or on account of the nobility of its race, or on account of some benefit conferred on his country, or on account of his power suitable to the occasion in ruling the mass so as to prevent the multitude from oppressing.¶ In case an individual

* Expos. Arist. III. lect. 12; IV. lect. 4; V. lect. 10; VII. lect. 2 and 10.
† Expos. Arist. XXI. p. 504.
‡ p. 507.
§ p. 528.
‖ p. 529.
¶ p. 585-6.

is found who excels all others it is right for him to bear rule as long as he continues so, and in case there is a succession of this race, it is well that one of them should reign. If it is found that several are equally qualified it is fitting that they should govern during their lifetime.*

When it is said that a kingdom is the best form of government, there is a question as to the manner of calling such a king to the government, whether by election or natural descent. Aristotle thinks that he ought not to be called by hereditary descent, because it is not certain what kind of a son will follow a father, and perhaps there may be no son. It may happen that a bad son would inherit the right to rule. This must be avoided, and therefore the ruler should not be chosen by heredity. It may be answered, when a father has a bad son, he should leave the kingdom to another. Aristotle replies it is difficult to believe that a father will pass by his son, even if wicked, and give the kingdom to another, because the father will naturally prefer his own child, for the son is in a certain way a reproduction of the father. It is better to choose a king, therefore, by election than by natural descent. But, it may happen that it is better at certain times to get one by natural descent. It is well to get a ruler in whichever way is more suitable to the people and the occasion. By election a better king can be obtained than by natural descent, because in most cases it is easier to find a good one among a great many, election being an intelligent way of expressing confidence. Yet it may be better to make the choice by heredity, for in an election a division may take place among the electors and sometimes the electors themselves are bad and choose a bad man. Again, the traditions and customs of rulers have an effect that makes one method of choice give place to the other. As long as the father continues to reign the son is accustomed to be in subjection, after the death of the father the people have an inclination to accept his son. It is often a difficult thing to find one who is qualified to be an equal of the people to-day and their superior to-morrow. Therefore it seems wiser to choose a ruler by natural descent rather than by election to avoid these difficulties and dangers.†

In ultimate issue two kinds of kingdoms. It is according to nature that he who is conspicuous for virtue should be lord of all; therefore if the virtue of one surpasses the others it is natural that he should be king. It is not fitting that such a person should rule over only a part, he must rule over all, and not simply for a definite time but always. A part is not formed to surpass the whole and if any one excel in political virtue then he should unite the whole in his government. Such a person should rule over all, and always, and all should obey him. When many are conspicuous in virtue and culture, one only must rule with the kingly power. Many a society is composed of virtuous people and as such has a peculiar dignity. Such is the society of free

* p. 673.
† p. 495-6.

citizens *multitudo politica*. Another kind of society differing from this is that which is appointed to absolute government. It is fitting for both societies to be governed by kingly power, because in both there is someone surpassing the others in excellence. There is a distinction however to be made, because the government of free citizens is very far from that of an absolute government; the second is very near it, because the one society is reasonable and the other not. There is also a distinction between the two kingdoms in this that the absolute kingdom is of longer continuance and less political virtue is necessary in order to excel in it. In the society of free citizens all have a share in reason, and there are many who might devise ways and means of banishing the prince because they can freely plan such means. In the absolute kingdom this is not so, because the members have little intelligence and therefore little foresight to enable them to work against the ruler. The result is that the absolute form of government is likely to endure longer than the government over free citizens.* The kingdom in both cases is the best form of state constitution, considered theoretically. It is evident that a system where the power is distributed according to the degree of political virtue and equally divided between the citizens who are of equal rank is in harmony with the principle of the superiority of virtue, which forms the basis of the philosophical theory of Thomas.

(b) In the *De Reg. Princ.* Thomas abandons almost wholly the theoretical domain of abstract philosophy and takes up the practical view. He does not determine the superiority of monarchy in this work upon the basis of equality or inequality of citizens, but upon the basis of utility. He acknowledges that there are many disadvantages attaching to monarchy, chiefly on account of its tendency to degenerate into tyranny on account of the great power entrusted to the king, and the tendency to place power before virtue.† Yet he concludes in favor of monarchy. The unity of government tends to preserve the safety of the people, because it preserves peace and prevents disorder which destroys and breaks up the social life. The end of government is to secure the safety of the people, their unity and peace. The best means to attain this end is the concentration of power. Just as the heart quells the passions, one *per se* maintains more unity than a number. In this way monarchy is preferable to all plural forms of government, because it is the best means to the end desired, on the principle of utility. This is confirmed in the natural constitution of physical and moral beings, where Science proves that unity results from the action of one superior force. The monarchy is the best form of government because it is best adapted to preserve unity and freedom in the state and among the people.

In determining whether one or more shall rule, it is appropriate to enquire what kind of a province or city it is that is to be governed? This is to be

pp. 501-2.

† Ia. 2ae. qu. 105, 2, 2.

decided by the aim of the government. The duty of a governor is to preserve what is given into his care. That is the more suitable which leads to the end. What is in itself a unit can better effect unity than several units. Consequently, the government of an individual is more suitable for a state than that of many. Again, several rulers do not keep the society absolutely firm, where they are themselves disunited. For with a plurality of governors there is needed a certain unity that they may be able to govern at all. The plurality is united as it approximates towards unity, therefore one governs better than several and more than one the nearer they come to unity. What is according to nature is always the best and all government in nature proceeds from one. All this rests on a fundamental principle, the works of art imitate nature, and a work of art is better the nearer it comes to its pattern in nature. That must be best in society that is governed by one. This lesson of nature is confirmed by experience. Provinces and cities which are not governed by one ruler suffer through disunion, and are in continual disquiet without peace so that there is fulfilled in them what God declares in the prophet's language, "many keepers have destroyed my vineyard."* It is just the opposite with provinces and cities under one ruler, quiet, peace, prosperity, righteousness, and abundance is the portion of all. For this reason the Lord promises his people through the prophet as a great gift, that he would place a head over them and a ruler in their midst.†

United strength is more effective in the production of an action than scattered and separate power. Much is done by united effort that could not be effected if these efforts were partial and individual. It is better that the power for good be unified in order more perfectly to work for the good. So the kingdom is better than the aristocracy, and aristocracy better than democracy.‡ Thomas carefully compares the advantages and disadvantages of different forms of government which he found in the history of the Roman people. He says that by reason of tyranny the name of king became hateful. The Romans appointed consuls and other magistrates to lead and govern the people. This changed the kingdom into an aristocracy, and according to Sallust's statement, it is almost incredible how soon the Roman state grew after it had acquired freedom. For the most part men who live under a king are less energetic in their strivings for the common welfare, in the conviction that their strivings for the common good will not redound to their own good but to another's, in whose power they see the common possessions. If however they see the common welfare not in the power of one, then they deem the common good not the affair of another, but everyone looks upon it as his own. Experience shows that a city which is governed by annual magistrates has often more influence than when a king has three or

Jer. 12. 10.
* De Reg. Prin. I. 2.
‡ De Reg. Princ. I. 3.

four cities under him. Small services which are required by kings are borne more grudgingly than heavier burdens if they are required by ordinary citizens, as was seen in the development of the Roman state. Those in service were remunerated by pay for their war service, and when the state treasury was not sufficient for the payment of the salaries, private treasures were used for state purposes, so that the senate itself had left no money save a golden ring and a golden case which were the insignia of their dignity. In the meantime they were exhausted as a consequence of partisan fights which rapidly developed into civil war. In this civil war freedom for which they had endured so much was torn from them, and they fell under the power of the emperors, who in reality did not call themselves kings, because the Romans detested the name of king. A few of these emperors were really kings, because they faithfully attended to the common good and by their exertions the Roman state was preserved and increased. The most of them however were tyrants in the treatment of their subjects and weak against their enemies. By these two causes was brought on the downfall of the Roman state.

The history of the Hebrew state was almost the same. While the Jews were under the rule of the judges, they were the prey of enemies, for each one did what seemed right to himself. Afterwards at their request God gave them a king. Through the wickedness of the kings they fell away from their reverence of God and were led into captivity. If tyrants are to be dreaded government by kings is after all the best.*

What kind of a monarchy does he speak of, absolute, limited, or tempered? The prince is only representative of the people. The king ought not to be a tyrant because tyranny is the worst of all forms. The people ought to choose a king who is not likely to degenerate to tyranny and they ought to limit his power for the same end.† He concludes in favor of monarchy on one ground, because presenting less danger of dissension, it less often engenders tyranny than other forms of government. This monarchy which is best, is one that is desired or elected by the people and one that is limited and tempered. Aside from the risk of tyranny, a monarchy is always to be preferred. Society should require guarantees, that the king may not easily become a tyrant.

Neither in his exposition of Aristotle nor in his own treatise on kingly power do we find the last word of Thomas in regard to the best form of government. In his *Summa* we have an indication of his thought upon the ideal form. He views the dominion of man over man now from the standpoint of his natural social being. There is a dominion of man over man compatible with human freedom, (a) because man is by nature a social being. There cannot be a social life if there is not a leader who strives toward the good of the community, for many strive according to the ideas of the many, but one

* De Reg. Princ. I. 4.
† Ibid. I. 6, 7.

according to the mind of one; (b) because when a man is conspicuously above others in scientific attainments or uprightness of character, in knowledge or justice, it would be unseemly if he did not use these gifts for the good of others. Therefore, Augustine says, the upright do not govern from a desire to rule, but from a sense of duty, to give counsel and protection to those who need it. Ideal kingship is thus founded upon a moral sense of right, peculiar to man's social being and independent, as Thomas points out, of sin and of slavery which results from sin.*

In the mixed government the chief ruler is chosen by reason of his virtue and his pre-eminent excellence, the inferior governors being chosen by the people, the people thus participating in the government. The most perfect form of government is not the monarchy, aristocracy or republic. It is that in which these three forms of government are mingled in such a way as to unite all the advantages and avoid all the disadvantages of the separate forms. This is the form most generally desired in civilized Europe, what we call constitutional government. This is one evidence that the old theological writers and Christian philosophers are favorable to the free political institutions of modern times and anticipated many of the practical forms in their thoughts and ideas. But how can such a commingling of forms take place? How can such a blending give us a perfect form? The chief point in the opinion of Thomas is that he regards it as a *politia bene commixta*, in which the chief who is supreme and is elected directs the general affairs of the state, while the inferior officials also elected concur with the head and aid him in the administration, and all the citizens, even the populace, are eligible, and have the right to elect, to all the magistracies, even the highest.

Two things are to be observed in what relates to the appointment of rulers in any town or nation. The *first* is, that the whole of the multitude should have some share in the government, because by this means peace is maintained among the people. The *second* has relation to the forms of government which are manifold. Yet, the principal forms are monarchy in which one man possessing the necessary virtues is the ruler of all, and aristocracy, that is, the power of the best men, in which a few persons possessing the necessary qualifications are the rulers. Therefore the best way of ruling towns and states is, that a person gifted with the necessary virtues should be exalted to preside over all, and that under him there should be other capable rulers; and yet that the princedom should appertain to the whole multitude, because the ruling members may be chosen from the multitude and because the multitude chooses them.

This form was established by Divine law. Moses and his successors ruled the people as possessing supreme power over all, which is a kind of monarchy. There were also chosen the elders of Israel, men possessing the necessary virtues, as it is stated in the book of Deuteronomy,† "I took out

* Ia. qu. 96, 3, 4.   † c. I. 15.

of your tribes wise and honorable men and appointed them rulers over you." This was the aristocratic element. But it was democratic in this, that the elders were chosen from the whole people, as it is said in the book of Exodus,* "thou shalt provide out of all the people wise men;" and they were elected by all the people, for Moses said, "give me wise men and understanding and I will make them rulers over you."† Therefore it is manifest that the appointment of princes and rulers according to the old law was the best of all.‡ The statement *ut omnes aliquam partem habeant in principatu* is significant, especially when it is added, *per hoc conservatur pax populi et omnes talem dominationem amant et custodiunt*, laying the basis for that share of the people in the government of the state which identifies the people with the administration of affairs, so that no one can say the government is not carried on for his interest being a part of the government as well as of the state.§ In such a government the monarchical element would be the single leader; the aristocratic, the elective magistrates; and the democratic would be found in the fact that all the magistrates could be elected from and by the people themselves. Such a political organization would be, *optima principum ordinatio*.

This account of the ideal government occurs at the centre of the treatise upon law. Thomas had begun to treat of the Mosaic law and he defends the political and civil constitution of the Israelites. He asks if the ancient law had properly organized a government? It is in answer to this question he reproduces the ideal form of government which is practically perfect. Moses and the judges who succeeded him are practically heads of the government; the elected lords who governed the tribes were under the chief ruler, and were taken from and elected by the people. God reserved to himself the election of the sovereign prince. It is thus from the Bible that he derives his democratic and republican forms of government. He does not take his model from the Greek republics where slavery existed and where the great mass of the people were excluded from citizenship, and where the social community included only the noble families in the state. He took it from the Hebrews where there was at that time no noble race by blood or lineage, all being of the same blood, and where the property of the state was divided among the people according to their families and their tribes. He gives to the people the right of suffrage in the election of the prince and of the magistrates, and he makes the citizens eligible for the office of state, reducing the whole commonwealth to a democratic institution.

4. *The worst form of government.* If the government of one is the best because and when it is just, it becomes the worst when it falls into violence and injustice. Tyranny is the most noxious according to the old maxim

* c. 18, 21.
† Deut. 1, 13.
‡ In 2ae. qu. 105, 1.
§ Pope, Prince and People, Pius Melia c. II.

corruptio optimi pessima. A tyrant looks upon his subjects as a flock of slaves. A tyrant's empire cannot last long, *non potest diu conservari quod votis multorum repugnat.** In the hands of a tyrant the forces that ought to be devoted to the common good, and the unity of the state that ought to promote peace, are utilized in the service of passion. The tyrant is not a man but a fierce creature; giving himself up to the passions of violence, vice, ignorance, and division, he becomes an enemy of the soul as well as of the body.† Tyranny is the absence of all security and the reduction of government to human caprice. The tyrant is an enemy of spiritual progress as well as of material, he aims at effacing virtue and takes away from the people the spirit of courage and magnanimity, standing in the way of everything that promotes amity and confidence among men. He often does not long enjoy the reward of his passions and God does not let him have the riches, glory and fame he desired. He is not so happy as the king because he has more fears and dangers. He acts against the liberty of all and thereby incurs the indignation of heaven, falling under the machinations of his own satellites. It is the degeneracy of royalty and is more unsuitable than any other unjust government, because it is so much more powerful.‡

Tyranny is not peculiar to perverted monarchy, it is the general term used by Thomas to designate degenerate forms of state government, although the tyranny in the case of a single ruler is the more dangerous and the more difficult to overcome. If the normal government becomes tyrannical, or usurpation arises in any of the forms, then we have an unjust and illegitimate government. Just as it is more in the interest of good to be unified, so it is more harmful when the power for evil is unified than when it is separated. The power of an unrighteous ruler works to the injury of society in that he perverts its welfare to his own private interest. The perversion in the unrighteous government therefore will be the greater just as it is more united and concentrated; tyranny is more harmful than oligarchy and oligarchy than democracy for the same reason. A government also is unrighteous when the welfare of society is neglected and only the private interest of the ruler is sought. The more a ruler withdraws himself from the good of the community the more unjust he is and his government. Now the welfare of the community is farther away in an oligarchy in which the good of a few is sought than in democracy in which the good of many is pursued. Farther still removed from good is a tyranny in which the interest of one is the aim, for the totality is nearer the many than the few, and the few nearer to the many than the individual. Therefore the government of the tyrant is the most unjust. As good comes into the world from a perfect cause and this perfect cause helps towards the good, so evil comes in a practical form.

* De Reg. Princ. I, 2.
† De Reg. Princ. I, 3.
‡ Ibid. I, 3, 4.

There is no beauty in the body unless all the the members stand to each other in the relation of self-dependence. Ugliness appears so soon as one member loses this relation. So it is with good and evil. God has provided that good from a single cause is better, that evil from more than one cause is weaker, that the righteous government carried on by one has the advantage of strength and so soon as the government inclines towards unrighteousness, it is better in the hands of many, because it is weaker and the rulers will check each other. Of the unjust governments the democratic is the most bearable, the tyrannical the worst to endure. This is evident if one considers the evil which springs from the tyrannical form of government. The tyrant despises the good of the community and aims at his own private good. Through avarice he robs his subjects of all their goods. When he yields to anger then he sheds blood without cause. Nothing can be sure which rests solely on the will or caprice of another. Tyrants suspect the good more than the evil, because the virtues of others are always a ground of fear. Therefore tyrants do not care to have their subjects become excellent of character, *virtuosi*, and so cultivate a courageous spirit and find out the injustice of tyranny. Their aim is to have no bonds of friendship among their subjects and no rejoicing over the benefits of peace, so that in general mistrust among the subjects themselves there may be nothing undertaken against the government. To this end the tyrants sow dissensions and foster them, prohibiting what leads to the unity of men, trying to keep them from becoming rich and powerful. Job says of the tyrant, "the noise of tumults is always in his ears."* Where the wicked bear rule men fall, because through the wickedness of tyrants virtue is destroyed and the people are led into the slavery of vice. This is not to be wondered at, because a man who rules without understanding is in no way different from a wild beast. To be subject to a tyrant is the same thing as to be thrown into the power of a wild animal.† In the Roman state the kings were expelled because the people could not any longer bear the arrogant assumptions of their tyranny. If too much reliance is placed upon the authority of kings then kingship is changed into a wicked tyrannical government.‡

If a monarchy is changed into tyranny is it a lesser evil than a government of several *optimates* which soon degenerates? The dissension which usually follows from a government of several is opposed to peace which is the chief good in the social union. This good would by the rule of a tyrant not be entirely abrogated but the good of many would be hindered. Therefore government by one is preferable when from both equal dangers arise. That should be avoided from which in various ways danger arises. Often greater danger arises from government by many than by one. It often happens that

* c. XV. 21.
† De Reg. Pr. I. 3.
‡ ibid. I. 4

one of several yields out of respect for the community, but this only one will do. When one of several rulers withdraws out of respect for the society, the danger of disunion threatens the subjects, for disunion in society is a necessary result of disunion among the rulers. If one alone reigns he generally regards the community, or if his mind is turned away from it, it does not follow that he will oppress the subjects, because this occurs only in the excess of tyranny and in the worst degree of wickedness in a government. It often happens that in a government by many there is a change into tyranny, for when disunion arises in a government of several, one rises above the others and usurps the government. This has been seen in the past. Almost every government by many has ended in tyranny. After the Roman state had been governed by magistrates, dissension and civil war broke out and the state fell into the hands of cruel tyrants. He who observes carefully past and present history will find that in countries governed by many there is oftener tyranny than in countries governed by one.* Thomas thus distinguishes between two forms of tyranny, (a) tyranny *in excess*, in which case the tyranny of one is the most unbearable, the tyranny of a few less unbearable and the tyranny of the multitude the most bearable; (b) tyranny *in moderation*, in which case it is better to endure the tyranny of one than that of a few or of the many, because the first form avoids dissension and promotes a greater unity among the subjects.

* Ibid. I. 5.

CHAPTER VIII.

RULE AND OBEDIENCE. LIMITATIONS UPON THE ACTIVITY OF THE GOVERNMENT AND STATE.

1. *Idea of the power.* We have seen that the idea of power is at the basis of civil society. The form of government is fixed according to the same idea of power. In all political forms we meet with the distinction between the just and unjust powers, the distinction between the two being intrinsic. The question of the limitation upon the activity of the government and of the state, resolves itself into two parts, (a) does all power, just as well as unjust, come from God and merit recognition in an equal degree? (b) Are subjects bound to obey all the powers unjust as well as just? The former question is answered by a consideration of the powers in themselves, the latter in the following sections by a consideration of the position and duties of rulers and of subjects.

The general statement of the apostle in Romans XIII. is accepted by Thomas, not in an absolute sense, nor without restriction, but in a qualified sense. (a) *Omnis potestas a Deo* is given in an unqualified form, no such epithet as *justa* or *legitima* being added. (b) *Omnis anima subdita sit potestatibus sublimioribus*, but it is not added, *dum sint justae aut legitimae*. (c) *Non bonis tantum et modestis, verum etiam discolis dominis reverenter subditos esse.* There is no restriction here upon the powers, just powers being set upon a par with just in the claim for recognition and obedience. Yet Paul has introduced certain restrictions derived from the nature, origin and use of the power. (a) The power in essence and principle, that is, the relation of superior and inferior, the principle of making laws, these evidence that the power is from God. (b) The means of acquiring the power may be just or unjust. (c) The use of the power may be legitimate or illegitimate. In the last two senses we have the two forms of perverted power, that which is unjustly obtained and illegally used. These powers come from God only in the sense in which they are permissive *sub providentia Dei*. These evil powers are often tolerated by God for the punishment of the wicked, and hence as instruments of his providential will are his ministers for good.*

Thomas thus limits the principle of the power and he carries the same

---

* Com. Sent. disq. 45 qu. 1, 2; qu. 4, 2

limitation into the results of the principle. In any political power we must consider apart from the power in principle two things, (a) the mode of acquisition, and (b) the manner of use. (a) In two ways power may be acquired in a manner in which it is not acknowledged as coming from God, (i) in the case of personal deficiency and demerit in him who acquires, and (ii) in case the title is defective. In the case of an unworthy individual acquiring the power, in form it is of God and to it man owes obedience, just as a slave owes obedience to an unworthy master. In the second case an individual usurps the power by means of violence or gets it by bribery or other corrupt means, and in this case it cannot be said there is a true ruler, and subjects are in no way bound to obey him or acknowledge his power, because they have in themselves the power, he having assumed it by fraud. Power that is acquired by unjust means may be legitimated by use, *per usum*, when subjects give their consent by yielding obedience to it, or when a superior who has the power of giving *dominium* to another confers such power. In these cases the form of the power is all right and obedience is due to such power. (b) In the use of power there arises illegitimacy in a twofold manner. (i) when the ruler in the exercise of his power ordains something contrary to virtue, in which case the command has no binding force upon the subjects, and the subject if he be virtuous must disobey the command, preferring to obey God and to adhere to the order of social virtue; (ii) when the ruler oversteps the limits of his dominion, assuming prerogatives which do not belong to him, for example, in imposing taxes which are not due and which he has no right to levy. In this case subjects are not bound to obey, but on the other hand they are not bound to disobey. The question of recourse against such a power of usurpation will be treated under the right of revolution. Thus the interpretation of the idea of power is very liberal in Thomas. He places limits to the absolute power of the ruler and places in the multitude the principle of sovereignty.

Taking monarchy as the better form of government in the *De Reg. Princ.* he considers what kind of royalty it is. He regards the prince as the representative, the choice of the people. The king ought not to be a tyrant, and the people ought to choose for a king one who will not be likely to degenerate into tyranny, and his power ought to be limited for the same end. This is done by the authority of the people as the sovereign power.

In his fuller consideration of royal power he presents another division of powers, namely, despotic and political. Despotic power is that of a master over a slave, *dominus ad servum*. Despotic power is the same as tyranny. Political power is that which is established in provinces, and cities, either of one or more than one, ruling according to laws and customs. It is the same as limited power. While distinguishing these classes of power we have in Thomas a confusing comparison of three powers, *despotic*, *royal* and *political* in the form of monarchy. (a) *Despotic power* is that of a master over slaves which with Thomas, as with Aristotle and Augustine, is perfectly lawful: Among men certain are qualified to command and others to occupy a servile position, by nature slaves to their master.* Despotic power is not to be confounded with tyranny—a despot being a monarch ruling with absolute power who may be a good king. A tyrant always conveys the idea of oppression; therefore every tyrant is a despot, but every despot is not a tyrant, although despotic power is liable to fall into tyranny. Every ruler must have due power. In this meaning only free members of a human society are subjects and rulers are the masters and lords.† Aristotle says that slavery as a result of war is unjust. Thomas says it is just as a means of inciting to courage in warfare, and it is just because it is a result of sin. There are therefore three classes of servile persons, those naturally slaves, according to Aristotle, those in slavery as a result of sin, according to Augustine, and those who are slaves by war and subjection, according to the Jurists. These classes under the despotic power are unfree and therefore excluded from the power of the state. This power is domestic and does not exist in the case of rulers and subjects, except in tyranny. Despotic royal power is for the good of the ruler and of all forms it is the worst.‡

(b) *Royal power.* He distinguishes regal power from domestic. As it is put by him *regnum non est propter regem, sed est propter regnum.*§ The royal power is to care for the kingdom and the security of its subjects, in this way reflecting the kingly administration of God over men. The royal power is that which is left to the wisdom of the prince and where the only limitation is the duty of copying the divine providence. Despotic power in this way may be introduced into kingly government; for example, the laws given by Samuel to Israel were despotic laws. Royal power implies a certain servitude on account of the corruption of sin, because since the fall man needs to be held more firmly in check. Therefore the despotic character of royalty springs from sin. Differences in the people give rise to royalty. Those who are free are inclined to political power while those people who are suited to serve are inclined to subjection to despotic royalty. Here we have the tendency to confuse despotism and monarchy.‖

(c) *Political power* is that which is limited by the laws. Thomas seems to indicate a preference for this form, because it is a better government, the rulers being temporary and their interests being those of the people. He cites the example of Moses who challenges Israel, "Have I taken aught from any man," and of the great Roman citizens who manifested a disinterestedness in their conduct of public affairs and in the wars for the establishment

* Ar. Pol. I, 8, 9, 10; III, 2, 9.
† In. qu. 96, 4.
‡ De Reg. Princ. II, 8, 9.
§ De Reg. Princ. III, 2.
‖ Ibid. I, 9, 10.

of the republic. The political power is limited by the laws and hence although tending to a mercenary character of itself it is kept in check by the conventions and customs of the people. This idea of political power is the practical application of the principle of Thomas that all government is limited and checked by reason and natural right.

The theory of the limitation upon the state and government arises from the fact that the state has a definite aim and that government is designed for the realization of that end. In the state as in the individual there are a series of agencies, one in subordination to the other and these in themselves form a check.* The ultimate end of the state as we saw is *æterna beatitudo*, and the general limit placed upon the action of the state and of the subjects of the state is *qui potestate resistit, Dei ordinationi resistit*.† To the supremacy of the king there is the general limit of the end of governmental power. This in the estimation of Thomas is a spiritual one, and hence the priests are over lords above the civil ruler. The destiny of man can only be realized by the supervisory direction of the Divine law.‡ The will of the prince has the force of law, *voluntas principis legis habet vigorem*.§ The limitation placed upon this exercise of sovereign power is that three requisites are imposed upon the sovereign activity, *justitia*, *auctoritas* and *prudentia*.‖ The *judex* is limited by the fact that *justitia* implies *reddere unicuique quod suum est et proprius actus justitiæ*.¶ *Auctoritas* depends as we have seen upon the acquisition of the power. In the exercise of the executive power the grand limitation is that the office implies the use of *prudentia*,** the absence of *crudelitas*,†† of animosity, rapacity and severity, and the exercise of *dominium* to the good of the citizens without any detriment or injury to liberty, *nullum præjudicium et detrimentum libertati*.‡‡

2. *Limitation derived from the position of the rulers.* Thomas establishes not only the power that is possessed by the ruler of the state, but also the conditions upon which such power is held, and the duties owed by the ruler to his subjects. A tyrant is one who gives himself up to self-pleasure and the pursuit of self-interest. Pleasure is injurious to the state. Men who live only for pleasure are dull in spirit, and they are unable to exercise sound judgment. So according to Aristotle, the reflections of a judge were corrupted by amusement. Men give up excessive pleasures out of a regard for virtue (*honestate*). Nothing is more likely to increase beyond limits than pleasure, although it is the means whereby virtue continues to exist, yet it often destroys virtue. Because nature is greedy of pleasure one by means of it is thrown into the charms of lust. It is therefore a task of virtue to abstain

* 1a. qu. 116.   ‡ 2a. 2ae. qu. 60. 2.
† 2 sent. disq. 44. qu. 1. 6.   ‖ 1a. qu. 21. 1; 2a. 2ae. qu. 58. 11.
‡ De Reg. Prin. 1. 14.   ** 2a. 2ae. qu. 60. 5.
§ 1a. 2ae. qu. 90. 1; qu. 92. 4.   †† qu. 157.
‡‡ 2 sent. disq. 44. qu. 1. 2.

from excessive pleasure, for if one avoids the excess one is more easily able to use the right means of securing virtue. Those who give themselves to excessive pleasure become timid and faint-hearted, so that they do not attempt what is difficult, they cannot endure hardship and shrink from danger. For this reason pleasures are injurious to the practice of war, because, as Vegetius says, they fear death least who have been conscious of little pleasure in life. Those who are entirely given up to pleasure are generally slothful, neglect necessary exercise and business, and turn their attentions solely to their own pleasure, while they are prodigal in spending what has been gathered by others. If they become poor, yet they cannot dispense with accustomed pleasures, but would rather steal and plunder in order to have the means of satisfying their lusts. Therefore it is injurious to the state to give facilities for injurious and excessive pleasures. Rulers as well as subjects are led into such excesses and become slaves to self.*

Motives that lead the king to rule well. Reward. They have an exalted place in heaven who worthily fulfil the calling of a king. If the reward of virtue is happiness, the greater the virtue, the higher the degree of blessedness that will be granted. It is a conspicuous virtue when a man tries to guide not himself only, but others aright, for even in physical virtue one is esteemed the more praiseworthy the more he overcomes or the greater the difficulties he can remove. So much greater virtue is required to govern a house than to govern oneself, and greater still to govern a city or a kingdom. It is a proof of excellent virtue that a king practises well the calling of a ruler, therefore to him belongs a great reward in heaven. In all arts and activities those merit greater praise who guide others well than those who simply follow the lead of others. It is more honorable to transmit a system of imparting truth than merely to be able to comprehend what has been taught by others. Among trades the architect is more highly honored and receives a larger price for the plan of the building which he designs than the workman who works mechanically according to the plan. In war in case of a siege, the general receives greater fame for his tact than the soldiers do for their bravery. So it is with the ruler of society in those things which have to be done with skill as with the instructor in science, the architect in building and the general in war. The king deserves greater reward if he rules his subjects well than does any one of his subjects who acts under him. Among men every private person is praised and accounted by God to be worthy of reward when he assists the needy, brings peace to the discordant, saves the oppressed from the power of the mighty, any one in fact who helps another. How much more is one to be praised by God and men who brings peace to an entire nation, who stops acts of violence, upholds righteousness and decides by his laws and statutes what men are to do. The great height of kingly virtue is shown in this, that the king is in a conspicuous way an image of

*De Reg. Princ. II. 4.

God and that he does in the kingdom what God does in the world. Therefore kings are called judges of the people of God. God is better pleased with them the nearer they approach the imitation of his works. Good kings are the most pleasing to God and best rewarded by Him. It is very difficult for princes, as Augustine says, to bear in mind that they are merely men and not be unduly exalted when they bear exaggerated expressions of veneration and meet with servile subjects. Many fall from virtue as soon as they come to a high position, although they appeared to be virtuous while humble. Here is the difficulty which princes find to be good. They are not to forget to come to God in humility and prayer. God himself promises a high reward to deserving kings. The house of David will be as God's house and all worthy kings shall reign with Christ. So the heathen conceived of rulers and preservers of states as changed into Gods.* Nothing can be so desirable as to be taken away from the glory of kingship and placed in the honor of heaven. Therefore kings have a great motive to lead them to avoid tyranny. Tyrants make a mistake when for the sake of earthly advantage they cheat themselves out of the great reward of righteousness, which if they had governed justly they might have received in heaven. Tyrants give up righteousness for transitory advantage.

Nothing in this world is to be preferred to an honorable friendship which unites virtuous qualities, preserves and promotes virtue itself. It is this that is needed in all human affairs in prosperity or adversity. One cannot rejoice without friends. This love makes the severity of life easy. In no tyrant is cruelty so great that he cannot appreciate friendship's joy. The history of Dionysius the tyrant of Syracuse proves this. He wanted to kill one of two friends, Damon and Pythias. The condemned one pleaded for a stay of the execution of the sentence in order that he might go home and set in order his affairs. The other begged to be taken as surety for the return of his friend. The appointed day came but the absent one had not returned. Everyone reproached him who had assumed the suretyship, but he said he was not troubled about the trustworthiness of his friend. At the very time he was to be executed he returned. Even the tyrant admired the friendship of these men and released from the sentence him who was so faithful in friendship, and asked to be admitted as a third party in the covenant of friendship. No matter how much the tyrant desired this he could not receive it, because he did not seek the common good, but his own, and so little could exist in common between him and his subjects. The subjects have no love for him, because they are oppressed by him; a tyrant has no cause of complaint because of lack of love, because he gives no evidence of loving them. Good kings work zealously for the common good, that through their efforts advantage may accrue to their subjects. In this kind of love the thrones of good kings are enduring; for their sake subjects are willing to expose them-

* Ibid. I. 9.

selves to all kinds of hazard. Julius Caesar loved his soldiers so much that when he heard of the murder of one of them, he would not cut his hair or beard till the murder was avenged. By a similar affection to Caesar his soldiers became devoted to him. So Augustus who governed gently was so loved by his subjects that on their deaths they ordered sacrifices to be offered in thanksgiving because he outlived them. It is not easy to shake the government of a king whose subjects love him with one accord. The government of tyrants cannot long continue because they are hated by society. Misfortune will come and the opportunity will be seized by some one, followed by many others, to take away the power from the tyrant. The government of a tyrant is not founded upon love, because there is little friendship between him and oppressed society. Tyrants therefore cannot rely on the fidelity of their subjects and they govern through fear and try to make subjects afraid of them. Fear is a weak foundation on which to build a kingdom for those who are subjects by fear release themselves so soon as an opportunity offers. The government of kings beloved by their subjects has the subjects as guards of honor, and they will not withhold their lives and treasures to defend it. To kings who seek righteousness God will add wealth. Good kings in life and after death continue to live in the praises of men and their memory is cherished; the name of the bad perishes and is remembered with contempt. Thus the moral force of love and the motive of a high reward should restrain kings from falling into tyranny.*

Love of what is right and fear of punishment. Continuance of power, wealth, honor and reputation are oftener the portion of kings than tyrants. That is, the price which a tyrant gives for his tyranny is the loss of these. No one departs from righteousness unless when he is lured by desire of something as gain. For this the tyrant robs himself of the blessedness of a prince, and worst of all he brings on himself the torments of eternal punishment. As he who robs an individual, enslaves or kills him, receives punishment from men, he who robs and destroys the freedom of a community merits punishment from God. When will tyrants repay all they have done contrary to justice? They not only sin themselves but repeat their sins in their posterity. They will be punished for their own sins, for the sins committed by others through their example and on account of the dignity of their position. Therefore kings receive temporal good as a portion in life and a prominent place in heaven; but tyrants rob to gain earthly good, exposing themselves to many dangers, depriving themselves of eternal good and have laid up for them most terrible punishments.†

Limitation in qualification for office. Power, love of ruling, and virtue. Aristotle says in electing a ruler one must look in two directions, (a) that in which the citizens can come nearer to the aim of the government; and (b) that in which

* Ibid. I. 10.
† Ibid. I. 11.

they are not in favorable circumstances to do so. The government finds its reason in its aim, and its aim is the reason of its being. Therefore he who governs is to use in governing what he has and in this the citizens all approach nearer the aim of the state. Thus it is in the manner of warfare, the conducting of an army, it is more a matter of experience than of excellence. For, through an experimental knowledge of government the aim of the state can be easier atttained than through virtue in warfare. Virtuous qualities are as a rule not much in experience in such matters, although in themselves they are much better. Therefore one must be chosen to rule over the military who has experience rather than one who has complete virtue and no experience. In the responsible position of preserving the state and managing the finances (oeconii) one must be chosen who has virtue, because to such an office virtue is more essential than experience. Theoretical knowledge is common to all, for theoretical knowledge the ruler must have as well in the leading of an army as in the governing of a state, otherwise they cannot arrange means for the attainment of the desired end. If one loves the state and desires to rule and has power why is virtue necessary? It seems unnecessary because by power and love of rule everything seems provided that is necessary in government. Aristotle says that next to power and love of ruling virtue is essential in government, if one would rule well, for it may happen one has power and love of rule who has no self-restraint and as such is opposed to the state. In spite of his love for ruling and his power he will govern badly because he has no virtue to guide and harmonize his actions.*

Constitutional government. Thomas indicates how a king should rule from different points of view. *The injuries which bring down a kingdom.* The king rules over subjects who desire him to rule over them according to the principles of good and virtue. Such a kingdom will not fall through external circumstances because there is harmony between the rulers and ruled. It is preserved by the subjects who desire the king to reign. Through itself, or internally, the kingdom may go to ruin in many ways, for example, when those who are near the throne or first in the kingdom rebel. Then by the power they possess they banish the king from the government. Or when the king wishes to rule as a tyrant and the subjects oppose him, then the subjects rebel against him and banish him, changing the constitution of the government.† Then Thomas indicates the best means to be used to preserve it. The kingdom is the best form of state-constitution. To preserve this is the aim of the king. It is preserved chiefly through moderation in governing in all matters that pertain to it. When something which the king who is governor of all does, seems oppressive and displeasing to the subjects, the king must either mitigate or abolish it. The less the king ap-

* Expos. Arist. XXI. p. 582.
† ibid. p. 593-596.

fears to rule the more enduring his government will be, and the less absolutely he governs, he will have occasion to give fewer decisions, more people will be interested in his government, and he will seem more on an equality with his subjects. This is proved by examples.

To make a kingdom enduring is to avoid being a tyrant. In a tyranny an individual reigns just as in kingdom, but he governs for his own good, and contrary to the virtue and will of his subjects. He tries to uphold his authority by keeping the subjects in ignorance, by keeping them from acquaintance with one another and by keeping them poor. The old form of tyranny uses as means to effect its purpose, the removing of those who are prominent by reason of wealth and power, killing the wise, allowing no associations, unions, or societies so that the subjects may not combine with one another, not allowing education, nor anything tending to knowledge, for the wise and educated could find many ways of rebelling and banishing the tyrant; therefore everything is prohibited which tends to make the subjects wiser whether in practical or theoretical science, in popular teaching or in power of speech. They permit no schools, no societies in which one may devote himself to science, for by wisdom educated men would be inclined to the performance of great deeds and carry out bold plans; such persons readily revolt. The king must so act as to avoid these tyrannical acts. He should encourage learning, strengthen the members by association and enable them to confide in each other. The king must so conduct himself that he will seem to care for the good of all and not expend aimlessly what he receives from his subjects. In this way he should render accounts of what has been received and expended, which means a regular public finance. The reason is that one manages and governs, when he seems to be economical, shows his care for the common welfare and acknowledges his representative character. In what concerns religion and culture the ruler must show himself zealous and reverent, because if the subjects believe that the ruler is religious and fears God they will not believe that he can do wrong. From godly men no one expects evil. The subjects will be less inclined to conspiracy, for if they believe God is favorable to the king, they will strive for him against conspirators.*

The king has all the necessary force to do good and he ought to use it actively and usefully, (a) in defence of the territory of the state, and (b) in assisting the feeble and especially the unfortunate. This is a new duty enjoined upon the royal power derived from Christian polities. It has been developed upon a Christian basis and Thomas sets it forth as a duty devolving upon the royal power to exercise public charity and to minister help to the weak and unfortunate.† These duties which kings owe to their subjects and in the doing of which kingly power is strengthened and made honorable

* Ibid. p. 335-339.
† De Reg. Prin. II. 11-14.

are moral duties viewed by Thomas from the moral standpoint of obligation. They act as limits upon kingly power.

3. *Limitation arising from the position of the subjects in the state.* The question is what obligation rests upon subjects to render obedience to rulers and to the human laws of such rulers. Human laws are not obligatory upon subjects as the legislation of men merely, because man is not always bound to obey man; but they are binding because they derive their force from and are in conformity with eternal right, and because such eternal law gives rise to such commands as are delivered by human authority. If they cease to be in conformity with the Divine law, they cease to have binding effect, that is, only such commands and laws as are just are to be obeyed by subjects.* So Augustine says, *lex esse non videtur quae justa non fuerit.* Unjust statutes or laws are not laws at all but a declination from law. There are many different kinds of unjust laws, such as contravene the public utility, such as express the caprice or will of the legislator, such as ignore distributive justice which is the presiding principle in all social administration—such laws have no compulsory force. Such commands have no authority and to disobey them is a right of subjects. Christian subjects are bound to yield obedience to the temporal authority of the rulers, but when they pass beyond this limit Christians are to obey God before man, God revealing Himself *in quantum ordo justitiae requirit.* If the prince's authority is illegitimate, and if the command he gives, even if his authority is just, be contrary to justice, subjects are not bound to obey. These are the fundamental rights of subjects which must not be invaded by the executive or legislative authority of the rulers. There is no passive obedience for in all that does not pertain to civil or military life, and in all that pertains to virtue man is subject only to God. Obedience is the queen of virtues in the social life, but unlimited obedience would destroy man's responsibility to God and make him the tool of another human will.†

The chief duties of the members of the state may be summarized, (a) subjection and obedience to the laws and to the lawful commands of the higher powers over them; (b) reverence, honor, and fear towards the rulers; (c) willingness to obey in the civil or military sphere of life; (d) leading a practical life of peace, justice and charity in common with all the other members of the community.‡ The fundamental principle of government is that the subjects of the state must exercise themselves to serve those who are set over them by nature to govern them, for this governing is just and a righteous war is carried on against those who show signs of rebellion. Such a relation is the foundation of all just government.§

* Ia. 2ae. qu. 96. 4.
† Ia. 2ae. qu. 90-97; 2a. 2ae. qu. 104.
‡ Melia, ch. 9.
§ Expos. Arist. XXI. p. 676.

Obedience is the general principle. But the question arises, how far shall subjects obey their superiors? What is the principle of natural right? Is obedience absolute? For two reasons it may happen that the subject is not bound to obey his superior in everything, (a) on account of the commands issued by a still higher power; (b) when he is commanded to do something which he ought not to do. In this case it pertains to the inner exercise of the will, something that man is not bound to do for man, but only for God. Man is bound to obey man in authority in what is external to the body; yet man is not bound to obey man in what concerns the preservation of the body and the generation of posterity, for slaves are not bound to obey their masters nor sons their parents in the intercourse of marriage, in the preservation of chastity, or anything of that kind. But in what belongs to the regulation of activity and human affairs the subject is bound to obey his superiors, as they are placed over him, as soldiers obey the general in what relates to war, the slave his master in what relates to his work, the son the father in what relates to the discipline of life (*disciplina*) and to what belongs to the house.*

The position and duty of the subject should prevent tyranny. Society should be on its guard in relation to the king that it may not find in him a tyrant. The first thing for those who have to do with filling the office is to elevate the kind of man to the office who is not likely to degenerate into a tyrant. Samuel praised God's providence in the appointment of the king. The government of a kingdom should be so ordered as to remove the opportunity of becoming a tyrant from the appointed king. At the same time his power must be so tempered (*temperatur*) that he cannot easily degenerate to tyranny. Provision should be made also as to how to act in case the king does become a tyrant. In the institution of government stipulations ought to be made limiting the power and providing for the case of abuse. If no excess of tyranny takes place it is better to bear moderate tyranny for a time, than by opposition to develop greater dangers. It does happen that those who oppose tyrants do not always succeed in getting the upper hand, and the excited tyrant is more enraged than before. On the other hand when the mastery over a tyrant is gained there is often the greatest dissension among the people. It may be at the time of the uprising or after his overthrow that the society divides into parties over the kind of government desired. It also often happens that those with whose help the society has expelled the tyrant get possession of the power and become tyrants themselves, and from fear that they will have to suffer from others what they have caused others to endure hold their dependents in a more severe bondage. It is usually the case in dealing with tyrants that the later evil is worse than the former, that in removing one form of oppression out of the

* *Sac.* Vol. III, pp. 579-89. *Parma.*

wickedness of their hearts they produce others. So the aged woman who prayed for the life of Dionysius when all Syracuse desired his death, said, "in my girlhood we had a bad tyrant and I desired his death. He was killed and after him came a much worse. The end of his reign I deemed a deliverance. The third one was worse still."* The popular will is thus a limit upon royal power, in the constitution and proper safe-guarding of the instituted Kingship.

4. *Positive limits. Right of Revolution.* The question arises is it permissible to free the state from a tyrant? Is revolution legitimate? Who has the right to exercise the power of revolution if it is legitimate? Thomas answers, "the reverse of tyranny does not bear the character of sedition."† We have seen there are circumstances in which subjects are in duty bound to obey. But not to obey and to use violent means to subvert the power are two different things. On this point Thomas does not conceive it to be a duty to be subject absolutely. What are the rights of subjects under an unjust government? What measure of obedience are they to yield and at what point are they to resist? Even the apostle acknowledges that there is a limit to the obedience of subjects, for man is to obey God rather than men. A government has no right to compel obedience in what is contrary to God's will or order. In commands and laws purely human the question is, is there any limit to obedience? It is a matter of conscience and Thomas does not hesitate to pronounce himself in favor of the freedom of the popular conscience which alone can determine how to act.

Thomas distinguishes between sedition and insurrection — the former he condemns, the latter he acknowledges to be lawful and in certain circumstances praiseworthy. Sedition he describes as *pugna injusta*, an unjust strife stirred up between citizens which is directed against the public peace and detrimental to the public utility and for this reason a grave offence. It is not directed against any special power.‡ If the power attacked is an unjust one, a tyrannical government, then the attack is not sedition and those attacking are not seditious. An independent people has always the right of destroying the kingship it has established, if the king fall into tyranny. Even if the subjects have sworn perpetual fealty, when the prince has violated his compact, the people have the right of revolution or insurrection. The tyrannical government is unjust because it does not act with a view to the common good, but for the good of the particular ruler. The reversal of such a government is not seditious, it is the tyrant who is seditious. On the ground of natural right revolution against an unjust government is allowable. In general, sedition is in a sense sinful. It is against the unity and

---

* De Reg. Princ. I. 6.

† 2a. 2ae. qu. 42. 2.

‡ 2a. 2ae. qu. 42. 1.

peace of society, that is, of the people in a state or city. According to Augustine, the wise do not call every union of a mass of people a nation, but only those associated together through harmony in subjection to a common law and community of interest. It is clear that the unity to which the sedition is in opposition is the unity of justice and the social union for the common advantage. It is clear that the sedition is against not only justice, but also against the common welfare, and therefore it is a deadly sin of its kind *ex suo genere*, the more so because the common welfare which is attacked is greater than the welfare of a private person, who may be attacked in a quarrel. The sin of rebellion lies chiefly with those who bring the sedition and secondarily with those who aid them. The opposition of these should be such as will defend the common welfare in so far as they can accomplish the opposition without sedition. Revolution against a tyranny does not come under the name of sedition, *perturbatio hujus regiminis non habet rationem seditionis*, except where the government of a tyrant is disturbed in such a disorderly way that the subjects suffer more from the revolution than they did from the tyrant's government. The tyrant is the insurgent because through him the people are encouraged in dissension. The distinction between sedition and revolution is marked by the language used by Thomas. *Seditio* and *seditiosus* are used in the bad sense of sedition which is not justified, whereas the word *insurgere* is used in the commendable sense of an uprising against a despotic government. This nomenclature is now adopted in the French and English languages as the scientific nomenclature to denote this distinction borrowed from the scholastics of the thirteenth century.*

Tyrannicide. The murder of a tyrant is not lawful chiefly after the insurrection against a tyrant or usurper has taken place. In the battle against a tyrant or usurper they are merely to be put to death when deeds of violence are done by them or they seek an unjust conquest of the country. It is difficult to determine however the boundary line between lawful and unlawful putting to death. Is there any recourse against a power that is legitimate but abused? Such power is permitted sometimes as a punishment for sin, but it is not always so. In such cases it is lawful to refuse even legitimate power when it is abused.† Thomas sets up constitutional regulations which will limit the power of the ruler, as we have seen. It is better to endure the tyrant and supplicate God's help against him. If the normal government becomes tyrannical he is in favor of opposing the tyrant, with certain reservations (a) that nothing worse come to pass than the tyranny opposed; (b) that there be some prospect of success; (c) that an individual does not appear as a private person against the tyrant, but that the opposition be common and carried through in a lawful way. It is wrong to act by private means or in a private capacity. It is lawful and reasonable only to

* 2a. 2ae. qu. 42, 1-3.

† Com. Sent. disp. 45, qu. 1, 2; 2a. 2ae. qu. 42, 3.

proceed by public authority. If by some fundamental law it is established that the people or some of them have the right to appoint a king, then the people or some of them, as the case may be, in a regular way may depose or restrain him and are not unfaithful in dethroning an unfaithful king. *nec judicanda est talis multitudo infideliter agere, tyrannum destituens, etiam si sidem in perpetuum se ante subjecerat, quia hoc ipse meruit in multitudinis regimine se non fideliter gerens (ut exigit regis officium) quod ei pactum a subditis non servetur. Si ad jus multitudinis pertineat sibi providere de rege, non injuste ab eadem rex institutus potest destitui.* If the people is independent it can in justice destroy the kingship which it has made, or recall the power if the prince abuse it, and in destroying a tyrant the people does not prove unfaithful; even in the case in which it has vowed perpetual subjection to a prince it is not acting unfaithfully, for the royal behavior has merited it, because the pact between him and his subjects has not been observed. So Rome banished the Tarquins when they fell into tyranny. In order to this, the monarchy, even hereditary monarchy, must be elective by the choice of the people.*

Thomas is opposed to the murder of a tyrant unless he has recourse to war and is killed in the lawful strife; but he thinks that he should be dethroned or limited in power. There is a lawful revolution as there has always been in history. But often as in the civil strife among the Romans that freedom for which they had borne so much is torn from them. Yet such a degree of virtue is not found in society (*in multis*) that it will refrain from casting off the undeserved yoke of bondage when the opportunity occurs. It will more probably be according to the view of society (*multi*) to consider it not at all against fidelity to oppose in any manner the misrule of a tyrant. A tyrant governs through fear and this gives opportunity to those who can release themselves from bondage to do so. Fear is not without danger, for by it many are brought to desperation and the desperate will venture anything. If one studies ancient and modern history one will see that the reign of tyranny has not endured long. Aristotle shows that the tyranny lasted longer where the tyrant imitated the gentleness (*modestia*) of kings. The same is the judgment of Scripture. God will not long allow such an one to reign, for after he has allowed the tyrant to punish his people he will overthrow him to bring rest to them.†

If the excess of tyranny is unbearable, in the opinion of many, it is proper and right for brave and virtuous men to kill the tyrant and thus expose themselves to the hazard of death for the freedom of society. We have examples of this in the Old Testament history. Eglon, King of Moab, held the people in hard bondage. Ehud killed Eglon and himself became judge of Israel. But this does not agree with the teaching of the apostle. Peter

* De Reg. Princ. I. 6.
† De Reg. Princ. I. 10.

teaches us with becoming reverence not only to be subject to good and gentle, but also to froward masters. For it is a grace of God to suffer wrong and bear it patiently. Hence when many of the Roman emperors tyrannically persecuted Christians on account of their faith, even when a multitude of nobles as well as the common people embraced Christianity, they patiently suffered death and were courageous for Christ's sake. In the case of Ehud it must be specially noticed that he killed an enemy and a tyrant over the people. It would be dangerous to society if from mere personal presumption (*privata presumptione*) a few could murder the rulers, even if they were tyrants. For most people would rather expose themselves to the hazardous undertaking for bad men than for good and it happens that under the government of a king there are bad men as well as under a tyrant. It is more just to proceed against the oppressors not according to the view of a few (*presumptione*), but by the public authority (*auctoritate publica*). (a) In case the right to choose a king belongs to the society then it can without injustice (*non injuste*) remove him or limit his power if he misuse it. Such a society does not act contrary to fidelity when it removes the tyrant, even when he is dethroned forever, for he has not conducted himself with fidelity in the government of the society as is required of a king. He has brought it on himself so that his subjects are no longer obliged to keep the contract. (b) If it is the right of a superior ruler to choose a governor it is expected that he will be a safeguard against tyranny. Archelaus who ruled in Judea instead of his father Herod whose wicked policy he imitated, when the Jews complained to Augustus, was deprived of part of his power and his title of king was taken away and the half of his wealth divided between his two brothers. As he did not however check his tyranny he was sent by the Emperor Tiberius into exile. (c) When no human help can be had against tyrants one must fly for help to the King of all, God, who is a present help in time of trouble. Tyrants who are not worthy of conversion He can put out of the world or place in a low condition upon earth. He saw the oppression of his people in Egypt and drowned Pharaoh and his army in the sea. He hurled Nebuchadnezzar from his throne and drove him from the companionship of mankind, changing him into the likeness of an animal. He can even yet free his people from tyranny. In order that the people may merit this favor they must forsake sin, because it was as a punishment for sin that God allowed the tyrannical to rule over them.

Thomas shows that, (a) royal power should be elective and limited, to prevent it from falling into tyranny. This is not possible in hereditary monarchy which is excluded. Prudence is the only check, because it is to the king's own interest to avoid such acts. (b) The authority of the king ought to be tempered to prevent tyranny, that is, certain limits are set to royalty. (c) Tyrannicide is condemned, but the right of deposing and banishing belongs to the multitude or to a superior power which evidently is the Church. In these principles we have the germs of the principles of freedom which are found in later ages, though the edifice is crowned by theocracy. There is no redress for misgovernment unless according to law.*

This doctrine is confirmed in the other works of Thomas. If any one begins a revolution in the state he must have a just cause and power to carry it through. Now virtuous people as a rule have not the power and do not believe they have just cause for revolution, and therefore they do not begin any. In case however they have just cause and power and no injury to the common welfare will result, they will begin a revolution with good reason and they would sin if they did not. The virtuous are the wise of whom it is said, the wise man loves the common welfare before his own interest.† If a monarch does not govern in the interest of the community efforts must be made to banish him. Revolution is thus permissible, but is to be avoided if possible, being a remedy to be used only in case of extreme necessity. Insurrection is always a dangerous experiment even in case of success. Often it leads to civil dissension and anarchy; oftener still to a new and worse tyranny. Yet, while Thomas counsels moderation he defends the rights of the people against the abuse of power, and the peace of the state against the disturbances of the revolter. In regard to Tyrannicide which was accepted by many of the Doctors of the Middle Ages he follows the same moderate course. When tyranny has passed beyond endurance and violates all human and divine laws it is permissible to reverse it. He regards tyrannicide as moved by a personal sentiment, *privata presumptione*, and a particular opinion cannot affect a public personage. It is to society alone the right belongs. Only in one case does he regard it with favor, when the tyrant has recourse to public war and is killed in the struggle ensuing. It is better to let the murder of the tyrant rest upon the judgment of God. Tyrannicide is expressly condemned.‡

The only authentic passage in Thomas dealing directly with Tyrannicide is in his *Commentary upon the sentences*.§ In this passage he approves of the position of Cicero in his *De Officiis*, in which sanction is given to the murder of Caesar and in which the murderers are praised. In this case the powers are usurped by violence. The one who killed the tyrant is praised and receives a reward. Thomas says the praise is not deserved because the act was not a praiseworthy one. Yet this passage was the basis of the doctrine of tyrannicide in the middle ages and especially in the sixteenth century. It does not however meet with the approval of Thomas, because he only refers to the incident, he does not commend it. The best way to avoid tyranny is to choose a proper king at the first and to limit his government in such a way that there will be no occasion for falling into tyranny, *sic temperatur po-*

* De Reg. Prin. 1. 6.
† Expos. Arist. V. lect. 1. 2.
‡ De Reg. Prin. 1. 6.
§ disq. 4. 8. qu. 2. 2.

cessus et tyrannicida ne tacite declinari non possit.* There are two possible cases of tyranny, (a) *usurpationis*, (b) *regimine* or *administrativa per lapsu manifesta in justos*.†

5. *To prevent corruption.* The king should guard the people from the misuse of office on the part of rulers and prevent his servants and officials falling into oppressive measures against the people. The sale of offices by the princes does not appear to Thomas to be unlawful, provided the purchasers seem capable of performing the duties of the office, and provided that the price of sale is not so large that it would amount to oppression or corruption. If this is not the case such a sale is improper for several reasons. It often happens that those who have ability to fill official positions are poor and cannot buy them. If they are rich they do not desire such positions and do not see any advantage in the acquisition. The result is that in the most of cases those persons get the offices who are of inferior ability and desirous of office and money. Of these it may be said that they oppress the subjects and do not care for the interests of the princes. It is therefore much better to select brave and capable men to fill the offices and if necessary to compel them against their will to do so. For by their bravery and zeal the princes and subjects will derive greater advantage than through those who buy offices. Thomas permits an additional loan to the princes by the officers. When people lend a prince money under condition that an office will be granted in return for it, this is without doubt a usurious traffic (*pactum usurarium*), because they have for the loan the privilege of office. Thus the prince presents to them a chance of sinning and they themselves are forced to hold an office which they have used for gain. If however the prince has conferred the office without price and afterwards receives a loan from what the office has yielded there is no sin.‡

Resistance to the judgment of a ruler. One who is justly condemned to death is not permitted to defend himself. When however he is unjustly condemned, such a judgment is similar to a deed of violence by a robber. "Her princes in her midst are like wolves, they rob the prey in order to shed blood, to get dishonest gain."§ As it is allowed to withstand robbers, so one ought in such cases to oppose bad rulers, except it be to avoid a scandal (*scandalum*) when a great disturbance is to be feared as the result.‖

Confiscation. Restitution. Can those who were banished in consequence of schism demand their possessions from those who remained behind? Either they were justly banished, being guilty, in which case they cannot recover what they have lost by confiscation; or they were unjustly banished, without

---

* De Reg. Prin. I. 6.
† Ibid. I. 6; 2a. 2ae. qu. 42. 2; qu. 67. 1; 1a. 2ae. qu. 96. 5.
‡ Essay on Jews. Vol. XVI. pp. 294-295. Parma.
§ Ezek. XXII. 27.
‖ 2a. 2ae. Vol. III. p. 220.

guilt, and in an unlawful way, so that they can recover in this case their lost property. If they have a superior, then they must through him ask for the return of their property; if they have no superior then they can themselves recover what they lost, if such restitution is possible.* When princes contrary to justice by their power take from others that which belongs to them they act unlawfully, commit robbery and are bound to give restitution. If princes exact from their subjects what justly belongs to them (*debetur*) for the preservation of the community, it is not robbery, even if force be used; but if they extort what does not belong to them, it is robbery. Therefore they are bound to make restitution, the same as would be required of robbers, and their sin is more heinous being more dangerous to public justice, because they are set to be the guardians of public right.†

* Summa Theolog. Vol. IX. p. 627.
† Ibid. Vol. III. p. 237.

CHAPTER IX.

THE RELATION OF THE TEMPORAL AND SPIRITUAL. THE CHURCH AND STATE.

1. *Temporal and spiritual power.* The relation of the temporal and spiritual powers opens up one of the most difficult problems of medieval politics and furnishes us with the weakest part in the political theory of Aquinas. Here Thomas leaves his ancient master, and in a sense departs from many of his former principles in order to crown the political structure with a theocracy. The general position he takes is that of the absolute supremacy of and consequently the temporal supremacy of the Church over the state and over all the states of the world. If kings and other rulers have a right to govern the states, God has a superior right over all rulers. God's rule over the universe is rendered manifest in the Vicar of Christ upon the earth. Earthly rulers govern to promote the earthly good of the states, but this is subordinate to the higher end of all men, eternal blessedness. God has entrusted the power to guide into this eternal happiness to the priests over whom presides the Pontiff. The result of this theory is a confusion of the two cieties, the Church and state, and of the two powers temporal and spiritual, as also the twofold law which is administered in these societies. The Church is a society similar to the political society or state, *civitas per se sufficiens et unita.** The divine law is ultimate and rulers in governing must have respect thereunto in order to lead individuals and states alike to the ultimate end of life which can be secured only through the Church. The Church is superior to the civil society and religious authority pre-eminent because of its end. The definite and final end of every man and society of men is not simply living according to virtue, but living according to virtue for the purpose of securing eternal life with God. Since it cannot be secured by temporal means it does not belong to the temporal ruler to secure it, therefore super-natural means must be used, *gratia Dei vita æterna*. To bring men to this heavenly end belongs to the Divine ruler, THE LORD JESUS CHRIST, who by the agency of his own righteousness and the sacraments of the Church prepares men for heaven. Although all disciples are kings and priests in the heavenly life, yet in the Christian community upon earth there is instituted the priesthood, chiefly the successors of Christ and his Vicar, the High Priest of the Church, to whose charge the Christian kingdom is committed,

* Psalm 45, 10; Eph. IV. lect. 2; De Reg. Prin. I. 14; 2a. 2ae. qu. 83, 9, 4; 3a. qu. 72, 11.

and to whom all rulers as well as subjects are bound to submit in all spiritual concerns. *Hujus ergo regni ministerium ut a terrenis esset spiritualia distincta, non terrenis regibus, sed sacerdotibus est commissum et praecipue summo sacerdoti successori Petri, Christi Vicario Romano Pontifici, cui omnes reges populi Christiani oportet esse subditos.* All Christians when baptized become members of the Christian Church which is organized as a visible unity under one head. All Christians are accordingly united with this community and in subjection to the spiritual power of the Head. In ancient Rome where Christians first became civil rulers these temporal rulers placed themselves under the spiritual authority of the Church. There are two kinds of law, natural and divine, and as these cannot be contradictory as coming from the same God, there cannot be any antagonism between the temporal and spiritual powers which are concerned with these laws. So Thomas says, *quod rex, sicut dominio et regimini, quod administratur per sacerdotis officium subdi debet; ita processu debet omnibus humanis officiis et ea imperio sui regiminis ordinare,* as the king ought to be subject to the authority and rule administered through the office of the priest, so he ought to have authority over all human offices and order them by the imperium of his rule. The temporal power has no right to interfere with the spiritual, because the Church was not established upon the temporal foundation; the temporal power, as Thomas says above, has a full and uncontrolled empire over all human affairs in relation to the good of the social community, even the priests being in subjection in all matters that do not antagonize their spiritual office; but the ultimate authority by means of which difficulties are removed and conflicts avoided, while each helps the other to secure the general happiness, is found in this that the spiritual power is concerned with the supernatural end and therefore with the highest aim of human life, *unde in lege Christi reges debeant sacerdotibus esse subjecti.**

Thomas is here separated entirely from Aristotle. In the ancient philosophy the priesthood was subordinate to the temporal power. Thomas sets up the theocracy, that is, the superiority of the political and civil power wielded by the priesthood, guiding all men, individuals as well as societies, to the supernatural end. In the pure theocracy the temporal power is not only subordinate to, but under the control of the spiritual, and is exercised by the spiritual functionaries. Thomas is not theocratic in this sense for the secular rulers exercise the temporal power and occupy a distinct position of superiority and authority in the state. Theocratic principles were found embodied in the constitutions of the states at this time, and Thomas reflects the spirit of his own age. The Pope is the head of the Christian community, occupying the summit of the two powers, *qui utriusque potestatis apicem tenet,*† The same principle was found in the organization of the nations and in the

* De Reg. Prin. I. 14, 15.

† 2a. 2ae. qu. 67. 1.

public institutions of state, for example, the clergy had seats in all public assemblies, and enjoyed high political privileges as spiritual peers, as well as exercised important functions in judiciary, testatory matters, military supervision and inquisitorial courts, giving external sanction and validity to the theoretical assumption that the spiritual is the greater, more dignified, and consecrating power, tending in great measure to confound the sphere and province of the powers. Thomas was the exponent of the Church doctrine in his age. He sanctioned the temporal authority of the Church, admitted the right of the priesthood to determine temporal matters; but his ideas were limited. What position then did he ascribe to the Pope and to the clergy respectively?

The great question is, what power did the Pope legitimately exercise over temporal governments and in the conduct of secular affairs in the state? Thomas does not give an elaborate account of the temporal power of the Church. His theory is contained in the *De Regimine Principum*, Bk. I, chapters 14 and 15. He first gives an account of the theory of government, governing being directing the governed to the desired goal. Just as in the management of a ship it is governed when by the efforts of the shipmaster it is brought safely to its haven. How much more in matters pertaining to God should pains be taken to reach the highest end. To determine the function of government is the same as discovering the end for which subjects are governed. When applied to man as an individual the functions are economic, medicinal, educational, reparative, which tend to preserve human society; but man has an end of a higher nature, which he can realize only through the ministers of Jesus Christ, to whom are entrusted spiritual functions. The highest happiness is the enjoyment of God after death. The spiritual end alone can perfect the state as it alone can perfect the individual, *idem oportet esse judicium de fine totius multitudinis et unius*. Men can as individuals only get real blessedness in society, and society being organized to perfect man, man must reach his highest in the social life. This natural end is to live virtuously and as it belongs to the king to promote such a life, it follows that as the virtuous man has an ulterior end which consists in the possession of God, society has the same end to attain. If one would attain this end by the virtue of human nature, it belongs to the office of the king to conduct men, for we call him king who has the supreme government of human affairs. Man can only acquire this by divine virtue. It is not human government which conducts to this end but divine government under him who is not only man but God, our Lord Jesus Christ, who leads men to heavenly happiness. Christ is the origin of the kingly priesthood in all believers in as far as the members of Christ are Kings and Priests. To separate the temporal things from the spiritual, the service of the eternal kingdom has been confided, not to the kings of the world, but to the priests and chiefly to the High Priest, the Roman Pope, to whom all kings of Christian peoples ought to be subject as to Jesus Christ Himself. Man's spiritual destiny requires a divine law in addition to human, and natural law is the highest. Thus it is solely in the interest of the supernatural end Thomas sets up this theocracy. Among the Gentiles and Jews the priesthood was subject to royalty, because religious worship was designed to secure natural earthly good, which relates to the welfare of society; while under the Christian dispensation the worship is more exalted and is appointed with a view to securing celestial happiness. The legitimacy of the theocracy rests upon the fact that the ultimate aim of man is heaven and the secondary end, earthly peace, must be subject to the higher one; therefore it has come to pass that by a wonderful providence, in the city of Rome we have the capital city of Christian people, *principalem sedem*. It has come about by degrees that rulers of states are subject to the priests.

The king rules the other functionaries because of the superiority of end implied in his office, but he is subject to the priest because of the superior end of the priest's office. Thomas ascribes not a direct power to the Pope, but only an indirect power, for the governments do not come from the Church but are subject to it solely for the sake of religion. The religious authority controls government and society without absorbing it, just as grace controls human nature without destroying it. He does not accept the doctrine of Boniface set forth in the *Unam sanctam* according to which the political and civil power emanates from the ecclesiastical which has the right to direct and even destroy it if it acts contrary, in which there is but one sole master of the universe, the pope, and all governors and rulers are his creatures. The Church is the heavenly hierarchy. It is necessary to have some supreme power in matters of faith and this authority is confided to the Pope, in whose person is represented the Church's unity and who realizes the divine presence and government. To him is given the power to revise and control Church laws, to promulgate new doctrines and to prevent the rise of error, and to issue anathemas for the excommunication of unworthy Christian sovereigns and the release of subjects from their oaths of allegiance. Absolute power does not pertain in government to temporal rulers but to the spiritual ruler who is directly appointed by God.* The secular and spiritual powers are united in the person of the pope by the will of Christ, who is both King and Priest. Such is Thomas's statement,† giving color to the statement of Bellarmine that Thomas supported the absolute theory of the direct institution and control of the temporal by the spiritual power, which however is a mistake. In the *Summa theologiae*‡ it is said that the temporal power is subjected to the spiritual as the body is to the soul, and therefore the spiritual

* Sum. Contr. Gent. IV. 76; 2a. 2ae. qu. 12. 2.

† Com. Sent. II. disp. 44. qu. 2. 3

‡ 2a. 2ae. qu. 60. 6

does not usurp when it takes charge of temporal affairs. But this implies that the relation of the temporal to the spiritual power is in the interests of religion. Thomas's theory is that man's supreme end is eternal beatitude and this can only be secured through the ministers of supernatural law; therefore these ministers have supreme authority over men as individuals and human society in so far as the interests of religion are concerned, so that wherever religion comes in the spiritual power has right, but in all that is beyond religion the secular is supreme. The king is to be instructed, it is true, in the divine law which is to regulate his efforts in keeping his subjects to an orderly way of living.* In regard to what refers to the safety of the soul the spiritual power is to be heeded, but in that which affects civil good the secular power is sovereign, this is seen in the relation of the infidel rulers to the spiritual power.†

The distinction of temporal and spiritual power lies in this, that in temporal government the use of reason is authorized, for human laws are an emanation of reason; whereas in the kingdom of the spiritual reason has no place, it does not decide whether truth and reason shall rule but has only to obey, and at best it is only permitted to prove this in a subjective way, that is, to justify what exists as far as it is possible. Reason is limited by the supernatural so that in the Church the spiritual government is absolute and not amenable to human reason. The Church is built on faith and divine reason. The State and Church occupy the same relation as the natural and supernatural, the state being subordinate to the Church in all cases where the end of the Church and its authority comes into question. Their relations are founded, (a) upon their respective ends, and (b) upon the respective means they use to attain these ends. The Church has a higher aim and uses higher means than the state. The Church must be free and independent in her spiritual work and must not be hindered in any way by the state, but rather helped; for the earthly government can help citizens to be subjects of the Church, by protecting with its power and legislation the laws of the Church and her doctrines, and by punishing enemies and apostates, executing the sentence of the Church with the secular arm.‡ If the Church could copy the example set before her in the first century it would be well for her; according to Thomas, the Church in her new position at that period had not the power to check worldly princes; if she acted similarly now she would not usurp an untenable position, and harmony would be restored between the society of the state and of the Church. The divine law is necessary to guide man to his heavenly end.§ This divine law is represented by the Church and the Church has her unity in the Pope. It is necessary to the unity of the Church that

 * Deut. 17. 18; De Reg. Prin. 1. 15.
 † See sect. 2.
 ‡ 2a. 2ae. qu. 11. 1; qu. 12. 2.
 § 1a. 2ae. Vol. II. p. 331.

all believers should be one in faith. Among believers questions arise which involve differences of opinion and the Church would become divided were not this unity preserved by the opinion of one person. It is therefore necessary for the unity of the Church that one who represents the entire Church should embody this opinion. Christ does not forsake his Church in her time of need, and therefore it cannot be doubted that according to the ordinance of Christ there is a leader and ruler of the Church.* It belongs to the Pope to ordain the Church's creed, *symbolum ordinare*. A new edition of the creed is necessary at certain intervals for the avoidance of errors that arise from time to time. It is the duty of those who are vested with the proper authority to decide what shall be the creed, so that all with unshaken faith may keep it. This belongs to the authority of the Pope to whom are referred the most difficult questions. The Church cannot be one in faith unless unsettled questions of faith are decided by him who is the head of the entire Church (*pracesse*); in this way his opinion (*sententia*) is firmly held by all. Therefore new articles in the creed are to be set forth only by the Pope's authority (*sola auctoritas*), just as everything that pertains to the Church is under him.†

2. *The faithful and unfaithful.* The next question arises, what relation do the faithful and unfaithful, the believing and unbelieving, sustain to the spiritual power? And do they stand in the same relation or in different relations? This question has an important bearing on the ecclesiastical politics of Thomas. The duty of the state is to adapt its legislation and power to the Church, executing the ordinances of the Church and shaping its policy according to the plans of the ecclesiastical authorities, and to the promotion of the true faith. A faithful king and faithful rulers will do this, whether they be aristocratic or democratic. On the other hand this cannot be expected from an unbelieving prince or ruler, chiefly if they are of another faith. Thomas in toleration allows that such a prince should be recognized if he is already in possession of power, for greater injury would arise from non-recognition than by acknowledging his true dignity. On the other hand, if a believing prince or ruler has fallen away from the Catholic faith and acts contrary to the true Church of Christ, then he is not to be recognized and he has forfeited the right to rule and enjoy his kingdom. The subjects are then authorized to refuse him obedience and may recognize another ruler. The Church does not tolerate other religions and all who have left the fold of the true Church are to be forced back by penalties of body and soul. The rights of unbelievers in relation to the faith are peculiarly precarious because the Church can suspend these rights by her decision. Those who have never been believers are safest, because with their rights and privileges the Church is not concerned, only the believing nations may declare war against the in-

* Sum. Cont. Gent. Vol. V. p. 357.
† 2a. 2ae. Vol. III. p. 9. Criticism of Aquinas' Theory of Church and State. Frohschammer, p. 486 sq.; Burri, c. VII.

fidel peoples if they refuse to suffer the preaching of Christianity in their countries. These views are represented and to be executed by the Pope.

In general this is the doctrine of Thomas. Thomas does not allow to the Church the right to condemn and depose infidel princes. Here he draws a distinction. Infidelity is not in itself contrary to sovereignty for it is of human law and comes from nature. On the other hand the distinction of believing and unbelieving is of divine right and springs from grace. And as divine right does not suppress human right, it does not belong to the Church to punish the unbelief of those who have never received the faith nor does it abolish the power of the unbelieving over the believing. Yet the Church which acts for God in the interests of religion ought to abolish such authority of unbelieving over believing, for it is detrimental to religion and infidelity destroys authority. In regard to those who have received the faith the Church has power in their relapse into infidelity to excommunicate them and release the subjects from their oaths of fidelity.* Apostacy entails along with it the destruction of authority. The example of Julian the apostate does not overcome this, because as yet the Church had not the power to restrain princes and therefore subjects were permitted to continue in obedience in order to avoid a greater evil. In support of this position he cites the authority of Gregory VII.†

This raises the question, in how far do Christians owe obedience to superiors in the world? Faith in Christ is the principle and cause of righteousness, therefore faith in Christ does not abolish the regulation of righteousness, but establishes it. The ordinance of righteousness requires however inferiors to obey their superiors, otherwise the condition of human affairs could not continue to exist. Therefore believers through faith in Christ are not released from the obligation to obey their worldly princes. Before this, Thomas objected, that the government by worldly princes is generally unrighteous, or has been in origin an unjust usurpation, and from this it would appear that Christians do not owe obedience to worldly princes. But, he says, man is only to obey worldly princes in so far as it is required by the ordinance of righteousness. When they have no regular government but are under a usurpation, or when what is unjust is commanded, then the subjects are not bound to obey, except in peculiar circumstances or to avoid great danger.‡

In regard to the distinction between Christians and unbelievers Thomas brings out the medieval conceptions in regard to the Jews. Through their guilt in regard to the death of Christ, they have fallen into endless slavery, but Christian mildness allows them to live together, and instead of being actual slaves they are domestic servants, *servos tributarios*. Only the traditional duties may be demanded and no unusual obligations may be laid upon

* 2a. 2ae. qu. 10. 10.
† 2a. 2ae. qu. 12. 2.
‡ 2a. 2ae. Vol. III. p. 380-1.

them, because what is unusual produces unrest. The mistake committed by the Jews in Brabant who make their living by taking usury,—that is, all their possessions were according to the view of the time unjustly acquired— is to be taken along with the mistake of the princes themselves in the imposition of special taxes upon the Jew. To avoid possible disadvantage the Jews should be made to bear some burden, for it would be better to compel the Jews to work for the earning of their maintenance as they do in Italy, than that they should live without work and enrich themselves by usury.* Another question is, is it right that the Jews should be distinguished from Christians by the wearing of a sign? Here the answer is clear and in accordance with the decision of a general council. Jews must in some outward manner be distinguished from other people. This is also commanded in their law that on the four corners of their cloaks they shall make fringes to distinguish them from others. This is the brand of their iniquity.†

Many unbelieving rulers have authority (*dominium*) over believers. If at the first establishment of the authority unbelievers are allowed to have power over believers, it is not permissible to make such a bargain. Only danger could in this way come to believers, for it would be easy for them if they were under the jurisdiction of another power to change from those to whom they were subject. In a similar way the unbelievers would despise the believers when they saw the defection in the position they occupied. Therefore the Apostle forbad believers to take their quarrels before unbelieving judges for settlement. So the Church does not allow unbelievers to rule over believers or in any way to be officially over them. The case is different when the establishment of power is already in existence. Here it ought to be considered that authority and superintendence are exercised by the power of human law, the distinction between believers and unbelievers being of divine law. The divine right which is of grace does not abolish the human right which is of natural reason. Thus the government of believers by unbelievers is not abolished by the distinction between believers and unbelievers. There can, however, by means of judgments and ordinances through the Church which has the authority of God be such an abolition of the right of governing, because unbelievers have lost through the guilt of unbelief power over believers, who have become the sons of God. Sometimes the Church does this, sometimes she does not. For unbelievers who in temporal matters are subject to the Church and her members, there is the ordinance of the Church. A slave who is a Jew is free without recompense, through accepting of Christianity, if he was born a slave or if he had been purchased; if however he is again to be offered for sale his master must do so within three months. The Church does no wrong here because the Jews are the slaves of the Church over whom she has authority. Worldly princes have given many

* Summa on Jews, p. 292-294. Vol. XVI.
† ibid. p. 292-4.

laws concerning the freedom of subjects. For the unbelievers who in temporal matters are not subject to the Church and her members the Church has no established rule, although she has the right to do as above in order to avoid offence, as the Lord showed in Matthew XVII. 26, that he might be excused from paying tribute because the sons were free, but commanded that the tribute be paid in order to avoid offence. So Paul when he says slaves should honor their masters, adds, "that the name of the Lord and his teaching be not blasphemed."* In reference to the relation of the Church to those who have never believed and to heretics and apostates, he says, among unbelievers who have never had the faith as heathens and Jews, such are in no wise to be forced, that is, they are to believe of themselves, because faith is a matter of the will. There are however among unbelievers cases in which power should be used to compel them not to hinder believers, *si adsit facultas*, but this is a case of protection afforded unbelievers.†

3. *Intolerance, Inquisition, Persecution.* If a believing prince has fallen away from the faith and denied the true Church of Christ then he is to be refused recognition, having alienated his right of rule and his kingdom. In such a case the subjects have the right of revolt against him even more distinctly than in case of tyranny. Naturally the Ecclesiastical autocrat will not delay to call forth positive insurrection or to pronounce sentence of excommunication and formal removal. He who is an apostate and a heretic from the faith has incurred the penalty of death, if he can be reached by the inquisition, for there is to be no toleration granted to heretics and apostates but rather excommunication and the death-penalty. Such is the general doctrine of Thomas on this point.‡

An important question is, *are unbelievers to be compelled to accept the true Christian faith?* Augustine asserted that a man can believe only willingly and that his will cannot be compelled in this matter. Jews and Gentiles therefore who have never received Christianity are not to be forced to accept of it and they are not to be subjected to wars or penalties by way of compelling them, unless they positively and openly hinder the progress of the Christian faith. But it is different in the case of those who have accepted Christianity, for if they depart from their profession of faith, they may be subjected to corporal penalties in order to force them to fulfil their promises. Such is the *Dominican* doctrine which gave scope to the persecuting spirit in the middle ages, Thomas himself being a *Dominican*. The Dominicans argued against the doctrine of Augustine, that to make a promise is an act of will, whereas to fulfil a promise is an act of necessity—to accept a faith is voluntary but to keep the faith is an obligatory act. Man becomes thus a creature of necessity the moment he has by consent expressed his assent. Thomas in theory

* 2a. 2ae. Vol. III, p. 44.
† ibid. p. 42.
‡ 2a. 2ae. qu. 11. 1; qu. 12. 2.

reforms and repudiates this distinction, holding that the spirit of God is the originator as well as the sustainer of faith in man. But in as far as he was a Dominican he was bound by the fetters of this belief, and his fine distinction between believers and unbelievers is at bottom nothing else but this fundamental principle which has been at the foundation of all the persecutions by the Church, in her false zeal and still more false idea of devotion to an unalterable belief.* In the case of unbelievers who never accepted the faith no force is to be used because faith is of the will. There are among unbelievers cases in which power should be used to compel them not to retard believers, even by open persecution. For this reason Christians frequently carry on war against unbelievers, not to force them to believe, but with the idea of compelling them to refrain from hindering Christians. There are also other unbelievers who at some time (*quandoque*) have received the faith and confessed it, as heretics and all apostates, these must be forced by means of corporal punishments (*corporaliter*) to fulfil what they promised and to retain what they once had.†

Thomas declares these ideas in connection with the fundamental principle of the intercourse of believers and unbelievers. The Church does not forbid intercourse between believers and unbelievers who have departed from the faith they once received, as heretics do, or who deny it as apostates do. For against both of these the Church expresses her opinion in the penalty of excommunication. That which concerns intercourse with those who have never believed must be decided by circumstances, location of the persons, the transactions referred to (*negotia*), and the times. If they are strong in the faith so that their intercourse with unbelievers may restore them rather than that the believers may be turned away from the faith, their intercourse with unbelievers is not forbidden, that is, those who have not accepted the faith as heathens and Jews, and especially when compelled by necessity. If however the believers are simple and weak in the faith and likely to be led astray, intercourse with unbelievers must be forbidden to them, and chiefly there must not be much of a confidential nature between them and no intercourse unless it is necessary.‡

Are the religious rites (*ritus*) of unbelievers to be tolerated? These rites are to be tolerated in so far as they contain anything that is useful or true for believers, as those of the Jews which as prototypes, types of Christianity, witness on behalf of the Christian faith. On the other hand, rites of unbelievers which have no truth nor anything useful in them are in no way to be tolerated, except to avoid an evil; for example, to avoid offence or disunion, (*dissidium*) which might ensue or to avoid a hindrance to the salvation of those persons in tolerating things which if tolerated might bring them to the

* Maurice, Hist. of Phil. I. 620 sq.
† 2a. 2ae. Vol. III. p. 42.
‡ Ibid. p. 43.

faith, for often the Church has tolerated the rites of heathen and Jews when the number of unbelievers was large.* In principle, that is, there is no toleration, but for human expediency if it is likely to lead to salvation there is toleration. Thomas condemns the compulsory baptism of the children of Jews, and other unbelievers against the will of their parents. The custom of the Church which is to be followed in all cases has never sanctioned it. It would be contrary to natural justice and might place the faith in hazard, because the compulsory baptism of growing persons who are easily led astray from their parents results in their falling away again, because the natural right of the child before it has the use of reason is to be under the guardianship of its father.†

Concerning heretics two things are to be observed, as to themselves and as to the Church. Concerning themselves they have sinned and deserve not only to be separated from the Church by suspension, but also to be excluded from the world by death, for it is very much worse to destroy the faith in which is the life of the soul, than to counterfeit money by which the temporal life is forfeited. If therefore forgers and other evil-doers are immediately condemned to death by the princes, with much more right should heretics who have been convicted of heresy be not only excommunicated but put to death. In regard to the Church she has compassion and is desirous of the return of the erring and so does not immediately condemn him, but only after a first and second admonition. If he still continues obstinate in his error, then the Church hopes no longer for his return and has care for the salvation of others in that she separates him from the Church by excommunication and hands him over to a worldly tribunal that he may be put out of the world by death (*exterminandum*).‡

The Church according to the command of the Lord loves all, not only her friends, but her enemies and persecutors. It pertains to love, not only to wish well to a neighbor but also to do good to him. There is a double welfare, first, a spiritual, the salvation of the soul, which love has especially in mind; therefore as often as heretics fall they should be received by the Church through repentance; the other welfare which love bears in mind is temporal good, as physical life, worldly property, good reputation and ecclesiastical or secular dignity. We are bound in love to desire these for others except when these imperil eternal salvation as well of themselves as of others. When therefore these possessions hinder in one or in many the eternal salvation, we must not (*non oportet*) desire through love to him that he should have them, but much more that he should not have them, because everlasting salvation is to be preferred to temporal good, and the welfare of many is to be preferred to that of one person. If heretics were always restored to the

* Ibid. p. 45.
† Ibid. p. 45, 46.
‡ Ibid. p. 48.

Church privileges when they returned and were allowed to keep their temporal goods, this would be prejudicial to the salvation of others, because they would corrupt others when they fall away again, and others would feel secure when they fell into heresy, that they would not be punished. Therefore the Church the first time there is a return after heresy not only receives to penitence but restores by dispensation to their former privileges in case of true repentance and in the interest of peace. If however they fall away again it is a sign of their instability in the faith and therefore those who have been far away and have returned are received to repentance but are not freed from the judgment of death.*

Does a prince on account of defection from the faith thereby lose his authority over his subjects so that they are not bound to obey him? Authority is not inconsistent with unbelief, because the authority is exercised in accordance with the right of the people whose human right it is. The distinction between believers and unbelievers however, is of divine law. One who has sinned through unbelief may through the voice of the Church lose the right of authority as well as by many other transgressions. The Church does not exist to punish unbelievers who have never received the faith, as the apostle says, "why should I judge them that are without?" But those unbelievers who have received the faith and denied it can be punished by the decree of the Church. What could more conduce to the destruction of faith than an apostate man who meditates wickedness in his wicked heart and sows strife with the intention of taking men away from the faith. As soon as the decree of excommunication is pronounced on account of apostacy, the believers are *ipso facto* released from his authority and the oath of fidelity with which they are bound is broken. The Church did not deal thus with Julian the apostate, because she had not the power to control worldly princes, and therefore she permitted believers to obey the apostate in matters that were not against the faith and so avoided a greater danger to the Church.†

Schismatics ought to receive secular punishment. The Schismatic sins in two ways, (a) because he separates himself from the society of the Church: his punishment for this sin is excommunication: (b) because he refuses to be subject to the Head of the Church, and for this it is right that he should be punished with the chastisement of the secular power (*coercentur*), because he will not be chastised by the spiritual power of the Church.‡

The relation of the Church to war is treated by Thomas. The Church does not directly take part in war, yet it exerts no small influence indirectly. A war is sinful if it is not just. A just war has three characteristics, (a) the will of the prince at whose command it is waged; (b) a just cause, that those who are attacked deserve the attack because of their guilt; (c) good intention

* Ibid. p. 49.
† Ibid. p. 50, 51.
‡ Ibid. p. 156.

in the conduct of the war, that is, either to secure some good or to avoid an evil. Bishops, clergymen, and spiritual persons are not permitted to take part in the warfare unless in cases of necessity, because war turns the mind away from the contemplation of divine things and fills it with thoughts of bloodshed. On the other hand, prelates shall not only oppose robbers and tyrants who oppress the people with spiritual weapons such as wholesome admonitions, pious prayers, and the sentence of excommunication against obstinacy, but they shall also exercise authority in regard to the means of attaining the end, that is, bringing back to virtue. Carnal warfare is considered however by a believing people to be related to spiritual good as its aim. Thus it belongs to the clergy to regulate and to induce others to conduct just wars (*disponere et inducere alios ad bellandum bella justa*).*

Views of inquisitorial power. The principle of the liberty of conscience began to be obscured when the Church and State were allied at and after the time of Constantine. Coming under the influence of the Emperors the Church fell in with the ideas that were prevalent in the minds of those who exercised the political power. Augustine was at first the champion of tolerance, but in later times he adopted the principle of *political intolerance*, according to which the interest of the state demands the preservation of the truth and the uprooting of error by force; and as a consequence the principle of *religious intolerance*, that the Church demands the state to protect her and to proscribe all beliefs opposite to those which bear upon the Church's interest in the salvation of men. In consequence of these views Augustine consented to the use of the military in the defence of the faith. Through the influence of Augustine and by the power of the states this idea of intolerance, aiming at the good of the community and the salvation of souls, was established and received public sanction in the canonical legislation of the twelfth century which held universal authority in the time of Thomas Aquinas. It was presumed that the freedom of the Church demanded the expurgation of heresy, that the hazard brought upon human souls by contact with heretics demanded their extermination, and on this foundation the inquisition was started some years before the birth of Aquinas.

Thomas gave to the secular power the task of executing the decrees of the ecclesiastical tribunals in all matters pertaining to religion, and he gave to the High Priest of Roman Christianity the supervisory control of all powers in matters of a religious character. As we have seen he treats of unbelievers under two heads, in the one class are heathen, pagans, and Jews, and in the other heretics and apostates. The first class should never be compelled to embrace the faith. They are therefore excluded from the category of persecution. However, such unbelievers ought to be hindered from opposing the true faith, for example, in case of blasphemy and efforts to pervert Christ-

---
* Ibid. pp. 136-139.

ians to paganism. Therefore in regard to them toleration is practised.* In regard to heretics and apostates, heresy is a corruption of faith and apostacy a defection from faith once embraced. He who enters the Church ought to be compelled to abide by it.† The Church is to have recourse to admonition, and if this fails she is to call in the civil power. The Church is to proscribe heretics and the secular power is to punish them, *haeretici saecularibus principibus exterminandi tradendi sunt*. This was the formula which expressed the policy of the Church. By a decree of the Lateran Council under Innocent III, in 1215 the Albigenses were placed under the ban of the Inquisition and handed over to the secular powers to be exterminated.‡ Of the sense of the word exterminate (*exterminandi*) there can be doubt, for after having stated that heretics are to be delivered to the secular powers after two admonitions, Thomas says that these heretics are to be excluded from the world by death, *per mortem a mundo excludi, occidi.*§ Still more emphatic is the statement that if a heretic who has relapsed a second time into heresy seeks forgiveness and indulgence, the Church is to pardon his sins but to deny him freedom from the death-penalty.‖ The ground upon which this rests is the interest in the salvation of souls, not only of the individual concerned, but especially of others, that they may be warned by the severity of the discipline to which heretics are subjected. Such men are dangerous to society as well as being sinners and since capital punishment is meted out upon the twofold ground of sin and perniciousness to society, the penalty of death is due to the heretic, because heresy is a sin and it imperils society.¶

Such is the inquisitorial spirit found in the writings of the great saint and scholar of the middle ages, read with profound regret, recorded not through reproach, but simply because it is believed they express the sentiments of the age in which he lived, in which the doctrines of political freedom were baptized in the blood of the martyrs of liberty, that the confusion of despotism and free institutions might be destroyed and the new-born child of blood given to the world in the ages of renaissance. The only justification of these sentiments is to be found in this, the social institutions of government were almost buried in the ruins of the first ten centuries, weak nations had perished, barbarian inroads had been checked, imperialism proved but an empty dream, and there was left only the ecclesiastical institution to represent advancing civilization; it usurped universal government, made itself or tried to make itself the imperialism of the world because no power was strong enough to resist it, and it kept alive the organic unity of men at the expense of its own despotic career in preparation for the stable institutions of later centuries. Thomas is in spirit tolerant, but he is the master mind of the Church and the exaggerations of this part of his theory may well be pardoned in the

* 2a. 2ae. qu. 10. 8, 9, 10.   ‡ 2a. 2ae. qu. 11. 3.
† qu. 10. 8.   ‖ qu. 11. 4.
‡ Gregor. Decr. Bk. VII. c. 13. ¶ 2a. 2ae. qu. 64. 2.

remembrance of his fidelity to political principles in other parts and in the thought that his genius kindled afresh the fires of liberty at the beginning of the middle ages.

CHAPTER X.

ECONOMIC VIEWS OF AQUINAS. GERMS OF NATIONAL-POLITICAL ECONOMY.

1. *Introduction.* The account of Thomas's views would be incomplete without a presentation of his economic ideas. Thomas starts with the activity of human beings. He takes for granted a material basis for a state, desiring even the most beautiful location, that the citizens may have the greatest possible, pleasure and enjoy every facility for health and comfort. In order to make material provision for the wants of the community he prefers a strong agricultural state, in which the land is fertile and productive, because commerce and trade introduce the selfish, mercenary spirit, and destroy the spirit of self-sufficiency which characterizes the best state. States should as far as possible produce what would support their own population and depend as little as possible on trade with foreigners, because foreign trade is detrimental to the customs and laws of a state. He maintained what are regarded as the foundation principles of modern state-civilization, private property and the family. Private property is not opposed to natural law, but an addition to it on the basis of human right. Private property arose chiefly from the desire to avoid the confusion involved in common property and to encourage individual activity and industry, because a man cares more for what is his own. Yet, the use of property should be common, because all have a right to be supported out of the excess in others' possessions. He acknowledges the value of wealth, and the excess of population is to be checked by necessary regulations in reference to marriage.

The end of man's life is not wealth, nor power, nor property, but a virtuous life. Only in the state which is the highest form of human society, and in a national state, can man really be a man. The whole state-regulation should be promoted as much as possible by the necessary subjection of every one; this state-regulation is specially manifest in the training and education of children for the state. The monarch cares for the individuals in the state as he would for the members of his own body. State constitutions are changeable, depending upon the location, circumstances, culture of the state; in the ideal state artisans, laborers and peasant-farmers are not citizens, but only the military and official members who must be landed proprietors are real citizens. The lower kinds of work, manual labor and industrial operations, are at a discount when compared with the higher occupations, military, scientific and contemplative. There is a division of labor, for the workman is naturally a servant of toil, and the virtuous man a master of employment, and governor of states, cities, etc. The nobility of virtue is above that of wealth, although the latter is generally the foundation of the former, because of the natural advantages afforded for a higher form of life. Slavery is a natural and necessary condition arising from the difference in the nature of men, and the result of sin. This marks off the population of the state into two classes, slave and free. The individual is merged in the state and the unity of the state is the great consideration in its policy and development. The owners of property are the citizens of the state, and those who are not owners are regarded as servants under the control and subject to the authority of the citizens. Thus the citizens alone are members of the state and under its control, the non-citizens being subject to the state and enjoying any rights they do through the citizen class.

Trade and commerce. It is fitting that a state which has not of itself all things that are needful for sustaining life, should trade, but only for itself, that is not as an enterprise for gain, but only so far as it can gain a sufficiency for itself, not for the satisfaction or benefit of other states and communities. Those who trade with all and at the same time have a market in their own state do it in order to get wealth, because they esteem wealth too highly which is a disadvantage to a just state-life. It is not well that a state should be located too near the sea, because in the case of such a sea-board state many enter the state who have been brought up under different customs and trained to different habits of life, and they tend to draw away the citizens from the observance of their own laws and customs. Foreigners who thus enter into the state should occupy the position of workmen, and only such foreigners should be permitted to remain in the state as are essential to maintain the self-sufficiency of the community. Commerce and the entrance of strangers as immigrants tend to the corruption of morals and make men avaricious. If the end of trade is legitimate, namely, to supply the necessities of the state, to support the family or to feed the poor, then it is to be regarded as honest and honorable.* When commerce is for gain then it is illegitimate. In order to make it legitimate it must be prompted by an honest purpose. For such an end it is a necessity, but the nation which relies solely upon trade and industry for support is unnatural, because it produces intercourse with outsiders which breaks down the public spirit of nationality. When the desire for gain becomes general then all political and civil virtue vanishes and the military spirit becomes weak; the city itself is a centre of constant warfare, and the peace of the state is broken by the continual tur-

* Expos. Arist. Vol. XXI. p. 630.

moil of trade and of traders. When the citizens are engaged in tilling the soil there is peace and no incursions of foreigners. Therefore, the chief resource of a state should be agriculture. He recommends that not only should men live in cities, but that the dwellings of the citizens should be built upon the plains where they can have around them sufficient lands to produce the means of support. In moderation there is permitted an external commerce to make up what is needful for the sustenance of the inhabitants.

One reason why he condemns commerce is because of the frauds committed in the markets by the traders. There is, he alleges, a natural price fixed for things to which there ought to be a general conformity and no such thing as prigging to raise or lower the price of goods should be allowed. In such merchandise as is carried on in which the seller profits at the expense of the buyer or the buyer cheats the seller out of a part of the natural price of the goods there is deceit and sin. Just as there is a natural right, there is a natural price for goods. This is the basis of the natural-economic views of Thomas as it is the foundation of his natural political-ideas.*

2. *State-regulation, Marriage, Education, Progress.* In the state the individual is subordinated to the state; the state is the highest community of human beings, and as such, its aim being for the best interests of man, its regulations govern all individual life and subordinate personal interests to those of the community. What rescues the individual from complete obscurity is the fact that the end of the state is the same as that of the individual, scientific contemplation, not industry nor labor, is the highest occupation of man as an individual, and only in the exalted condition of human life is man really anything in the national state, the nationality of the state being either natural or historical. The aim of the state is to secure the common welfare. Each member is a part of the state and is to surrender himself in the state whether small or great, to the regulations of the state in regard to life and law. Thus man lives and labors in the higher spheres of life, as a citizen, and in more menial services of manual labor and servitude, with a view to promote the general welfare, and through this his own interest, utilizing individual aptitudes and activities in a common service which develops the best nature of man. The ethical virtue of the state is made up of the virtues of the citizens in their parts. The arrangements of the state are the best because therein the happiness and good of all is promoted. A mistake is made when many of the state regulations are not in accordance with the highest good of all.† Education is fitted by the state for the best end; marriage is regulated so as to produce the best results; religion is to promote the state-good and to develop virtue among the citizens; the treatment of the Jews and Gentile strangers is to be regulated by the state for the good of all, for when the Jews give themselves to excessive greed in making mon-

* De Reg. Prin. II. 3; Sum. 2a, 2ae, qu. 97, I. 2. 3.
† Expos. Arist. Vol. XXI. pp. 635-658, 678-9.

as to avoid possible disadvantages they are to be compelled to bear the burden of toil and taxation in order that they may live honorably and honestly like other citizens. It is the duty of the state to provide for the wants of the members so that none shall suffer through lack of the necessaries of life.*

Marriage. Thomas expressly defends the view of Aristotle that the women should marry at eighteen and the men about thirty-seven years of age. For, when we consider the good condition of the spouses and the good future condition of those who are to be brought up and consequently the general welfare of the state, it is better that this union should take place when the bodies of both parties are in a perfect condition. Circumstances may occur in which this union may take place earlier or later, in cases where the bodies have more slowly or more quickly developed, or where there has been immoral intercourse (*fornicatio cum alienis*) or something of that kind exists. Thomas says, some may refer to the Roman laws as against Aristotle, which gives as a rule that the common welfare demands that women should be twelve and men fourteen or thereabouts before marriage takes place. On the contrary Thomas objects, justice does not require that the marriage should take place when the male and female are fourteen and twelve years respectively, but that this is the earliest period at which marriage is competent, because at these years the earliest mutual consent can be given by the use of their reason.† Thomas prohibits intercourse outside of wedlock, and only monogamous marriages are allowed. In the companionship of husband and wife, nature has for its aim the perfection of posterity; all sexual intercourse which takes place outside of that relation is against nature (*innaturalis*).‡

The state is a society which has sufficient within itself to support life, and therefore the citizens should have a sufficiency and not be in poverty. The state must be on its guard to prevent want from coming into its midst. This may arise from its having too many children to inherit the patrimony. For when a large inheritance is divided among many children it is very small for each individual, especially when it comes to the third or fourth generation.

Aristotle is dissatisfied (*non placuit*) with the law which gives to the firstborn the entire inheritance. He would have the inheritance divided among all according to the Greek usage. Thomas regards the overthrow of the succession law of nobility, as a proof of its impracticability. The reasons for the overthrow were, (a) the firstborn is only one child, the later children are many and the consequence is the majority are poor and the few rich; (b) the owners of property are members of the state, non-owners are not, therefore the property must be in the hands of the citizens. If now the later children did

* Sum. Jud. Vol. XVI. pp. 292-4.
† Expos. Arist. Vol. XXI. p. 686.
‡ ibid. p. 686

not inherit a portion from their parents, the greater part of the children would not be citizens and so would be excluded from the state. (c) The later born children may be as fully qualified by nature for doing great things as the first born. If therefore they have no means with which to work, then they are forced to get means where they can find them (*accipere undecumque*), by waylaying citizens and others, robbing and murdering them, or by combining with enemies and doing what is unprofitable and injurious.

Are there any means to be used to limit the number of children? Thomas denies that Aristotle permits the use of abortion, since he only mentions the custom as prevailing in some nations. It is the opinion of Aristotle that to limit the population means should be taken to limit the males to the ages of between thirty-seven and fifty-five years, and the women from eighteen to thirty-seven years in the bearing of children; for both men and women are then in their most perfect condition. For this reason and in this way not only are better children born but they are fewer in numbers (*pauciores*).*

State education. Thomas considers that the nurture of children belongs to the mother. Yet no one who has the right use of reason can doubt that the legislator who esteems the welfare of the state must specially look after the education and regulation of the youth. To neglect to provide for the training of the young and to let them behave as they wish is to injure and destroy the state. Aristotle says that the legislature must have absolute control of the training of children and that it must not be left to others as is the case in many states, where each one cares for his own children as seems best to him, so that one trains them in one way and another in a different way. Where the training is common there is a common care, and pains are taken with all, such as are appropriate to all. All in the state should have the same training and the same rational aim. Thomas does not follow Aristotle fully. The text says, one cannot believe that among the citizens each one is for himself (*sibi esse*) but that they all belong to the state. In the exposition Thomas puts it *for himself alone*, which rescues individuality, for although it is for the state it is for himself also. It is to be observed, he says, that not only does a citizen belong to himself and exist for the sake of himself (*esse sui ipsius solum, neque gratia sui*), but that all belong to the state and are for its sake; consequently the provisions and regulations for each individual citizen are made in respect of his relation to the entire state and its welfare. So the youth are to be provided for and regulated by the entire state, having for its aim the welfare of the community. For all that pertains to youth must be measured and determined by its utility to the state in attaining its end, which is the perfect possession and use of reason.†

The liberal sciences are those according to the ancients which dispose man to work and act according to reason. Those are illiberal sciences which

* Ibid. pp. 688-687.
† Ibid. pp. 692-695.

simply regard the welfare of the body and are called servile, because they are concerned with external good. Thomas wants only the liberal sciences, for it makes a difference what is the end for which one learns and practises science. If he does it to attain excellent virtue, then it is not illiberal, whether he seek to attain personal excellence or the good of others, *for a friend is like a second self*. If some one learns the sciences and is diligently engaged for the sake of others, it is different from the case of those who pursue them for the sake of advantage and external possessions, as do many lawyers and physicians; such is the work of an hireling and is servile. He who engages in science for the love of truth and virtue and for the love of benefiting others, without making it a source of greedy gain is worthy of praise.* He thus emphasizes the duty of the state to encourage learning and to provide for the education of all its members.

Education proceeds on the basis of capacity. There are many so circumstanced by nature that it is difficult for them to become good by education; this natural position which is caused by the condition of the brain at birth gives an inclination towards good or evil, but such an inclination carries with it no necessity in regard to intelligent action.† A child imperfectly formed at birth is not fitted for intelligent activity or state life and is not to be educated with the same care as the perfectly formed children; but Thomas does not accept of the position of the ancient philosopher that such children are not to be reared, for Christianity has changed the view in regard to the preciousness of human life.‡ His idea of state-education results from his view of the family. It is an imperfect society, not of itself self-sufficient, but simply a part of the perfect community, the state, and subject to it. If the family master and head has a wide power over the females and children in the household, he is in subjection to the power of the state, and acts as it were in the family circle as an official of the state, subject to the surveillance of the government.

Progress. In the principle of education we find the predominating element is progress. It is natural to human reason to go from imperfect to perfect. We see in the speculative sciences the first philosophers have transmitted to their successors an imperfect knowledge, transmitted to them to perfect it. In the practical sciences it is the same. The first who considered the welfare of the human community created imperfect institutions which require much modification and enlargement by their successors.§ There is a natural progress among the sciences and arts among men, seen in the changes in human laws and institutions effected by human reason in conformity with the changeful circumstances of the times. Human nature and its capacity

* Ibid. pp. 626-7.
† Ibid. p. 609.
‡ Ibid. p. 682.
§ In. 2ae. qu. 97, 1.

for development is the basis of education and progress in laws and institutions. This principle of elasticity applied to sciences, arts and human life is one of the best features of an otherwise stiff scholasticism. At first man makes an invention and he transmits it incomplete for perfection by successors.* The idea of imperfect and perfect as stages in human life and progress, a conception applied alike to the hierarchy of Church and State, gives the possibility of constant development. Humanity is compared to a single man who in childhood received from the divine Being a law suitable to his life, to the feebleness and insufficiency of childhood, to the vigor of youth and to the perfect constitution of manhood.† The ancient law was not absolutely perfect, it is perfect according to the time and circumstances, suitable to the age and condition of the people. The law of Moses in like manner was perfect in its suitability to the Hebrews, forming the intermediate link in the chain that had as its first link the revelation of nature and as its last the revelation of grace. There is thus a natural progress in the evolution of law conformed to the evolution of man and to the environments of human life. Progress is led by man for human reason is the captain; it is limited by man for man's circumstances condition it; and it is perfect at each stage for in man's perfection it secures its perfection. In this view the whole theory of Thomas occupies its natural place in the historic development of truth.

3. *Wealth. Taxation. Money.* On the subject of money the works of Aristotle presented materials for attacking the abuses of the middle ages. The coins were depreciated by the arbitrary action of the rulers who appropriated to themselves the difference in value in the coins which they put in the market and the standard measure. Aquinas is the first to make such an attack upon political abuses of the currency. The king or whoever has the right to rule ought to see that proper money is used and that the weights and measures are of the proper standard. The special use which money serves is that it is a standard by which value is measured. It is the rule of measurement in prices and as there is a natural price for marketable commodities the standard ought to be fixed and rigid. If values are changeable at the pleasure of the prince then the commerce of the state is reduced to the arbitrary will of the ruler and money is no longer sacred. Money is of value because it is an index of price.‡

Money is the index of resources. Aquinas's idea of wealth is that of natural riches, natural resources. In a kingdom in which the people under the government of a king are aiming after the proper end, the preservation of society and the establishment of peace and unity, the making of wealth is not the chief end; but there is a nobility of wealth in the state, which in general is synonymous with the nobility of virtue. The owners of the property

* Expos. Arist. III. lect. 8. 1.
† 2a, 2ae, qu. 98. 2.
‡ De Reg. Prin. II. 12, 13.

of the community alone are citizens. Unless there is a sufficient supply of victuals the state cannot survive, because the support of physical existence is the first condition of human life.* It is necessary that the state abound in temporal riches, called natural riches, chiefly a suitable land with flocks of cattle, herds of sheep, etc.† It is also essential that the state abound in artificial riches, such as gold, silver and other precious metals, because these are specially useful in fortifying the kingdom and preserving it from external attack.‡ Another part of the wealth of the state is its buildings, fortifications, and its public roads, all of which are necessary for the state-life.§ In regard to the value of private property, he says, few have property in common compared with those who have separate possessions and so fewer quarrels take place over property, when it is held in separate possession.‖ True wealth consists in the things with which the requirements of nature can be supplied. This is true wealth, when in that which one has there is no want, there is satisfaction, enough to supply what is demanded in a right way of living. It is clear that he is richer who has a superfluity of the things which are really necessary to life, than he who has a superfluity of money. That is not true riches which when circumstances are altered has no value or use for the necessities of life; in some circumstances money is valueless and useless for the supply of the necessities of life, as for example, when the king or community decree that the money shall have no value.¶ Not the temperate life which may be also miserable because it is in want of many things can be the just measure of property. There should be sufficient property to enable one to live moderately and generously. To live in moderation is to be moderate in desires for food and the enjoyment of the luxuries of pleasure, in the effort to attain which many exhaust their property; to live generously is to be in a position to offer hospitality to the deserving and to cultivate the virtue of charity.**

Taxation. Being asked by the Duchess of Brabant if the sovereign has power to impose taxes upon the subjects, Thomas answered in a letter, that princes and governments ought to be satisfied in general with the proceeds of the private domains in their possession and with the revenues fixed by usage, but in cases of extraordinary necessity, when the public good is at stake, they may add to the public charges upon their subjects, because they alone who are charged with the public welfare and have sole charge of the public affairs, have the right to impose taxes. Taxation is one of the rights of public authority, but it is limited by the twofold fact, that it must be in the interest of the public community and its amount must not exceed the value of the subject's property, because to destroy the community by taxation is to

---

* Ibid. II. 3.   ‡ Ibid. II. 11.
† Ibid. II. 5 and 6.   § Expos. Arist. Vol. XXI. p. 412.
‡ Ibid. II. 7.   ¶ Ibid. pp. 386, 389.
** Ibid. p. 418.

destroy the kingdom which the king is in duty bound to preserve.* We have here two doctrines of public finance, (a) taxation must be for the public good; and (b) it must not be arbitrary or extortionate, but of definite, limited amount.

The *sixth* question was, are you allowed to make demands upon your Christian subjects? Here you must consider that you are appointed by God, not to seek your own advantage, but to act for the welfare of the people. In a reproachful speech to certain princes, God said, "Her princes in her midst are like wolves ravening the prey, to get dishonest gain."† Revenues have been appointed for the princes of the land upon which they may live and refrain from robbing their subjects. Yet it often happens that princes do not have sufficient incomes for the protection of the state and other matters which naturally devolve upon princes. In such a case it is right that the subjects provide the means for the performance of what is necessary. In some countries according to an ancient custom, the rulers lay upon their subjects certain taxes, and when these are not excessive they can do so without sin, for according to the apostle no one serves at his own cost. Therefore the princes who serve in the interest of the community should have a living from the community (*de communibus*), and take charge of the business for the community, from certain revenues or when that is not sufficient out of what is raised from each individual (*colligatur*). The case is similar when something new arises, or when more must be spent for the common weal or to maintain the standing of a prince, and for that the incomes or usual revenues are not sufficient; also when an enemy makes an attack upon the country; then the princes can in a permissive way demand something above the usual allowance from their subjects. If they wish however an increase above what is usual out of mere greed or on account of expenses, then it is not allowable. The revenues of the princes are the same as their wages. They must be content with what they receive and not require more, unless for the reasons named above, and when it is for the good of all.

The *seventh* question was, when your officers have unlawfully (*absque juris ordine*) extorted from the subjects that which comes into your hands, or perhaps does not, what ought you to do? If it has come into your hands, you should restore it to the persons, if possible or spend it for some pious purpose, or for the common good, if you cannot remit it to the particular persons. If it has not come to your hands, then you must compel your officers (*compallas*) to make a similar restitution and also when the persons cannot be found from whom it was taken, for the officers should gain nothing by their wicked acts, they must give it up, and you must severely punish them for their injustice, so that in future they may abstain from anything of the kind. Thus the sub-

* Aquin. Oper. Romæ. Opuscular XXI. qu. 6, 7 in Vol. XVII; Parma Ed. Vol. XVI. p. 292-94.

† Ezek. XXII. 27.

jects are to be protected from arbitrary oppression at the hands of the king's officers.

4. *Usury and Reasonable Price.* *A. Usury.* With Dominican strictness he condemns the taking of interest, because he regards it as the price of the use of things consumed in the using. To exact first the price of the thing and then the price of the use after, is to sell the same thing twice over. In the old Testament Thomas explains, the Jews were not allowed to take interest from their fellow Jews but were permitted to take it from the Gentiles, yet they extorted that to which they had no right. *permissum fuit eis usuris et quibuscunque exactionibus extorquere ab injuste possidentibus quod eis juste debebatur.** This is an important point because it is the central point around which medieval economics circles. Aristotle had decided against taking interest because money is barren; the Church fathers had refused to accept the doctrine of usury because the command of Scripture enjoined abstinence from taking interest. Aquinas takes different ground in his opposition to it. It is interesting to read his argument as to whether the taking of interest for the loan of money is a sin. (a) That it is not a sin it is argued is proved in the fact that to take a price for something which one is not bound to do or give does not appear to be a sin. One is not under obligation in every case to lend his neighbor money, even if he has it. Therefore at times one may take a price for a loan. (b) Again, there is no distinction to be made between coined silver or gold and gold or silver vessels. One may take a price for the loan of coined metals as well as for the precious vessels; therefore the taking of this sort of interest is not sinful. In Exodus XXII. 25 it is said, "if thou lend money to my people that is poor by thee," that is, who are living with you, "thou shalt not be to him as an usurer, neither shalt thou lay upon him usury." Thomas decides, that to take interest for the loan of money is in itself unjust, because by it there is a sale of what is not there; therefore it is plain that an inequality exists which is contrary to justice.

He distinguishes between two things, (a) that which is consumed by use, *consumptibilis*, so that the article and its use cannot be separated. When wine is sold and afterwards its use then the same thing is sold twice, or what is not there is sold. A sin of unrighteousness would plainly be committed in this case. Similarly it is unjust when wine or wheat is loaned and a double return is required, either a return of the same or a price for the use which is called interest. (b) It is otherwise where the use is not the same as the thing itself, *inconsumptibilis*, as in the case of renting a house, where one receives a price for the use of the house and at the end of the time stipulated the loaned house is returned. Money according to Aristotle is chiefly for the completing of exchange and belongs to the class of things whose use implies their consumption, so far as it is given in exchange.† Therefore to take a

* Com. Sent. disq. 47. qu. 1.
† Ethics, V. 5; Politics, I. 3, 6.

price for the use of money which is called interest is not lawful, and since a man is bound to return what has been unjustly acquired he is under obligation to return money received as interest. On the other hand an appeal cannot be made to human law, for human laws allow often a sin to go unpunished on account of the condition of imperfect men, in which many advantages would have to be given up if it were decided to accompany all sins with punishment. Consequently human law has permitted interest, not because it is believed to be according to right, but that men may not be deprived of whatever advantages it has.

In opposition to the *first* of the above arguments in favor of interest, it is said, he who is not bound to lend can require a restitution of what he has given, but he cannot demand anything more. It must be a return according to the equality of right, if one is to receive the same as he lent. If he in addition requires something more for the usufruct of the article, which has no use apart from the consumption of its substance, he may require a price for that which is not in existence at all, and such a requirement is therefore unjust. Against the *second* argument Thomas says, the cases are not alike, because the chief use of gold and silver vessels is not their consumption. Therefore their use can be bought with the reservation of their property, just as the dominium of a house is retained when it is rented. There is also a secondary use that can be made of gold and silver vessels, when there is a lack of money they may be used in exchange; in such a case it is illegal to take anything for the use of them. Similarly there is secondary use of coin, when one makes over coined money for displaying in a shop, or a deposit for a pawn. It is lawful to sell such a use of money because the dominium is reserved.*

May there be an evasion of the prohibition to take interest? Is it lawful to ask a profit under any circumstances for a loan of money (*commoditas*)? It is answered, (a) every one is allowed to provide for his indemnification. Many suffer damage through lending money. Therefore it is lawful for any one besides collecting the loaned money to exact (*exigere*) something to recoup for damages sustained. (b) Everyone is bound in honor to do what is pleasing. In this case it seems lawful that the receiver should consider himself bound by what is according to natural right. (c) He removes himself from his money who lends it more than he who entrusts it (*committit*) to a merchant or trader (*artifici*). One can however receive gain from money which has been given to a trader, therefore one may also receive gain from loaned money. (d) For money that is deposited one may take a pawn, the use of which can be sold for a price; for example, when a field or house that is inhabited is given in pledge. Therefore one may receive gain from a loan of money. (e) It often happens that one in case of a loan (*ratione mutui*) sells his article dearer or buys it cheaper than he could otherwise, or on account of delay the

* 2a. 2ae qu 78.

price may increase, or by reason of haste the price may be lowered. In all these cases the reimbursement should be equal to the loss sustained by the loan of money. This seems lawful. It seems also lawful to demand a profit for loaned money, provided it do not amount to extortion. In opposition to all these reasons given in favor of taking interest there is this that is said of what a just man should require of another. "He that hath not given forth upon usury, neither hath taken any increase, hath executed true judgment between man and man."*

Thomas distinguishes between the reasons given in favor of usury and the contrary reasons. As all money is just whose price can be paid with money, he sins against righteousness who for a loan of money or something else receives what has been consumed in use and a price for it and is silent in regard to the matter of having received more. If however he receives something he did not demand, not by reason of his own silence or express agreement with the other, but as a free gift from the other, he does not sin, for before he lent the money he could have received something as a present, and he has not done wrong in lending the money and taking a present after the loan. A return of what cannot be purchased with money may be required for the loan (*exigere*), for example, good will and love for those to whom a loan is made and something of that kind.

Against the *first* argument above Thomas says, whoever makes a loan can, without sin in the agreement with the receiver of the loan, bargain for restitution for damages according to what is right (*debet*); for that is not selling the use of money, but avoiding injury; and it is possible the receiver of the loan avoids a still greater injury than the lender does and to the receiver offsets (*compensatio*) the profit of the one against the damage sustained by the other. But reparation for the damage in so far as it can be taken into account, and as the lender gets no gain from the money, is implied even though it is not brought into the agreement. To the *second*, he replies, according to strict justice the receiver of a loan of money or other perishable goods is not to be bound to more than a simple return of what is borrowed. To the *fifth* he replies, the lender conveys the property of money to the receiver, therefore the receiver has the risk and is bound to return the sum in its entirety but no more. He who however entrusts his money to a merchant or trader in the form of a trading society (*societas*) does not make the money over to him, but it remains with him in property, so that the merchant does the business at his own risk and also the risk of the trader and he can lawfully require a part of the gain. To the *sixth* he replies, when any one has pledged an article for a loan of money which can be valued in money, he must consider the use of the thing in the arrangement of the loan; if he does not, it is the same as taking interest for his loan, and it is like the customary usage among friends to give the use of an article without compensation as when a

* Ezek. XVIII. 8.

book is borrowed. Respecting the *seventh* he says, when one wants to sell his article dearer than the just price, waiting a time for the purchaser to pay, this is a clear case of desire to take interest, because such a waiting for payment is a deferred payment and falls under the class of loans. What therefore is the just price for the delay is equal to the price for a loan and is the same as taking interest. It is similar when the purchaser wants to buy an article cheaper than its just price because he pays the money before the article is delivered to him. It is also the same as taking interest, because it falls under the category of loans, since a price is taken for the article which is subtracted from its just price. If however one will remit part of the just price in order to get his money sooner he has not committed the sin of taking interest.*

Is it lawful to lend money on interest? No man may lead another into sin, but it is lawful to use the sins of others for good, because God uses the sins of all men for some good purpose. In the present case it is not lawful to mislead, by lending money for interest, but it is lawful in the case of one who is prepared to do it to take a loan in the interest of something good, for example, for the assistance of one's own or a stranger in time of need, or if one has fallen among thieves to relieve the goods he has which is the sin of the robbers when they take them, his aim being to secure that he be not killed himself.† One may under certain circumstances deposit money with a usurer. If any one entrusts his money to a usurer who has not already other money from which interest accrues, or entrusts it to him with the object of getting profit by usury he creates an opportunity for sinning and himself takes part in the sin. However should any one entrust his money to a usurer who already had carried on that trade with the impression that it is more safely kept by him (*tutius*) he does not sin, but uses a sinning man for good purposes.‡

Aquinas sees that no trade could be carried on without interest and hence he says that where there is risk (*periculum*) then a compensation may lawfully be taken in return for the hazard involved in the transaction. In the same way the money changers do not act illegally when they change the coins of other countries and charge a profit, because it is not the price of the use (*interesse*), it is not the usury on a loan, but the price of risk (*ratione periculi*), because one is not to take the hazard of changing money without payment for it. It is not the price paid for the purchase of money, but the price of risk in changing.§

The theory of Thomas is based upon the distinction according to the Roman law of *res fungibilis* and *res infungibilis*, the former being the subject-matter

* Ibid. pp. 280-281.
† Ibid. pp. 282-283.
‡ Ibid. p. 283.
§ De Usuris, c. 6.

of an obligation returnable in the same kind, quantity or measure, the latter requiring the return of the specific subject; also between *res consumptibilis* and *inconsumptibilis*, the former being consumed in use, the latter remaining in substance after the use is exhausted. In the case of *infungibiles* and *inconsumptibiles* the use is different from the thing itself whereas in the *fungibilis* and *consumptibiles* the use and the thing are indistinguishable. Money is used for exchange purposes and is *consumptibilis et fungibilis*; therefore in lending money when the money is returned all is returned that belongs to the lender, the price for the use being unlawful and hence called, *usura*, *pretium usus*.

II. *Justum pretium. Reasonable price.* There was no market competition to determine the price of goods. The government deemed it in the interest of all parties to prevent such competition in the buying and selling of commodities; the theologians supported this idea of the times, on the ground that such variations in price from the reasonable or natural value were fraudulent and to be prevented. The result was that by state-ordinance regulations were ordained fixing the reasonable price of marketable goods, so that the markets became a department of national administration.

In Aquinas we find the best and fullest statement of the theory of reasonable price prevalent in the middle ages; for this reason we give a full account of his theory. *Question I.* May any one lawfully sell a thing for a greater price than he paid for it? Is it permissible to sell anything for more than its value? He gives the reasons alleged for the supposed permission. (a) It is in harmony with the civil law upon which justice is based. (b) Everyone is anxious to purchase cheap and to sell dear. (c) If any one receives a gift from a friend and feels bound to make a return for it, what is given in return must be measured by the benefit conferred. Now the benefit may be of more value than the substance of the gift. If it is permissable to do this in the case of friendship, it is also allowable in case of a sale. Against this permissibility he alleges, that the gospel commands, "whatsoever ye would that men do to you do ye likewise unto them." No one wishes to pay more for a thing than its worth. To buy or sell for more than the worth is not allowable, because if it were by fraud it would be sinful. Buying and selling is carried on for the benefit of the community, that is, of the contracting parties; that which is done for the benefit of the community, of contracting parties, must not be done more for the oppression of one than of another, and there must therefore be an equality in the matter of business between them. Commerce can only be of equal advantage to both if each one gets his share of the equal value. The thing will be rated according to a given price, and when the price is greater than the value of the article or the article of more value than the price the equality of justice is annulled. Therefore it is unjust and unlawful to sell dearer or buy cheaper than the worth of a thing. There are peculiar circumstances however to be considered; for example, when buying and selling is profitable to one and disadvantageous to another, as when some one desires a thing very much and another is a loser by parting with it. In this case the just price will be, not what the thing sold appears to be valued for, but the value *plus* the loss which the seller sustains by the sale. In this case compensation for damage may be demanded. Also a thing may be sold dearer than its worth, as well as for less than its worth to the owner. If however one is satisfied with the thing he has received and on the other hand the seller has suffered no wrong, when he parts with it he must not oversell (*supervendere*), because the advantage which comes to the other is not from what is bought, but proceeds from the position of the buyer. No one may however sell what does not belong to him although he can sell to him the damage he sustains.

He refutes the three arguments in favor of permitting to sell for more than the just value. (a) Just price is a matter of conscientious duty, not a legal matter. Human law was given to the people among whom were many who had departed from virtue. It was not given merely to the virtuous. Therefore human law has not forbidden everything that is contrary to virtue; it is enough if it forbid what disturbs the common social life of men and tends to break up society. Other things have been permitted (*habent quasi licita*), not because they were reasonable, but because they were not punishable. So then if the matter does not lead to punishment, the case is allowed where the seller without deceit overbuys, or the buyer under buys (buys too cheaply) the excess will then be too great, because then the human law presses for a restitution; for example, when anyone is cheated to the amount of half the price. The divine law does not let those go unpunished who act contrary to virtue. Therefore it would be according to the divine law, not to permit in buying and selling, a failure in the observance of the equality of justice, and this failure has done much to establish what is detrimental in cases where the damage is considerable (*notabile*). (b) The fact that a vice is common to all does not make it just, because the masses are generally vicious. (c) The justice demanded in commerce is different from the virtue of friendship. In the case of commerce there is demanded equality in the things themselves, in friendship it is equality in the quality of the virtue or relationship.

While a just price is the true value, it is not destroyed by a slight variation, because just value depends upon an estimate, so that a slight addition or subtraction does not abolish the equality of justice. A just price is *quantitatis valoris rei*, the quantity of the value of a thing. This may be determined according to common usage (*æstimatio communis*), or more properly by legal regulations fixing the *legitimum pretium*. Therefore the *justum pretium* comes to mean the *legitimum pretium*, which price the government is to fix; but after all there is no unchangeable standard, for the just price is to be reckoned according to the true value of the thing in so far as it is affected, whether lowered or raised in value, by *copia aut inopia*, both of goods and of money; money or labor spent in importing and transporting, damages for loss and compensation for risk and variations that are of a local character (*ratio loci*). These are the circumstances which are to be considered in fixing the price. All that is arbitrary is the removal of competition and the placing of the power to fix the value in the hands of the government.

Question 2. Does a defect in the article sold invalidate the bargain of sale? There are three reasons that lead to infer that it does not. (a) If the article satisfies what a man wants with it, it is not unfair to sell it although it is not the proper substance; for example, if the gold of alchemy is as good as the pure gold for the purpose for which it is wanted, there is nothing wrong in selling it. (b) The measure of quantity in things differs from place to place, therefore an inadequate measure in one place may be adequate in another. (c) It requires much knowledge to discriminate variations in quality and those who can judge quality are rare. In answer to these Thomas says, it is a rule that deviation from justice or positive injury to anyone is sinful. Therefore to sell one thing for another, if it is not the proper substance, quality or quantity is unlawful, because it is fraud, and he who thus defrauds is bound to restitution. One does not dare to sell a halting horse for a swift one, a defective house for a perfect one, poisoned food for good food. If these and similar defects which bring damage or danger to the buyer are concealed and the seller is not discovered, then the sale is unlawful and fraudulent and the seller bound to make restitution. He refutes the arguments used in support of its lawfulness. (a) Gold is of value not only for the uses to which it is put, but for its purity and also for medicinal uses. (b) If the measures are variable the government ought to fix the standard of the weights and measures. (c) In reference to the quality the buyer and seller can agree as to its use in the particular case.

Question 3. Is the seller bound to declare the fault in the article before he sells it? In general he decides that the seller is bound to declare all defects, but in particular the seller may keep silent in order to avoid damage to himself, provided his silence does not result in positive loss to the buyer. If the defect is apparent, as when the horse is one-eyed or the article does not suit the seller but might suit some one else, and he deducts from the price what ought to be added to it (*oportet*), on account of defects, he is not obliged to make public the defects of the article, because probably the buyer would desire a still greater deduction in price beyond what there should be. Thus the buyer can be indemnified for the damage or defect which was concealed (*sub modtati sane*). Often the price of an article is less than it would be were it defective in any respect. For example, a seller brings grain to a place where there is a lack of it and he knows at the same time that many others are coming with grain to the same place. If this were known to the buyers they would give a lower price for the grain. The seller however says nothing about it. This case is different from that of the concealment of defects, for in this case it is to be expected that by and by through the arrival of oth-

or merchants the grain will be cheaper which fact is at present unknown to the buyers. Therefore when the seller sells his article at the current price, he does not act contrary to justice if he does not give information respecting what will or may happen later. Should he however give the information of approaching fall in price by reason of a plentiful supply of grain, he would prove himself to be a man of unusual virtue. But he is not under any obligation to do it.

Question 4. Is it right and lawful in trade to buy cheap and sell dear? He gives three arguments of those who oppose it. (a) Chrysostom says, to buy an article and sell it without changing it in any way at an increased price is unlawful; it is lawful however to do so after altering it. To buy and sell simply for gain is evil. (b) He who buys cheap and sells dear, either sells it above its value or buys it below its value, both of which are unlawful. (c) As Jerome says, one should avoid a clergyman who out of poverty becomes rich; so one ought to be avoided as something pestilent who becomes rich among the laity. It is lawful Aquinas admits to engage in trade but only to provide the necessaries of life. It belongs to traders to make an exchange of possessions. According to Aristotle,* there is a double exchange of this kind. One is natural and necessary, it is the exchange of one thing for another, or of articles for money to secure the requirements of life. This exchange does not pertain exclusively to traders, but rather to stewards and officers of state who have to provide the necessaries of life in the household or state. The other kind of exchange is that of money for money or of articles for money, not on account of the requirements of life, but for the sake of gain. This kind of trade pertains to the traders. The first kind of exchange is praiseworthy, because it provides the necessities of life; the second is justly censureable because it serves to gratify the desire for gain which is never satisfied. There is therefore attached to this kind of trade a certain stigma, because it does not lead to an honorable and necessary end. Yet when the gain which is the aim of the act has nothing in it contrary to honor, or what is necessary, there is nothing in the transaction blameworthy or contrary to virtue. Thus when the gain tends towards an honorable and necessary end, the trade may be allowed, as when one by means of trade acquires a moderate gain and uses it for the support of his family, of the poor; or when some one undertakes to trade on account of its advantage to the community, that by means of it there may be no lack of necessaries in the nation; in this case gain is not really his aim but wages for his work. He answers the objections. (a) Lust for gain is manifest when one sells an article dearer without alteration in it; for if he had improved the article and then sold it dearer, it would only be the price of his work which it is lawful to strive after. Although it is not the very highest aim, yet it is an honorable and necessary one. The rise

* Pol. 1, 5, 6.

in price in such a case is the reward of labor. (b) Yet not everyone who sells an article dearer than he bought it trades, but only those who buy with the intention of selling dearer. If anyone buys an article, not to sell it, but to keep it, and then for some cause sells it, it is not trade, even if it be sold dearer. One can do this lawfully, either because he has improved it or because the price of the article had risen from a change of time or place, or on account of risk, or because the article has been transported from one place to another. (c) It is not sinful because the clergy cannot do it, but rather it is due to a necessity of trade. The legality of trade it would seem from Thomas depends upon two things, (a) its necessity, and (b) the intention of the trader, not upon the trade itself.

Question 3. Is it lawful to require a higher price when one is not paid the price in money at the time, but postpones the payment till a future time? Thomas regards such a transaction as equivalent to a loan (*mutuum*) and to raise the price is to require money *quasi pretium mutui* and therefore is sinful. Similarly if a buyer pays less than the *justum pretium*, by paying in advance, it is equivalent to paying *interesse* and unlawful. Thus the doctrines of credit and discount are placed in the same category as usury and reasonable price in the economics of Aquinas.*

It is interesting to note the humanitarian idea which governs the thoughts of Thomas in regard to trade, reasonable price and interest. In buying and selling, in trade and business, the aim should not be to gain, but to supply human needs, and the motive of the transaction ought to be the fulfilment of a duty that is due to humanity. He could not carry out logically this idea, and hence he gave it up to admit contrary customs of trade. In fact the idea of humanity was lost in his whole system which reduced itself to a national economy under the supervision and control of the government. Yet there was an elasticity depending upon the will of the governors of the state according to the time, place, and circumstances which in a large measure determined the view of price and interest. The government would be or appoint a standing commission in the bureau of markets for the fixing of the just and reasonable price.

* 2a 2ae. qu. 77. 1-5.

CHAPTER XI.

CONCLUSION.

1. *View of the anonymous continuator of Thomas.* Without doubt the closing part of the second book and the whole of the third and fourth books of the *De Regimine Principum* were written not by Thomas Aquinas, but by a Dominican follower of his. Apart from the reference to a period and events of that period subsequent to the death of Thomas, the spirit of the writing and the principles developed although scholastic are distinctly an advance upon the views of Aquinas as hitherto set forth. Instead of presenting the ideas and principles of social politics on the foundation of reason as Thomas had done, vindicating political rationalism, the continuator presents them as matters of fact, true because they have always existed. The power is no longer regarded as a natural quality of man, it is a divine, direct institution, and it is elaborated upon the most rigorous view of Divine Right. Tradition as manifested in history is his great judge upon all questions and matters of fact. From the very beginning of history God chose a special race of men to govern the world, as the prototype of the universal kingdom of Jesus Christ in the world. This power first given to the chosen race has often changed hands in the past history of the world, nation succeeding nation in its possession and exercise. Nimrod was the first world-ruler; succeeding him were the Assyrians, after them were the Medes, then the Persians, then the Macedonians, and last of all the Romans, from whom it passed to the Sovereign Universal Pontiff. Jesus Christ instituted St. Peter his Vicar and communicated all his power, temporal and spiritual, to him and his successors, and that the temporal power received its actual existence and form from Peter and his successors, as the body from the soul. According to this theory the temporal power originates directly from the spiritual power, the sacerdotal power being the supreme one. There is in man two natures, two ends in life, two orders of virtue, two grades of happiness,—to these two parts of nature, life, and end correspond the two powers and of necessity the spiritual is the superior. This superiority is not simply moral and religious, it is political also because all power rests in the representative of Jesus Christ, the Sole King and Priest of the world.* *Temporalis jurisdictio principum per spiritualem Petri et successorum ejus.* Jurisdiction is the test of superiority as Thomas himself

---

* De Reg. Prin. III, 10, 12-16.

says, *per jurisdictionem constituitur aliquis in gradu superioritatis.*" The summit of the hierarchy is in the pope, and just as matter ought to obey spirit, the body the soul, so the terrestrial powers must be subject to the divine power, *ex summo pontifice est plenitudo gratiarum ut computat sibi quod de primo Principe Domino dicimus, quia de plenitudine ejus nos omnes accepimus.*†

Added to the authority of reason there are the Biblical arguments used by Gregory VII, drawn from Scripture which establish, it is alleged, the supremacy of the sacerdotal power and raise it as a divine institution above the human institution of kingship. In kingly power the grant is only made for life, in the case of the spiritual a perpetual grant has been given to Peter and his successors.‡ The sacerdotal supremacy is a fact and it is consecrated as well as proved by history. Here are introduced the visionary pretensions of the canonists of the middle ages which gathered around the pretended donation of Constantine, the pretended cession of the Western Empire to Pope Sylvester, the translation of the empire from the East to the West, from the Greeks to the Germans by Adrian, accomplished under the authority of the Papacy, the deposition of emperors by papal power, chiefly that of Childeric III. by Zechariah and the crowning of Pepin, the elevation to the empire of Otho IV. by Innocent III. and of Frederick by Honorius. The early pagan Emperors were in revolt against the kingdom of God and for a time persistently persecuted it; but reparation was made when Constantine placed himself in subjection to Pope Sylvester. All the Emperors after Constantine with the exception of the Apostate Julian were in submission to the spiritual power, until Charlemagne was advanced to the Emperorship by the authority of the Pope. When the Greek Emperors became too feeble to defend the Church against the barbarians then it became necessary to seek new lieutenants. If the papal power could institute and remove the representatives of the temporal power then the spiritual has absorbed the temporal within itself, becoming the embodiment of that single sovereignty which Jesus Christ has established upon earth, which alone has supreme power of judgment over monarchs and subjects alike. History therefore establishes that the pontifical power is above all others and that the Pontiff is in the temporal order as he is in the spiritual *"le roi des rois."*§ As there is but one supreme power so there is in human society and human life but one great end, eternal salvation and virtue.

In such a theocracy politics becomes entirely subordinated to the Church-power. Monarchy is no longer regarded as the government of the single wise man in political virtue, it is the only lawful government having the divine sanction. Subjects are to be in obedience to the kings who are unlimited

---

* Sent. dis. 18. qu. 2; 19. qu. 1.
† De Reg. Prin. III. 10.
‡ Ibid. III. 10, 16.
§ Franck, Pub. et Ref. Moyen Age, p. 48.

in power and prerogative, save by the pontiff. Servitude marks off the two classes of men, those fitted to command and those competent only to obey, slavery marking the degradation of sinful men who have by fall been deprived of freedom.² Thus reason, scripture and history unite in giving their unanimous testimony on behalf of the papal supremacy over all temporal as well as spiritual power. At that time it would seem as if history did confirm this opinion. The Empire may be said to have expired with Frederick II, who was declared deposed by Innocent III.

At the time when Thomas wrote his book the title of King of the Romans and Imperator was claimed by two candidates and it was not till the beginning of the 14th. century that a new Emperor was crowned. Consequently before the opening of the 14th. century it seemed as if the spiritual power had conquered and merged in itself the temporal authority, as a Universal Emperorship, over and above the petty national states of the civilized world, as the arbiter of the peace and the basis of unity in the states of Christendom. As Poole suggests, this idea of a spiritual imperialism indicates that the followers of Aquinas had learned what civilians did not know, "that the world had outgrown the imperial conception." A revolution was at hand in the political relations of the European states, the results of which were to be felt during the next five hundred years in preparation for the downfall of the spiritual imperialism, that upon the ruins of pagan and spiritual empire there might be reared up the statehood of nationality, only vaguely dreamed of as a vision in the dark night of ages in the mind of Aquinas. A people that values its free institutions will not forget that the saint and scholar of the 13th. century is the bridge between the old and the new, and that he saw the light although he could scarce distinguish it amid the darkness which surrounded decaying institutions, and that in his writings there are found germs of that newer condition of things which he could not see clearly, because bound by the chains of the old order. We reverence the genius of that political philosopher who ranks next to Aristotle, if not above him.

2. *Close.* Thomas properly belongs to the philosophical school of political philosophers. His political theory pure and simple, divested of all its intricacies, is based upon the law of nature which presents the social condition of men and places organized society under the natural hierarchy of government to perfect its being. The consequence is that experience, tradition and history play only a small part in the process of upbuilding, and that the principal weight is given to authorities as expressing the universal sentiments of man, conformed to nature and reason. Yet the actual events of the day and the conflicting issues of the time color the logical and metaphysical conceptions of his writings. The *De Regimine Principum* is a standing witness to the fact that the political questions of the day are treated with fairness, and that the customs and institutions of the time are thoroughly

² Ibid. III. 17 sq.

understood by him. He does not, it is true, concern himself with everything that goes on around, otherwise his book would have been full of stirring reminiscences and interesting details. The missing links and the lacunae in the work of Thomas are many; he takes no notice of representation, except in stating that the supreme power represents the people, gives no account of the assemblies of the people, takes no notice of that idea of imperialism which was beginning to gather together its forces in his own day for the struggle with the spiritual power,—all this is explained by the fact that science to Thomas is contemplative and profoundly speculative. This is all the more natural, when we consider that he combined in himself the conceptions of the great Master of antiquity, the sentiments of Christianity gathered from the sacred writings, and also in a lesser degree the teachings of the canon and civil systems of law. The sacred writings and the doctrines of Aristotle hold a chief place, but he is not ignorant of the civil law, although it has been asserted by some writers that he never shows any knowledge of it. It was in imitation of the glossators that the *Summa* was first introduced and even through canon law he could not be ignorant of the Roman Jurisprudence. His conceptions of right, justice and institutions are Aristotelian, showing a marked veneration for antiquity and ancient ideas, not surpassed in the renascence of classic literature. It was the age of revival and that revival gave to the political ideas of the time an antique cast repeated in all the writers of medieval ages. The political science of Aegidius Romanus the publicist of French monarchy, of Bartolus the civil jurist, and of the Spanish Jurists—all present the same ideas of antiquity which had first received expression in occidental language in Aquinas.

One result of this was the freedom which always attached to political ideas inherent as it was in the politics of the Greek republics; such doctrines as the sovereignty of the people, the illegality of tyranny and the right of removing a tyrant kept alive the spirit of independence that was to struggle with the absolute monarchies of later centuries. And there was not only the old; the equality and fraternity which entered into the conception of justice, as a Christian idea, forms in Thomas the connecting link with the newer civilization of social order such as the 17th. century developed. He commends the new order of civilization in preference to the old because it rules by love, not by coercion, but this new law which he describes as, *lex nova is supereterem odderc, quu debuit circa exteriora agenda.**

Thomas falls short here in the judgment he has formed. The law of salvation, as he conceives it, makes no change in temporal things, save in introducing them entire into the supernatural, spiritual order. He did not conceive of a Christian politics or a Christian state, on parallel lines with a Christian theology and a Christian Church, each equally independent. His politics becomes a department of theology, and his state a part of the Church.

* 1a 2ae qu. 108 2

Had he adopted the idea of a Christian state, purified as the Church from ancient errors, of a Christian polities elevated above partisanship, tyranny and bigotry, and made socially as well as morally just, without transferring these *in toto* to the sphere of religion and the Church, his view would have been complete. The keynote of his error is sounded in the words quoted above. Despite his errors and mistakes, we honor his genius and revere his memory as the Aristotle of the new dispensation, occupying as he does a deservedly high place in the temple of political fame.*

* Franck, Moyen age, pp. 59-60; M. Jourdain, La Philos. de St. Th. d'Aquin, 2 Vols. Paris, 1858; Riezler, Die Literarischen Widersacher der Papste, pp. 37-39; Poole, Illustr. of Hist. of Mediæval Thought, pp. 240 sq.

PART III.

POLITICAL THEORY OF THE LATER SCHOOLMEN.

CHAPTER I.

ÆGIDIUS ROMANUS AND TRIUMFO (TRIUMPHUS).

1. The Middle Ages have been called the age of the Christian Theocracy. It was not a pure Theocracy in the same sense in which the antique system of Egypt or the modern system of the Jesuits in Paraguay may be characterized as pure theocracy, for the temporal power was always in a measure self-existent and self-controlling, however much subjected to the spiritual power. Yet, although not distributed nor guided by the spiritual power the temporal power was in a great measure the instrument and tool of the Church. But in the sense in which religious power is brought in, more or less, in the direction of the affairs of the temporal state, it is true of these ages, that theocracy did prevail. Catholic Europe in these ages may be viewed as one immense theocracy, for if a certain independence was enjoyed by the two powers, in ultimate resort that hierarchy whose head possessed the power of benediction, excommunication, and dispensation, whose members ranked as a spiritual aristocracy in the temporal state, and whose judicial power was felt in the Inquisition as well as in temporal affairs of a testamentary and marital character, could not but claim a certain precedence

This question divided the political writers following Aquinas into two schools, the advocates and the opponents of the theocracy. It is on this point alone that the great philosophers of the later middle ages have an independent opinion. It was a problem unknown to the ancient world. The question therefore of supreme interest, outside of what we have seen to be the universal polities of the school as set forth in Aquinas, is, has the papacy supreme temporal power as well as spiritual, or what power has it? The Church and its defenders have entered the discussion, as they allege, by supernatural right, and they have failed to solve the problem because they treated it as a problem of theology, a matter for the consideration of Churchmen, rather than a question of social humanity.

It is in this age in the vehemence of the spiritual supremacy theory and in the opposition that sprung up from the very heart of the Church itself that we date the beginning of the freedom of politics from theology, little by little accomplished as the people and the popular will come upon the scene in the struggle hitherto confined to the pope and the Emperor. It is when the people begin to be regarded as a third party that the new era opens. There arise the questions of liberty, equality, freedom of thought, and in the discussion of these the foundations of political independence are laid upon natural law, preparing the way for the establishment of the modern state upon the citizenship of man, not upon the dictatorship either of pope or emperor.

This change was accomplished by three potent factors. (a) The assertion of national consciousness. In the struggle between the empire and the Church two nationalities were developed both of which manifested an independent attitude towards the papal claims. These were England and France which became powerful monarchies. Neither of the two kingdoms were closely allied to Rome, and in both the clergy under the royal direction manifested an independent spirit, while the kings and the people claimed the rights and liberties of nationality. (b) Imperialism had become little more than a dream. At the best the imperial dominion was purely accidental. At this time *Imperatorship* of Rome is simply a title and at most a dignity, without even the semblance of power. Its holder is the sovereign of a principality and it is because of precedent national sovereignty that he is elected to the emperorship. In the matter of legislative, executive or judicial power he is really *non est*. (c) In the decline of the Empire the Church is gradually asserting her supreme prerogatives, not as a Church but as a state, finally to rank as one state among many states. The papacy had reached its zenith in Innocent III. In the struggle of Philip the Fair with Boniface VIII., French nationality comes to the front and combats an imperial papacy as well as an imperial empire, bequeathing to the Kingdoms of Europe as a result of that struggle, the idea of independent nationhood. The papacy had attempted to bolster itself up by false spiritual pretensions, false writings and by diplomatic intrigue.

This three-fold foundation of papal claims became the subject of an attack by some of the clergy themselves, and also by the defenders of universal temporal empire. Hence we have in these succeeding centuries the preparation for the reformation, in the discovery by members the Church as well as by others, of the untenable character of the church's position in the light of reason, history and the nationality of the kingdoms of Europe. Wyclif in England, Savonarola in Florence, Rienzi in Rome, Huss in Bohemia, are the representatives of that spirit, called by the Church heresy, but stirred up by the church herself at the first through the indefensible claims and pretentions of Boniface VIII. and John XXII. In the struggle carried on by these two Popes we have political philosophy represented in Aegidius Romanus and Augustinus Triumphus. In later times Ockham, Marsilius and the poet Dante represent the freer spirit that inscribes itself upon the political philosophy, the schoolmen, as they oppose the power that claims to give and withhold temporal dominion at its pleasure.*

2. *Aegidius Romanus, or Colonna, or Gilles of Rome, 1250-1316.* He was a member of the order of St. Augustine, and attended to the teaching of philosophy and theology as a follower of Aquinas with such distinction in the University of Paris that he received the appellation of most profound Doctor. He attracted the attention of the King of France, Philip III., who made him tutor to the young heir, after Philip the Fair. He wrote his chief political thesis in imitation of his master Thomas, entitled *D Regimine Principum*, as a book of instruction to his royal pupil. In 1285 Philip the Fair succeeded to the French monarchy. Aegidius became Archbishop of Bourges, and died in 1316, leaving on the monument to his memory the noble inscription, *lux in lucem reducens dubia*, light bringing to light dark things.† His work is perfect in form and its arrangement is scientific.

1. *Ethical basis of political theory.* In philosophy Aegidius laid the foundation for his political theory. There is a human science or philosophy quite distinct from and independent of divine revelation, which has as its primary source reason. Authority is not the primary, but only a subordinate basis of philosophy, and only a secondary source in so far as it conforms to reason. *Non credimus philosophos nisi quatenus rationabiliter locuti sunt.*‡ He sets such a high value upon reason that even apart from revelation it is possible to secure salvation from condemnation through natural law, *potuit salvari in lege naturae*. Reason is the basis of human freedom.§

His *De Reg. Princ.* is a general treatise on natural law as applied to the relations of the individual, the family, the state, in which he developes a three-fold classification of government according to these three societies and kingdoms. The first book treats of monastics or ethics in their application to the conduct of princes, consisting of a subtle blending of Aristotelian ethics and christian principles. In the second book he treats of the economics of the family, in relation to property and slavery, master and servant, male and female, parents and children. In the third book politics is treated of, in which he sets forth the fundamental conceptions of society, government and obedience, in presenting the relations of the government and the state, citizens,

---

* Poole, pp. 241 sq.; Janet, Vol. I. pp. 475-485.
† Bulaei Hist. III. p. 671; Sammarthan in Gall. Christ. I. p. 179.
‡ Mag. Sent. I. II. qu. 1. 2.
§ Ibid. qu. 1. 2.

and rulers, governors among themselves, and lastly the relations of war and peace within the state and in the state's public relations with other states. In this book we have the outline of a complete treatise upon the laws of nature and of nations, professedly based upon human reason independent of theology, but like all the works of the 13th century based largely, despite the author's profession to the contrary, upon authority. Still it is an honest attempt to give an independent account of a new science.

In the first book the author views individual morality as an indivisible totality, consisting of goodness and virtue. He applauds Aristotle for placing contemplation above activity, and consequently virtue above pleasure. According to him activity is feeble and even to be avoided as perilous unless it is actuated by goodness and charity. The ancient philosophers do not set up charity, because felicity is said to consist in acting prudently in as far as the act is impelled by love. It is not enough for princes and kings to seek goodness in pleasures, riches, honors, not even in civil power which sees the subjects in obedience to his authority; not even in the right exercise of power is happiness placed because this leads to fortitude not to justice, whereas justice is greater than fortitude; the soul of a ruler ought to seek the highest good in the contemplation of truth and in the acts of prudence in the political life, vivified by the love of God, for the king is a minister of God and a director of the multitude, God himself being universal good. The more elevated a man is in rank the nearer he comes to God, and the more he should seek the rational, common good of those placed under him between whom and God he himself stands. The foundation of the first book is that no one can govern others unless he can first govern himself.*

There are three powers of the soul, the natural, the sensitive, and the appetitive. The first two are in common with the brutes and have no moral value; in the last there are intellectual and moral virtues and some which partake of both of these characteristics, the moral and intellectual. Prudence is the virtue, according to him, which is both intellectual and moral, although the intellectual element prevails; justice is the moral virtue. Justice moderates the passions, *moderat ipsas res et ipsas operationes exteriores fecit enim quod cuilibet tribuatur quod decet*. Prudence tends to the good of reason, rectifies reason and is found in the perfection of reason.† Prudence is the directive virtue. Without it kings cannot rule according to truth, and without it kings readily degenerate to tyranny.‡ Justice is legal and equal; in the former case it is general, and is the fulfilment of legal principles, in the latter case it is special and renders to each one what is equal. Legal justice avoids vice and seeks good; equal justice promotes special good for individuals, giving to each what is due. The leader of the state is the dis-

* De Reg. Princ. Bk. 1. Pt.i. c. 1–12; 14–1.
† Ibid. I. ii. 2 & 3.
‡ Ibid c. 6 & 7.

tributor of justice to the individuals.* Justice is necessary to the existence of a kingdom. Without legal justice there can be no order among citizens, without special justice which is commutative and distributive there can be no kingdom, because commutative justice demands that the citizens be like members of the body, and distributive justice gives to the individuals the dignities and honors of state.† In the rest of the book he treats of other virtues and qualities as they exist in kings and citizens, showing the identity of goodness with the higer degree of moral perfection, in the avoidance of ignoble passions and in the cultivation of good manners, alike in young and old, princes and subjects.‡

II. *Economic basis of political Theory*. When the family and the state are compared we find that the household is the most elementary form of association. (1) The household community is the first. Individuals are united in three forms of societies, according to Economics, conjugal society in which we find the relation of male and female; paternal society in which the relations of parents and children are established; and lastly, domestic society in which there is the relation of master and slave, proprietor and goods; but the names of husband, father and master indicate one person who is *imperans*. Man is naturally a social animal, *societas* being natural to him, (a) for the supply of good, (b) for the provision of clothing, (c) for the defence against enemies, and (d) for speech and discipline. He who lives not a social life is either a beast or a God. The household is necessary as leading to the *civitas* and ultimately to the *Kingdom regnum*. The household is not sufficient in itself and hence the village is constituted of many households, the multiplication of villages leads to *civitas* and *regnum*, *communitas* being the basis of all these societies. One community leads to another as the imperfect to the perfect, as a lower end to a higher, therefore house, village, city-state, is the natural order, and all are needed to perfection.§

The domestic community is the basis for the supply of daily needs.‖ Conjugal society is natural to man not only because human nature demands it for its continuation, but also because the species is divided into male and female, the one being fitted for active work outside and the other for housework.¶ Marriage is indissoluble in the interest of the spouses, because apart from such a relation fidelity is impossible; and in the interests of the offspring for their upbringing.** Marriage ought to be monogamous, because neither husband nor wife is respected under polygamy, and the children are not well raised. The birds give to man an example of solicitude for the welfare of offspring. Kings ought more particularly to respect marriage.†† So also ought wives to be content with one man, and marriage ought not to be

* Ibid. c. 10.   ‡ II. i. 1-3.
* Ibid. c. 11.   ‖ Ibid. c. 5 and 6.
§ Ibid. I. iii and iiii   ¶ Ibid. c. 7.
** Ibid. c. 8.   ** Ibid. c. 9.

of near kin because marriage destroys the respect existing between certain degrees and also because a man ought to increase his circle of friendship instead of limiting it by marrying a relative.* This is the first defence of monogamy on the ground of human nature and human reason. In the choice of a wife, chiefly in case of a king, the husband ought to see that she is of noble race, as well as a splendid physique, and having many friendly alliances as a plurality of riches.† Aegidius's sentiments of women are those of a man devoted to the monkish life of a cloister.‡ It is the men who are to rule the house. They are not to take counsel with their wives unless in cases when prompt action is needed. The husband is not to confide in her secrets.§ Yet, he is to treat her as a companion, *uxorem non se habere ad vicinio quasi servam sed quasi sociam.*∥

2. The position of parents and children determines their respective duties. In giving life to another a parent undertakes to provide for its necessities, to educate it and protect it from danger, till it is able to look after itself. This obligation gives him as parent power to command obedience. Kings are specially anxious to govern their children for their intelligence and goodness and for the good of the kingdom, because a kingdom is good only when those in it are good.¶ Paternal rule originates in love such as induces children to obey.1 This rule of love is specially concerned in the instruction and discipline of the young.

The system of education Aegidius recommends is that found in the Universities of his own age, the *trivium* and *quadrivium*. In addition to these which are ancient studies he says it is necessary to teach them theology, a knowledge of God and angels, ethics, economics, and politics so as to qualify them for their places in the household, and kingdom.2 He divides the educational career into three epochs, from nativity up to the seventh year, from the seventh year to the fourteenth year, and over fourteen years to adult age. During the first period the physical nature alone should be attended to, the supply of physical wants by good food and moderate exercise; also the learning of some fables to develop memory and imagination, and the elements of music; but theoretical study should be entirely avoided. During the second epoch, the body, the moral nature and the intellect should be attended to, for the physical system a variety of exercise is required and good manners and proper dress; for the moral nature the will should be exercised in the government of the passions; for the intellect there should be education in language. During the third epoch care should be taken in the cultivation of good dispositions, the development of the faculties and the subjection of the

* Ibid. c. 10, 11.
† Ibid. c. 12 and 13.
‡ Ibid. c. 18.
§ Ibid. c. 23.

‖ Ibid. c. 20.
¶ II. ii. 1 and 2.
1 Ibid. c. 3, 4.
2 Ibid. c. 5 and 8.

passions by the exercise of courageous efforts.* Female children are also to be trained particularly in lawful and honest employments, *nolunt otiose vivere s*[...] *s*[...] *exerceburi circa opera aliqua licita et honesta*. These honest employments are, weaving, sewing, spinning.† In the case of females of high rank they may study literature but they must learn that in female life silence is the art of perfection.‡

3. The position of property and slaves under master and owner. Man and woman live together in one house. Man is the master; but the wife is his comrade because she is raised from degradation. But it is necessary that they have servants and possessions in order to support the house. Property is an indispensable element of the family. He who would be the head of a house must learn to govern, having knowledge of what is sufficient for life and of the arts of building, making money and keeping possessions as well as knowledge of controlling slaves and servants.§ A man as well as a king ought not to have a lust for riches or property. Economic money is *laudabilis*, the other kinds are *vituperabilis*, and are described as *campsaria, usura, obolostatica*.‖ Government is duplex. So is the art of governing a house. Accordingly property in the family such as possessions, houses, money is individual; these are called inanimate property; slaves and servants are animate property; slaves and servants are animate property and to be governed as such.*

Man was made in the similitude of God, and as such he is the master of the universe and has a lawful power over inferior creatures. Sin has lessened this power, but it still belongs to man. That which is best and most perfect ought to rule over the lesser and less perfect or imperfect. So man rules over plants and animals by natural right. Man's individual right of property is necessary, (a) to promote man's individual activity, (b) to prevent contests, and (c) to prevent society falling into civil anarchy.** Property thus depends upon utility.

Slavery is also natural to some. Man has destroyed the light that was in him, or departed from the original order appointed by God in human nature. Therefore one race of men is destined to liberty another to slavery, and this is for the good of the slave as well as of the master.†† In addition to natural slavery there is a just legal slavery which is founded upon the right of war and binds the conquered *a secundo* to be slaves of the conquerors when their lives are preserved. The Roman jural idea of slavery is here strongly supported and is an indication of the new element of civil law brought into Scholasticism. It is just because it incites to courage and is needful in the

---

* Ibid. c. 15-17. † Ibid. c. s 10.
‡ Ibid. c. 20. § Ibid. c. 2.
‖ Ibid. c. 21. ** Ibid. c. 5-7.
†† II. iii. 1 ** Ibid. c. 13.

defense of a country.* There are also servants who are not slaves, some condemned to service by law, because of their conduct, others from choice the best and most virtuous class of dependents.†

3. III. *Political Theory of Aegidius*. The rest of the book treats of the political conditions of the state and kingdom, *civitas et regum*. Aegidius adds the *regum* to the three forms of Aristotle. In his time the French Kingdom was a reality; its nationality was asserted in the consolidation of the entire community for defence under a single prince. Nationality had amalgamated the lesser feudal Barons with their vassals under a single great lord or ruler. There is in all by nature an impulse to community. The community of the state is for the highest good, being superior to the household (*domus*) and village (*vicus*). Without such a life of community man cannot live socially. Man requires a state as much as a house or village, for the purpose of living the best life.‡ This is proved, (a) from what the state embraces, the house and village; (b) from its end, which is to live the true life in the enjoyment of everything necessary for such a life. The natural impulse to society and speech proves the necessity of the state.§ In the congregation of a number of villages, it is easier to have all the necessaries of life; so in the congregation of a number of states into a kingdom the entire community is better supplied with all that it needs, because every state does not abound in the same thing. It is better also to live in a Kingdom for the purpose of having a common law to guide in being virtuous. In a confederation of states there is better defence against aggression on the part of enemies, when all are united under one king whose office it is to protect.‖ The state is therefore necessary to physical preservation and also moral perfection.

The modes of formation of states are three. By the overflow of the house the village is formed, and in the same way the overgrowth of the village furnishes the state. This is the natural mode of development. In another way, for the sake of peace, men constituting different divided states lay aside hostility and unite together. This is the artificial work of man. It is natural also because human impulse is at the bottom of it, but not so natural as the first. Another mode is *simpliciter violentus* according to which men are overcome by violence and compelled to form a state or part of one.¶ Accordingly, political theory is divided into three parts, (a) the philosophy of civil organization and rule, (b) the best politics in time of peace, and (c) the policy of war.

(a) Aegidius distinguishes with care civil law and civil organization from civil authority and religious authority. In opposition to Plato he contends that there is no necessity for perfect unity and equality in the state in every mode. The communism class distinctions and other leading features of Pla-

* Ibid. c. 4. ‡ Ibid. c. 1.
† Ibid. c. 15. § Ibid. c. 5.
‡ III, i, 1 2. ¶ Ibid. c. 6.

to's Republic are argued down on Aristotelian lines in set scholastic style. (1) A state is a diversity because it is composed of many villages, many houses and many men. To say it is a unity is to deny that it is a kingdom. (2) In an army many men make war, so is it in a state. (3) As the members of the body are many so are the parts of the state. (4) The end of the state is to live well and have sufficiency in life; this implies diversity of ends. (5) The fact that there are princes and subjects gives it the character of multiplicity. (6) In melody there is a multitude of voices; so the state or kingdom is a diversity in unity.*

It is not proper that all things be held in community, because all citizens are not equally prudent and good, and community of wives and children destroys the principles laid down above and raises disputes as well as exalts the vile to a level with the noble.† The state should not be so arranged that women would need to go to war to fight like men, because they lack courage and strength.‡ The kings and princes ought to see that the state is not always under the same magistrates, (1) because it is not good for the community that magistrates assume such powers; (2) they are apt to fall into evil and injustice if they know they are to be perpetual; (3) to change magistrates is to distribute the offices and keep down sedition.§ The citizens should not be so distinguished so that the warriors are separated from the rest of the citizens, for there is danger in keeping so many men and paying them. In fixing the number of warriors respect should be had to the size of the state, its position and circumstances in respect of enemies.‖ The ruler does not require to divide the possessions of the state equally among citizens, because unless there is community of children no right of equality exists and virtues are different, not equal in citizens.¶ The chief duty of a legislator is to repress concupiscence because wherever man is guided by his desires there can be no peace.1 The distinction of citizens into three classes is reprehensible because it could not be maintained with the popular election of the prince. If the warriors were in the first class they would have greater power and then the two other classes, agriculturists and artisans, would have no share in politics, they would be excluded from the election of a prince. The judges are not to be independent of one another in their judgment, each one giving his judgment *per se*, because if they do not confer in judging then discord and degeneracy will result. The laws ought to be made by the wise and they should be profitable to the state.2

(b) *The government of a kingdom in time of peace.* The state is governed in time of peace by just laws. In the rule of the state there are four elements, *princeps, consilium, praetorium,* and *populus.* It is required in the case of just

* Ibid. c. 8. † Ibid. c. 14.
† Ibid. c. 9, 10. * Ibid. c. 16.
‡ Ibid. c. 12. 1 Ibid. c. 18.
§ Ibid. c. 13. 2 Ibid. c. 20.

laws, that they spring from wisdom and that they be well-guarded by civil power, and that the laws be well administered and applied in cases of dispute. The prince is *custos* of these laws; in order that they may be well-founded he has the *consilium*; that they may be properly applied he has the *praetorium*; and for the observance of the laws he looks to all the citizens, *populus*. The end of legislation is to avoid evil and promote good, the *consilium* discovering the good and evil and remedying the evil, the *praetorium* deciding what is just and unjust, and the *populus* determining what is laudable and what is *vituperabile*. These are the different branches of the government.*

There are three good and three bad principates,—the kingdom, aristocracy and polity being good, and tyranny, obligantia and democracy being bad. If a single ruler governs for the common good of subjects that is monarchy or kingdom; if he oppresses by civil power he is a tyrant. If a few virtuous rulers act for the common good, it is aristocracy; if they are rich and oppress them it is obligantia because it is a principate of riches. If many act with the consent of all the people for the good of all it is called *polity*, because it is *ordinatio civitatis quantum ad omnes principatus*, if against the common good of all, it is *democratia* because it is *perversionem populi*.† Monarchy is the best form of principate, because there is more likely to be peace and unity when one rules and when the princeps has all the power of government it is more effective, also from the fact that nature and experience teach the value of unity in the government of states.‡ The kingdom in which monarchy is hereditary is the best. Abstractly it is better that the prince should be chosen by election, but, because men are apt to be corrupt, it is better practically that choice should be by heredity, because it is more likely the good of the kingdom will be the king's when father and son are united in making it the best, because an adventurer is more apt to be elated at the prospect of a kingdom, and because to the people custom is like second nature, teaching them obedience without a scruple.§ A good king wishes to be loved by the people, to procure the common good and to punish seditious and troublesome persons; to this end he excels in *beneficium*, distributing gifts, in virtue as an example to the people and in dignity and power by which he corrects abuses. A tyrant seeks his own good, aims after pleasure and money instead of virtue and uses his power to oppress.‖ Tyranny is the worst government and care should be taken lest princes fall into it. A good government is founded upon reason, a tyranny upon passion and caprice.¶ The king is to act like God, the King of all the kingdoms of nature. He must have virtue, knowledge and external possessions, encourage the study of literature and the practice of virtue.** Everything good is perverted to the use of tyranny, whether tyranny of one, a few or many.†† There are three modes in which corruption

* III. ii. 1.
† Ibid. c. 2
‡ Ibid. c. 4.
§ Ibid. c. 5.
‖ Ibid. c. 6, 9.
¶ Ibid. c. 7
** c. 8
†† Ibid. c. 11, 12

takes place, (1) *a se tyrannide in corrumpi*, (2) *a tyrannide alio*, (3) *a regno*. Evil perverts one to injustice, or one is corrupted by another tyrant, or on account of the kingdom itself.*

The prince ought to take the advice of his advisers, *consilium*. Every *consilium* has some *quaestio* so that it may be defined as *quaestio agibilium humanorum*. Counsel is taken in regard to what is not yet determined and care should be taken that the secrets of such a counsel are kept and that truth not flattery is the subject of advice.† Goodness, friendship and wisdom are essential in counsellors. Counsel is taken by the princeps in whatever concerns the interest of the kingdom for its peace and unity, the subsistence and the resources of the country.‡

All matters are to be determined according to the laws and the judgment is to be in the hands of judges who form the *praetorium*. Judges are to judge according to law, and if they do not act in this way they are corrupt and should be removed. As little as possible should be left to the discretion of the judges by the legislators. Punishment should not be left entirely to their *arbitrium* lest they be swayed by opinion. Law should determine as much as possible because judges must form an opinion suddenly and are apt to err.§ When a matter is in *judicis* passionate speeches before the judges ought to be prohibited, for the judge should be left free between litigants to form an impartial judgment, not to be moved by passion.‖ Judges require authority, knowledge of law and experience of human actions, as well as moral qualities of justice and equity.¶

There are different kinds of laws, some written and some unwritten, common and proper, natural and positive. There is also a difference between *jus naturale* and *jus gentium*. Properly there are four kinds of jus, *animalium, naturale, civile* and *gentium. Jus naturale* is what accords with reason or to which there is a natural impulse. *Justa positiva* is that which is just by agreement or institution of man, these may be *naturalis traditis, positive statutum*. These different forms may be reduced to natural which is *non scriptum* and positive which is *scriptum*.** Jus naturale in this wide sense is not peculiar to human beings but common to animals, because nature teaches it to all creatures; *jus gentium* is peculiar to the human race and implies the conventions adopted by men in society.†† *Lex humana* ought to be conform to natural law, useful for the people in securing their common good, possible of fulfilment and obedience according to the manners and customs of the people.‡‡ Laws have no force unless promulgated, for since law is the mandate of a superior for the guidance of our acts, there is no law unless it is

* Ibid. c. 14.
† Ibid. c. 17.
‡ Ibid. c. 18, 19.
§ Ibid. c. 20.

‖ Ibid. c. 21.
¶ Ibid. c. 22.
** Ibid. c. 24.
†† Ibid. c. 25.
‡‡ Ibid. c. 26.

notified to subjects.* He distinguishes human law and civil power from divine law and religious authority. The first is concerned with the defence of society and aims at relative perfection, to encourage all the virtues which aid and to discourage the vices which hinder social order. It does not command every virtue or forbid every vice. Divine law, however, proposes absolute perfection and opposes evil in thought as well as in word and action, and recommends virtues which society ignores.†

The last element in the rule of the state is the *populus*. The state or kingdom is something natural and a natural impulse constitutes it, yet this is not effected or perfected without work and industry on the part of men. What is accomplished by human art is best seen in considering the end and the good which are ordained in the state. There are six good ends for which the state is ordained. (1) The state is ordained for the social life of men living together and enjoying the pleasures of society; (2) for the preservation of life itself and to aid one another in preserving life; (3) for the sake of warfare necessary to repel injuries; (4) for the sake of contracts and exchange, because no one has a sufficiency of life unless there is barter to get what is needful and to dispose of what is not necessary; (5) for the sake of the marriage relationship; (6) when men live virtuously together the state can better punish delinquents, *communicatio civium propter bene et virtuose vivere et propter perfectam et per se sustinentem vitam*.

What is a kingdom, *regnum*, as opposed to a *civitas*? Kingdom is above *civitas*. *Civitas* is a multitude of *nobiles et ingenui*. A kingdom includes a greater multitude of *nobiles* and *ingenui* than a state, living according to virtue, arranged under one best man, that is, under a king. A kingdom is the confederation of many camps, and many cities under a single prince or king, a confederation useful in making war against enemies and in warding the dangers which menace family and city life. In other words it is the kingdom of the feudal regime. To live according to virtue is the end of citizens in a state and kingdom. The state has the same end as a single citizen. The people in a state are those dwellers in a kingdom ordained to a good and virtuous life. A citizen abounds in houses, possessions, but more in virtuous acts and in observing the laws and statutes of the kingdom.‡ The best state is that which is composed of many middle class persons, *multis personis mediis*, because they live more rationally, less enviously, and have more mutual love and respect. The very rich and poor, the extremes, do not live rationally, because of *nocumenta* hazards to the national life. The poor envy the rich and the rich despise the poor; *mutuus amor intercires* when they can freely associate with one another.§ Citizens are to reverence the king and to

* Ibid. c. 27.
† Ibid. c. 29-30.
‡ Ibid. c. 34.
§ Ibid. c. 33.

observe with great diligence the laws: from this springs peace and prosperity.* The chief duty of kings is to induce the citizens to practice virtue and therefore to love and fear themselves; the chief duty of citizens is to abstain from provoking the anger of the king because he is more excellent than others in the kingdom.†

(c) *Policy of war.* Here Aegidius reproduces the ideas of Vegetius in regard to the government of a kingdom in time of war. *Militaris prudentia* is a special kind of prudence. The soul has two kinds of virtue, (1) that which seeks the good and avoids the evil; and (2) that which attacks the evil. The state needs this military prudence to check and overcome enemies. It defends the common good by warlike operations. War and the military spirit are necessary as a utility in defence of the stability of the state.‡

IV. *Ecclesiastical politics.* In another writing which is unpublished, *De Ecclesiastica potestate*, extracts of which are given by Ch. Jourdain in the *Journal general de l'Instruction publique et des Cultes*,§ Aegidius reduces the philosophy of pure politics as based on reason and natural right to an Ecclesiastical system. He treats of the question of the relation of the temporal and spiritual powers. It is probable that this treatise was written during the quarrel of Boniface and Philip the Fair, being dedicated to Boniface. Philip was to get a small portion of land from the papal dominions and Boniface contended this could only be done under the seal of the Head of the Church. Aegidius speaks of Him as the Sovereign Master of men as well as of societies and the state. He is the arbiter of peace in the temporal as well as in the spiritual domain; to him belongs the right to appoint kings and to depose them when he judges them unfit to rule in the interests of the Church. The twofold power is in the hand of the Lord's Vicar, although he does not exercise the two powers in the same way. He delegates to the temporal princes secular power that it may be exercised by them under his supervision; the spiritual he holds and exercises himself. True government consists in placing all temporal kingdoms in relation to the papacy, just as the body is to the soul and matter to spirit. The Church only recognizes such authority in human society as acknowledges her dominion, for she is over man in all relations and conditions of life. Therefore the individual and the state hold their property under the sanction of the Church, so much so that the individual cannot hold a vine or plant except with her consent; the relation of marriage is sacred because of the Church's benediction; the position of offspring is secured in succession to the parent because the Church admits hereditary succession; and testamentary rights are valid only when judged so by the ecclesiastical court. Heretics and all who have committed mortal sin

* Ibid. c. 31
† Ibid. c. 35, 36
‡ III. iii. 1-5
§ XXVII. 122 sq. 1859

or are in opposition to the Church are declared unfit to be owners of property and all such as hold property are declared no longer proprietors but detaining in unlawful possession. Ultimate ownership of all temporal possessions is vested in the Church; this right is *de jure* and although it may not be recognized *de facto* the right remains notwithstanding. The reason of this is that all goods relate to the body, in use, the body is for the soul, and the soul is placed under the control and guidance of the Pontiff. The entire system of secular government and temporal power is placed at the feet of the pope who alone possesses sovereign authority upon earth. In this Aegidius consistently carries out the ideas of Boniface to whom he dedicated the work, reproducing almost the exact language of his famous bulls particularly the *Unam Sanctam*, 1302. But the time for such assertions was past because Philip was firmly established on the French throne. This does not however prevent him from recording his opinion, *patet quod omnia temporalia sunt sub dominio ecclesiae collata, et si non de facto, quoniam multi forte huic juri rebellantur, de jure tamen et ex debito temporalia summo pontifici sunt subjecta, a quo jure et a quo debito nullatenus possunt abulci.**

4. Augustinus Trionfo (Triumphus), 1244-1318. He was the contemporary of Pope John XXII, and wrote in defence of the Pope and papal claims, dedicating his work to him in the contest between the Pope and the Emperor Louis. His work is entitled *Summa De Potestate Ecclesiae* and it ascribes to the papacy the very highest prerogatives, setting the pope in the place of God as his sole representative upon earth with sovereign power for God. If God alone is entitled to divine honor and worship, the character and position of the pope entitle him to an adoration that is superior to the angels and to the saints, because the papal power is universal over men whether the pope himself be good or bad personally, his personal character making no difference as to the transmission and enjoyment of the power.† The two swords of the scripture symbolize the two powers deposited in the hands of Peter and his successors, the one power being delegated by him to temporal rulers that it may be exercised for the good of man and the advancement of the Church, the other being retained in the hands of the pope.‡

This prerogative possessed by the Supreme ruler independent of his character, whether he be good or bad, is in opposition to the prior scholastic view of Thomas in which he makes the good ruler first of all and chiefly a good man. His divine right as successor of Peter according to Triumphus is independent of man. He cannot be elected either by the king or the people, nor can he be removed from office by either. In the case of heresy his deposition may be enacted by a general council, but this does not remove him from

---

* Bk. II. 4; Journal general de l'Inst. pub. p. 138, v. 1. Janet, Vol. 1, pp. 402-415; Franck, Ref. et Pub. Moyen age, pp. 71-102; Riezler, pp. 139-140.

† De potestate Eccles. IX. 1, p. 72.

‡ Ibid. I. 1, 3, pp. 3, 4; pp. 54, sq.

office: the heresy itself *ipso facto* removes him from the position of head.*
His judgment is final on any issue, as final as God's decree, for his decree is
God's, and there is no appeal from his decision to the judgment of God.† To
make such an appeal to heaven against a papal pronouncement is an act of
defiance against God and renders him who makes it an outlaw from the
kingdom of God.‡ The papal power is the only real and effective sovereign
power upon the universe because it acts in the name of the divine government
upon the earth. The emperor is in subordination to the Pope and may be
deposed and a new one elected by him in case the electors make no choice,
choose an unqualified one, or in case he can secure the service of a powerful
man of pre-eminent ability by whose efforts the Church's welfare may be
promoted, her peace maintained, or her adversaries brought to subjection.
He can abolish any secular government distasteful to him or repugnant to
the Church. The true foundation of secular power and the true character
of temporal government depends upon papal sanction. He may by an act of
will transfer the right of election to whom he wishes, overturn and change
a constitution that is antagonistic to the Church, and modify any human
government so as to bring it into line with the policy he dictates as the sovereign authority among the kingdoms of the world.§ The characteristic of
a true temporal power is that it has been blessed and established by the
Pope who received through the donation of Constantine, the restoration of
his right to actual and direct government of the entire western world. The
interpretation of constitutions and the extent of allegiance due by subjects
to their rulers is to be determined by the papal decrees.∥ The division of
territory and the assignment of the limits of kingdoms depend upon his sanction and the emperor has permission to act in such matters only with his
concurrence. The papal *curia* is the universal appellate court in the world
and the pope himself supreme judge and arbiter of kingdoms.¶

In the work of Jacques de Viterbe, the same sacerdotal idea is fully carried
out to its extreme, *De Regimine Christiano*. The Christian Church is the most
glorious kingdom, being one, universal and apostolic. Jesus Christ is the
sovereign ruler and king, and the Pontiff is his Vicar on earth. Christ has
delegated his power to the Bishops and secular princes, yet the sacerdotal
and temporal powers are united in the hands of the Bishops, whose head is
the Chief Bishop of Christendom. The spiritual power has the right to cor-

* Ibid. II. 7. s pp. 25 sq.; V. 6. p. 54.
† Ibid. V. 1. p. 50; VI. 1. p.56.
‡ Ibid. VI. 2. p. 58
§ Ibid. XXXV. 1-8. pp. 206-211; XL. 1. pp. 230 sq.
∥ XXXVI. 1. p. 212.
¶ XLIV. 1. p. 240; XLV. 1. 3. pp. 246-249. Poole, pp. 253-255; Friedberg, II. 3. 19. Oudin.
L. c. 509; Chronicon.Ed. by Potthast, Triumphus; Zeitschrift f. Kirchenrech , Friedberg.
93; Riezler p. 286.

rect and also to depose the temporal ruler, in the interests of the Church, he being the supreme arbiter in all human affairs secular as well as Ecclesiastical.1

* Janet. Vol. I. p. 415.

CHAPTER II.

DANTE. MARSILIUS. OCKHAM. WYCLIF.

1. *Contest of the 14th. Century. Nationality.* During the 14th. Century mysticism began to separate itself from and to protest against the dry doctrines of the Schoolmen. Petrarch from the side of Classicism and polite literature, Eckart and Ruysbroek from the speculative side of Theology which despised everything worldly as phenomenal, and Gerson following in the wake of St. Bernard and Hugh St. Victor in emphasizing the experiences of men set themselves to oppose the 'reconciliation' politics of the greater Schoolmen. These men were not strong enough to work a revolution, because they were opposing practical issues with speculative ideas which rend man away from the world of reality.

Another class of men did the real work of opposing the theocratical doctrine although they hailed themselves from the very centre of Scholasticism. The crisis precipitated by the violence of Boniface VIII., who in the pride and presumption of his own heart arrogated to himself almost superhuman dignity. From 1296-1302 a series of papal Bulls were issued in which the Pope claimed the prerogatives of sanctioning the payment of taxes by the Church members to secular rulers, of establishing and destroying temporal sovereignties and of absolute dominion, *subessa Romano Pontifici omnem humanam creaturam declaramus*. This amounts to a claim of universal dominion by the Popes. It is met by the practical sagacity of Philip of France and Louis of Bavaria, and the spirit of nationality in France and England, around which the literature of the Schoolmen circles at this period. Nationality is one of the grand issues of the 14th. Century as may be seen in Dubois and other writers. The great names of Dante and Ockham are inseparably associated with the theory of the Schoolmen in reference to this papal claim. Across the border the voice of Marsilius is heard, and in the reforming spirit of Huss in Bohemia and Wyclif with his russet friars the doctrine of nationality is proclaimed in the island Kingdom of England.

At the time when Boniface was making his violent attempts to snatch a victory an interesting writing appears under the name of Peter Du Bois of

Normandy in the year 1300, in the interest of the French nationality and Empire. His aim is to establish the French Kingdom in a state of peace and thereby to secure freedom from war over all the world, bringing the other kingdoms into subjection to France. He claims that the French are peculiarly qualified to act reasonably, with impartiality and right judgment. France is a kingdom peculiarly adapted for the nurture and training of kings. He acknowledges that the Pope has a right to all the lands known as the papal dominions, granted to him in the Donation of Constantine. At the same time the Pope is unfitted for temporal kingship, because being generally old and infirm before he reaches the papal chair, he cannot avoid the disasters of war which destroy so many of the subjects. Therefore he advises the Pope to be content with the guardianship of souls and to leave the bodies and temporal interests to strong and well-equipped rulers. He then reviews the position of the different kingdoms and asserts that by delicate diplomacy, secret treaties and some minor concessions everything might be arranged satisfactorily so as to secure a French monarchy over the whole civilized world, while the Pope might be content to accept a satisfactory pension in return for the yielding up of his claims, and attend to the spiritual interests of the Church. He thus represents the idea at the opening of the 14th. Century of the papacy as a state among other states of Europe, of the Empire as nothing more than a petty principality, and of the temporal dominion of the Pope as the cause of immense evil to society. Obedience he asserts to be due not to the temporal power for the sake of the spiritual, but to the temporal for its own sake as a duly constituted earthly power. It is impossible to reform society by reforming the abuses in the Church and placing it as a purified organization at the head of all powers. He asserts the nationality of the French Kingdom. It is different from and independent of the Empire. The latter is under the surveillance of the Pope, who as temporal chief crowns and confirms the Emperor; there is no such thing in France, for France is free from any subjection as a kingdom to the papacy. It is because she is not subject to the trammels of Roman Espionage that in the enjoyment of national freedom she is fitted to be the leader of the world and her king the universal earthly ruler. This idea was developed during the remainder of the Century under the sanction of the University of Paris, then the light of Europe, from which came forth all the learned Doctors of the School.*

Another writing that is to be noticed is *De Utraque potestate*. It is the work of a learned man equally theologian and jurist who can manipulate facts in defence of his position, skillfully hiding the Scholastic bent. It was pub-

---

* Poole, pp. 256-260; Wailly, Memoire sur un opuscule anonyme in Memoires de l'Academie des Inscriptions et belles-lettres, t. 18; 435-494, 1849; Quaestio de potestate papae. Enquiry touching the power of the Pope by du Bois, printed by Dupuy, in Acts et Preuves appended to Histoire du different d'entre le Pope Boniface VIII et Philippes le bel. Roy de France, pp. 683-684, 1655; Riezler, pp. 143 sq.

issued in 1304 in connection with the controversy between Boniface and Philip. It has been ascribed to Gilles of Rome by nearly all the Gallican writers. But it is impossible to ascribe it to him.* He declares that there is no single power sovereign and absolute in jurisdiction. The two powers are distinct, the spiritual having no jurisdiction in temporal affairs.

He maintains the independence of the temporal power (a) *philosophically*. This proof is drawn from Aristotle. In the soul two faculties are distinct which differ according to their acts, their objects, and their ends. In the temporal and spiritual powers there are different ends, objects, and acts, so that they are not to be confused, nor is one to be subordinate to the other. (b) *Revelation* confirms the voice of reason. In this connection he proves from the duplex character of objects presented in Scripture, earth and sky, two orders of creatures, two worlds, two luminaries, the difference in the two powers. (c) This conclusion is ratified by quotations from the *Civil law*, and (d) from *Canon law*. He then goes on, having established the distinction of the powers, to show (a) that both powers are divine in origin and institution; (b) that they are independent of one another having different organizations and laws, needs and ends, the one securing temporal peace the other spiritual; (c) that spiritual power having its concern in the eternal life of men has no authority over temporal things; (d) the spheres of each can be easily distinguished. He distinguishes in human affairs three sorts, the purely spiritual such as marriage, divorce, heresy; the purely temporal as the feudal rights and the right of taxation; and the mixed in character as the feudal oath of fealty which is religious in appealing to God and temporal as a tie between vassal and lord. Civil and religious society have each their own domain. (e) He claims for the King of France the same independence as he grants to the Emperor. France existed it is claimed before the Western Empire was established, before Charlemagne became Emperor over it; it was a nation before the Roman Empire. He traces their origin to the migration of Trojans after the destruction of their city by the Greeks to the region now known as Hungary, from whence they moved, because they refused to be subjected and forced to pay tribute by Valentinian, to the borders of the Rhine territory, passing into Gaul and founding the kingdom of France. The French nation was always independent and never in vassalage to the Empire. It is an interesting idea that is here developed, that of nationhood.†

Another work which is anonymous but has been ascribed to William of Ockham deserves honorable notice. It was produced in 1303 in the quarrel between Philip the Fair and Boniface VIII. The writing is in the form of a dialogue between a cavalier and a priest in which the respective rights and

---

* M. Jourdain, on Gilles of Rome; also Journal general de l'Instruction publique et des Cultes XXVII p. 122, sq.; Riezler, pp. 139 sq.; Poole, p. 255; De Monarchia, Goldast, II. 95 sq.

† Goldast, Monarchia, s. 1. III, p. 105; Franck, p. 119.

powers of the spiritual and temporal princes are discussed. The priest meets the cavalier and questions him on the position of the Church. There is a satirical representation of the contest in which Boniface is the chief figure. The priest then claims that Jesus Christ has committed all the power he himself possessed to his Vicar the Pope. The soldier says he distinguishes two conditions in Christ, that of humiliation and exaltation. Peter is the Vicar of Christ only in His humiliation and not in His glory.*

This writing formed the model upon which in 1376 another work was produced, the *Songe du Verger* (*Somnium Viridarii*) by Raoul de Presles.† This writing is allied to Scholasticism, because its author was the translator of Aegidius Romanus, and the translator of and commentator upon Augustine, from whom he largely drew the inspiration of his work. The author sees in vision two queens appear before the throne of Charles V., the secular and the ecclesiastical powers, the end being to secure peace and amity between them. The one has the power of the priesthood, the other that of civil command; the one pardons sin, the other reprieves and punishes attacks upon the social order; the first is guided by the Canon, the second by the Civil law. The rights of each are inviolable, the temporal functions do not pertain to the spiritual power, the temporal power is associated with the social order of the state. The King of France appoints two advocates, a priest and a cavalier, the one to plead the cause of the Church, the other that of the state. In two parts the discussion proceeds: in the first the priest attacks and the cavalier defends; in the second the cavalier attacks and the priest defends. In this work we have a summary of all the arguments used by predecessors, taken from Scholastic writers, jurists, papal constitutions and imperial rescripts. It may be regarded as a review at the close of the 14th. Century of the position on both sides of the controversy. In it there are maintained and defended many of the free doctrines of later times, individual liberty, the independence of the kingdom, the distinction of the powers found later in Montesquieu, the rational basis of monarchy and of the succession to the crown as established by the Salic law, the limitation of war to the promotion of the peace of the state, natural nobility as the basis of political nobility. These are some of the liberal ideas contained in this remarkable writing of the 14th. Century.‡

2. Dante Allighieri, 1265-1321. He was the poet of Scholasticism, the author of *Divina Comedia*, jurist, theologian and Schoolman. In early life he was a poet, but through his study of the Schoolmen, he became a zealous philosopher and an eloquent lecturer at Paris and Bologna. At first he was a Guelf,

* Goldast, Monarchia I. 17; Dialogus, printed in English by James Savage, London, 1848; Riezler, pp. 276 sq.

† Franck, Réf. et Pub. Moyen Age, p. 219 sq.

‡ Janet, Vol. I. pp. 440-3; Franck, p. 209 sq.; Academie des Inscriptions, 1785; Riezler, pp. 225 sq.; Goldast, Monarchia, I. 58; Manuscrits francais, Vol. IV. 239.

but being compelled to retire but exile through the division among the victorious Guelfs, he avowed the Ghibelline party in the struggle and became an ardent believer in the unity of Italy and in the strong position of a powerful Emperor, independent of the Pope. The civil law having reached its preeminence in the Bologna School, and the Emperor Henry of Luxembourg having the desire to re-establish the imperial dominion over Italy, was entrenched in his position against the Pope by the civil law which furnished him with a powerful weapon to establish his sovereignty in temporal matters. In opposition, the School of Canonists supported the supremacy of the Pope in all matters. In Thomas Dante found the conflict of the temporal and spiritual. In the Italian republics there was the division into factions and in the Neapolitan Kingdom there was usurpation, while the papacy was in exile at Avignon. The only central power in which there was any hope for unity in Western Europe was in Henry VII. Dante during his exile meditated on these subjects as is seen in his *Convito*,* *Paradiso*† and in his *Purgatorio*.‡ He became a patriot for Italian freedom. In the year in which Henry VIII. died he wrote his famous work *De Monarchia* in which he presents the substance of his meditations, not on monarchy compared with other forms as the title seems to indicate, but in an account of the disputes of the times from the standpoint of philosophy, revelation, and history, the demonstration of the fact that in the Empire of the Universe God has no superior, and likewise the Emperor upon Earth in the temporal kingdom is supreme governor. He puts his theory in a single phrase, the most perfect happiness is realized when the Church as wagon rests upon the Empire as beam. He is a strong and ardent follower of Thomistic politics and his chief merit lies in this that he accepted the Scholastic principles, and used them to build up Imperialism against Rome.

His work was chiefly critical. The most distinguished humanist in the age of revival he writes the Epitaph for the dead system, refuting one impossible theory by propounding another equally impossible.§ He like the Scholastics dealt with a theory that fitted into ancient history, but was out of place in the history and circumstances of his own time. If he did not give life to the dead he showed the people that a new regime was much needed. He is the earliest defender of nationality in Italy. He is a follower of Thomas and Aegidius. Man's goal is happiness both earthly and heavenly. He attains the former by the proper use of reason and those virtues which are dependent upon the guidance of reason; man's normal condition in life is peace and it is preserved and secured by the State. The State should be a monarchy to avoid the confusion of dividing the power. Weary of an age

* V. 167.
† 27th. Chant.
‡ 16th. Chant.
§ Bryce, Holy Roman Empire, 265 sq.

of disorder and tyranny he raises his voice against lawlessness on behalf of
unity and peace for Italy and the world. But he goes on to add his own contribution to the discussion of politics, princes as well as subjects need to
preserve peace, and in order to the preservation of peace in the multitude of
states, a universal Emperor is required, a prince of princes. This Emperor
is the feudal lord of the pope in reference to his temporal possessions, as
much as in the case of the temporal princes. Heavenly happiness comes
through grace and revelation by means of the spiritual institutions in the
hands of the Church, which is controlled by the Pope. The more he confines
himself to spiritual things and uses spiritual means to attain human happiness the more success will he have and the greater honor among temporal
rulers. The *De Monarchia* is a kind of philosophy of history in which Dante
treats of the science of history and of politics. The work is divided into
three parts which consist of the answers to three separate questions.*

(1) Is universal temporal monarchy as represented in the empire necessary
to the good of the human race? Monarchy is the empire of a single chief
over all men who live in his time, and therefore over everything temporal.
Monarchy therefore embraces the universal human race, human interests
and temporal concerns. To discover the character of government among
men one must find out the aim of political society. Politics being a practical science is concerned with actions. Actions are determined by the end in
view. A man builds a house suitable to his object. In human beings the
end is not individual life nor intellectual knowledge of life; but it is common
to all men to seek and to find the realization of their hopes not in a single
being but in the unity of a multitude of men. There are two degrees in the
activity, the practical and speculative; according to the first, man is active
in doing or working, and according to the second he is knowing, which is more
perfect than doing. Accordingly to the individual knowledge, not action, is
the highest, that is, rest is before activity; likewise in the race, peace is the
best condition. The exile feels that there is need of peace in the war
of pope against emperor, faction against faction in the city, republic
and kingdom. The human race has a common end, and this it aims after.
Temporal universal monarchy is essential to peace, to the general agreement
of individuals and of states; peace is the most blessed condition and is the
most favorable to the progress of civilization and to the advancement of
man in intelligence and culture. Just as all members of the body are subject to the soul, and the entire universe in subjection to one God who is a
unity, the human race has been destined by God for such unity. In
every multitude which has a common end there must be a chief; the faculties
of man are led by one, the family, the commune and the city have each a head.
The more a society resembles God, the more perfect it is for its end. In

* *Bk.* I, 2.

such subjection mankind is made more like God.* In order to avoid disputes and to settle litigation there must be judgment and to settle such contests between persons, there must be one supreme judge. The world is organized under justice. Justice is most perfect when it rests in a person who has the greatest freedom and the largest power.† The distinguishing quality of man is understanding, and understanding is best realized in a single man, hence the strong in understanding are natural rulers.‡ The whole race is ordered to some end, and some one must guide to this end, therefore monarchy or empire is necessary to the welfare of the world.§ The world is made up of parts which are related to some one thing, therefore the mass of mankind is ordered in relation to a prince.|| Justice is the basis of the continued existence of the human race, and such justice can only be truly of value when the authority of all is united with the will of the best one.¶ The human race is most happy when it is most free. Under a monarch men are most free, because liberty consists in living for oneself, not for another; in monarchy the ruler is for the citizen, not the citizen for the ruler. What is done by one is better than what is done by many. In common interests the single ruler can best furnish general principles; the practical application can be left to the individual princes. Good states aim at liberty; nations do not exist for the good of kings but kings for the good of the nations. The monarch therefore is bound by the end which is appointed to him in legislation.** One who is the best fitted to rule can rule others best, because rule is the reflection of the ruler. A monarch is best fitted to rule, because in him judgment and justice, the preeminent virtues of a king are best displayed.†† In the universal empire the totality of power placed in the hands of one always seeks the good; the contrary is impossible, because when one is made supreme ruler, he loses all desire for self and throws his entire force and influence into the effort to bring the most good to others. There is the absence of jealousy, or envy because he has no rivals; there is no desire for competition because he has no equals; and his love to all is preeminent because he is above all others. There is a gradation among beings and this depends upon the will of one who directs all.‡‡ It is also the pledge of liberty for all as well as for the peace of society; for in the exercise of imperial justice, the inferior powers are committed to all and they are retained in subordination by the sentiment of love. That government which best conserves unity is the best.§§ In history we find confirmation of this theory, for there never has existed a better or more just government than that of Augustus under which the whole world was in subjection and willingly gave obedience to the laws. It was at this very time that Jesus was born when unity and peace reigned in the

* I. 8.
† I. 10.
‡ I. 3, 4.
§ I. 5.
|| I. 6.

¶ I. 11.
** I. 12.
†† I. 13.
‡‡ I. 16.
§§ I. 14.

whole world, in the fulness of times.* The right and proper form of government then is that of one universal state under one sole universal governor.†
One might ask in considering Dante's theory, does this not require homogeneity on the part of the entire race of men?

(II.) Did the Roman people who held this universal monarchy and who gave it its form legitimately and of right possess Imperial power? Has it been transmitted from the Eastern to the Western Empire? This part of the work is of interest as being the first systematic application of the historical method to the study of politics. Dante shows that the Roman Empire is by right superior to every other, proving this by human reason and God's authority.‡ His interpretation of history is the discovery of the will of God in the events and occurrences in Roman history.§ At first this wonderful supremacy was secured by the force of arms and bloodshed, but the destiny of providence is marked out in this course of usurpation by force. It is not really usurpation but the right given by God. There are two forces that guide this tendency to supremacy, reason and divine authority. The right belonged to God. But men are to seek it in the will of God, and that will of God is discerned by reason in human history. Man is led by signs to the discovery of God's will in the events of the world. What are these signs?‖ The Romans were justly invested with the empire of the world; they derived it first from the right of birth because they were always of noble lineage.¶ They were the descendants of Aeneas who represented all parts of the world, being raised among the princes, the heir of three continents, Assaracus and Creusa representing Asia, Dardanus and Lavinia, Europe, and Electra mother of Dardanus, daughter of Atlas, and Dido representing Africa. The world is his by legitimate inheritance, and he being the father of the Romans, therefore the Romans are the most noble people.** The wonderful achievements wrought by Romans in conquering other nations give evidence that God approved their dominion and ruled other nations by them. The miracles and miraculous acts that were performed under the spell of their universal empire gives further evidence, the shield that fell from heaven in the days of Numa, the miraculous deliverance of the Capitol from the Gauls, and the tempest which retarded the progress of Hannibal and his conquering army after Cannae.†† Whoever works for the good of the state works for right as his end. The end of all right is the common good. In subjecting the world the Romans aimed at such a common end. The Romans were a people sacred to the Gods, generous even to sacrifice, and having in all their conquests, which ultimately extended to the civilized world, the laudable end of securing peace for all nations under the guidance of just and equitable laws. Free from the avaricious spirit of the world her heroes were men of disinterested patriotism, marked by universal sympathy, neglecting their own interests to care for the world and the concerns of other nations. Such were Fabricius, Brutus, Camillus, Mucius, the Decii, and Marcus Cato, illustrious men realizing the fulfilment of the lines of the Aeneid of Virgil, in which the race of Aeneas was destined for universal empire on account of their valour and nobility.

> Tu regere imperio populos, Romane, memento;
> Hae tibi erunt artes; pacisque imponere morem,
> Parcere subjectis, et debellare superbos.*

The Roman people therefore in following after the common good of all mankind fulfilled the order of nature and thereby attained universal empire.† The history of the Roman people ought to be looked upon as a long continued combat on the field of the world in which the race of Aeneas gained the victory under the sanction of heaven. All the conflicts of history have been conducted under the sanction of religion. For God's will is revealed to men by means of signs in order to satisfy human reason.‡ The single combat is the favorite method of settling disputes because it is a duel between man and man. The history of the Romans attests this. Aeneas first conquers Turnus; the Horatii then triumph over the Curatii; Fabricius conquers Pyrrhus; Scipio conquers Hannibal § Rome triumphs over the Samnites and Sabines; Augustus becomes Emperor of the world, for by a series of duels with Sabines, Carthaginians, Greeks, Assyrians, and Egyptians Rome attained universal dominion. The result of the combat being favorable to Rome indicated God's approval. The result of a combat is right. When two nations quarrel they are by discussion to try to settle the dispute. Only when this is hopeless may we resort to a trial of strength, of soul as well as body; and this contest must be entered upon by common consent not animated by private hatred or love, but simply by an eager desire for justice.¶ Here we have in Dante the first idea of arbitration and a just war. In this empire Jesus Christ is born and to it he yields submission, acknowledging the legitimacy of the power of Cæsar; for when he is condemned by a Roman governor in a Roman praetorium he recognizes the jurisdiction of the tribunal and submits to be put to death according to its decree.** In Justinian we have the realization of the destiny of providence in regard to the Romans. The Roman people legitimately held world-empire, the earlier emperors were depositories of this power. It is transmitted to the later emperors with the consent of

* Virg. Aen. VI. s. 81-3.   De Monarch. II. 5.
† II. 6. 7.
‡ II. 8.
§ II. 11.
‖ II. 9.
¶ II. 10.
** II. 12. 13.

the people. The Romans have given up their authority by the voice of election, *lex curialis*, to the emperor; so should the Italians by making choice of Henry of Luxembourg.*

(III) Is the authority of the Emperor of the Romans, who has been shown to be the monarch of the world, derived from God or from the vicar of God, and does it depend upon God directly, or upon the Vicar of God the successor of Peter?† Dante takes as his foundation principle, that what is contrary to the design of nature is against God's will.‡ The answer to this question is critical, being an answer to the arguments of opponents who had tried to establish the superiority of the pope over the emperors as the heir and successor of the Roman emperors. Dante reproduces and answers (a) the arguments from the Scripture, (b) those from history, and (c) those from philosophy, as used by the decretists the papalists, and false philosophers. His refutation is based on the truism "the overthrow of an argument is the discovery of the defect in it."§

(a) Arguments from Scripture. It is said in Genesis that God made two great lights, the greater to shine by day and the lesser by night. These symbolize the pope and emperor, the spiritual and temporal powers, the latter receiving its light and authority from the former. To this Dante replies, such an analogy cannot apply to man or to any society of men because man was created on the sixth day while these lights were on the fourth day. An accident does not exist before its essence, and as the two powers exist to remedy the accident of sin, they cannot be symbolized by the sun and moon, because they existed before man and before his fall. The temporal power does not receive its being from the spiritual, nor its authority, yet it should receive the means of exercising its authority more efficiently from the spiritual through the agency of grace.‖ Again the decretists said that Levi was born before Judah, therefore the sacerdotal tribe represented by the former has precedence of the royal represented by the latter. Dante says, the fact of the priority in birth is true, but it does not justify the conclusion; priority in generation does not imply superiority in dignity, otherwise Reuben would have the supremacy.¶ Again, it is alleged, Saul was appointed and deposed by Samuel, God's representative. Dante says, on this special occasion Samuel acted for God, but not as a priest, only as a legate in a particular matter, and in this there does not appear permanence of power.** The incense and offerings presented by the wise men to Jesus indicate his double sovereignty. This argument, Dante shows, rests upon a false syllogism consisting of four terms, — God is sovereign in the temporal and spiritual, the Pope is Vicar of God and therefore sovereign in the temporal and spiritual. There is a fal-

* Paradiso, c. 3 and 6. † III. 4.
† III. 1.   ‡ III. 5.
‡ III. 2.   § Soph. El. II. 3.
** III. 6.

lacy in the reasoning because God in the major is not the same as Vicar of God in the minor premise. A Vicar does not possess the power of him who is represented, but only a part.* Again, it is argued, "thou art Peter and on this rock will I build my Church," "whatsoever ye shall bind on earth shall be bound in heaven," and the saying of Peter, "here are two swords," gives the basis in the life of Christ for the supremacy of the Church. Dante replies, that these words refer entirely to the spiritual kingdom, as Christ declared he had nothing to do with earthly dominion, "my kingdom is not of this world."† Dante's answers are characterized by subtlety and finesse and gave materials to future theorists for some centuries to come.

(b) Arguments from history. The defenders of papal supremacy depended upon the donation of Constantine and the translation of the empire from the Greeks to the Germans by Pope Adrian. Dante does not seriously consider the accuracy of these supposed historical foundations, but he proves that they have no real foundation as a basis of right. He repudiates the donation of Constantine to Sylvester, on the ground that Constantine had no power to alienate the rights and liberties of the Empire and that the Church had no right to be a party to such a transaction. It is the design of the Imperial Empire to protect the territory and to preserve the laws of the Empire. If the Emperor attempt to divide the Empire then he is abandoning his duty which is to keep the dominion under a single ruler. It is contrary to the human right of an Empire to divide, or destroy, or alienate it. In abandoning his duty he acts *ultra vires* and in destroying the rights of others nullifies his own acts. The property and liberties of the Empire are inalienable. Therefore the Donation of Constantine is illegal and the Church cannot receive the *imperium* because she rests it upon an act that is void. To destroy the Empire is contrary to human right. Not only was the Emperor incompetent as a divider of Empire and bestower of it, but the Church was unqualified to receive it, because she is expressly forbidden by Christ to receive temporal power. Therefore the gift was invalid both in giving and receiving.‡ In regard to the translation of the Empire, Dante declares usurpation is not a ground of right. Even if Adrian crowned Charlemagne, transferring the Imperial dignity from Michael Emperor at Constantinople to Charles, the fact is not sufficient to establish the right, nor does it destroy Imperial independence. It could likewise be shown that the Church depended upon the Empire, for Emperor Otho established Pope Leo VIII. on the papal chair and deposed Benedict, condemning him to exile in Saxony.§ Therefore historical proofs fail.

(c) Philosophical Arguments. In this he introduces the finesse of philosoph-

* III. 7.
† III. s. 9.
‡ III. 10.
§ III. 13.

ic thought. All things, it is argued, belonging to one genus are to be brought under one head, which is the standard of all under it. All things that are of the same kind ought to be reduced in subjection to a unity.* All men are of the same race, genus, therefore they ought to be reduced in subjection to a unity which becomes the measure of all. And since the Emperor and sovereign pope are likewise men they must be reduced to subjection under a single man. But the pope cannot be subjected to the Emperor, because he cannot be subject to any man; therefore the Pope must be the measure and rule of the Emperor. So argue the Pontifical devotees. But, says Dante, there is a fallacy in the argument, for it distinguishes in the genus of man the quality of Pope and the quality of Emperor. They refer not, as they allege, to the genus of a common individual, but of a perfect man. Hence they cannot be merged in any single individual man, the only being to whom they can be united on equal terms is God. To be a man is one thing, to be a pope or emperor quite a different thing. A man exists in essence, but a pope or emperor in the quality or accident; therefore as they owe their existence to the papacy or empire they fall under the category of relation; both being relative they are relative to each other and fall under a higher genus or unity which is God.†

Conclusion. Dante does not carry out his ideas into practical life. He is a reformer, but a reformer who remains in the Church he is trying to reform. It is reserved for Marsilius and Ockham to present the more practical side of the theory. Yet Dante has a grand ideal. He does not desire the emperor to be in vassalage to the papacy, nor does he wish to see the pope in vassalage to the empire. He desires an Emperor who is a true feudal sovereign and yet spiritually a true son of the Church. The authority of the empire does not spring from the Church, because the empire had its power while the Church was either not existing at all or had no power of action. The authority of the empire springs from God directly. Christ acknowledged the power of the empire to judge, submitting to its judgment. Paul says, "I stand at Cæsar's tribunal where I ought to be judged."‡ He wishes these two to abide independent, since they derive independent power from the same Divine source. The good of man and the welfare of the state demand the independence of Church and State. This ideal is the dream of fancy kept before the eye of a poet, his arguments the lines of thought that lead up to it.

The earliest germs of International law were found in the conception of the world as an Imperial Empire in which the different states were united under one world governor. Starting from human Christian community which found its unity realized in the superior power of Ecclesiasticism, Aquinas ex-

* Arist. Metaph. X. 1.
† III. 12.
‡ III. 13.

pressed these sentiments; but the first to delineate the world of states was Dante in his *De Monarchia*. Nationality was beginning to assert itself in the changed condition of institutions and chiefly in the decay of feudalism. To prevent the nations crumbling to atoms Dante conceived the plan of uniting all the nations, still preserving nationality, in one great world-empire. He places his ideal monarchy, the Universal Empire, side by side with the Church as the instrument of the Divine will. His Empire he defines to be a state above everything temporal in the world, concerned with the government of all secular affairs. His idea of war too as an appeal to force, after every other peaceful means had failed, resorted to by consent of the parties, gives us in germ the two great principles for which International law has contended, the necessity of declaring war, and also of consulting peace before war is declared.*

3. Marsilius of Padua, 1270-1342. Among the political opponents of the supremacy of the papacy there figures a name that has been almost forgotten in history, that of one whose personality occupied a large place in the struggle to eliminate from Ecclesiastical policy the pretensions to control and subject the temporal powers and to give to the secular prince his rightful place. Marsilius was a man of passion and vehemence and he created a stir in the school and in the world in which he figured. Marsilius or Marsiglio was born in Padua. He is surnamed Patavinus. It is asserted by Papadopoli, the historian of Padua,† that Marsiglio was a member of the Franciscan order and attached to the faction excommunicated by John XXII. On the other hand Wadding in his *History of the Minors*‡ denies that he was a Franciscan. It is probable that he was not a member of any religious order as Michael Cesena does not allude to him and Ockham does not refer to him, and his name is not mentioned in the Papal bull of Excommunication of 1327. He seems to have been the chief in an independent group along with his comrade and friend, John of Jandun. Marsilius studied at Padua medicine and philosophy. He was naturally a distinguished orator. From Padua he went to Milan and from thence visited other cities in Italy. In 1312 he was Rector of the University of Paris when William of Ockham reigned in the intellectual world there ‡. In his high position he devoted himself to the study of Theology but particularly medicine. No doubt his contact with Ockham served to give him an insight into the political doctrines of Ockham himself. The ardent nature of Marsilius would act as a magnet in the political friendship of the two. They did not rest satisfied with mere speculative

* Pulszky, pp. 91-95; Janet, I, pp. 433-445; Erdman, I p. 474 sq.; Franck, p. 163 sq.; Henck, de Rom. Script. II c. 42, p. 491; Poole, pp. 262 sq.; De Monarchia, translated, F. J. Church and R. W. Church, London, 1879; Bryce, Holy Rom. Empire, pp. 265-269. Analysis of De Monarchia: Trans'n of A. Torri, Leghorn, 1844, Riezler, pp. 169 sq.

† History of the Gymnasium of Patavinus.

‡ Annales Ordinis Minorum, Bk. VII, 85.

§ Du Boulay, Hist. Univ. Paris, IV, fol. 264.

ideas. When the conflict was started between Louis of Bavaria and Pope John XXII., Ockham and Marsilius left the university home of liberal speculation to devote their giant intellects to the cause of independence and enlightenment represented by Louis, heedless of the ostracism it implied and the anger of the papacy it provoked. Marsilius with his companion John of Jandun led the independent order of defenders that followed the German prince. When Louis was excommunicated in 1324 Marsilius took the counsel of Jandun and with him formulated the plan of the great work which afterwards became the *Defensor Pacis*. In two months he produced the treatise as a defence of Louis and as an attack upon the very foundation of the papal power. It is the most clear defence of constitutional right that has yet been written; it stands to-day as a witness to the truth that it was impossible to effect a compromise on the lines of the old established order of society and that nothing less than an entire reconstruction of society can place it in its rightful position. It was a prophecy of the new order as Dante's work was the epitaph of the dead system of Medievalism.

Very soon after this Marsilius and his followers retired from Paris to the court of Louis at Nuremberg. By the eloquence and activity of Marsilius many friends were gained for the cause of Louis. The Pope vainly tried to anethematize and arrest the progress of the work. To Marsilius and his co-workers is due the policy as well as the scheme of the Emperor to deliver the empire from the hands of the Pope and to vindicate the independence of the empire. Louis was too weak to conquer such a foe. He gained a temporary victory and became possessor of Rome. A new Pope was set up in the city and Marsilius was appointed the Pope's Counsellor and Vicar in Rome. This state of affairs was of short duration, for in 1330 Louis was again baffled, compelled to retire to Germany and his followers were excommunicated as heretics. In 1336 Louis was reconciled with John XXII. But Marsilius and his genius were forgotten, he was forsaken by the Emperor on whose behalf he had wielded such a mighty influence, anathematized by the Pope, reproached by the Sorbonne, and forbidden to enter the University of Paris.*

The *Defensor Pacis* is unlike any other work of the age. It is divided into three parts. (1) Book I. treats of political right in general. (2) Book II. considers particular rights, especially the Church organization, in which Marsilius comes out boldly against the organization of the Catholic Church and against the temporal and spiritual sovereignty of the Pope as pretended head of the Church. (3) He presents the chief principles developed in the former part of the work, giving some conclusions that mark him off from the political writers of the age in which he lived, the principal one being the doctrine of the sovereignty of the people and that of universal suffrage. The

---

* Baldassare Labanca, Marsilius de Padona, 1882; Riezler, pp. 40 sq.; Examen Judiciale Franc. Veneti Marsil. de Padua, Baluze, Miscell. II. 280; Marsiglio de Maynardina, Dr. Friedberg II. 24 sq.; Goldast, II. 154 sq.; Albertino Mussato, Latin poem to Marsiglio; Poole, pp. 263–266.

work makes almost no allusion to the stirring events of the times. It follows in general the lines laid down in Aristotle.

(1) *General Theory of the State.* The *defensor pacis* commences with the foundation principle that government is established in the state with the object of preserving and securing peace. The end proposed is to discover what is the goal of society, in what the good of society consists, the welfare of the state. The good of the state is simply the good of the members of the state, physical and moral good, such as was in view in the first institution of the civil society. Its existence is simply to promote the peace and the good of those who make it up.* Marsilius gives the cause of the origin and the origin itself of civil society. If men had not felt the need of mutual helpfulness and of associating in a large community where that aid is pledged and organization is perfected for its exercise, they would not have been able to rise above the union of the sexes in the family, of families in the tribe, of tribes in the city and from these to kingdoms and large empires which have taken such a conspicuous place in the history of the world. Man's civil association is a natural society. He adopts the idea which Aquinas opposed, that civil institutions are a result of sin. Adam was made in innocence and with perfect integrity. In his fall civil control is utilized to bring him into subjection. The cause of the origin of the state is to enable men to live the best life; and in order to live such a good life man must engage his time and attentions in meditation and activity, cultivating virtue of soul, and manifesting virtuous thought in a life of action.†

The state is not simply an association of individuals, but is also a collection of separate estates, as they were called in the Middle Ages, or professions of which the individuals are members, and in which they are associated together. The peace of society depends upon the proper harmony of the different classes in the state. There are in all six estates, three general and three particular. The three general estates or public professions are, magistracy, military, and ecclesiastical offices; the three particular estates or professions are those of agriculture, industry and commerce. These public and private functions are to be discharged in the interests of all, for the common utility—thus in marked contrast with the classes of the middle ages which always acted in private or class interest. These six classes form the civil society, form the organic elements in the living organism of the state. When each of the estates keeps its proper place and does its own part, as organs in the body of the community, there results that condition of social health which we call peace, harmony leading to material prosperity, moral force, and the general good order and security of the state. As the estates are not perfectly separate, there is a tendency to confusion and commingling in the performance of duty and the exercise of power,—the one over-

* Def. Pac. I. 4.
† I. c. 4.

stepping the limits of its authority and the other falling short in the performance of duty. Hence springs up disorder in the state. In such a case the social body is diseased. Consequently, ther is required a *legislative* power to make laws to regulate the functions and the duties of the different estates and an *executive* government to see to the execution of these laws.*

To whom then belongs the legislative power and in whom is the executive authority of government vested? He gives the classification of Aristotle in regard to the various forms of government, stating that perhaps the most perfect form is the royal. He does not however decide very strongly in favor of the monarchy, although he dedicated his book to the Emperor. He simply indicates his preference for this form, without any of the servile royalistic sentiments which are generally found in the Imperialistic writers. In the definition he gives of law and in his idea of sovereignty as inhering by nature in the state he limits the prerogatives of the monarch.†

(1) *The legislative power.* The foundation of the social structure of the state which others had failed to recognize, in ascribing to the prince the attributes of the state, he asserts is to be found in the principle that the sovereign power of the state vests in the people, and that legislation springs from such sovereignty, and laws depend for their force and validity upon the legislative power of the people. Legislative power, like sovereignty, pertains to the entire people, or to the majority which evidences its will in the public assembly of or representative of the people. The people alone have the right to impose laws upon themselves and if absolute unanimity is impossible then there should be a majority of suffrages. It is upon the principle of injustice that one or some should make the rest of the people slaves, for all men are equal among themselves. When the whole people legislate the laws are most legitimate, and they are more likely to be obeyed, for every man will obey his own will. To make one or a few the absolute masters of legislation is to employ constraint in commanding obedience.‡ The nation or people itself is the source of all power and right, it alone has the authority to legislate for the people, *humanus legislator fidelis superiore careus.*§ He shows the difference between the making of laws and the judging of their goodness or badness, justice or injustice, utility or disadvantageousness under certain conditions. The making of laws belongs to one wise man or a few wise men, but the judging of their applicability or suitability rests with the whole people. He claims for the people the right of accepting or rejecting laws framed in advance by the powers named as legislative officials or draft legislators. In other words draft laws should be submitted for approval to the people. As in the case of codification, a drafting or codifying commission should prepare the laws and then submit them to the whole people. For if the few had ab-

* I. c. 5-8.
† I. c. 9.
‡ I. c. 12.
§ II. c. 21

solute power in law-making we should be subject to the mistakes and even to the selfishness of that few, constituting an oligarchy. The people best know their requirements, what will satisfy their purposes. Therefore the mass of the citizens or the majority expressing its opinion by electing its own representatives possesses the sovereign power of the state.*

(2) *The executive power.* If wisdom belongs to a few, the incorruptible sense of justice and right belongs to the whole body of the people, and the just and proper combination of these two elements, the wisdom of a few and the justice of all, produces the best laws. Legislative power thus belongs to the entire nation. But the people require officers to execute their will. Therefore they choose executive persons and entrust them with governmental powers. *Cujuslibet principatus, aut alterius officii, per electionem, instituendi, praecipue vim coactivam habentis, electionem a solius legislatoris expressa voluntate pendere.*† We regard, he says, the second power in the state as an instrumental or executive power, which commands in virtue of authority accorded to it by the legislator, *secundarium vero quasi instrumentalem seu executivum dicimus principatum per auctoritatem a legislatore sibi concessam.* This executive ruler or rulers are charged with the execution of laws, *per ipsum executio legalium.* The executive power in whatever manner it is constituted has simply the authority delegated to it by the entire people, that only being legitimate which the people gives and grants. Whatever the executive does is subject to the will of the people in which we notice the marking off the state from the government clearly, in which case the government is the official servant of the state.† Elective monarchy is the preferable form in which the choice of a chief ruler is made, the hereditary is not consonant with the idea of popular sovereignty. He cites the papacy as an example of elective monarchy, in which the principle of election works better than heredity. The same principle was exemplified during the present century in the Italian cities of Florence, Padua, and Pisa. The government must have a unity somewhere, not necessarily however a numerical unity, official unity is sufficient. Unity may be secured when the government is conducted by an executive body as well as by a single king or ruler; in the case of the body the entire committee or council act unitedly or by the majority, not by any individual separately or on his own responsibility. The unity of government is not, according to Marsilius, that of numbers, it is a unity of principle and policy, in quality not in quantity.‡

(3) *Military and official power.* If a king is chosen as the chief ruler then he requires defense and the means of supporting his authority. This is done by means of an armed body of men at the command of the ruler. In numbers they must not be too great or so strong as to give to the king a position inde-

* l. c. 12.
† l. c. 14.
‡ l. c. 15.
§ l. c. 17.

pendent of the people, nor must they be too few or too weak so as to place him in the power of scheming men. So soon as he has been elected to office in the state, not before, these forces must be accorded to him, because they are intended to support the royal dignity bestowed by the people on a person of distinction, not as resources to wrest the power from an unwilling nation.

The king has in reality no prerogatives because he owes his kingship to the people's choice, and the people reserve the residuary power of sovereignty to themselves. Kings derive their authority from the *fons* of power, and they are responsible to the same people. Therefore the king acts as a chief in interpreting law and directing the state according to the people's will.* Subordinate officials of the state equally receive their authority and office from the people, although the king may deliver the seals of office to the holders, yet he does so in the people's name, executing all the necessary arrangements for the good government of the state. The people in last resort is supreme in everything. They supervise the king and his subordinates, and if he should overstep the limits of his commission, although he is above the law in his executive capacity, yet he is not above the lawgiver, but amenable to the will of the people. The people may depose him for violation of the terms of his election. The popular will is the controlling force in preventing despotism.†

(II) *Theory of the civil and religious orders.* One of the six classes in the community requires special attention because of the difficulties and dangers associated with its existence, namely, the priesthood. It is not absolutely essential to the existence of a properly organized state, that there be such a priesthood. For while it is the special province of the clergy to educate the people so as to prepare them for a future life, they whose commission was and is to preach the gospel and instruct the ignorant, have abandoned their spiritual vocation and usurped authority over temporal affairs, even over the emperor himself. The present disordered state of society is due largely to this usurpation. Marsilius has laid the foundation for his treatment of the religious office in its relation to the civil state, in the distinction he has drawn between public functions and public powers. The state and the Church are parallel organizations, the former embracing all the people as citizens, the latter all the people as Christians. In the secular order it is civil or human law that guides the executive in governing, in the religious order the only guide is revealed law or the Bible. The word Church is used in a non-apostolic sense, as he says, in that age, embracing the clergy and other Church dignitaries; whereas it ought to include, in its apostolic application, now as then, the whole body of Christians, all the members of the Church being alike included, priests and laymen, *viri Ecclesiastici.* Church dignitaries have usurped the title Ecclesiastics which belongs of right to all Church

* l. c. 15.
† l. c. 15-18.

members. It is absurd and wrong that clerics should usurp sole prerogative in the Church of Christ as alone possessed of sacerdotal power. In the Church as in the state the people are and have the real power.*

Civil power is concerned with the temporal welfare of society and its preservation from the dangers that arise in the worldly relations of men, and the sanction upon which it acts is corporal punishment in the sphere of the human life by the exercise of coercive power equally against Ecclesiastics and laity, when they break the laws of civil society or revolt against social order in the state. Divine law is limited in its operation to the souls of men, and to those means of a spiritual kind that promote the salvation of the soul, being limited to spiritual means, spiritual rewards and spiritual penalties with respect to the future life. All the power even of a spiritual kind which the Church officers possess is included in the promise of eternal life, and the denunciation of eternal condemnation. Excommunication from the Church is not a penalty that can be imposed by a single priest or council of priests. The priesthood as Doctors of Divine law exercise the functions of advising what should be done and avoided in the interests of the salvation of souls; they are entitled to be consulted as experts in regard to charges against the unfaithful, but the decision of such a charge rests with the congregation of which the culprit is a member or with the general council of the Church, not of the clerics alone. The clergy act not in the manner of judges, pronouncing a penalty, but as physicians prescribing remedies in the interest of health. The priests are the physicians of the soul as Jesus professed to be and their acts should not have a material character lest it hinder salvation. Clergy are not entitled to be called Ecclesiastics exclusively, nor are they just in arrogating the name of spiritual to all that attaches to them, such as revenues, lands, and other temporal perquisites, and to all their actions even of a temporal kind. They are not entitled to freedom from legal burdens. Their office is spiritual in the Church but in all relations outside of the Church in regard to land, finance, and temporal things they are subject to the same laws as the common people in the state. In the Church they are Churchmen, in the state they are citizens of the commonwealth; their temporal affairs are subject to civil law and their crimes are punishable by common law, but with greater severity because they are crimes of educated men.†

Citizenship with all its rights and duties is independent of a man's religion. The clergy in this respect stand on an equality with all others in civil relations and as citizens are treated in all respects alike, claiming and receiving no exemption on the ground of religious office. It is even the duty of the executive to regulate the number of clergy in each district, lest an overgrowth of clerics tend to disturb the peace of the society by an unequal dis-

* II. c. 2.
† II. c. 8.

tribution of cleric and lay elements in the population. The power of the priesthood is strictly spiritual. Temporal punishment does not belong to them. The gospel is doctrine, not law, and no force is authorized by it to compel its acceptance. The priest may admonish and even denounce spiritual threatenings, but he has no temporal power to enforce them. Heretics and unbelievers so far as the Divine law is concerned are only responsible to God, and only can be judged in the future life. The priest has the right to forewarn of what they shall receive hereafter at the judgment of Christ, the sole judge of heresy. If a heretic becomes dangerous to social order he may be tried by the civil tribunal, but only upon social causes; errors of opinion and unbelief are *ultra vires* of any human judicature. The only ground of human punishment is *contra praeceptum humanae legis*. The civil tribunal should never pronounce any sentence against heresy, errors, or any infraction of matters of belief. As is often the case the civil law interdicts spiritual crimes and so oversteps its authority.*

Marsilius thus teaches in plain terms the doctrine of toleration which has triumphed in modern civilization. He attacks the spiritual hierarchy in its ascending scale of powers and dignities, as destitute of scriptural authority. Bishop and priest are interchangeable titles in the New Testament for the same officials in the Church; and the popedom has no foundation in fact, for Peter had no supremacy over the other apostles and gave no such primacy to a successor or successors. Christ gave the Church no head upon earth. The papacy springs from the fact of the Church being identified with the imperial city and empire in the temporal domain, and results from courting the favor of and then conquering the emperor. The supreme power of the Church is deposited in the Church itself, that is, in a general assembly of clergy and laity, convened by the legislative power of the civil state, that is, not by the executive but by the legislative power which is in the people. The Emperor as representative of the people has the right of calling and dissolving assemblies of the Church. Such an assembly has power to decide all ecclesiastical matters, and representing as it does the whole community has power to suspend and depose the executive ruler and to suspend the operation of his commands which are beyond his jurisdiction. Such an assembly is the sole authority in matters of faith. It has jurisdiction also over the pope, because he cannot claim any supreme authority over clergy or people in human affairs. Church and state are reconciled in the fact that they are ultimately the same body of the people, with different functions, spiritual and temporal. Priests have no temporal jurisdiction for they received none from Christ. In regard to the ceremony of crowning Emperors, it has no validity in fact or right, but is at best an act of recognition. He rejects all ecclesiastical assumptions and prerogatives as a departure from the primitive simplicity of the Church of the Apostles and an attempt to attach to a purely

* II, c. 9, 10.

spiritual organization temporal sovereignty, temporal functions which are inconsistent with the spiritual nature of her officers, duties, assemblies, and ends. He thus declares long before the reformation the principles which he applied in politics and theology alike, a protestantism which gives a harmonious theory of Church and state, equally independent and exclusive.*

(III) *Conclusion.* In the last part of the work we have a summary of the conclusions reached by Marsilius, conclusions which mark the first dawn of the political renaissance. (1) He distinguishes *theology from politics* and the sphere of the temporal from that of the spiritual power. He defends the civil power and separates it from the Church. He maintains liberty of conscience. To be compelled to observe precepts of divine law by punishment or temporal penalty is not allowed. A priest has no temporal jurisdiction, his province being to guide men to seek eternal life. The ministry is to serve the Church; the assembly of the clergy and laity, is to stand where the hierarchy has stood; no autocrat is to be permitted to rule either in Church or state.

(2) *The State is an organization of free men.* There can be no freedom when one or some are *despotes aliorum.* Men unite in society to obtain common advantage and there can be no obedience on the part of citizens if they do not themselves make the laws. He might have adopted the language of Rousseau who seeks "to find a form of association in which everyone united to all obeys only himself."† People best know what is for their advantage and disadvantage, and such knowledge is the surest safeguard of well-being in the state.

(3) *The people is sovereign.* The opinion of Aristotle and truth itself (*secundum veritatem*) establish that human legislators are to be the *Universitas* of citizens, or the majority of them, through their elected representatives. All know what is best for them and no one willingly injures himself, *nemo sibi nocet sciunter.* The sovereignty of the people is manifested in appointing and also in removing the executive as well as in making the laws. He presents the division of the powers essential to a true democracy. (a) legislative power belongs to the people; (b) the people in their legislative capacity institute the executive; (c) similarly it exercises judicial power, for it is the supreme court before whom the executive is placed upon trial for failure in duty. Thus Marsilius laid the foundation of the modern constitutional state which he prophetically forecasts in his book.‡

4. William of Ockham, 1280-1347. (1) *Position in Imperial contest.* The great English schoolman, the disciple of Duns Scotus, lived through most exciting times, as a man, a politician and a philosopher of exceptionally

---
* II. c. 15, 16, 18, 22.

† Contrat social, c. 6.

‡ Franck, pp. 145-150; Janet, Vol. I, 457-464; Poole, pp. 265-276; Riezler, pp. 193-233; Friedberg, II. 32-48; Goldast, II. 154.

wide sympathies, and involved in interests that covered a large area. He was a man of action more than of speculation and his political theory comes out in the practical issues of his time. He was lecturing in Paris during the celebrated dispute between Boniface VIII. and Philip the Fair, but he did not take any part in the controversy. The greatest intellectual genius in an age of intellectual disputation, he figured as a prominent personage in the sceptical movement that swept over the field of theology, in the political struggle between the pope and the Emperor, which developed the liberal doctrines of politics; and also in the struggle between the papacy and the extreme order of Franciscans on the question of poverty and the right of the Church to hold property. He is best known for the courage he displayed in opposing the tyranny of the papal over the civil power. Louis of Bavaria had been legally elected to the Imperial dignity; the pope, John XXII., refused to own him, claiming that he had a right to veto his election. This contest was waged for over 25 years and the principal interest of it centres in the writings it produced. The men who espoused the Imperial cause found a shelter at Munich and published their works in defence of the law of the civil order *versus* the hierarchical despotism. Oekham published several treatises during the struggle.

He was contemporary with Marsilius and his colleague in the University of Paris. Pope Clement III. charges Oekham as the teacher of error to Marsilius. His writings however are all subsequent to the *Defensor Paris* and are more theological, as well as treating of the controversial details of the time in which however the grand purpose is the same as that of Marsilius, to cut short the temporal and spiritual power of the pope. Marsilius no doubt learned much from Oekham. Oekham on the other hand fell under the spell of the Italian orator's political enthusiasm. Marsilius elaborated his theory in Paris and as a result of his supreme faith in it cast in his lot with Louis. Oekham after fighting in the thickest of the struggle accepts and formulates his ideas as the result of the part he played in the melee. Marsilius stands like a itary figure looking backward and pointing forward; Oekham on the other hand with torch in hand makes his way onward, carrying the trend of thought from the greater schoolmen to the lesser, pioneering the progress of reform, till it meets the passionate soul of Huss, the popular spirit of Wyclif, and the reforming genius of the German and Swiss anti-ecclesiastics.

Oekham's chief work is *De potestate Ecclesiastica et sæculare*, 1326, in which he attacks the temporal sovereignty of the pope and declares the independence of kingly power as a divine institution, inveighing against the vices of Rome.* From the very nature of spiritual truth and from the agencies it uses to apply itself to the hearts and lives of men, it must be subordinate to the principle of authority in any state where it is accepted as the foundation of a national religion. On account of the boldness of this writing he was forced to seek refuge in France for a time.

* Goldast, Monarchia, I. p. 44

In his work *Disputatio super potestate praelatis atque principibus terrarum commissa* he declares that no power can be exercised except in accordance with its natural and lawful attributes as a power; hence the French king does not possess superior authority over the Emperor, neither can the Emperor exercise superior power over the French Monarch; that temporal rulers have no right to intermeddle with spiritual affairs, neither have spiritual officials any right to control temporal matters. Hence the spiritual ministers ought to confine their attention to the things that concern salvation, leaving to the princes of the temporal kingdom the government of the state, the conduct of war and the preservation of peace, as well as all executive administration. The pretension of the Pope is not founded upon fact and as a right it seems too absurd to need refutation. He declares that the priest is a citizen as much as ordinary subjects, and as such is to be subject to the temporal authority, to pay his share of the taxes and charges of government, as he shares its benefits and to support the civil institutions upon which the state is founded and by which its existence and peace are preserved.* In his *Super potestate summi pontificis*, 1339-1342, he places the temporal power above the spiritual.† He still more strongly insists on this principle in the *Tractatus de Jurisdictione Imperatoris in causis matrimonialibus*, 1342, in which he ascribes to the Imperial authority the right of declaring the degrees of affinity in marriage and of deciding judicially all contested cases.‡ The independence of the civil power and the rights of election he asserts plainly in his *Tractatus de Electione Caroli IV*.§

(2) *Position in the Franciscan struggle.* Ockham was closely associated with Michael of Cesena, and Francis of Ascoli in the order of Franciscans. His life is largely bound up in this controversy, which arose between the Dominicans, of which St. Thomas was a representative, and the Franciscans represented by Scotus, the predecessor and teacher of Ockham, in the time of Thomas. Ockham was the greatest pupil of Duns Scotus and upon him fell the mantle of his master. The Franciscans were mendicant friars and taught humility, bringing in the new doctrine of poverty, in which they declared that as Jesus Christ Himself had no property neither should the Church entangle herself with this worldly burden. They appealed to the Pope to sanction this new departure, but the Pope and a general council decided against them, the pope at the same time fulminating his anathemas and decrees against the order. When they were handed over to the power of the Inquisition in the hands of their Dominican opponents, Ockham went

* Scriptores Ordinis Minorum. Ockham. Rome 1650.
† Goldast, Monarchia, I. 558-617; Riezler, p. 249.
‡ Goldast, I. 21-24; Riezler, p. 254.
§ Riezler, p. 274; Lindsay, "Ockham and his connection with the Reformation." Brit. Quart. Review, July 1872; Lelland, c. 326; Account of writings of Ockham. Riezler, pp. 241 sq.

over to Louis of Bavaria who was himself in conflict with John XXII. in regard to the supremacy of the papal power over the imperial power, and joined issues with him, "defend me with the sword and I will defend you with the pen," the words he uttered on arriving as a fugitive at the Emperor's court being the motto of their alliance. Francis had based the order of Minor Friars he instituted upon the principles of humility and the renunciation of all property, individual and common; every individual was a brother or sister; the brotherhood was a conglomerate mass of individuals united on the extreme conception of charity, with little discipline or authority. The followers and successors of Francis were divided into a number of sects, many of them yielding themselves to great excesses in belief and practice, finding refuge in mysticism and monasticism, in which they despised all authority, temporal and spiritual, each individual being his own priest. Wadding tries to distinguish the Franciscans from these extreme factions, but they were all united on a common basis of poverty. It is in this connection that Cesena and Ockham appear as their defenders against the papacy.

In 1316 Michael of Cesena, the general chapter of the Minor brothers ordained a more strict adherence to the doctrine and practice of evangelical poverty; and with a view to restore the extreme sects called by the general name of spirituals, he appealed to John XXII. to ordain the dissolution of their separate orders and to impose severe penalties upon recalcitrants who refused submission. This measure reunited the order. But it opened the way for the opposition of the papacy. In 1322 a Franciscan was seized by the Dominican Inquisitors and through the intervention of one of the Franciscans the question of poverty was raised. It was carried to the papal court and the Doctors were set to investigate whether Jesus and his apostles had property. The order of Franciscans held a chapter general at which they decided, that having examined the proofs relative to the question, it was true, they believed, that Jesus and his apostles had no right of property, general or individual, and therefore the principle of poverty is sound Catholic doctrine. To this decision Ockham appended his name as one of the provincials of the order; in fact he wrote the resolution of the order himself. The Pope deposed Cesena, and declaring him a heretic deprived him of all office and dignity in 1329. He retired to Louis at Munich, who made him his adviser and in whose cause he wrote while defending himself against the attacks of the Pope and the Council of Perpignan, in which he declares that the Pope has forfeited his right to share in the government of the world in the interests of Christianity, and that it remains with the emperor to govern the world in the interests of the cause of the poor.*

Ockham entered into this controversy with all the enthusiasm of his being.

* Goldast, Monarchia, III. 1331-46; Wadding, Ann. Ord. Minorum, Anno. 1322, No. 53, 131; VII. 2nd. Ed.; Fleury, Eccl. Hist. 92, c. 63, 94, c. 16; Smith's Eccl. Hist., Vol. II. Pt. II. p 382; Franck, pp. 153-170; Riezler, pp. 59, sq.

The manifesto drawn up and signed at Perouse is the motto which guided his facile pen in elaborating his principles. He published a defence of poverty in opposition to the errors of John XXII.* In this writing he becomes the champion of spirituality, in which the rule of Francis is pushed to its farthest limit in defence of the Fraticelli who proclaimed themselves the enemies of all property, individual and collective. He sets forth at the same time the doctrine of equality in the Christian brotherhood which has no distinctions and makes no differences among individuals. On these two points he bore against the papacy, for the foe of property is the adversary of the papal dominion and the friend of a Church organization purely spiritual; and the friend of brotherhood is the opponent of hierarchical dignitaries and despotic actions in the name of Christianity. He is led to rebel against the authority of the Church and to lay stress upon the lay element just as Marsilius had done. An outlaw from the Church he continued to reside under imperial favor as a defender of civil independence in respect of the Ecclesiastical power, withstanding the encroachments of the papacy and censuring the excesses of the monks.

(1) *The nominalistic ideas of Ockham at the basis of Politics.* Nominalism was not merely a pet theory with him, it exercised an influence upon his political doctrines and his idea of natural right. Knowledge exercises an influence upon the religious and moral order. Knowledge springs from a double source, intuition and abstraction, called *vis intuitiva et abstractativa*. By the former process he means the experience which results from observation, whereby the faculty of the mind apprehends what is presented to it in evidence whether external to the senses or internal to the mind, and judges of its existence; by the latter process he understands the capacity of abstracting the particular facts or ideas with their special circumstances, which we have perceived, and considering them by themselves in separation from all others. It is in this way we particularize objects and ideas, the qualities pertaining to them and the circumstances connected with them. According to this the nature of knowledge presents ideas as nothing in themselves, simply a quality of the mind, which cannot be separated from it, excited by the external object; there is no intermediary between the object known and the subject knowing it. Hence general ideas are simply signs by means of which particulars are united by their similarities in a common term. All that is universal exists only in the individuals quite distinct from one another. We know nothing, for example, of universal humanity except what we know of the individuals as they are distinguished from one another. All our knowledge therefore which is real comes directly through the senses or through the mind; whatever else we know is abstraction. In this case the moral qualities are known only in their particular aspect, and there can be no moral duty universally binding upon

* Published by Brown, in the appendix of Fasciculus rerum expetendarum, II. p. 436, London, 1690; Riezler, p. 246; Singulare opus ordinis S. Francisci. Venetiis, 1513, III. S. 28.

all rational beings. Hence we cannot know virtue or science absolutely, but only as they are particular qualities of a human soul.

Instead of uniting and reconciling human reason and faith, as did Thomas, Ockham separates these, denying to reason the right of speaking concerning anything touching theology. He does not use this to destroy religion or religious liberty, because however much he has been opposed and subjected to the penalties of the Church for insubordination to religious authority, his philosophy has not been placed under censure. Ockham accepted this position in all sincerity, as giving to faith a more secure position, with less hazard, and in this he was followed by some of the purest spirits of the 14th. and 15th. centuries. Reason is relegated to that which is relative and temporal, in order that faith may be reserved for the absolute and divine. How does he apply this? By emphasizing the principles of his own order. When faith unquestioningly accepts the instructions of the Scripture, abandoning at its call all worldly goods, even life itself, to obey the voice of the Master, he has the best defence he could make of poverty, and consequently against property. In the same mystic spirit the voice of revelation interdicts all worldly power so far as the Christian is concerned; as a result the voice of God commands the head of the Church to abstain from all temporal authority and to give up all temporal possessions, in order to devote his spiritual office to a spiritual end.

Thus he sets up the power of the temporal rulers independent of the Church. The temporal power is a secular one and as such the Church can have nothing to do with it. In defending the temporal sovereign he has less respect to the temporal power than to the spirituality of the Church and her separation from the world. The Emperor and all human princes are like reason, the pope, clergy and all Christians are like revelation. The earthly ruler is confined to earthly concerns and objects, and governs in conformity with the rule of reason, the spiritual officer governing only by spiritual means, so as to promote the salvation of the soul. The result is that spirituality alone is perfection; all property is to be despised in order to attain such a condition. The soul is to have free play, but the body needs clothing and nourishment. To secure these one needs earthly goods and the help of others, physical as well as spiritual. Unless there is the title to these goods, who has the right to buy them? According to Ockham, the only right to property in a spiritual being is that of *charity*. In his abstraction he has forgotten that man is a creature of the earth as well as a being for heaven and that property is necessary to realize personality. His idea is that of the monk.,

(II) *Theological politics.* Ockham is a theologian and he commences from that point of view to develop his politics. His opposition to the papacy is based upon the papal condemnation of the new doctrine of the Franciscans

* Haureau, Schol. Phil. II. 450; Franck, pp. 184 sq.

concerning evangelical poverty. To deny the clergy property is to strip them of temporal authority and to lay low the Church of Rome. Ockham interpreted the course of history; for while the simple political theories of Marsilius were forgotten, the theory of Ockham is alive and is vindicated in the religious reformation of the 16th century. It was as he had predicted two centuries before it took place, a theological revolution that shook the temporal power of the papacy, and wrought or at least opened the way for the accomplishment of the political changes in Europe.*

(1) *Liberty.* The Christian system is appealed to as a law of freedom in which there is introduced an entirely new element. If the pope, he argues, possesses such large powers, then all Christians who are under him must be his slaves, and one only can be free, for the pontiff, according to this idea of supreme prerogative exercises over all, kings and subjects alike, a power in respect of goods and property as well as of persons, not less despotic but more arbitrary than that of the master over his slaves. Christ in freeing Christians from the bondage of the law has rescued them from all servitude; and his law is not a law of liberty if they are freed from one servitude to be subjected to another. It is objected by some that Christians are not entirely set free from domination, because it is permitted to Christians to be themselves and to have slaves. It is true that the new law of Christ does not rescue man from every kind of service, because Christians are permitted to be serfs and villains; but it does not permit them to be placed in a greater degree of subjection than were the Jews. This does not imply that Christians are the slaves of the pope, for while Christians are permitted to have and hold property in earthly possessions, slaves and serfs are not. The Christians by permission of the imperial laws have possession of goods so that the pope is not the sole owner. Likewise Christians are permitted to have serfs whereas serfs have no liberty to possess slaves. Christians, therefore, are not serfs or slaves of the pope, but free men, and that by the law of Christianity. Therefore Christian liberty is the foundation and guarantee of civil liberty, religious freedom the basis of political independence on the part of the citizens, and consequently Christian freedom is one of the essential principles of a free state. The principle is that a free soul demands a free body. Christianity enfranchises the soul from sin and servitude to the Mosaic law; therefore it ought to free the body.

History has illustrated this principle which Ockham did not fully comprehend himself, the progress of Christian civilization having been the means of rescuing humanity from servitude. Ockham does not measure the full consequences of his principle, for while he declares that Christians ought not to be slaves, he permits them to have others as slaves. He gets over this however by discriminating between two classes of human beings, as most of the Schoolmen had done, the believer and unbeliever, the Christian and

* Compend. error. papae I. 5; Goldast, II. 958 sq.

the barbarian or foreigner. It is not yet the freedom of man as man, but of man as a Christian, that is the foundation of civil freedom. It is theological or Christian liberty that is introduced into politics.*

(2) *Authority. The Pope or the Emperor.* It is difficult to get at the definite views of Oekham. According to his method which is set forth in the treatment of the subject of power, the ecclesiastical and secular power ought they to be united in a single person, he asks. In answering he gives the affirmative and negative reasons, going back over every answer to give the arguments for and against. His opinion can only be gathered from the weight he attaches to the answers and arguments. He strenuously repudiates the imperial authority claimed by the pope, as a usurpation; and at the same time he does not express his wish to give it to any other person or body of persons. It is enough for him to take away the autocratic power from the spiritual head, he does not transfer it to the emperor although in some respects the emperor he allows is above the pope.†

Not only is the pope deprived of his supreme power, the general councils are placed in the same category.‡ The assembly of the Church is to be composed of representatives, not of clergy alone, but also of the lay element, men and women alike being represented. Even to such a representative council of Christians, representative of all, male and female, lay and clerical, there does not pertain absolute authority in the matters of faith.§ The emperor in a sense as the supreme power, entrusted with it by the people under certain limitations, is the natural final judge in ecclesiastical and civil matters, the pope himself being subject to him.‖ The assembly of the Church is regarded as an Ecclesiastical Council, not as a representative of the legislative power of the people, and its functions are purely Ecclesiastical. It cannot be said that supreme power in matters of faith belongs to any earthly power. With Oekham this council is an Ecclesiastical tribunal to be used only in case of the pope becoming a heretic or incompetent for his office. Women, he admits, to this Ecclesiastical council as members, *propter unitatem fidei virorum et mulierum, quae omnes tangit et in qua non masculus nec femina, . . . non est mulier a generali concilio excludenda.*¶

It is human to err, hence in man we naturally find an element of error. Therefore no form or organization or system of man can be said to contain perfect truth.** Inspired truth alone is infallible. The tradition of the Church and the decrees of Popes and councils are tainted with imperfection. Hence the infallibility of popes or councils is no part of Oekham's creed.†† He is not carried away with the imperial idea, nor does he place absolute confidence in unity, that is numerical unity in power, for he regards it as better

* Dialogus III. tract. i. lib. II. c. 5-8.   ‖ Dial. III. II. III. 17.
† Dial. III. i. I. 9-16.   ¶ Dial. I. i. VI. 85. Goldast. II. 605.
‡ Dial. I. i. V. 1-5; III. I. III. 8-13.   ** Dial. I. i. V. 25-35.
§ Dial. I. i. VI. 85.   †† Dial. III. i. III. 1-4

in certain circumstances that there should be several popes and likewise several princes.*

In political affairs he prefers the nationality of the state, such as he found it in his own native land and in France where he spent a great part of his life to any fanciful imperial conception.† In history there is a progress that is moulded by the circumstances of the times; no state of society, no human institution can presume to be absolutely final in form, that is, there is no absolutely rigid and unchangeable form of government, no divine right of any special theory; and no single individual be he pope or emperor can impose his will as a barrier to the progressive adaptation in form of government to the conditions of society.‡ If the empire at present is worldwide, it is suited to the necessities of the world; but it is not universal, for it does not include everything, for spiritual concerns cannot be subordinated to temporal sovereignty. Neither can the pope claim to exercise the pope's spiritual power in the temporal domain. The state is an organic independent organization, free in its own domain, subject to the will of the entire community; the Church is a spiritual organism independent in spiritual concerns, also subject to the popular will of Christendom expressed in the general assembly or council of the Church.§ Each power has its own definite position and sphere, free and untrammelled.

The independent Franciscan spirit of Ockham draws upon the apostolic examples. Deep as his reverence is for spirituality he is in favor of free thought and denies to the Pope the right of trenching upon the liberal ideas of philosophy or theology. The state is in its sphere independent of and superior to the Church. In the Church the pope he acknowledges as the head, but he is subject to the voice of the Church and there is a right of appeal from him to the general body of Christians, to the society of Christendom, in whom the residuary spiritual power resides. If the pope errs every wise man is bound to resist him as far as his circumstances and ability will permit. If he is an heretic he ought to be judged by the Bishops. In default of ecclesiastical judgment he may be judged by the secular power, if he is guilty of any serious crimes. Ockham has already defended the independence of the Ecclesiastical and civil powers, but now when crime or heresy endanger society and the Church action is necessary somewhere. That action is imperative on the part of the Emperor, but also on the part of the people as a whole, in order to prevent the overthrow of liberty, truth and authority. It is the first sign of a popular, independent movement in the settlement of the question of the age, the Schism between Church and State, and the Schism in the Church itself. It bore fruit in the reforming Councils of Basle and Constance

* Dial. III. i. II. 28-30
† Dial. III. ii. I. 1-12.
‡ Dial. III. ii. I. 5.
§ Dial. III. ii. II. 6-9.

and prepared the way for the general reformation of Church and State, enfranchising the people, all the people, as members of the Church and as citizens in the state.*

5. John Wyclif, 1324-1384. Wyclif has been called the "morning star of the Reformation." A brilliant scholar and Master at Oxford, a hard-working parish cleric, and a most energetic organizer he left his impress upon the English Church, people and nation. His preaching friars in their russet gowns were themselves witnesses of the activity and enthusiasm of a man who perhaps next to Chaucer, the father of English verse, did more for English manners, language and civilization than any other before the reformation of the 16th. century. The share he took in opposing the pretensions of papalism and in asserting the independent nationality of the English people and the national character of the English Church has given him an imperishable place in the memory of the Anglo-Saxon race. In the contest between Pope Urban V. and the King of England in regard to the payment of the annual tribute promised by the weak King John as an acknowledgment of the Pope's feudal superiority, Wyclif defended the English monarchy against papal usurpation. There was but one Church in his time; while in that Church he cries out vigorously against her abuses. The papacy at this time was more than anything else a great political institution, claiming to regulate the affairs of all Christendom. It sought to exercise certain prerogatives over the English national Church which were offensive to the secular rulers, claiming in fact the island as its property.

Wyclif was the representative of the School when he made his attack on the papal excesses. The seeds of liberty he sowed excited the hatred of the Roman priesthood, a hatred manifested not only during his life by constant annoyance and vexatious decrees, but even after his death in cremating his corpse and scattering its dust upon the waters of the Swift, a branch of the Avon, to be borne on the tide into the bosom of the ocean. Wyclif was not only a saint, scholar, and evangelist, he was a Churchman and Scholastic. Like Marsilius and Ockham, Wyclif represents a national opposition to the papacy.

About 1366 he published his work entitled *Determinatio quaedam de Dominio* in defence of the English Parliament which repudiated the power of the papacy to exact the tribute promised by King John. In it we find the earliest traces of his doctrine of lordship, *dominium*, in which he presents the idea of a spiritual feudalism on parallel lines with the temporal feudalism; and in which he sets forth the grounds of his antagonism to the papal claims, which he based not upon theological, but upon political grounds. He denied the right of the spiritual authority to interfere in temporal affairs, which led

* Riezler, pp. 258-274; Goldast, Monarchia, II. 399-992; Fabricius l. c. III. p. 466; Janet, I. 445-457; Poole, pp. 277-284; Franck, pp. 48,-260; Haenel, Catalogi libror. Manuscript, in biblioth, Galliae, 53 and 56.

him to the Franciscan doctrine that the Church ought to have no temporal possessions, but ought to be purely spiritual.* His doctrine of *Dominium* he is said to have derived from his predecessor and teacher, Richard Fitz Ralph, Archbishop of Armagh, a doctrine which Fitz Ralph had used in opposing the friars and in supporting the beneficed clergy.† Wyclif does not accept his theory *in toto*, but rather modifies it by the Franciscan conception of spiritualism *versus* temporalism. He really established a theory of his own which is religious-political. In substance it is, (a) man has lost by sin all right to the possession of anything; (b) the consequence is, all property should be held in community; (c) the spiritual power is quite distinct from the temporal, and in overriding the limits of its authority it subjects itself to the temporal authority, because of usurpation; (d) the Church ought to have no property and ought not to pronounce the sentence of excommunication in the case of any temporal offence; if it does so there is really no excommunication. Wyclif sets forth these ideas in his treatises *De Dominio*.‡

His theory was vastly different from that of Marsilius and Oekham, his predecessors, and in fact from that of the men of his own age. Other theorists were groping in the mine of Aristotelian philosophy to discover, or hewing from the quarry of Old Testament Theology, a system to graft on to the modern society; while the jurists were culling selections from the civil law to support the imperial idea, and the papal devotees from the canonists. There was no attempt to formulate a theory on the basis of the then existing constitutions. There was one theory, however, preposterous as it may seem that adjusted itself to the conditions of feudal society and presented an ideal picture of what society ought to be. It was not a practical theory, and it was based upon as impracticable an idea of the Scripture theory as that of any of the hierarchical writers. Pure and simple as understood at the time it was Christian socialism. The doctrinal theology of Wyclif was orthodox, his character sustained, but he had an ardent desire as a Churchman to reform the papacy and to establish it above the reproach and the corruption into which it had fallen.§ His political and theological ideas are contained in the word *Lordship*, *Dominium*, the title he gives to his theory. He develops this lordship in two directions in his two works, *De Dominio Divino*, Divine Lordship, and *De Civili Dominio*, Civil Lordship ‖

(1) *General theory of Lordship*. God and humanity are inseparably united. Their

* Printed by J. Lewis, Life of Wiclif. Oxford, 1820, Appendix, pp. 349-356 from M. S. in Bodleian Library, Oxford, arch. Seld. B 26, ff. 54, sq.

† See F. D. Mathew, in Introd. to English Works of Wyclif, p. 34, 1880.

‡ De Civili Dominio, edited by R. L. Poole, 1885; De Ecclesia, by J. Loserth, 1886.

§ Lechler, Johann Von Wyclif und die Vorgeschichte der Reformation, I, 573, n. 2.

‖ Published under the Wyclif Society by R. L. Poole from the original codices in the palace Library at Vienna, the De Dominio Divino from Codex. 1339 corrected from 1294 and 395; the De Civili Dominio from the only extant copy, Codex 1340 containing book III, and 1341 books I. and II.

union is effected by means of lordship and service. The idea of lordship does not pertain to the natural order of existence, for lordship is correlative with service and there was no possibility of service until God by an act of creation, depending upon an act of will, produced creatures capable of standing in relation to Himself as creatures.* The Elohim God of Genesis I. is presented as the Jahveh Elohim, Lord God, in Genesis II. The self-existent being, self-sufficient because of plurality, becomes the Lord, I am as I am, because he has creatures in the position of service to him; just as man is lord over the lower animals by his creation. Lordship and service therefore imply mutual relations of beings, and are corresponding terms in denoting the two sides of the relation. Lordship implies authority and right and something more, because lordship cannot exist unless there are subjects in obedience to it, over whom it has rights and upon whom it exercises its power. Lordship, therefore, implies the use of power and the exercise of rights; for rights and powers may exist without the enjoyment of the one or the use of the other. On the other hand, lordship being more than a right or power, is an inherent characteristic or habit of the rational nature and manifests itself as a habitual element of nature in the fact of its superiority over other inferior creatures. *Dominium est habitudo naturæ rationalis secundum quam denominatur suo profici servienti.*†

Divine lordship belongs to God by virtue of his creating power and the act of creation, and it shows its power in exercise in the control of the universe and the government of man for His own purposes. The Divine is the only sovereign lordship, because it is universal; and while it is not required on the part of God that he receive service from man, though he is independent of man's service, yet it is of such an absolute character that all creatures offer him homage.‡ God acts immediately in his government of man and the universe, neither requiring nor using the mediation of others in establishing and sustaining his lordship over all, but holding all things in immediate relation with himself. God is the sovereign lord, all creatures are his immediate vassals. In feudalism there was a series of subinfeudations, the king being chief vassal, his vassals immediate the greater barons, their vassals immediate and the king's mediate being the lesser barons, and so on down the scale of vassalage. Divine feudalism views God as the supreme Lord and every creature his immediate vassal by the same kind of tenure, each one holding directly from the supreme Lord. Every individual is dependent upon God and upon God alone, no one is an intermediary between God and man.§

Here we have the substance of Wyclif's independent theory as distinct

* De Div. Dom. I. 2.
† Ibid. I. 1-2.
‡ Ibid. I. 3.
§ Ibid. I. 4, 5.

from the theory and practice of the age in which he lived. As Ockham laid low the priesthood by *nominalism*, Wyclif strikes out the priestly power and denies priestly interference by placing all men on an equality before God and making them all hold equal rank as citizens under the sole universal lordship of God Himself. Every one "holds" from God in the language of feudalism.

(II) *Application of the Theory of Lordship.* He applies this doctrine of Divine feudalism to man and every man in his remarkable treatise on *Civil Lordship.* (1) No one who is guilty of mortal sin has any right to enjoy the gifts of God and every recipient of grace possesses all these gifts as well as the right to use them. To sin is to reduce oneself to absolute nothingness, and therefore he who sins has not any right to anything. Possession implies right; right presupposes a title, and a title to possession comes directly from God and depends upon his will. God cannot approve of a sinner, therefore he cannot approve of a sinner's possessing anything; He abhors a sinful dominion and domination. Such a possession may be held *de facto*, but not *de jure*. God gives to man, as the chief over-Lord, all possession and lordship on the basis of man's allegiance and obedience; if man sins a sin that is unto death, then he has broken the tie of feudal vassalage which was based upon obedience, that binds him to God, the governor and proprietor of all things, and he has forfeited his right to possess them.* He distinguishes between the true Church of Christ and the actual Church. In the pure Church of Christ all the members are faithful; in the actual Church in human society there is a mixture of wicked and good, the wicked retaining membership in the society for the sake of the benefits it yields. To the members of the true Church God gives the possession and domination which belongs to the righteous; the unbelieving who are members only in name share in this possession by reason of their nominal relation to the Church, but their title is not deserving of recognition.† All dominion of man comes from God and is conferred upon condition of service; the failure to yield such service by commission or omission amounting to mortal sin acts as a forfeiture of any and every right of *dominion* given to man.‡

(2) *Righteousness is the fundamental principle of Lordship*; consequently every righteous person is lord in the visible world. This lordship is not limited to a part or a few things in the sensible world, but extends to all things; for if a righteous man has a right to enjoy anything he has the right to enjoy everything, because all things are gifted by God, and God gives everything to a truly righteous man by first giving Himself. Even in adversity the righteous are lords of all the world, because all things work for the good of the righteous and serve him whether they are in harmony with his present position

* De Civ. Dom. I. 1.
† Ibid. I. 2.
‡ Ibid. I. 3.

or whether they afflict and trouble him.* Seeing that there are many righteous ones and as each one is entitled to the lordship of the whole world (*dominus universitatis*), there cannot be any private possessions, everything in the shape of goods or possessions ought to be held in common, for the good and service of all (*Omnia debent esse communia*).† The consequence of this doctrine is twofold, (a) all lordship, possession and government is founded upon grace, not upon moral nature, but upon moral nature regenerated by grace from God (*si est in gracia est dominus universitatis*). (b) Only the subjects of this divine grace have any right to lordship, or possession, or control of anything; therefore the wicked when they do enjoy them usurp their possession or control. This is the natural result of the doctrine that domination of man over man was introduced by the sin and fall of man.‡

(3) Following from the last principle is another, that the *gospel law alone is necessary in the exercise of that lordship*. All ordinances and laws of a human kind are, if not superfluous, at least not essential but accidental. Such human laws and arrangements result from the fall, giving rise to tyranny according as men arbitrarily seek a self-interested dominium. Accordingly there is a distinction between *natural lordship* and *civil lordship*, the latter being subordinate to the former, springing up as a consequence of, and possessing only a relative character, depending upon and varying with the changing necessities and circumstances of men in society. Natural lordship is *dominium divinitus institutum*, civil lordship is *occasione peccati humanitus institutum*. All human institutions are variable and fallible; and consequently in civil lordship there is no inflexible and unalterable form of government. The fact that a certain form is assumed or that a certain ruler is chosen by a people to govern in a certain way does not make the government conform to the law of natural lordship. Natural law with Wyclif is different from the natural law of the other Schoolmen: natural law is the law of the gospel laid down in the distinction of righteous and wicked.§

Like Aquinas he goes to the Old Testament for the model of the best government. It is a kind of righteous Aristocracy in which the administration and legislation depend upon judges who are chosen in a plurality from the people and by them, because such a government in the abstract comes nearest to natural Lordship. His appreciation of the Republican form arises from the fact of the history of Israel, that the origin of the republican form was in God's own appointment, while the monarchic sprung from the will of the people, when they fell away into defection from the divine form of government. He depreciates the priestocracy, because he says that the final form of degenerate government in Israel was that of the priests in which

* Ibid. I. 7.
† Ibid. I. 14, 15.
‡ Ibid. I. 5.
§ Ibid. I. 17-19, 34.

were introduced more of human ordinances, the introduction of which led the people first of all to captivity and finally to entire disintegration. The ideal form of government then in natural lordship is the Aristocracy. But when it comes to the practical application in civil lordship, he thinks monarchy is the best, because seeing that all men are sinful and tendencies exist among all men to degeneracy and corruption, a strong government is needed to check excesses and to prevent decay. Such a strong government is more easily found in the single will of a powerful ruler.* He discusses the respective merits of succession by heredity and by election in the transmission of lordship. Hereditary succession tends to develop tyranny, because the certainty that the son or heir will follow the present ruler gives him a security in the government which one depending upon personal merit does not enjoy. This is confirmed by the medieval idea that a hereditary prince has the *dominium* of his kingdom and cannot be deposed even for tyrannical use of his power; that the society can only depose one whom it has elected, not a hereditary prince. On the other hand such an idea of transmitting to his son or heir his rulership may and ought to exercise a beneficial influence upon the conduct of the ruler, that he shall make the best possible use of his trust and receive the highest approbation from those whom he governs. Popular election is vitiated by the results of the fall, the consequence being that often, even in the majority of cases, the vote of the people, even of all the people is given in support of what is evil, so that the electing power of the community is used in elevating the wrong person or persons to the rulership. Neither heredity nor election however gives absolute title to lordship, unless the person so succeeding is a subject of grace and so qualified as a righteous person to exercise the lordship.†

(4) *Lordship presupposes and implies its correlative, service.* That is, those who are themselves lords are bound in service to God from whom they derive their lordship and to whom they are responsible.‡ This is the means of keeping them from excess, because as custodians of power received from God, they exercise it in his service. Kings are limited by their responsibility to God. The absolute lordship of God alone is unconditional and unlimited, authority in the hands of man is limited and conditional. All men are the ministers of God and servants of one another.§ Even the Pontiffs acknowledge in their bulls and decrees that they are servants of God. And since they are servants of God, they are not infallible or sovereign, and as lords they are stewards.‖ All men who are just and faithful are co-participators in lordship, and hence all power is in common, and all property is held in common. To take possession of power or possessions by force is illegitimate, because contrary to the commands of God's word; and to alter the form of society, im-

* Ibid. I. 27.   ‡ Ibid. I. 11.
* Ibid. I. 29–30.   § Ibid. I. 19.
† Ibid. I. 14.

perfect and unformed though it be, is illegal because the divine being has given his sanction to the present constitution of human society, and a change is contrary to his will. It is a part of the plan of providence which orders all things for the good of the righteous. The righteous may not enjoy all things in the present life, but they have a right to them, although they are not to exercise their right to enforce possession from present possessors; their right will become actual possession in the life to come. It is enough to be conscious that as Christians we are entitled to all things, and that the wicked whatever they have, have no right to its possession; they have their enjoyment and possession here; in the future it is cut off, and in the removal of sin every wrong is thoroughly rectified.*

Walsingham charges to the communistic doctrines of Wyclif and his disciples the peasant's revolt of 1382. Ball boasted that he had imbibed the views of Wyclif upon property ownership and civil power. It is but justice to Wyclif to say, that such violent measures never entered his mind, and no word that he has written can be construed into an incitement or encouragement to the use of violence, for his first principle clearly laid down is that force is contrary to the law of God.†

(5) *Summary.* The one idea running through the whole theory is the distinction of the righteous and the wicked; the righteous have a natural right to everything, but it is founded on grace; the wicked have no rights natural, all their enjoyments and possessions being civil. Every distinction in society and among men is based upon this primary conception. It gives rise to the tyranny that is found so often in society and in history, the fact that enjoyment and possession are always with the wicked a usurpation. Feudalism is the theocratic conception that realizes the relations of lordship and service, this feudalism being determined by two factors, (a) every relationship of lordship and service among men implies and presupposes the over-lordship of God and the service of man; (b) the determining element in man's character is not his outward position of office, but his inward relation of heart and soul with God. While every individual has a natural right to all things and all power, he may not use his power or enjoy his right in opposition to the present form of the civil structure of society, nor may he refuse to acknowledge the civil governor, even though he be a tyrant, because he rules in accordance with divine permission. Wyclif goes so far in this permissive will of God that if the devil should usurp authority in the world, God ought he says to obey even the devil. Tyranny or usurpation of power gives no excuse for disobedience, for refusal to acknowledge it or for tyrannicide. The fact of the existence of a power gives the right of obedience which must accordingly be passive.‡

* Ibid. I. 9, 12, 16.
† Poole, p. 269.
‡ Ibid. I. 28.

He distinguishes between the temporal and spiritual powers, and limits each to its own province. In the present condition of life and state of society the temporal is sovereign in secular affairs, and the spiritual in religious matters, each being independent and free from interference in its own department. No bishop or pope can exercise any secular office, because to enter upon any temporal function is to degrade the sovereign dignity of the spiritual office received from God.* Yet he does not proscribe the pope's benediction or grant, because only by the blessing of the Pope does God give his special favors to men.† He regards all human legislation as accidental and arising from the necessities of a sinful condition of man. In the future state, or the external order as he calls it, the power of the righteous will be established; human ordinances will no longer be necessary, because sin will be eradicated and man will return to the divine, eternal law. He concedes the necessity of civil society as a providentially permissive necessity.‡ Meanwhile the present order is one of confusion; the conflict of the temporal and spiritual powers is due to sin and sin's selfishness and tyranny. Them isuse of the power of the pope has brought him and the papacy into discredit. So much has the Pope interfered, especially in England, in regard to temporalities Wyclif is led to assert the complete independence of the nation in temporal things; and even within the sphere of the Church herself he joins Ockham in questioning the utility and the indispensable character of the popedom in spiritual matters. Temporal revenues are to be restored to the temporal province and the Church limited to spiritual things.§ He questions if the time may not yet come when Ecclesiasticism will be abolished and the Church return into the hands of the laity.‖ An office does not give an individual any superiority, unless he has an excellence of character to back it up. He arrives at the conclusion that man is an individual, his liberty, responsibility, and authority are individual, so that toleration and qualifications for office in Church and State depend upon the personal status. Consequently in Church or State the individual is independent and self determining, so far as the organization to which he attaches himself is concerned, and the organization itself is free from the interference of every other such organization. Yet a person is nothing and has no power by right unless he belongs to the body of Christ, and receives through grace a qualification of character that gives him a right to all the gifts of God. He thus becomes the advocate and exponent of Christian individualism and Christian socialism as the two great principles in politics and religion.¶

* Ibid. I. 11, 17.
† Ibid. I. 13.
‡ Ibid. I. 17.
§ Ibid. 11, 12.
‖ Ibid. I. 15.
¶ Poole, pp. 295-307; Smith's Eccles. Hist. Vol. II. Pt. II. c. 39, p. 630 sq.; Life of Wyclif by John Lewis, 1719. Robert Vaughan 1828 and 1853. Le Bas, 1832; Lechler, Johann Von Wiclif und die Vorgeschichte der Reformation, Leipsic 1873; Beacon Lights of History, Vol. II. c. 24, p. 435 sq.; Works of Wyclif edited by F. D. Mathew; D'Aubigne, Hist. of Reform. Vol. V. c. 7 and 8, p. 108-140, Edinb. 1853; Poole, Wicliffe and Movements for Reform. Epochs of Church History, London 1889.

CHAPTER III.

THE SPANISH JURISTS. VICTORIA. SOTO. SUAREZ.

1. *Introduction. Humanism. Spanish Jurists.* The fifteenth century produced some learned Scholastics. It was the period in which Scholasticism became disintegrated through the influence of mysticism and rationalism. This was the age of brotherhood or community, asserting itself equally in Germany, France, Italy and England. Above all it was the age of Humanism; that revival of letters and literature called Classicism which was the prelude of the Reformation in the 16th. Century. Among the first, perhaps the first, both in point of time and in excellence of spirit and work was the poet and philosopher Dante. He had a conscious purpose of banishing barbarism, and in the dawn of an awakened interest in literature to prepare the way for the revival of science, the revival of rational philosophy and the reformation of society. One of the brightest stars in the humanistic sky was the successor of Dante, Francis Petrarcha. To the revival of purity in the Latin tongue and the perfection of Italian poetry may be added the grace and elegance with which he clothed morality in some of the choicest flowers of literature.[*] This was the age of the conquest of the East by the Turks and the exile of the Greek scholars in Italy and Western Europe. Greek Literature which had lain in silence for centuries arose with fresh light to revive the world. The Italian poets, having created a taste for literature, left the task of encouraging it to the laudable rivalry of princes, and especially to that humanistic prelate, Nicolas V. whose patronage made Rome the home of learning. Lorenzo de Medici, the prince of Florence, expended the wealth of his noble family in procuring the most valuable manuscripts which antiquity possessed. In the latter half of the 15th. Century John Argyropolus taught the philosophy of Aristotle under the authority of the Roman see at Rome. Laurentius Valla the most celebrated Latin of his age refuted the absurdities of the barbarians, resurrected Italian literature and the Latin tongue and gave to Italians their former splendor of eloquence, contributing to learning this, that learned men after his day were compelled to use accurate language in speaking and writing.[†]

Following upon this revival of learning scholastic philosophy was attacked in two different directions, by the followers of pure peripateticism and by the followers of platonism. The Greek refugees finding that Aristotelianism

[*] Squarzafich, Vit. Petrarch. Oper. proem.
[†] Erasmus, Epist. VII. 7.

had become corrupted through Arabian translations, used their influence to introduce Aristotle himself and to throw out the Arabian and Scholastic adulterations. The platonists seizing the opportunity of appealing to the impiety cultivated by the doctrines of Averrhoes, recommended their system as better adapted to religion. Among the Scholastics themselves one deserves special notice because he united in himself scholastic training and tendencies of a humanistic kind. This was John Herman Wessel of Groningen. He was a brilliant scholar having studied the Greek, Hebrew, and Arabic languages, and he taught at Groningen with great distinction. He died in 1489 after discovering the weaknesses of Scholasticism: "the doctrines of Thomas Aquinas, Bonaventure and other modern disputants of the same stamp will be exploded by all true Christian Divines," were his prophetic words to one of his disciples.* Another link between the scholasticism of the past and the modern renaissance is found in Ludovicus Vives, a native of Spain, educated in all the refinements of Scholasticism at Paris, who devoted himself to the destruction of corruption and to establish purity of Science and learning. He was the friend of that great Humanist, Erasmus of Rotterdam, who declared him well informed in every department of philosophy. One of his chief writings is a commentary upon the *De Civitate Dei* of Augustine which shows a wide knowledge of ancient philosophy. His work *De Corruptis artibus et tradendis disciplinis*, Lugd. 1551, displays a knowledge of philosophy and an estimate of education far in advance of his own age.†

Scholasticism although subjected to much opposition did not die, at least in its principles. The shell or form in which the truth was encased became old and it passed away. In Spain we have the lastest survival of the system as such. In no other country was there such a close investigation of the subject of politics. In the very heart of the Inquisition we find some of the ablest expositors of the principles of government and of freedom in the history of the middle ages. The grand mistake made in Spain is found in the fact that the knowledge of these doctrines is purely theoretical. The spirit of casuistry is there and the doctrines are fully stated even with the minutest detail; but they end in speculation, they have no practical bearing upon life and government. Spanish political philosophy is overwhelmingly theological. This is largely owing to the influence of the writings of Aquinas upon the Spanish philosophers. The Spanish Jurists were adherents of the Thomist School, and naturally they followed the principles of their Master, elaborating them in their discussions of Scientific topics. And yet, although the Spanish Universities were under the complete spell of Thomism, they exhibit in dealing with politics which is a favorite subject among Spaniards, a wonderful degree of toleration and liberalism.

* Suffr. Petri de Ser. Fris. doc. VIII. p. 46; Adami Vit. Phil. p. 21.
† Nich. Anton. Bibl. Hispan. I. p. 160; Calones. Hisp. Orient. p. 223.

We are now passing from the distinctively Scholastic times to the last stage of Medieval history, in which attention is directed to the great world upon which human life exists, and particularly to what must be regarded as of greater importance, the little world of human beings that inhabits the greater world. Men begin to be viewed, not as mere generators of power, but as individuals of passion, desire, and inclination; and in the reaction against the rigid Ecclesiasticism of the purest schoolmen, the philosophers tend to subordinate every human relation to a two-fold legalism in its almost infinite varieties, the *jus naturae* and *jus gentium*. This movement of political thinking develops in three directions. In the *first*, the politics of the Jurist-theologians is developed in harmony with the Church as represented in Aquinas. In the *second*, we have anti-Ecclesiastical writers who break altogether with the Church, openly opposing the Church's politics; and in the *last*, we have the political writers who simply disregard the Church in dealing with politics. The first class embraces the Spanish Jurists and Jesuits. The second class includes the reformers who break with the Church, inaugurate and carry through the religious reformation of the 16th Century, and Machiavelli of Florence with his school. The third class is represented by Bodin, Gentilis and Grotius, the trio of independent politicians whom we consider in the next part.

The *Spanish Jurists* follow the lead of Aquinas. The political theory of Aquinas, as elaborated by the Spanish Jurists, may be reduced to two main propositions, referring to power in relation to God, and power so far as it relates to man. God is the constant direct source of power, and just as He sustains the physical universe by his presence and influence, so he sustains and develops the moral world by His presence and power. He is the great centre from which all the radiations proceed as rays of light from His moral being, to vivify and fill with enthusiasm the moral natures of men in their social relations with one another. Without this constant outpouring of the divine element man's society would be an utter blank, for all authority among men springs from and is delegated by the divine being. Unless man is guided to unfold the divine character of his authority in all human institutions, government, and legislation, he will fall into defection and thereby into a state of rebellion and tyranny. Divine revelation opens up a channel whereby the Divine mind is brought to bear upon the human mind in legislation and government. The grand design of the political life and of civil government is to elevate man to a higher life of perfection. He concentrates all his energies upon this more perfect life, and in the social and political sphere he is guided by the power of intellect or reason.

Legislation is the chief province of the governor in the state, who tries to harmonize the actions of all so as to attain the end set forth. To possess true political knowledge and to impart it is the duty of the legislator. This political knowledge must be purely intellectual and develops in three directions, (a) an examination of the political causes which determine political action; (b) an abstract conception of the moral nature of man, apart from the sensuous nature, for legislation must depend upon the former if it is to be in a measure perfect and preserved from sensuous corruption; (c) to reach a perfectly clear political knowledge it must be viewed in its spiritual relations, apart altogether from material things and relations. Legislation to be perfect in a word must be abstract, ideal and religious, moulded by revelation. To perfect legislation and through legislation to perfect men in society is the end of God's delegation of power to men in civil society.

These Spanish Jurists were Jesuits. One great design in the origin of the society of Jesus was a political end, to bring all nations into subjection to the Roman see as the channel through which all political power is dispensed by God. This is the realization of the doctrine that God is the direct source of all power. The first Jesuit School was opened in 1546. It was soon created a University by the Papal Bull and the rescript of the Spanish king. The establishment of the Jesuit school was like the establishment of the Bologna School for the revival of Roman jurisprudence and it was an attempt to counteract the effect of the Reformation which had already been felt in Europe. While the kings and potentates whose empires had been shaken by the reformation were seeking to find some power to strengthen the unstable political structure, the pope was equally concerned to support and strengthen his own temporal and spiritual position. The Council of Trent, 1546, is an evidence of this desire; the existence and recognition of the Jesuits is another evidence. These Jesuits were tenacious and persistent in their efforts. One feature of their whole course and system, if they ever had a system, is its variable character; they have lost the strict rigidity of Scholasticism and in their political speculations they are guided largely by expediency and temporizing expedients to gain success. Pope Clement felt that they were a thorn in the Church's flesh, for he declared that "they troubled the entire Church." The main object of the society was to secure the recognition of the Pope as the holder of universal political power and to exert their influence upon kings and governors to secure this end.

In their opposition to the Reformation which preached the gospel of Christ, and consequently of free conscience and liberty of action, they dwelt earnestly upon the duty of obedience and enforced the moral side of religion, opposing the democratic tendency of the reformation by political expedients to secure obedience to Rome. In turn they used war, imprisonment and the torture to bring Protestants and Catholics alike to subjection. In their zeal for truth, as they conceived it, they declined Ecclesiastical preferments, and threw themselves into the task of educating in the Universities and public schools. As educators they exercised a good influence upon Europe, taking advantage of the opportunities opened up by the revival of letters to spread their intellectual acquirements with great zeal and much talent.

Europe owes much to the enthusiasm of the men who willingly travelled into every country to communicate the knowledge they had themselves acquired. We do not palliate any of the crimes of the order, nor commend the secret intrigues that were followed by the majority of the members. We look to the noble and self-sacrificing minority of nominal members of the order who were above the order itself, and whose writings present to us the last feeble, yet living and transforming views of the Schoolmen of Medieval ages.*

2. Victoria. Soto. We come to a class of men who expound justice, morals and politics. Ferdinand Vasquez was the first to distinguish formally between the law of nature and the law of nations, or the particular ordinances of states, these two forming the wider, *jus gentium*, International Law. But the earliest exponent and systematizer of the general principles of Spanish Scholasticism was Francis de Victoria, who when he died was a professor in the University of Salamanca, in 1546. He was a man of exceptional ability and genius in Spain, then one of the most enlightened and powerful of European nations. He took as his guide the works of the Latin Schoolmen, chiefly the treatise upon laws in the *Summa* of St. Thomas, the method he followed being casuistical.

He was the first to elaborate these primal principles which later became the foundation of the law of nations. The independence of the national state was asserted and vindicated by the establishment of the Science of International Law, which set up a determining authority to settle questions of right between those States. International Law and its advocates were the real promoters of nationality and independence in the State. In order to secure a solid foundation upon which to rest the principles of justice and right among nations, Victoria placed the sanction of the obligations upon a theological principle and enforced it by appealing to the moral sentiments of the body of mankind in all ages and in all countries. His sentiments upon national honor and justice are exceedingly liberal and laudable. Theological casuistry was the foundation upon which was built up by means of local statutes and the loose practice of nations this system. It was recognized that not alone in peace, but also in war were there rights and duties belonging to and encumbent upon states and princes, and even enemies in combat were entitled to receive a certain consideration at the hands of their opponents on the principle of reciprocity. Ancient and medieval history and especially the tenets of the Christian faith supported this principle. The Spanish colonization movements of this and the preceding century gave rise to new principles of procedure in government and legislation. The discovery of America placed the old world in a new position, and demanded a new policy in administration and in the consideration of territorial nationality. Europe seemed awakened to a new interest in politi-

* Die Moral und Politik der Jesuiten, Ellendorf, Darmstadt, 1840; Ludovicus Vives, Relatio gestorum Patrum Societatis, 1596; Blakey, Hist. of Pol. Lit. II. p. 365 sq.

cal questions by the opening up of new fields of enterprise and political problems assumed a new aspect in the light of developing trade and expanding civilization. Victoria was among the first to condemn publicly the policy of Spain in her sanguinary contest with the American races, even when that policy was dictated by a pretended desire of extending Christianity among the barbarous races in the new world. He refused to acknowledge this as a sufficient ground for a just war.

The chief work of Victoria is, "*Relectiones Theologicæ,*" in which he attempts to restore the supremacy of Theology. This work was known to Grotius. Dupin gives a brief summary of the work. In the work there are thirteen treatises upon different topics. The *third* relection is entitled, *De potestate civili,* in which he declares that government and royal power originate immediately from divine institution. The majority of a state may elect a king and to him the minority must be subject. Likewise the majority of Christians may choose a universal emperor and subject all others to him. In the *fifth* relection he presents the various titles upon which the king of Spain claims to rest his sovereignty over the new world and its inhabitants. He vindicates the natural right of the Indians to the sovereign control of their own territory and to the supreme dominion in their own government, denying the alleged dominion which is based upon the infidelity and the barbarism of these people as non-Christians. He refuses to acknowledge the statement of the jurist Bartolus, that the Emperor is sovereign of the whole world, or that the pope had any right to give the dominion over Indians, barbarians, or infidels to the kings of Spain or any other Monarch. He asserts that the title of the King of Spain over the new world rests upon what he designates the *natural right of intercourse and society* which permits the Spanish people to trade with and to enter into the country of these natives for the purpose of trading, without inflicting any injury upon them. The refusal of permission to trade and to hold intercourse with these native barbarians is a just cause of war and gives the right to the King of Spain to acquire the sovereignty over these parts by means of arms, but this conquest must be validated by cessions such as were made by the Spanish allies among the native chiefs.

In the *sixth* relection he treats of war. While admitting the justness of war to compel the infidels to trade, he denies that their refusal of Christianity is a just cause for declaring war; yet they ought to be compelled to permit those among them who are willing to hear the gospel to receive it at the hands of the missionaries; and that the force of Spain ought to be used justly in preventing the infidels from persecuting the converts to Christianity among them. Fearing lest his permission might seem to justify the excesses of his countrymen, he limits even this permission by declaring the unwarrantableness of using violence, which in the name of religion might be practised in an avaricious and a worldly spirit. Christians are justified, he thinks, in declaring war in order to defend themselves from attacks, in order to meet the force of the enemy which threatens their lives and properties and in order to retake what has been taken from them by an enemy. Defensive war is justifiable on the part of Christians. Offensive war is also justifiable when it falls within his definition, which is, that which seeks reparation for damage or injury received at the hands of others. He argues these questions scholastically, giving the arguments on both sides. He supports his own views by Scripture references and quotations from the fathers. He permits a private warfare, provided it be used only in defense of property or life. Private war is limited to self-defense, and does not extend to the avenging of a wrong already done, or to the recapture of what has been already lost. Private defence is to prevent a present impending calamity, not to redress a prior wrong. A state however has the right of war in defense and also in offensive warfare to redress the wrongs that have been done to the state or the members of it.

The power to make war is a prerogative of the state in its sovereign capacity. In order to determine who possesses this authority he defines what a state is. It is a perfect as distinguished from an imperfect organization, possessing independence, and separate from any other community, having its own executive, legislative authority, and governed by its own laws. Such is the Republic of Venice or the Kingdom of Arragon and Castille. This is a national state. There may be an imperial state in which a number of perfect or imperfect communities are associated together under the control of a single ruler, in whom is placed the sovereign authority of the united states, but each state under such a union does not possess the right of declaring war. He proceeds to state what are the just grounds of war. Religious belief is not a just ground of war, neither is the fact that a nation or race of people reject Christianity, neither is personal or public ambition or desire for conquest, or extension of territorial control, just ground for war. The prince or rulers in the state ought to be actuated solely in government by the desire to promote the common good of the community. Government is a public, not a private trust; the aim of government therefore is public utility. A good king governs for the good of the state, a tyrant in his own personal interest. Hence the tyrant reduces his subjects to slavery by imposing on them unbearable burdens, and by engaging in useless and wrongful wars. The only justifiable cause of war is an injury done to a state, and not every injury inflicted upon a state, because as every crime of an individual is not worthy of capital penalty, so every crime of a state or race against a state does not merit the condign punishment of war. In reality the justice of war can only be determined by the wise men. Hence there is need of the wisest counsels on the part of princes before entering upon war. Subjects are not bound to support their sovereigns in a war they believe to be plainly without just cause. No authority can command to do an unjust act, therefore the sub ject is warranted in refusing to follow his monarch when he manifestly departs from justice. Yet if the sovereign has taken the advice of his chief counsellors, and if they decide upon the justness of the war, subjects are to abide by this decision, that the authority of the wise may not be brought into disrepute.*

Another Spanish jurist and professor of considerable repute is Antonio Augustino, the author of *Emendationes Juris Civilis*, 1544, and a smaller writing on *the principles of government*. He presents some most liberal and profound ideas. All sovereign power is directly derived from God and it must be exercised so as to harmonize with the will of God. Everything that tends to violence or cruelty, every act of self-will must be avoided. The Creator alone has the absolute disposal of human lives and he delegates his authority to the rulers of states to be exercised by them only to the extent of preserving the life of the community. The goods of individuals and the property of subjects are absolutely free from the control of the sovereign and not subject to his impositions. The interests of human society and the welfare of the state demand such a principle. Rulers have no power over the individual members of the state, beyond what is demanded for the public good. The same standard of right and wrong, virtuous and vicious applies to the sphere of politics as to that of morals; hence the principle of determining what is good and what is bad in the conduct of individuals and of societies is of the same nature. What is right for the individual is right for the society and for persons in the social life. Personal will only regards one's self and therefore any action guided by such self-will is injurious to the society and wrongful to man. Man acts rightly when he is actuated by the common good and guided by the interest of the community. The public-political policy of the ruler ought to be controlled by the welfare of the entire state, hence legislation must promote the common weal.†

Dominic Soto, 1494-1560, was the greater disciple of his great master Victoria. He was Dominican confessor in the Court of Charles V., and in such high repute at the Roman see that when sent as a theologian he was the adviser of the Council of Trent. His famous work is *De justitia et de Jure*, being the lectures he delivered in public at Salamanca. He published it in 1560, dedicating it to Don Carlos. Hallam says it is the first original work of any reputation on Ethical philosophy since the revival of letters. It is the connecting link between the Spanish writers of whom he is a representative and the purely systematic treatises upon Ethics that were to follow by the writers of the revival. Every subject is discussed carefully and in judicial detail. It is a scholastic compound of morals. It gives evidence of the

* Tractatus Tractatuum, Venice 1584; Hallam, Eur. Lit. I. 324; D. C. Heron. Hist. of Jurisprudence, pp. 297-304, Blakey, Hist. of Pol. Liter. II. p. 384; Summary in Wheaton's Law of Nations.

† Blakey, Hist. of Pol. Liter. II. p 384.

enlightenment produced by the revival of learning and of the deepening interest taken in the political issues of the time as well as the liberal tendencies introduced into the scholasticism of St. Thomas, whose works are the basis of his treatise. Justice is to him the foundation principle of all Ethics. *illustrissima justitiae virtus, fidei nostrae legitima proles, spei robur charitatis pedissequa, caeterarumque virtutem clarissimum jubar, quamcum profana tum cum primis Divina oracula super aethera tollunt; ut pote quae homines, civile animal, in unum congregat, ab injuriis vindicat, amore conciliat, in pace, retinet, victutibus ornat, ad aeternam denique felicitatem divino numere subvehit.**

In regard to the doctrine of tyrannicide and the limits of the kingly power. Soto declares, "the king cannot be justly deprived of his kingdom by the community at large, unless his government becomes tyrannical." Victoria had already declared unlawful the Spanish war against the native Americans. In the celebrated dispute between Sepulveda and Las Casas the Emperor Charles V. appointed Soto as arbiter and his decision is given in conformity with his humane conception of political Ethics. *neque discrepantia ut reor est inter christianos et infideles; quoniam jus gentium cunctis gentibus equale est*, "there can be no difference between Christians and pagans for the law of nations is the same to all nations."

He deserves to be kept in remembrance as the first philosophical thinker who employed the principles of Christian liberty to brand the African slave trade as illegal and unjust. The same Scholastic principles with which Aquinas had covered the slavery of nature and conquest yielded in the hands of Soto an unquenchable antagonist to the slave traffic, to which the Spaniards clung until recent years with fearless tenacity. The new political science was becoming the instrument of freedom. "If the report which has lately been current is true that the Portugese traders entice the wretched natives of Africa to the coast by amusements and presents, and every species of seduction and fraud, and compel them to embark in their ships as slaves: neither those who take them, nor those who buy them from the traders, nor those who possess them can have clear consciences, until they manumit these slaves, however unable they may be to pay the ransom price.† He excuses in the sovereigns of states many defects, and he thus pleads for tolerance towards them by their subjects. "We ought not to censure the conduct of princes too freely and publicly; they are often honest in their intentions, but prove unjust and oppressive by being deceived and surrounded by their ministers who are not qualified to discover the truth. We ought rather to accuse ourselves of not having the courage to declare to rulers what is true and expedient to be done. The love of our country is almost extinguished now; everyone thinks only of himself and how he may aggrandize his power and fortune careless of the sufferings and privations of others. Kingdoms

* De Just. et de Jure, Medina, 1580.
† De Just. et de Jure, IV. qu. 1, 2.

perish more through want of having good subjects than because there are often bad sovereigns."*

Such men deserve remembrance for introducing such humanitarian ideas in an age of cold-hearted political and religious indifference. In recognizing the equality of men, in repudiating the cruelties of slave-traffic and in commiserating the condition of rulers, as well as presenting a system of morals equally adapted for the confessional and the political life, Soto brings before us his desire to adapt the ancient doctrines to the conditions of men and society in his own age, and especially to introduce that democratic sentiment which not only emphasizes the rights and liberties of the individual but also especially calls attention to the duties and responsibilities devolving upon men as men in every relation of life.

The earliest dawn of this idea is found in the writings of these Spanish writers. The schools had been tending to greater independence, partly due to the equality of justice springing from the movement of humanism, and partly from the conception becoming clearer to the minds of the wise that institutions must in some measure be in harmony with existing conditions of society. Instead of commentaries on ancient works the writers digest into manuals the prominent moral principles, guided in their discussion of principles not only by the Schoolmen, but by the canon and civil law; these principles are presented in the form of ethical rules for the guidance of the moral and religious cleric in the confessional, and when the era of war arrives the same method is employed to distinguish between just and unjust use of arms. Militarism united with the confessional may be said to have produced these adaptations of Scholasticism to the times. The work of Soto is scholastic in form and method. He treats the subject in ten books, discussing the classification and definition of the different forms of law and of justice, and also the divisions of dominium, and kindred subjects.†

3. Francis Suarez, 1548–1617. Jesuitism has emphasized three points, the reaction against protestantism, the defence of the doctrine of free will, and the support of the papal power. Against the doctrine of the divine institution of the state, they place its human origin, by means of an early social compact; against the inviolable majesty of the sovereign in contrast with his subject, they set up the doctrine that when the ruler proves himself unfaithful to the commission of the people, they may resume the power entrusted to him; in support of the papal power they allege the divine institution of the papacy and assert that the pope cannot be deposed. At this point Suarez comes upon the scene, the most prominent writer in the era of Scholastic reaction, the greatest writer among the Jesuits and the representative of

* Opera Vol. IV, p 216.

† De Just. et de Jure, Lugduni, 1569. Antonii Bibliotheca Hispana Nova, Madrid, 1783; Church. Philosophy, pp. 109–110; Heron, pp. 404–5. Edinb. Review, Vol. XXVII, pp. 239 sq.; Hallam, Europ. Liter. I. 209; Blakey, II. 386.

conservatism and conciliation, the last prominent representative of the schoolmen and a worthy disciple of the schools. The position he occupied is that of a philosophical jurist. The basis upon which his theory rests is that all paternal and legislative power is derived immediately from God and the authority of every law resolves itself into the authority of God. He is the last link in the old and the first link in the new chain, being the precursor of Grotius. Taking Aquinas as his foundation he becomes the channel through which takes place the transmission of scholastic doctrines to Grotius, who declared that Suarez had hardly an equal among the theologians and philosophers. The basis of his treatise of laws is that of Aquinas whose system he reproduces with slight modifications. He is the only writer who gives a complete system of politics and natural right based upon philosophy and in complete accord with theological beliefs.

He was born in 1548 of a noble family of Graanda. He gave himself to the study of law at the University of Salamanca and entered the order of the Jesuits. Under the direction of the celebrated Rodriguez he soon became an expert in philosophy and theology. He became Professor soon after and successively filled the theological chairs in Valladolid, Alcala, Salamanca and Rome. He was regarded by many as a reincarnation of the celebrated Master of the Schoolmen, being the most erudite and profound scholar of his age. In response to the invitation of Pope Paul V., he wrote his work against James I. in defence of the Catholic faith against the error of the Anglicans, in which he made an attack upon the crown rights of James I. Afterwards he retired into the Jesuit convent of Lisbon where he actively wielded a powerful pen. His *Tractatus de legibus ac Deo Legislatore* published in 1613 is his Masterpiece, an encyclopaedic volume upon law and politics in which natural and positive, civil and canon, human and divine law are classified and discussed in an elaborate way, the principles, consequences and relations of these being set forth. His method is the scholastic, in which we find careful systematization, and a multiplicity of divisions in exhibiting the principles in every possible light. He first states the proposition he examines, next gives the opposing opinions and concludes by presenting his own ideas. It is a splendid plan to avoid omitting anything but it tends to confusion by such a variety of divisions and subtle distinctions. His work is burdened by the weight of authorities referred to, Church fathers, canonists, schoolmen, casuists having an almost equal share of the weight. In method he evinces a desire to show that the elements of morality and politics have always been found in the writings of the school. His whole work is free from the excesses of the extreme school of Catholic theorists represented by Mariana and comes much nearer the modern democratic views in regard to the relations of ruler and ruled. He views these from the standpoint of morals, jurisprudence and politics. The importance of Suarez lies in this, that he collects, condenses and compares what has been written already by all the writers in the different schools, including the Christian fathers, the ancient philosophers and later writers on justice and right, so that to comprehend what Suarez has written is to digest the entire doctrines of the middle ages, upon Ethics, Jurisprudence, and Politics.

(1) *First Principles.* Suarez distinguishes between morals and politics; in the former the legitimate foundation of natural law is the chief question, in the latter the foundation of positive law is the main problem. Morals in other words deals with ethical obligation, politics with the principle of sovereignty. He thus discriminates between ethics and political science, but he unites them under the general head of law. God is the supreme legislator, and the ultimate end to which all creatures tend. If law is divine it comes from God; but if law is human it comes from man as the minister of God and Vicar of God. The leading principle is that all power of government comes from God, proceeding either directly from Him or indirectly from Him through man who represents him on earth.

Civil laws deal with the natural order of man in the world; canon law looks to the supernatural. We must distinguish between two things; (a) in every Ecclesiastical state there ought to be constituted a political order, to guard peace and justice and temper by right reason every thing which looks to the external Ecclesiastical form. (b) All things which bear on divine worship and the salvation of souls, purity of faith and morals, fall rightly and prudently into the purely Ecclesiastical sphere.* The end of civil power is peace and temporal felicity in the human republic; therefore only laws that involve and have principles of justice in them and preserve felicity belong to the civil power, that is, the peculiar virtue of the state is justice.† Civil laws not only enjoin right in the matter of justice but of all other moral virtues, and can forbid vices contrary to all virtues. Civil law cannot fulfil its end unless it enjoins the matter of all virtues, temperance, fortitude, prudence which are all necessary in a commonwealth for the common good. In so far as they are for the common good civil law takes cognizance of them all. Human external power only takes cognizance of external acts and human acts of the human community. No one naturally is subject in soul but only in body, only indirectly can pure human law bear upon internal actions.‡

The two fundamental principles of Suarez are, (a) man is a social being; (b) and he is under the influence and force of law. Man is a being of law. The human commonwealth is one of law; law is the ruling principle in all man's relations, monastic (single), economic (family), and civil (state). Thus everything is brought under the notion of legalism, everything rests on law. His idea is that of a society of right and the subjects in a society of morality.

* De Leg. proem.
† De leg. III. 12. 3.
‡ Bk. III. 13. 14.

He works in the system of Roman law in his treatment of *dominium, justitia restitutio*, etc. This is seen also in the case of tribute. The power of the prince is the foundation of right. But if there is a new tax and it is not agreed the prince has power to levy it, he asks the question, *quid agendum in dubio?* He carries out legalism in his answer. *In dubio melior est conditio possidentis*, because subjects are assured of one thing, that they possess their goods and their liberty, but they are in doubt, they are not assured that they owe this part of their goods to the prince. This question is to be answered in a legal spirit according to law.* The Science of civil right is *prudentia juris civilis*, it is a certain application or extension of moral philosophy used to regulate and govern the political morals of the state. That is political science. He gives us thus from the standpoint of law the details of his system of morals, the science of jurisprudence and political philosophy.†

(II.) *Law.* This is the predominating element in the entire system. Hence Suarez treats in the various books, of laws in general, their common character, their causes, effects and end; the forms in which they are promulgated, with the definitions and divisions of former writers: natural law and the law of nations; civil law in its relations with natural law; canon law in relation to natural law; the principle of penal laws; the interpretation of laws; unwritten law or custom; the laws of immunity or privileges; the revealed laws of the old Testament and the law of the gospel. All law presupposes justice of which it is the measure or rule, *mihi lex esse non videtur quae justa non fuerit*.‡ Hence Suarez says law is a certain measure of moral acts of such a nature that by conformity to it these acts are morally right, but if contrary to it they are morally wrong, *lex est mensura quaedam actuum moralium, ita ut per conformitatem ad illam, rectitudinem moralem habeant, et si ab illa discordent, obliqui sunt*. Law is a certain measure and rule according to which anyone is induced to act or restrained from acting, according to Thomas. *Lex est quaedam regula et mensura secundum quam inducitur aliquis ad agendum vel ab agendo retrahitur.*§ After giving a number of references to what might be embraced in the definition of law, Suarez says the proper and absolute term of law pertains to morals.‖ Justice, that supreme law which presupposes the other laws, is nothing else than natural law, that is, reason itself or the light which distinguishes all rational creatures, the internal voice which points out to all free beings the usage which makes for liberty.

Suarez analyzes the conceptions of *jus* and *lex*, distinguishes the different senses in which they have been used and confused by preceding writers. According to Thomas *jus* is not the same as *lex*, but is *quod lex praescribitur*. *Jus* is what is prescribed by law, which is to be understood of laws respecting special justice, as distinct from law in general, which respects all the vir-

* Bk. V. 18. 14.   † August. de lib. arb. II. 1.
‡ De Leg. procem.   § Sum. Theol. 1a. 2ae. qu. 90. 1.
‖ De Legibus 1. 1. 5.

ties. *Jus* may signify the object of justice (*objectum justitiæ*), or a certain moral faculty of possessing a right which any one has in what is strictly his own and what is owed to him by another.* Isidore compares *jus* and *lex* as genus and species, the former consisting of laws and customs.† Suarez however says, that, laying aside all metaphysical meanings and subtle distinctions, in the present treatise he uses *jus* as a term which is interchangeable with *lex*, because *lex* in final resort is *in imperio* or *in jussione*.‡ Law, then, is necessary and absolute, that is, *per se*; but this can only be so of God, because all law implies creation or a creature, so that law is necessary in regard to its end. Its end is *utilis* and *bonus*. There are four kinds of law, according to Plato, *divina*, *cœlestis*, *naturalis* and *humana*.§ The second kind is omitted by theologians, because it is a kind of legal fate used by the heathen.

Suarez adopts the following classification. (1) *Divine Law*, or eternal law with Plato, is reason governing the universe, existing in the mind of God. Theologians call it *lex æterna*, as existing in God, opposed to *temporalis*, which is *extra Deum*. Plato calls it *lex divina*, and it is with him *ratio gubernatrix universi in Dei mente existens*. From this idea of Divine or Eternal law may be inferred the first division of *lex* into eternal and temporal, for we suppose nothing is eternal which is *extra Deum*, but many laws are *extra Deum* and they are therefore *temporalis versus æterna lex*. Suarez describes positive Divine law as that immediately promulgated by God, *lex positiva divina quæ ab ipso Deo immediate lata est et toti legi naturali addita*.∥ Our duty to such law is simply to know and obey it. Eternal law is the free determination of the will of God ordering a rule to be observed either generally by all parts of the Universe, as a means of common good, or in respect of parts of it, or to be specially observed by rational creatures in their free operations.* This eternal law is not directly known to man in this life, except through or in other laws. Men can learn the Divine will only by the effects or signs of it. All cannot distinguish causes from effects and although no creature possessing reason is left ignorant of this law, yet it is not known directly. Some attain the knowledge of it by natural reasoning, others by the revelation of faith.**

(2) From the last two kinds of law in Plato we get a second division of *lex*, which is a subdivision of created law, into *naturalis* and *positiva*. All the theologians acknowledge this division whether as *lex* or *lex positiva et non talis*. First as to *natural law*. There are inclinations to certain ends in all who are ruled by the providence of God, and therefore natural law represents the share these have in eternal law, according to Thomas. Jurists say, this includes not only men but animals. Natural law proper is that

* Bk. I. 2, 4, and 5.   ‡ Bk. I 3, 5.
* Bk. I. 2, 7.   ∥ Ibid. I. 3, 6; 3, 14.
‡ Bk. I. 2, 6; I. 2, 11.   * Ibid. I.3, 5.
** Ibid. II. 4, 5.

which settles in the human mind so as to enable to discern honest from base, because there is no such law in the irrational creatures. So Thomas speaks of *participatio legis æternæ* as being *in rationali creatura*. This law may be either *cum natura* or *gratia*. That which is not so given, but is added as it were by an addition to *naturalis* by an exercise of power is *positiva lex*. It may be either divine or human, that is, immediately added by God or by man. Natural law is simply the moral sense of right or wrong, it is the principle in the human mind by which the just or good is distinguished from the unjust or bad.* Positive law, on the other hand, is the fixed law of human enactment, existing as it does by reason of this positive force, called positive because added to, not flowing from natural law.† Natural law may be distinguished as *duplex*, one form purely natural, another simply supernatural but natural in comparison with grace ‡

(3) By the theologians there is handed down a third division of law, namely, that of *lex positiva* into *divina* and *humana*. *Lex positiva divina* is immediately given by God and in addition to natural law.§ *Lex humana* is that law derived *proxima* from man, proxime because all law is from the eternal law. The necessity and utility of human law arises because it is derived from known principles of morals, necessary to preserve and govern the state. How does human law arise? Man is a sociable animal, his nature demanding civil life and communion with other men, and so it is necessary to live rightly, not only as a private person, but also as a member of the community. A man is therefore to consult not himself, but the peace and justice of others, in order that what tends to the common good of the community may be observed. It is of the essence of law that it be made for the public good.‖ It is difficult to know when laws are for the common good but as such they are positive, useful and necessary. This positive human law is ultimately divided into civil and Ecclesiastical, according as it concerns temporal or spiritual matters. Civil laws relate to political government in the state, to the defence of temporal rights and to the preservation of the republic in peace and justice. In addition to these Christianity acknowledges Ecclesiastical or canon laws, not human but divine, because specially derived from the power of God and referring to divine worship and the salvation of souls.¶

In answering the question, what is necessary to constitute a law, what acts are essential in the mind of the legislator to make a law, he says, (a) law is said to be the result of *an act of the intellect*, because law instructs and orders. Law is a rule because no act of will can be assigned as law, will is not necessary to it. Others says it is an act of intellect because it is by imperium, although not of God. (b) Law is said to imply *the act of the will* of the legislator which places imperium in will. Intellect rather directs than

* Ibid. I. 3. 9.
† Ibid. I. 3. 13.
‡ Ibid. I. 3. 14.
§ Ibid. I. 3. 11.
‖ Ibid. I. 3. 17.
¶ Ibid. I. 3. 20.

moves, the force of obliging is in the will, because the *exercise of dominium is an act of will*. Law is the act of legal justice and the prince looking to the common good respects legal justice and legal justice is a virtue of will.* (c) Law is said to involve *both an act of intellect and of will*. Law requires the two for unity, direction and motion, goodness and truth, right judgment and efficacious will. Hence the arbitrium of the prince is an act of both faculties. The two sides of law, accordingly, are *movendi* of the will, *dirigendi* of the intellect. This controversy about the necessary act or acts involved in a law arose in the effort to distinguish natural from positive law. In the case of positive law there must be both intellect and will, in the case of natural law simply intellect.†

In regard to the use of the term law, it seems to refer rather to the external imperium, and to be the ostensible sign of the commanding will. Law has its source in intellect but is made law by being made a rule according to the will of the lawgiver.‡ Law in the proper sense is only for man and may be said to be purely human. Is law for individual man or man in the community? Thomas says, all law is for the common good. What is imposed on one person is not law, that is, law is given in fact to the community which is perpetual. The question is, has law its end in the common good or in the individual? Law has its final end in the public good and its reason in the public power, because it requires a power to impose it. Every precept is not a law, though every law is a precept, so that there is a difference between preceptive and legislative power.

Justice. There are three kinds of justice. (a) legal justice, which is for the common good. It is peculiar *to lex* to tend to the preservation of the rights for the common good. (b) Commutative justice, to which the legislator looks. This justice is chiefly necessary to strengthen law. If princes make laws not for their subjects but for themselves they violate commutative justice. (c) Distributive justice is required in law, because in ruling a multitude distribution is made of the burdens of the republic in order to the good of each and all.§

Eternal law is *per essentiam*, all other law is *per participationem*. Law has a double status, in the mind of the legislator, and in relation to the subjects. Therefore all law is the effect of eternal law. All law must be just and according to reason, but man is just by participation with God and reason is the image of God's being. Human law comes to subjects through the medium of man and its obligation springs from the will of man who has power to constitute new laws. That is, its proximate obligation is in man, the ultimate in God.

Natural law is the light of reason which reveals the propriety or improprie-

* Ibid. I. 5, 8. ‡ Ibid. I. 5, 25.
† Ibid. I. 5, 20, 22. § Bk. I. 9, 12, 13.
‖ Ibid. II. 4, 8.

ty of actions, interpreting eternal law in the soul. With the idea of natural law is associated the author of it; so when man is brought up to God, it is impossible not to love God. There is in us a natural love inborn by our Creator. Every act which is conformed to natural law tends directly to God and to bring man nearer God, which is his final aim and the end of law.* Natural law is rational in a double sense, (a) understood from nature, according to nature, according to which some actions are convenient and some are not; (b) understood from nature itself by the action of judgment which is also natural and in respect of which it has the reason of law, because natural reason furnishes natural law. Natural law cannot be said properly to be divine, as from God the legislator, because natural reason which furnishes natural law is a gift from the Creator. Natural law indicates good and bad just as vision sees black and white.† Natural law not only indicates good and evil, but commands, by the prohibition of evil and the injunction of the good.‡ There is presupposed an intrinsic right and wrong in actions themselves to which is added the special obligation of a divine law. God is therefore the final legislator of natural law.§ Natural law teaches what is in harmony with rational nature and forbids the contrary; that which natural law prohibits is bad and what is necessary and honest is good. A thing is prohibited because it is bad and enjoined because it is good, supposing the act or object honesty or dishonesty, goodness and badness; whereas in other laws what is commanded is good and the forbidden bad.‖ Natural law has been proven alike by pagans and Christians. Natural law is the judgment of the mind, but is it the mind of the legislator or of the subjects? In the legislator who is God it is the same as eternal law, in the subjects it is the same law revealed in the soul. It reveals itself to each of us and appeals to us as the voice of nature or nature's author.¶ Natural law is not conscience, for the first is a universal sign to all men of what man should do and not do, the second is the particular reason in each of us, conscience applying the general rule to the particular case. Conscience may err, and may be influenced by opinion, natural law is infallible, for God is its author. Conscience has a wider domain, for it applies as well divine and human law as natural law. Law judges actions to come, conscience actions past. Natural law therefore is reason in the moral order. The foundation of natural law and of honesty of action is the rational nature. Natural law is very wide; it includes primary rules of conduct, such as doing to others as we wish them to do to us, and such consequences as flow from these in condemning crime, even those which require the use of reason, the whole decalogue being embraced within it.** Although natural law is one and the same in all men

* Ibid. II. 6. 2.   ‡ Ibid. II. 6. 1.
† Ibid. II. 6. 2. 3.   ǁ Ibid. II. 7. 1.
§ Ibid. II. 6. 5.   ¶ Ibid. II. 7. 4. II. 8. 5.
** Ibid. II. 7. 4-6.

and in every state of nature yet there is a double state of nature, the pure and the corrupt. So there is a difference in natural law; in the one case *jus naturale* seeks the liberty of all men, in which all are equal; in the latter case corrupt nature seeks servitude and division of goods. Distinction is not necessary, however, because in war and peace *jus naturale* is the same.* It is not in the power of any person, not even in the sovereign pontiff, to abrogate or enfeeble one of its precepts, or to give dispensations which permit its violation, *nulla potestas humana, etiamsi pontificia sit, potest proprium aliquod praeceptum legis naturalis abrogare, nec illud proprie et in se minuere, neque in illo dispensare.†* The obligation of natural law is absolute and without exception.

Suarez distinguishes between what is imperative and permissive, or between that which is preceptive and indicative, the former showing what is good or bad, the latter ordaining the doing or not doing of certain things. The divine command is imperative and no human authority can interfere. The permissive is subject to human authority. Primarily, by natural right all goods of the earth are in community among men; similarly, all men created in God's likeness are independent, entirely free, possessed of absolute liberty, —this is permissive. The permissive command has simply realized itself in individual property, and in the slavery of some men under changed conditions. So dominium in property and the loss of liberty are dependent upon human changes. It is impossible to enjoy society without restricting the absolute dominium or freedom. Hence the state has the right to fix the conditions of property, the laws of contract, etc. Liberty is simply a moral property and receives its form under the action of the state. Therefore the state ought to sacrifice all particular rights to the common good, *natio ipsa ut sic dicam potest cedere juri suo propter aliud bonum majus.‡*

Having thus placed all human rights at the will of the state, he has left to man individual only moral duties which he owes in obedience to this natural law. Are these duties universally obligatory? In theory they are, in practice they are not. Can God permit by his law actions against natural reason? No other power can change natural law save the legislator of nature; therefore, the question is raised, can God change the laws which he has given and which he continues to promulgate by the voice of reason? May he dispense with them for the time? Here we have in Suarez the casuist and the philosopher, playing a double role. He gives several opinions on this point. Every legislator can dispense with his own laws. This is the general proposition which raises the difficulty. It is seen in God's dispensation to Abraham. He distinguishes three orders of natural precepts, some are universal principles, some are immediate conclusions and wholly intrinsic, as the de-

* Ibid. II. s. s-9.
† II. 14 s.
‡ II. 14. 18. 20

calogue, some are far removed from first principles. There is no exception in the first class. The controversy among the Doctors concerns the decalogue chiefly. (a) The first opinion affirms God can dispense with all the precepts of natural law and even abrogate them. Good and evil are not founded in the nature of things, but depend upon the will and pleasure of God, so that natural law depends upon the will of God, and if God had willed it so evil might have been good and good evil. This opinion is absurd, says Suarez, and false.* (b) The opinion of Duns Scotus, who views the decalogue as the best expression of natural law, dividing it into two tables, the duty of man to God and of man towards his fellowman. He declares that the first table is irrevocable but that the second ought to depend upon human nature.† (c) Durandus declares that the positive precepts of the decalogue are revocable, the negative irrevocable, because the positive precepts can be fulfilled only under certain conditions of human life and incertain circumstances of society and history. The law does not exist where these conditions and circumstances are absent, and therefore it is not universal. (d) All the precepts of the decalogue are declared irrevocable even by the power of God which is absolute. The fundamental reason is that those things which contain intrinsic reason of justice and duty are indispensable. Of such a character are the precepts of the decalogue. Suarez answers these opinions. (a) there is a good and evil in essence, because if not God would act unreasonably; the good and evil depend upon the reason and nature of God as well as upon his will. Following Aquinas he declares, law is strictly immutable. The pope cannot dispense with the law of nature. (b) The duties we owe to man are according to reason as obligatory as those we owe to God. All the articles of the decalogue are equally binding. The natural law contains the Mosaic and evangelic principle, to love our neighbors, without which human society could not preserve its own existence nor preserve order within it. (c) All law is eternal, so that in similar circumstances the same law is binding upon action and the same duties obligatory. The relations of father and son are not universal but where they exist the duties are unlimited. Suarez accepts the *via media*, that natural law is both *indicative* and *preceptive*, for it indicates what is good and bad and also prohibits the bad and enjoins the good. The will of God supposes a good and evil to which it enjoins obligation, therefore natural law is a true law of which God is legislator, for it rests in the nature of things and the will of God. To Suarez the love of our neighbors is the universal duty, the common principle and the necessary condition of justice. Duties to man and to God are equally sacred and inviolable and therefore all the laws equally binding ‡

He goes on to distinguish between God as supreme legislator and as Sov-

* Bk. II. 15. 1-5.
† Bk. II. 15. 6-12.
‡ Bk. II. 15. 8-11; II. 16. 21. 26.

ereign Master, Lord of all things. As legislator God is supreme reason and therefore he cannot change natural law which expresses the justice of reason: but as absolute Lord of all men, creatures and goods, he may delegate part of his power and give to man the right to do what He does Himself. So he commanded Abraham to take away the life of Isaac, without breaking natural law, because He did so as proprietor of the life of Isaac, as owner and lord having the right to take away life. Thus what cannot be justified by natural right can be accomplished by a positive command, implying the delegation of power from the supreme proprietor. Natural law binds the conscience because it is the law of God. It cannot be dispensed with by any human power, even by the Popes, because they cannot dispense with divine law, much less natural law. Can God dispense with natural law? It seems so, because among men every legislator can dispense with his own legislation. We distinguish three classes of natural precepts, or moral laws, (a) Universal principles. God cannot dispense with these. (b) Direct conclusions, altogether intrinsic, as the precepts of the decalogue. Ockham and Gerson say He can dispense with these, because they are prohibitions he has himself imposed; but there is an intrinsic goodness in actions independent of God's commands. (c) Other precepts farther removed from first principles, not belonging to the decalogue. God cannot dispense with these though he may change the circumstances upon which rests the binding obligation of the law, as when he releases from a vow. Scotus said God could dispense with the second table; but all precepts of the decalogue are indispensable even by God. God cannot change any precept of nature, all he can do is to change its matter or circumstances.*

As we have seen *jus* is used in the same sense as *lex*, to signify the rule of acting honestly and the principle of equity. We may speak of *jus* as *utile secundum honestum* and *reale secundum legale*. In this sense *jusutile* is divided into *naturale*, *gentium* and *civile*. *Jus utile naturale* is spoken of because it is given by nature itself or comes with it. Whence liberty may be said to be *ex jure naturali*. *Jus utile civile* is so called because it is *jus praescriptionis*. *Jus utile gentium* is so called as derived from its common use among *gentes*. This division of *jus* pertains to the object of justice.† *Jus* is a species of *lex* and even in the sense of *jus legale* it is true that *jus* has three divisions, according as it is gathered *ex praeceptis naturalibus, aut gentium aut civili*. This division therefore we accept as good because it is generally accepted. (a) According to some of the Jurists, *jus naturale* is common to men and animals, *jus gentium* peculiar to men. In this sense there are two divisions of *jus*, *civile* and *naturale*, the last one being either common to men and animals or peculiar to men.‡ (b) The opinion which distinguishes *jus gentium* from *jus naturale*,

* Bk. II. 15. 20.
† Bk. II. 17. 2.
‡ Bk. II. 17. 3.

saying that the former has intrinsic necessity in its precepts and only differs from the latter because the latter is *sine discurs: vel facillimo discurs: innotescit*, while *jus gentium* is gathered *per plures illationes et difficiliores*.* Soto and later Thomists interpret Thomas as distinguishing *jus gentium* from *jus naturale*, because nature gives the natural law by reason without any difficulty in understanding it, whereas *jus gentium* is collected from many examples and is more difficult to understand. (c) Another opinion declares that *jus naturale* obliges without dependence upon human power while *jus gentium* does not. The former embraces things so necessary that no supposition of human society or fact of human will is needed to furnish or suggest it, but it follows from plain principles of nature. Other principles do not follow simply from nature but suppose human society and other circumstances which give rise to necessity for precepts and laws. Even this is not a just distinction for many things embraced in natural law do not oblige nor have they a place unless something is supposed to be done; for example, we cannot suppose theft unless there is a division of goods; obedience to masters has no place unless masters and servants exist, etc. To distingush *jus naturale* from *jus gentium* it is necessary that what is supposed to be natural do not follow by evident consequence, but from others less certain as human will and moral good rather than necessity; therefore *jus gentium* does not enjoin anything as of necessity nor prohibit anything as *per se* bad, but all such pertains to *jus naturale*; and in this sense *jus gentium* is not comprehended under *jus naturale*. *Jus gentium* differs from *jus civile* in that it is established not in the written law, but in custom and not only that of one state but of many states. It should be concluded that *jus gentium* does not enjoin anything so much for its necessity to honesty or prohibit anything because it is evil intrinsically, these pertain to *jus naturale*.† We cannot distinguish *jus gentium* and *jus naturale* as concessive and preceptive with Vasquez, for the former differs from the latter in the consent of men. To distinguish between *jus civile* and *jus gentium* the former is mutable *in totum*, the latter only in *parte*. *Jus gentium* is the medium between *civile* and *naturale*.

What is the end of civil law? Some say it is not only eternal peace but the felicity of man. But human happiness is of two kinds, present and future, natural and supernatural. Civil power has only to do with the natural, such power has nothing to do with the supernatural. Civil law is constituted by the will of the princeps.‡ Law is *signum voluntatis principis*; law must be sufficiently promulgated before it has force. An unjust law is not a law, because it enjoins what is evil, and therefore it is not binding, even it it has been accepted.§ Change in law is twofold, (a) change in the legislator either in will or intellect. Such is unreasonable because it is not a mere matter of will, but ought to be governed by reason; therefore unless the prior will was

* Bk. II. 17. 8.   ‡ Bk. III. 15. 1.
† Bk. II. 17. 9.   § Bk. III. 16. 1.

unreasonable it cannot be changed. (b) When the dictamen of reason is changed there can be a just change of law. Who can abrogate a law? Three points in such a change we note. (a) the founder of a law may abrogate it because a thing is *nascitur* by the causes by which it is *dissolvitur*; but the will and power of a legislator are the things upon which law hangs. This is clearly so in the case of a supreme prince who owns no superior and has power to change laws. This power vests in his successor. (b) The Superior can abrogate the law of an inferior. (c) Legislative power is more proper in a prince than dispensative.*

(III) *Civil society.* Suarez treats of political association. There are not only laws, there is a power to make laws. In general there is a human society and civil legislation has an end altogether distinct from religious legislation and society. In the latter the salvation of the soul is the end, sanctity and true faith leading to a heavenly life; civil society and human legislation consider the common interests of all the members of the association, that is, the good of the political and temporal state of which the first condition is justice and, conformed to it, peace and unity. The ultimate end which these two societies have is the same, the advancement of Christianity, although the civil law in its external end takes less cognizance of the province of conscience and is concerned with the temporal.† Society according to Suarez is the natural state of man, man being a social and legal being; apart from this fact there is no family, no association of similar beings, no means of education, no material preservation of society. Society therefore is legitimate and of divine purpose.

Civil society, therefore, is based upon two natural facts, (a) man is a social being, and (b) man is a being of law. This is a certain advance upon Aristotle and Aquinas, according to whom man is a social and political animal; right or law according to Suarez, instead of political organization according to Aquinas, being the end of man. The law or right must have its realization in the political organization. Is then the legitimate power of making laws, which is found in the civil power, of natural right or not? Some think it is not, because man naturally is free, unorganized and unlimited; while in civil society man is limited and each man reduced from natural tyranny to subjection. Suarez replies to this, man is a social animal fitted for life in a perfect society, and every such society presupposes a power which governs the community. But how is this realized? He says, it is realized, (a) in natural law: man is not subjected to the authority of a chief; but authority is by virtue of the act of submission itself; (b) governments have often in fact been founded by force, in bringing subjects into subjection, but that is not the essence of society; (c) Augustine says, that domination was introduced by the fall; but that refers only to master and slave, not to ruler and subject in the state.

* Bk. VI. N. 2.
† Bk. III. 11. 8-19.

Law is said to relate to a community, not collective but distributive. What is a community that is fit for proper law? (a) In general community can be distinguished into two kinds:—*first*, there is a natural community by the convenience of union, based in the rational nature, such community of the human race as is common to all men alike; but, *secondly*, there is community which may be said to be political or mystical by special association in a moral combination. Natural law respects the first community and it is propounded to each man by the light of reason. (b) A later community is to be distinguished of a particular kind. Some understand by it an addition to nature, yet not by human right but by divine, because instituted by God himself. More perfect is the Catholic Church which is not for one people but for the whole world as appointed by Christ. (c) In addition to these there is a community of humanity congregated together, which is called *coitus*, the association or meeting together of men, such as are associated by means of right; it is called *civitas*, in which it is not enough to have a multitude of men. There must be in order to community rulers among them, the members by some *faedus*, treaty, being joined for a certain end and being under a head. So Aristotle says a state is a multitude of citizens having a moral bond uniting them. But communities are distinguished by the moral philosopher into perfect and imperfect, the perfect being capable of political government. The state is a perfect community and *a fortiori* a kingdom or a part of it will be a perfect community. Thomas says that which is a part of either is imperfect. Among communities some are definitely marked, some local, because enclosed by some real boundaries; others are said to be personal because they consist more in persons than in places; as is the case in some religious orders or fraternities which ought to be placed among the perfect communities, if they have a perfect rule and moral union. But an imperfect community is different; the reason being the community is not self-sufficient, and because in it the individual persons are not united as common members composing one political body, but only as inferiors who are found in the service of the master and under his dominium; and such a community is not ruled by a proper power of jurisdiction but by dominium as in the case of slaves, a wife and family. Wherefore it has not perfect unity nor uniform power nor do its members share the political power, and hence the community is said to be imperfect.

Human laws have properly a place only in the perfect, not in the imperfect community. This is proved by the fact that every perfect community is a proper political body and governed by proper jurisdiction, having legitimate coactive power. So precepts and rules of living are proposed to such a community, if they possess the other conditions requisite to laws, such precepts or rules having the reason of law. As that community is perfect, the precept imposed upon it may be called a common precept, that is, law. The community of a single house is not sufficient for proper law, because in such a community there is not proper jurisdiction nor coactive force such as is required in a proper ruler. But the real reason is found in the imperfection of such a natural community, because it is not sufficient of itself to procure human felicity. Parts of such a community are not capable of giving the help which human society needs to secure its end and to preserve itself; such a community being part of a whole, the legislative power is not in such a community, such as it is in states subject to civil law. This applies to Ecclesiastical power, because though Ecclesiastical legislative power rests, not in the community but in Christ, yet it is communicated and distributed according to the common good. It is plain the statute of a house is not the law of the imperfect community, because that community is part of the perfect community in which there are a great number of such imperfect communities.*

The end of the human state is true political felicity which cannot be secured without honest morals; by means of civil laws the state is directed into that felicity, and therefore it is necessary that these laws tend to moral good. When Aristotle distinguishes a good citizen from a good man he does so, because more is required in order to the virtue of a good man than of a good citizen; for, though the virtue of a good citizen is moral and honest, it is not sufficient to make a good man. So if any one were alone he could be a good man but not a good citizen. He who is part of a state will not simply be good, although he can be a good citizen though he is not a good man. Canon laws make a man good simply but do not make him good in everything, for example, in citizenship.† Among men we find three types, (a) Monastic, the rule of a single life; (b) Economic, pertaining to the rule of a family; (c) political, which pertains to the rule of a state or perfect community.‡ We must distinguish four classes of persons in the state, (a) those *inferior* to the legislator, that is, subjects; (b) others *superior* to the legislators; (c) those *indifferentes*, who from the nature of their being, are neither subjects nor superiors, but are equals; (d) the legislator himself. We omit the class of superiors in considering society because they are not bound by the law of inferiors.§

Suarez often refers to the pact between the prince and the commonwealth, as the basis of civil society, according to which the ruler governs and his subjects obey. The constitution of kingdoms and the power of kings are not immediately of natural right, but immediately the concession of the people; therefore, the extent or restriction of power is not a matter of *jus naturale* but depends on the *arbitrium* of men and upon ancient convention or pact between the king and the members of his kingdom.

Monarchy may be established in two forms. (a) The prince may make laws by the consent of the people or Senate on behalf of those who have a definite franchise (suffragium). He does not deprive society of its rights: all political

* Bk. I. 6. 18-21 * Bk. I. 14. 7
‡ Bk. III. 11. 1. § Bk. III. 31. 1

power is founded upon its vote and ought to be by an act of will on the part of the state. (b) Power may be simply and solely in the prince though he ought to use the counsel of his advisers and the members of society. The latter form is more characteristic of monarchic rule and more consonant with prudence, justice, and obedience on the part of subjects.*

The creation of kings and of power is not *jure gentium*, but *jure civili* or *naturali*. Whence though in general it may be said, the division of kingdoms, states, magistrates or rulers is *jure gentium*, yet in constituting civil rule, conducted by many or by a few or by one, with so much or more power, is not *jure gentium*, but arises from the proper rights of distinct communities and has in principle its origin either in voluntary pact or in a just war or is sanctioned by an ancient custom.† That is, as we would say, the municipal law of a community settles the form of the society and its government, as well as the distribution of power in the state, whereas public or admininistrative law settles the principles upon which those entrusted with governmental powers are to conduct themselves and administer affairs in the exercise of the functions of their office.

(IV). *Sovereignty and temporal power.* There can be no society without laws, and there can be no laws without a power which makes and commands respect of the laws, that is, there must be a sovereign authority of some kind by whatever name it is known and in whatever way it is exercised. To whom then belongs the sovereignty, or the power of making laws? Suarez concludes that sovereignty resides in the people, in the civil order, or in other words, the temporal power rests upon the same basis as does the civil society itself. Civil society and sovereignty have their basis in natural law. Power is preceptive and legislative. Preceptive power, as a generic expression, is both economic and political, or the power of a dominus and a sovereign; and we may speak also of jurisdiction as distinguished by a certain dominium into jurisdiction proper and proprietas. The power *dominaticus* is found in imperfect communities and over single persons. This may originate in *natura* over children, in *pact* over a wife and in *jus gentium* over slaves, captives, or in contract with other men when slaves are sold. The power of *jurisdiction* on the other hand respects perfect communities for it implies the government of political communities. In jurisdiction there is much more power of coercing and compelling; it springs from primitive institutions and *per se* is for the public good. Divine laws proceed from a being who has not only public power but also supreme being; and so by essence the Divine being is sovereign as governor and men are naturally subject to Him. Viewing however human society, legislation is the most powerful act by which the republic is governed because the governing power of the republic seeks to promote the common good. The power of jurisdiction is public, and therefore is found

* Bk. V. 17. 3, 4.
† Bk. V. 17. 5.

only in that power which is capable of making laws. A distinction exists then between *dominus* and *potestas jurisdictionis.*

What power is supreme to make laws? Whence does this supreme power derive its authority? (a) *Per se*, by essence God alone is supreme. (b) Sovereignty is communicated to kings and rulers by such a participation in the supreme power of God, that they can make laws according to the measure of the power given. In every community there is some power supreme relatively, in the Church the Pope, in the kingdom the king, in the republic all the republic, for no body can be without a head except it be a monstrosity. The power of making laws is in the supreme head or authority.*

What is the title of sovereignty? The temporal authority, says Suarez, is in origin uniquely divine, because it is natural and indispensable to civil society and the same quality appertains to it under any form; "all power comes from God," says the Apostle, but this does not mean an express delegation of power, that is incomprehensible to human reason and above all rights. No doubt in certain cases given in Scripture there was an express appointment by God, but this extraordinary sanction of God was not the general order, but the exception to the general rule. The sovereignty in the temporal is in the people naturally, and they delegate a part or the whole of it to the kings or rulers. Some casuists allege, the sovereign power resides in a supreme prince to whom God has given it and who transmits it by succession. Suarez says, sovereignty does not reside in a man but in a collection of men, that is, in society as a whole or the people. For the idea of the sovereignty of the people, he cites the Doctors of the School, the jurists and the canonists. It has been so obscured by the conflict between the Emperors and Popes that it has never risen above the surface. He traces it back to the definition of Justinian, *lex est constitutio populi qua majores natu simul cum plebibus aliquid sanxerunt,* which gives a feeble expression to the popular idea of Roman republicanism.†

Suarez then proves that sovereignty does not reside in any one person. All are born and are by nature free, no one having power naturally over others. It is alleged that this power over others was given to Adam and has been transmitted by heredity ever since, or in other words sovereignty is patriarchal. Suarez refutes this theory. Adam possessed economic or patriarchal power but not political power. Such an idea has neither foundation nor authority. Theologians, civilians and casuists agree that the prince's power of making law is derived from the people's consent. The state first arises from the consent of many families. The head of the family is not the chief of the state and cannot give a royal right to his posterity by primogeniture. When the number of families increased each head of a household had the same power. Political power only began when men collected into a com-

* Bk. 1. 8. 5-10.
† Isidore of Seville. Origines. 1. 5. 10.

munity. Therefore as this did not take place till long after Adam's time, he had nothing to do with the royal power. There is no record in Scripture that God made Adam king of men as he made him lord of the animals and of the material world. So sovereignty does not belong to a single person. If it does not belong to one it must pertain to all.

This is only a negative proof. Suarez gives a positive proof. We may consider the multitude in two ways, either it is a single aggregate without order, physical or moral, and therefore it needs government, because there is no body politic; or else it is collected together by the will of men who consent to unite into a political society and form a body mystical which comes to be a body moral. A body politic cannot exist without a government of the body, and the creation of a common body requires the creation of a common power. Therefore the creation of the political society and of the governing body is one and the same act, both originating in the people who create it or give their consent. Sovereignty therefore is in the universality of the people. This sovereignty does not reside in the entire population of the world, but in the peoples grouped into nations according to local divisions. Immediately this power resides in man in political society, because it springs from the will of man, united with fellow-men. Mediately it comes from God who is the source of all power. The power by the very nature of the thing itself is immediately in the community and in order that it may be in the hands of any person legitimately, for example, in a supreme prince, it is necessary that it be given with the consent of the people.*

The temporal power is only a condition of human society, not the origin or cause of it. Therefore the temporal power should be subordinate to the interests of the society and subject to its will. Society has its foundation in nature and the civil state derives its power from a delegation of power, not on the part of the general society, but of the special nation or people constituted into a state. Sovereignty is originally in the people, and they alone can give it. Society may delegate it to one, a few or many, for a time or in perpetuity, in whole or in part, reserving it or part of it to exercise in its collective capacity. The power therefore is either exercised by itself or by others in its name, and hence the civil laws framed by legislation are obligatory upon the whole society.†

Sovereignty implies the promulgation of law. Law demands obedience of subjects and this cannot be expected unless the law is clearly set forth. Law is a precept of the prince and ought to be spoken by the king as a public person. The sovereignty of the people is maintained and proved by the limits placed upon Supreme rulers who have and exercise temporal power.

Can a man command other men at will? Man by nature is subject to no one save his Creator, being a free being; therefore a human principate against

* Bk. III 2 and 3; 4. 2.
† Bk. III 4. 1

reason is against the order of nature and is tyranny. The sovereignty of the prince is limited by the following facts, (a) that an unjust law is not law, because it exceeds the power of the legislator; (b) if a law is found to be hard, it cannot be supposed to be the will of a prince to bind absolutely but only to make an experiment; (c) when the law is not observed by the people or the majority, it cannot be supposed to be the will of the prince to bind one or more when it is not kept by all. Also if its observance in the kingdom engenders disturbance tending to popular sedition or scandal it cannot possess sovereign authority.* No human legislator has a perfect will, because God alone has such; therefore a legislator has not power to bind by unjust laws. Every power is from God, therefore every human legislator is limited by the will of God as superior.† The people who create the king may also dethrone him.

To the question, whether the people possesses or reserves to itself part of the sovereignty, Suarez has two answers to give. (a) Against a king who is legitimate but who ordains unjust laws there ought to be no recourse save by passive resistance, that is, by disobedience to the unjust laws. Because an unjust law is not a law. Against a tyrant or usurper there is the right of war because he is a public enemy; yet unless the tyrant is a usurper and the tyranny unbearable, submission is better because insurrection is often much worse than a moderate tyranny. He does not admit this power against princes who impose taxes against the will of the people.‡ (b) Against a royal power that claims unlimited authority, he allows recourse only when the faith of Christianity is to be defended; a tyrant or usurper ought to be killed by the citizens if they have no other means of opposing his aggression. *Hanc tyrannum quod titulum intellici possa a quacunque privata persona, quae sit membrum reipublicae quae tyrannidem patitur, si aliter non possit rempublicam ab illa tyrannide liberare.* In the case of a legitimate king who abuses his power, he distinguishes two cases,—in the one the abuse of power is a menace to an individual's own life, or some of his relatives; in the other, the entire community's liberty and existence is endangered. In both cases the king may lawfully be killed by the sword of an assassin; in the last case it is legitimate for any citizen to kill him.§ Where there is only injury done or danger threatened to one self or his friends, he may for the public peace and in response to the call of charity give up his right of tyrannicide. If however the country is imperilled the murder is legal, even private murder, if it is the only means of ridding the country of the tyrant; for every one ought to take arms to avenge the public wrong.‖

This is the extreme doctrine of tyrannicide which appeals to the sovereignty of the sword, even of the private sword. The desire of Suarez was

* Bk. I. 7; III, 19, 11, 13; III, 22.   ‡ Bk. III. 10, 22.
* Bk. I. 9, 3, 4.   § Bk. VI. 4, 5-7.
‖ Bk. III. 3, 8; IV. 8

to protect popular rights and popular liberty from the excesses of usurpation and tyranny. He does not go so far as to say that the popular sovereignty depends upon force and force adequate to conquest, like some more modern theorists; force is the guardian of popular rights with him. This same principle has a bearing upon his theory of the relation of the civil and ecclesiastical powers.

The sovereign power includes the power of life and death over the citizens, because a citizen belongs more to the republic than to himself. An interesting question in regard to sovereignty arises, does law bind a legislator? The constant doctrine of the Schools is that the legislating power is held bound to observe its own laws, only the schoolmen distinguished between directive and coactive power. Directive force is equivalent to natural law, and to this the law maker is bound; coactive force is the authority the ruler wields, to which he is not subject, except to God whose representative he is, or else subject to the spiritual power of the Church which is unlimited. The answer is twofold:—in the case of a community which is supreme the law of the community binds the whole community; in the case of a prince having received supreme power, if the law is for the common good, then as a member of the community the prince is bound, but if not then natural law gives him the right to be above it. If a tax is imposed upon things which are common and the prince has private domains, he sins against justice if he exempts himself; but if he makes a law against carrying arms, then he is exempt because it is not meant to include himself. In general power is universally binding upon the whole commonwealth. God gives this power to princes, that is, power to legislate, *vis directiva et vis coactiva*. Directive power directs those it commands, coactive power is of constraint, attaching to legal obligation a necessity. Some allege that it is by a kind of pact that submission to the laws is required of the legislature as well as of the people. Suarez does not accept this explanation from the nature of a pact, because the obligation comes from God who is the first cause of the power; the king being God's minister he is subject only to the true legislator. Hence law ought to *dominari in republica* as Aristotle says,* Hence Thomas says the prince ought to subject himself to it because if he does not the law is rendered useless and the peace of the state is disturbed. The prince is not bound by law so far as it is coactive, because that would imply he was bound by force which is exercised by his own law. The prince is bound *civiliter* to the laws because he is bound to stand to a contract having force and value as a bond of civil law; this arises from the directive force of law which rests with the prince. An action *in judicio* compels the debtor; therefore, it cannot be allowed against the prince, and so he cannot in this sense be bound *civiliter*. Yet, if by the opinion of the judge there is declared *jus creditionis* against the prince, so that judicially he is bound to observe it, and cannot

* Pol. III. 7.

deny it without injustice, an action can be given against him so that he is bound to admit or permit it in conscience. In this way he is bound *civiliter sive coactione*. In this case however the question is, is the price bound by the law, does he incur a penalty by the law, or by not executing the law? In all cases he seems free from the force of law because he is judged by an authority superior to the laws, as the minister of God and is responsible to him and to the pact by which he rules.[*]

One of the chief attributes of sovereignty is the power of taxation and this point really determines whether the prince is sovereign or not.[†] Interpretation of the law is another prerogative of sovereignty. The imperator who has power to make law alone can interpret it. There is a double power in the legislator, (a) a *natural* one, of willing or not willing, which we call *potestas facti*, (b) Another is superadded, *jurisdiction to bind others*. The political power is entrusted with the defence of human rights, (a) punishing evil-doers and administering the law of life and death; (b) avenging injuries. These rights come from God to the political body. God creates the civil power as a quality which springs from human nature and according to the law of reason, in order that society may not be left without the right of governing itself. God does not by a special act create the power, but when the political society is formed the sovereignty is attached therewith by divine institution, as a result of reason and springing from the nature of such a body as civil society.[‡]

This analysis of political sovereignty which is distinguished from the power of government or legal sovereignty, is the most acute that we have as yet found in the history of political theory up to the age of Suarez. He elaborates the principle of contract, in which he gives us the genesis of the contract of society, and of government. Government results from the institution of civil society and the civil society originates in the consent of the people, naturally social beings as yet free allying themselves under the dominion of human law, as distinct from natural law. According to natural right one man has no dominion over another man or body of men; neither is it according to divine law as a direct institution; accordingly sovereignty resides in the whole body of the society, whether general or particular. The people are brought together and by agreement they delegate the sovereignty or part of it to the ruler or rulers.

(V) *Government, its elements and its forms*. The civil power considered naturally and absolutely is in the hands of the whole people who are sovereign, the determination of the exercise of it, by whom, in what way, and to what extent it is to be exercised must be solved by the sovereign body politic.[§] The question arises, if the people is sovereign and if each individual is free and subject to no one but God, is not the principate of man a tyranny and

[*] Bk. III, 35, 22, 23.
[‡] Bk. V, 17, 18.
[†] Bk. VI, 19, 11.
[§] Bk. III, 4, 1.

against nature? Civil government in the hands of magistrates with temporal power to rule over men is just, especially in conformity with human nature. God approves of it in sending judges and kings to the Jews who undoubtedly had the principate and temporal power, and held such in veneration. If it is said they possessed it in a special manner, this did not prevent them from possessing the power itself. It is also useful in the rule of a human community and therefore has the consent of nature itself; and this amply confirms the custom of men that kings were sacred and highly reverenced in Scriptures.

The argument of reason is taken from Thomas. Man is a social animal; he naturally and rightly desires to live in community. Community is double, imperfect as in the family, and perfect as in the political society. The first is natural because made and female unite to propagate humanity in society; but this community is not self-sufficient and it is necessary for the good of man that political community be constituted as a state, in the coalition of many families, because no family can in itself have all the ministries and all the arts necessary to human life, and much less is it sufficient to secure the knowledge of necessary things. In single families peace could not be preserved nor injuries avenged. There is nothing better than that man should unite in a perfect political society or *civitas*. This community can be enlarged into a kingdom or principate by the society of many *civitates*, which union is more useful for the human race. In a perfect community of this kind it is necessary that there be a power to which the community looks for government. Where there is no government, the wise man says, the people become corrupt. Nature does not fail; therefore, as the community is perfect in reason and competent in natural right, so the power of governing it is there without which there would be confusion. The necessity of government is seen in all other human societies, the husband has power over the wife, the parents over the children, the master over servants; so likewise we find in such community some one family, though it is not found in the marriage relationship, but in the race of human society, that takes the lead. No one can preserve order unless some one is chief to whom pertains the power to procure and to will the common good; as in the natural body so in the political body experience teaches that single individuals are the best to consult. In order to promote the public good it is necessary to have a public power to which it belongs ex-officio to attend to the common good of society. Therefore there is a necessity for the civil magistrate, because by the name nothing else is signified than men or a multitude of men in whom is the power of ruling a perfect community, for such power ought to be in men because men are not governed politically by angels, nor immediately by God. The human magistrate, if he is supreme in his order, has the power of making laws according to his own judgment of the civil or human in the preservation of the force of natural law and the other conditions necessary to law. The civil magistrate is necessary in a state for government and tempering its relations; but the most necessary part of the government is the giving of laws; therefore in the political magistrates there exists the power of legislation, for he who receives an office receives all the power necessary and exercises such power. This power of law making belongs to the perfect jurisdiction of the chiefer magistrate or public power. It has the power of obliging and compelling for these two are necessary to law; therefore the magistrate having the sole power in the republic has the power of making laws human or civil. This superior power is a species of that dominium. It has not such a dominium as answers to despotic power in servitude; but in civil subjection it is the dominium of jurisdiction. The power of making laws implies the power of executing and also of jurisdiction, because jurisdiction without *coercitio* is nothing. Man is not born subject to a prince but he is born *subjecibilis*. Tyrants are not necessarily of the essence of kings because kings who rule not according to the will of God are tyrants.

Human principate is not *congenitus* with nature, but it is not contrary to nature. Even among angels there is a principate. It is not therefore founded upon sin, but in the natural condition of man, because man is a social animal and demands the mode of living in community which necessarily gives to the king public power.*

To whom then belongs the power of making laws, *legislative power?* (a) It is said to be in one man, the supreme prince and that by succession from God. (b) It is said to be in no single man, but in a collection of men, because by nature all men are born equal, and no one has political jurisdiction over others. We do not know that God gave it to any one man, nor did men at any one time will to raise any prince above the entire race.† Power is given immediately from God, and not given by men themselves because never was there such a uniting of men to give it. It is given by God in the same manner as property, following nature, but it does not take effect till men unite into a perfect community and so the governing power is not in a single man, nor in the entire mass of men but in the political body. It is by the consent of this political community such power is given and taken away. Evidence of this is given in the Pope who is elected by the people and when elected has power. The difference between him and a king is that the people cannot take away the power from the pope or his dignity, whereas in the human community the people can transfer the power to another person or to the community itself. It depends therefore on the will of men.‡ Legislative power is ultimate and derived, in the people and in him or in the persons to whom it is given.

Political government may be threefold in form, monarchy, that is by one

* Bk. III, 1, 1-13.
† Bk. III, 2, 1-6.
‡ Bk. III, 3, 1-8.

head; aristocracy, that is, by a few wise men; and democracy, by many and these the people. By the law of nature men are not bound to have any special form, because each may be good and useful. Therefore it depends upon the human will. Yet, there is one form of government which deserves the preference above the others, because it is most useful in the interest of the people, more efficient in preserving the existence and good order of society. That form is monarchy. The monarch ought not to forget that he is the delegate, mandatary of the people, and not the representative of God. Therefore all his acts ought to have as their end the bringing authority into accord with the will of the people; that is, to what would be just according to the consent of the people which is the source of power. A monarchy is simply the persistency of common consent to the profit of a dynasty which retains it by heredity or the translation of the mandate of the people from the prince to his descendants. Every dynasty implies a first prince who has received his authority from the nation, or at least usurped it, and that he transmits to his descendants these rights. Similarly, when a right is derived from force of arms, it derives its importance from the source of sovereign power, but it is by force it is wrested from them. It is the mode of seizing it that is violent; all the same it comes from the people.* Government is put into the hands of some or one, yet power resides in the community by nature. This title may be transmitted by hereditary succession, may be attained by *justum bellum*, but if *injustum* it is tyranny. But it is said, because it is derived from God and by election, therefore it is independent of the people. It is so in so far as it keeps within the will of God. It is held mediately from the community, just as the pontificate, though there are many electors, is held immediately from God. He does not regard monarchy as the only legitimate form of government, but simply as the preferable form, the others being useful and even necessary in certain conditions of society, the preference depending upon human right, not upon natural law.

In solving the question, who is supreme and sovereign, the government or the people, Suarez gives us the distinction between power which is delegated and power which is alienated, that is, the mode of constitution. All power of sole jurisdiction is *delegabilis*. The transfer of the power from the republic or state to the prince is not delegation but alienation, or the perfect transfer of all the power which was in the community in so far as the community could give it. Bartolus distinguishes between the community and the prince; the community can delegate power because it has the power in ordinary and can use its discretion regarding its disposal; but princes are persons to whom is entrusted this jurisdiction and therefore they cannot delegate it. Rulers to whom this authority is given with the highest powers may delegate it.† The supreme power of making laws is in the prince with common consent

* Bk. III. 4. 6.
† Bk. III. 4. 12.

under condition of bestowal and transfer through the community. What of princes who are not supreme? Magistrates and governors who are constituted by kings have authority under concession or by permission of the supreme prince, in as far as he grants it. Communities which are governed aristocratically or popularly retain in themselves the supreme governing power, not giving it to any prince. Hence in Venice and Genoa the people retain in themselves supreme power which, though they elect a leader, they do not transfer to him. Here the sovereign power is not in the prince only or in the community but in the whole body with its head (*in toto corpore cum capite*). Yet in the state it would be possible to give all such power to the head. In all states except democracies the people transfer supreme power to the prince or rulers either with or without the power of advice of the senate, and so it needs no acceptance of law enacted by them before their legislative enactments are binding on the people.

Who are eligible for office in government? Women are excluded from government. It is beyond the capacity of a female to make laws and so be supreme; they can neither be kings nor magistrates nor judges nor officers of any kind because these offices are and ought to be be exercised in all communities by men. Suarez speaks of *civitates* as *maximae*, *majores* and *minores*. There should be no religious test required in governors. Neither the law of nature nor the divine law nor ecclesiastical law require faith or morals on the part of a holder of the *potestas* in order to make laws, because kings who were evil in the Old Testament were not removed from their offices.

Alienation or delegation of power to the government. In theory the people is sovereign and superior to the prince. But when the contract is made between prince and people it is a contract of alienation, not of delegation, unless it is stipulated that reservation is made of ultimate powers, so that the prince becomes supreme legislator, executive and judge subject to residuary sovereignty in the people. The people generally transmits the power absolutely to the prince, at least in hereditary monarchy. In the case of what we call limited monarchy and democracy the people still retain the power in its final form. In theory however the people still retain the power and the government is the servant of the political body. In the absolute monarchy which is preferable on grounds of utility the prince becomes superior to the people and obedience is due from the people because they have been deprived of absolute freedom. The prince is possessor of the dominium by proprietorship and cannot be deprived of it unless in case of tyranny, in which case the kingdom is reduced to a state of war, this state of war being really a popular limit upon the absolute sovereignty of the prince. This exception which Suarez admits, giving the right to the people to judge the government in case of tyranny shows that it is not after all an absolute alienation but really a delegation of power, residuary power being retained in the people. In regard to the act of the people in entrusting to the government its authority, Suarez says, that the people can alienate absolutely the sovereignty and give up its freedom in favor of one, liberty being of natural right and capable of alienation by free will; and the people having received legislative power from God can if it wishes transfer it to another person or to another community.

In connection with the power of the government the question arises, does the legislation of the government require to be accepted by the people before it is binding? *Is legislative power absolute?* Canonists have two opinions on this point, that law has no force without acceptance, and that law when sufficiently promulgated implies acceptance and is therefore binding. In support of the former opinion, the majority of the Doctors allege, that governors have no power to impose laws upon the people without the consent of the people, because they hold the legislative power from the people and the prince is not presumed to bind the people against their wish, since they have placed him in the government to rule on the basis of the common interest. Suarez supports the other opinion, that acceptance is implied in the imposition of laws by the properly constituted authority of the people themselves, that is, the prince. Consent of the people is of the essence of law, but it is given in the case of absolute principate in and with the appointment. In other circumstances the people do give their consent separately, when legislative power is divided between the king and the kingdom, *regnum cum rege* being the legislature. In any of the forms of government, monarchy, aristocracy, or democracy or mixed, that power which is sovereign can impose laws and exact obedience. In any case the people does not give a formal acceptance, because it appoints some one or more to legislate as representing it and this implies consent. In principle in absolute monarchy consent is necessary and is given already, for the people have alienated this power to the prince, the act of cession is consent. Suarez admits certain objections to this presumed acceptance. In the case of an unjust law, which is not a law *per se*, having no obligation even if accepted; in the case of a law that bears hard upon the people because the prince does not presume to oppress the people; if in fact the majority of the people cease to observe it the minority is no longer bound. This places in the hands of the people the power of examining and judging the validity of laws, making the people the supreme court of judgment as to the question of constitutionality, replacing in this form of examination and rejection of law what he had swept away in the form of consent.*

(VI). *The Civil and Ecclesiastical.* The political theory of Suarez comes out more clearly when he examines the relations of the temporal and spiritual powers. He discusses the two extreme theories of canonists, jurists and theologians, which assert respectively the universal dominion of the *Sovereign Pope* and of the *Sovereign Emperor.* He lays it down, that the pope is not by right the universal lord of the universe, not having temporal sovereignty and only interfering indirectly in temporal affairs by virtue of his relations to

* Bk. III. 4. 1-11.

the spiritual order, *ordine ad spiritualia*. This indirect sovereignty involves the power to abrogate laws, but not to establish new laws in the civil domain. He asserts that this indirect temporal sovereignty is inherited not from Christ, as the other schoolmen asserted, but from the gift of the Emperors themselves who placed it in the hands of the Popes. The temporal power does not depend for its sanction upon Christian faith, nor solely upon the customs according to which the princes exercise it. It is a natural right sanctioned by human law and pertains to the unbelieving as well as the believing and does not rest upon faith or grace, but upon nature. He does not support the claim of Gregory VII. to absolute power over kings and rulers as derived from the apostles of Christ. He does not even with Thomas subordinate the temporal to the spiritual on the analogy of the body and soul. He apprehends the changed position of affairs and in a certain way meets it. The reformation has broken with the papacy. He recognizes the work of the reformers, although not in the way of accepting what they had done. The opinion of some obscure sectaries that grace has broken the Christian away from all obedience to the temporal authority, he alleges to be improper, because without the temporal authority there is no society possible.* He does not stand on the old ground of the papacy which declared the pope to be armed with two swords, and kings to be subject to him even in temporal affairs. He maintains the rights of princes, even when they are infidels, because their authority is uniquely based upon nature, was exercised before Christianity and has not been abrogated by the religion of Jesus Christ.†

What is the position then of the papal and civil powers? God put the spiritual power in Peter and his successors and it cannot be changed by man.‡ All the faithful are said to be freed from the law in the writings of Judas the Gallilean, the precepts of the Scripture which teach them to obey Christ frees them from natural, much more from civil law. But the gospels enjoin obedience and kings are true kings if they possess a just title. On conversion to the Church kings do not lose their civil power, because grace does not destroy nature. The civil kingdom is founded upon nature not on grace, that is, it comes from God as the God of nature. The end of civil law is good *per se* and this end is necessary for Christians, therefore the laws which are ordained to that end, and the magistrates by whom they are established are necessary to the state and Church alike.

As to the Emperor and the Pope. Many Doctors say the sovereign pope has power to make civil laws for the Church and also for the whole world. If so, it includes the believing and unbelieving which is clearly false. Christ never gave this power to the Church save in respect of the believing; he did give

* Bk. III. 5.
† Bk. III. 19, 2 and 3.
‡ Bk. III. 2, 4.

them the power and right of preaching to all outside of the Church in the whole world, but that is all. Hence Innocent III. declares, canon laws do not bind pagans outside the Church. Princes who are infidel are not bound to recognize the pope as a superior prince. In the Christian world the pope has universal power by the gift of Christ, and therefore it extends to all the world, if all the world has received the faith; but only in parts where the Church exists is there such a power. The sovereign pope has not direct temporal power in all the universe, but only in that kingdom or those provinces of which he is the temporal lord. He has temporal power by which he can govern civilly all the Church, not on account of the temporal power of the Church but on account of the spiritual power. Christ only promised Peter the keys of the kingdom of heaven. But if he has supreme temporal power then it would exclude all the rest, because there only can be one supreme power. Christ did not give such universal power. No dominion is given to the Roman Church, but that which it has in lands subject to it temporally, by the donation of Emperors and princes. Such universal power is not necessary at any rate to the propagation of the faith nor to the good government of the Church; it is not necessary that such power should be divinely given to the pope. Although the pope has no direct temporal power over princes, we cannot refuse to him an indirect power, as the common father of all Christian people, the pastor of the body of Christ. As such he can abrogate civil laws which seem to be susceptible of leading souls to ruin.*

Can the Emperor as Master and Prince of all the world bind all the world by his civil laws? The Doctors of Civil Law said that Emperors have *jus* and *jurisdictio* over all the world. But the Roman Emperor did not derive such a universal power from God or by the election of man and no one can take it to himself. Neither Emperor nor any single man has power of making laws for all the world. No one has in reason a title to claim temporal subjection from all the world. The pope has crowned Emperors, yet he is not to change at will, nor subject temporalities which are free, but only when the spiritual good reasonably demands it. The Emperor therefore cannot make civil laws to bind all the Church or all the world, but the subjects in the Roman dominion. If there is any supremacy in Emperor or Pope it is hedged in by limits on both sides.† The princes and kings have supreme power in the civil order of law-making, but it is limited by the mode in which and by the condition on which it is given and transferred from the community. The civil law has to do only with the natural in the life of man, the Ecclesiastical has to do with the supernatural, that is, it refers to the future life. Civil law, moreover, does not have anything to do with spiritual happiness in this life.‡ Civil law is all human law, because it is the minister of God in the

* Bk. III. 6, 1s.
* Bk. III. s. 9.
† Bk. III. 11. 1-12.

hands of his servants and binds even the conscience of men, and they are bound to observe the precepts given in the divine and human law as Christ said, "if you wish to enter into life, keep the commands."*

Do the civil laws bind ecclesiastical persons? Ecclesiastical persons are bound to observe civil laws because these are approved by canon law. But the Pope is exempt from all civil law, not only because he is supreme in his own lands, but because of his spiritual dignity *jure divino*. When the Pope is in other kingdoms he is not bound to observe the laws of that kingdom, because he is a person so excellent that he is not bound to conform to special statutes and laws of his interiors. Churches and Ecclesiastical communities are exempted as far as they enjoy a special privilege, for which reason a special disposition of law cannot be accommodated to them; it will be so in case of any special spiritual dignitary to whom is given a like privilege. In regard to all other Ecclesiastical persons there is equal reason for observing such a law. The Pope has the right to see that unbelieving princes command nothing contrary to the faith and good manners. It is his duty to make war on the prince who opposes the Christian faith and to bring down the throne by force of arms when he seeks to turn his subjects from their duty to the Church. As to apostate princes and heretics the Church has direct power over them. It may inflict a penalty for heresy in excluding them from the throne and also their descendants till they enter into the grace of the Church and the sentence of excommunication be revoked.†

Some have denied the right of the Pope and the Church to make laws because they are simply men, and have no power over men as such. But there is in the Church a peculiar authority for rule. The Church is sent as was Christ, and Christ was sent a legislator and governor as well as teacher. This did not close with his life, but it is perpetuated in his apostles. In Scripture such a power is used at the Council of Jerusalem, "it seemed good to the Holy Ghost and to us." This is the truth of tradition and custom as well as of the fathers. This Church power is truly and properly legislative; but legislative power requires directive and coactive power. It is perfect governing power and must do so by means of laws. The apostles had this power; therefore the Vicar of Christ has it. It is spiritual and supernatural.‡ The Church is more ancient than the law of grace, because it began with Abel. This is proved by the fact that there has been a mystic body, distinct formally from the body politic and tending to a different end, namely, supernatural felicity, united by a different bond and specially adapted to the worship of God. Yet, perfect power is in the Church by the grace of Christ. Perfect knowledge of God is not in nature, therefore not *lex naturalis*. Yet, the nature of man in this as in the case of the political power reveals this idea.

* Bk. III, 21, 1.
† Bk. III, 31, 22.
‡ Bk. IV, 1, 1-10.

because there is no nation which has not some religious worship. In the republic of Rome there was religion under the kings and emperors who in the exercise of natural powers had the care of religion. But nature is elevated by grace so as to attain supernatural happiness. Since in the community there is this external profession of faith and worship of God, there is necessary in the Church a power Ecclesiastical, a magistracy to which the care of these things is entrusted. The Church was not so perfect a unity in the state of nature as it is now because it has through Christ its power.* This power was given immediately to Peter by Christ, given to him as Head because it was becoming there should be in the Church of Christ a perfect mystical unity and a perfect rule, which is accomplished by instituting Ecclesiastical monarchy and giving the supreme power to one. This power includes universal law-making. This power was given immediately to the other apostles, but in a less perfect manner and in a different way. The apostles were not equal in jurisdiction, because Peter was their Head. In Peter there is a power of succession to perpetuity, in the other apostles it is a personal *munus* and *legatio*. The primacy was given to Peter and this included for him and his successors universal legislative power in the universal Church of Christ.† The other Bishops have power in their own dioceses, subject to the supreme power of the pope. The laws of a council do not bind unless the pope sanction them; because a council is under obedience to the pope and has not immediate jurisdiction, *jure divino*, over all the Church.‡ The Ecclesiastical power in the gospel law is far more excellent than the civil power, because it is in the supernatural order, the civil being in the natural; it is more excellent in *esse* and *substantia*. The end is more excellent because supernatural, the civil being confined to the order of nature. The one is spiritual and eternal, the other material and temporal; the end of the civil being the highest natural felicity of this life, only perfect in relation to the community. God is the author and supernatural governor, and immediate origin of the spiritual; but as author of nature he gives civil power and it is given not *per se*, but *per medium proprietatis* from nature itself.

The spiritual exceeds the temporal power because civil power is immediately in the community of man, but spiritual power resides principally in the Christ-man. Civil power can be in any person even an unbaptized, but baptism is the door of the Church. Civil power can be in men and women, Ecclesiastical power can only be in men. Civil power can be in a layman, Ecclesiastical power only in the clergy.§ Although the spiritual is more excellent, this does not imply that it is superior in jurisdiction or order of power. In the old law kingly power was not subject to sacerdotal law. In the New Testament Christ did not institute any superiority. There is only one power in the Pope and that is spiritual and extends to the temporal. It

* Bk. IV, 2. ‡ Bk. IV, 6.
* Bk. IV, 3, 1-15. § Bk. IV, 8, 1-8.

has the two swords, spiritual and natural, because it is necessary that in one body there should be one Head: it is necessary that the Vicar of Christ should have all power to rule over the body. Even kings and emperors are under Christ as sheep, therefore it rests with the Pope to ordain anything in regard to kings as to other men. This is confirmed by the usage of the Church and the institution of Christ. The two keys were promised to Peter and therefore the supremacy of the Pope is established.* These two powers are neither necessarily conjoined nor separated, because neither is according to precept or prohibition of the divine law. The Church for a long time had no temporal power as far as the Civil rule of a state is concerned and only as kings were converted to the faith was there a change.

In the new law of Christ Ecclesiastical power is not natural, but supernatural and specially given by Christ, but it is never given to earthly kings nor does Christ enjoin that it be united with kingly power. Yet the Civil and Ecclesiastical may be united in the same person, for the pope is king in his own lands. It is therefore not illegal but admissible because it leads to reverence for the Ecclesiastical prince. Christ did not give it but He did not forbid it.† *Whom does Ecclesiastical power bind?* In general the same persons as the civil, all those in the territory, whether living permanently or temporarily in it. A question arises in regard to the position of princes who are *infideles*, not Church members nor of the Ecclesiastical community. Though bound by the civil laws they are not bound by the Ecclesiastical laws, because they are not subject to the Church jurisdiction. But heretics retain the character of baptized persons, because baptism is the *fundamentum jurisdictionis*. They accordingly retain the sign of Ecclesiastical jurisdiction and are therefore bound to obey the Church's precepts. In distinguishing between *fidelis* and *infidelis* the mark is the form of baptism by the Church, which places under Church jurisdiction. Canon laws bind Christians everywhere and are not like civil laws which bind only in the state, because the power of the pope is universal in the Church. The laws of the Bishops and councils bind within the territory over which they have control, kings as well as subjects if they are Christians.‡ The Pope has, as a temporal prince, power to levy taxes in his own territory, not in the spiritual unless it is necessary to defend the Church from infidels or heretics, because in that case he has supreme power, even in temporal things.§ The power of dispensing belongs to the pope and emperor equally, the princes in the Ecclesiastical and Civil spheres respectively, because the power of dispensing belongs to him who has the power of legislating.‖ Civil and canon law are not subordinate *inter se*, for though the canon law is more dignified formally, it has not superior jurisdiction, for the civil is supreme in its own order. Yet, in order to the good of the soul civil law is subordinated to the canon and in this respect the Ec-

Bk. IV. 9. 5-7   ‡ Bk. IV, 19. 4-6.
† Bk. IV. 19. 1-5.   § Bk. V. 14. 3.
          ‖ Bk. VI. 14

clesiastical can abrogate the civil. If the civil law treat of spiritual things under the guise of temporal, as in the contract of marriage, and if the civil law even in purely temporal concerns is *contra bonos mores* or implies danger of life, then the canon law may abrogate it.*

Christ is not only Saviour; he is also true and proper legislator and king as is proved by the title of *rex* given in Scriptures to him. This is confirmed by the Canons of the Council of Trent. As King and Judge he perfectly rules his subjects and governs his kingdom; therefore the law of Christ in the New Testament is properly law. He instituted his Church as a spiritual commonwealth in which he rules (*ipse*). In this way the unity of the Church is declared and its rule is under a pastor, Christ Himself or His Vicar.† Although in theory the temporal prince is independent, this wide power which is called spiritual, given to the pope, of examining and judging whether civil laws are detrimental to the faith, and of dethroning princes who antagonize Christianity, practically makes him King of Kings. The one power is human, fallible and limited, the other is divine, infallible and unlimited. It is an advance to take away the temporal power from the latter, but it is reverting to the old order to give it back under the name of spiritual power; however this of itself is a preparation for the entire separation of the temporal and spiritual, the admission of such devout canonists as the Jesuits carrying along with it immense weight.

Is there a liberty of conscience? The civil law in some Christian states punishes blasphemy with severe penalties and inflicts upon heretics the severest penalties. Is this just? It is not, says Suarez, from the point of view of natural law; but it is legitimate from another point of view. This power comes from God alone to the Church, who is not only legislator but sovereign Lord; and in the latter capacity God gives this power to the civil society through the preservation of truth and Christianity.‡ Suarez distinguishes the infidel from the heretic. All men are subject to the law and bound to obey it and after the advent of Christ there is a new law to which those are subject to whom grace is given. Those who are *extra Ecclesiam* are bound only by the law of nature.§ In regard to the infidel princes the Church has not power to expel them unless they oppress their Christian subjects, in which case the Church may declare a just war against them. As to heretics the Church has the right, on account of their apostacy, to take away from them their kingdoms, only they are not dispossessed *ipso facto*, and according to the judgment of the Church they retain their power. As far as unjust kings are concerned the Church has power to remove them and depose them *ipso facto*. In such a case the subjects have a right of revolt against the princes and disorder would ensue. Out of this would spring peace.

(VI) *International law.* Suarez does not make much advance upon his pre-

* Bk. VI. 26. 3.
† Bk. X. 1. 3.
‡ Bk. III. 11. 10.
§ Bk. I. 18. 5.

decessors in the matter of the law of nations. He however saw clearly its importance as a science and gave it a place in his legal system. His anti-imperialistic views led him to the conclusion that national states were the best. These national states, *inter gentes*, seemed to point to the fact that there is a law of nations distinct from the law of nature, based upon the very same principles, which laws have arisen from the usages and concessions of separate communities and are as binding as the laws of natural right. He was able to see that there is a difference between the law of nations and International Law properly speaking: the first springs from the nature of reason as manifested in the necessary relations of human societies, these human societies, just like individuals, possessing certain inherent rights founded in natural law and human law which brings these states into existence, such as independence, local law, etc.; whereas international law has its foundation in positive conventions, treaties and arrangements actually recognized or established in the international relations which nations sustain to one another, as the measure of their common relations. Suarez was the first to see, if only imperfectly, that international law consisted not only in the principles of natural justice applied in the intercourse of states, but also in the customs and practices being observed in that intercourse as the foundation of that system of customary law and case-made jurisprudence derived from precedents which has since been recognized as the international law of the Christian nations in the civilized world.* He says that by the bringing together of the separate nations these positively recognized rules ought to increase and that the ultimate consummation ought to be attained some day of a confederation of states, embracing the universality of nations and uniting these nations in one grand society under an International system of law.†

He justifies war as legitimate in case of defence. War is his justification of slavery which finds a place in civil law as an institution of utility to the state. Slavery is the penalty which civil law attaches to him who takes up arms in an unjust war and is to be respected as a part of the human penal code.‡ In war he sees the battle of liberty and servitude, the result being that he who has the force to gain a victory is rewarded by liberty and he who is conquered in feebleness is punished by slavery. The harshness of this is somewhat mitigated by the fact that he distinguishes between a just and unjust war, inculcating the precepts of morals and justice in the determination of what is a just war as well as in the conducting of it. His respect for force is softened by the light of the Christian law which he enjoins and enforces. He adopts the definition of *jus gentium* given by Justinian, because the precepts of *jus gentium* are established by custom, not in one state alone but in many states. The law of nations is founded upon reason, for although

* Bk. II. 2 9.
† Bk. II 19. 9.
‡ Bk. II. 18. 9.

in the world there are a great many different states and nations, yet humanity is one, not only theoretically, but practically. The principle of natural law which is natural love to all mankind unites men, however they may be divided into perfect political communities, in one great human community. This is evident in the readiness with which at all stages in history nations and races have sought alliance and help from their powerful and favored neighbor states, at times for their own preservation, at times for their moral good; and in this they show their dependence upon the superior guidance and strength of those into whose care they entrust themselves. The world of national states is thus tending towards International unity.

Scholasticism has spoken its last word. We have seen that its doctrines are much confused, yet they are democratic in the main. Suarez with all his inconsistencies is honorably remembered as the last exponent of the system, in which we find all the germs of the new system. He repudiates the Divine Right of rulers, and the patriarchal theory of monarchy he refutes. He builds the society of the state and the government upon the same foundation, the consent of the people. He accepts in all its fulness the principle of the sovereignty of the people; no doubt it is marred by his doctrine of absolute alienation, but in the last resort even such alienated sovereignty when it becomes tyrannical is subject to the judgment of a residuary power in the people. His state and his government are legal; so much does he emphasize this legalism, that with him, an unjust law is null and void, being no law at all. The international relations of the states of Christendom are regulated by the principles of justice and the customs of International courtesy, the law of nature and of nations so much spoken of in more modern times.

We are now prepared to pass to the school of the renaissance as found in Grotius, who lives and writes at the same time as Suarez; ridding himself of the scholastic element he presents the democratic views adopted by Suarez with slight modification and rational explanation.*

We have attempted to show that there is a continuity and a discoverable coherence throughout the whole range of the political writings among the Schoolmen. Living as they did through the age of darkness and using a method that was cumbrous and unphilosophic, we are surprised to find that so many bright and beautiful germs of truth have been buried beneath the mass of details found in all their works. This study has produced in us the conviction that all the modern doctrines of politics are not new and that the originality of modern writers must yield the palm to ancient philosophers and thinkers whose

* Suarez, De legibus ac Deo Legislatore; Janet, H., pp. 55-76; Franck, Ref. et Pub. 17 Siecle, pp. 13-51; Hallam, Lit. of Europ. II. pp. 122 sq.; Blakey, Pol. Lit. II. pp. 39-64; Heron, Hist. of Jurisprudence, pp. 59, 305-309; K. Werner, Franz Suarez und die Scholastik der letzten Jahrhunderte, 2 Vols. Regensburg, 1861; Stockl's Hist. of Phil. in Middle Ages; Popedom and Politics of the 16th Century, History of the Jesuits, A. Steinmetz, 2 Vols. Phila. 1848.

memories are almost forgotten. It has impressed also upon our minds the thought that the truest philosophy is that which is justified by history: in crude and uncouth forms the great doctrines of politics appeared long centuries ago: with the increase of knowledge and the advance of civilization, these doctrines have laid aside their uncomely form, and are now presented to us in the bright attire of modern language, and cast in modern moulds. We should never forget that we owe a debt of gratitude to the men who in darker days saw ahead of their own times into the far distant future and preserved for us and our posterity the fundamental ideas of politics and political institutions, the full meaning and significance of which they were unable to grasp. The reputation of these men has received a bright resurrection from the oblivion of the past and as we pass from the memorials of the massive and monumental genius of these men we pay our respects to their memory, and turn to the future with fresh hope and a larger inspiration, because we can carry with us the thought that what has survived the iron age will not die but rather increase in vitality and freshness in the newer age of soft and silken manners.

COLLEGE DEGREES AND HONORS.

Glasgow University, undergraduate Arts course, first class in Classics, Mathematics, Logic, Metaphysics, Rhetoric, Moral Philosophy, English Language and Literature, 1881-85; first honors and University prize in Mental Philosophy, 1883; University Foundation Scholar in Mathematics and Natural Science, 1884.

R. P. Church Scholarship at Glasgow University, 1881—1885.

Professional course in Divinity, Glasgow University, honors and first class in Divinity, Biblical Criticism, New Testament Greek and Ecclesiastical History, with special University Prize in Oriental Languages, 1884-5, 1889-90.

Original Secession Seminary, Glasgow, 1884-5-6

Reformed Presbyterian Seminary, Belfast, 1885-6.

Glasgow University, A. M., 1889; B. D., 1890.

Member of Glasgow University Council for life, 1889.

Henderson fellowship in Theology, (Thesis, Sabbatism of Hebrews iv:9), 1891.

Professional course in Law school, Glasgow University; first class, (with first place) in Philosophy of Law, Political Philosophy, Public and Private International Law; University Medal in Jurisprudence; Special Prize in Feudal Law and Scottish Law, and University Prize in Constitutional Law and History, and Conveyancing, 1890-92; LL. B. with honors, 1892.

University Fellow in Political Philosophy, Faculty of Political Science, Columbia College, N. Y., 1892-3.

Student in post graduate School of Theology, National University; Fellow, 1893; D. D. (Thesis, "The Christian Sabbatism,") 1893.

Publications: —

Theological Essays and Discussions, *Covenanter*, Ireland, 1888; *Witness* Scotland, 1893; Joint Editor of *Glasgow University Magazine*, 1891-2, (Editorial and Literary contributions); Joint Editor and Review Editor of the *Christian Nation*, N. Y., 1892-94. (Editorial, Review, and general contributions.)

www.ingramcontent.com/pod-product-compliance
Lightning Source LLC
Chambersburg PA
CBHW022117230426
43672CB00008B/1420